Entrepreneurship

AND SMALL BUSINESS MANAGEMENT

SECOND EDITION

Earl C. Meyer, Ph.D.
Teacher Educator—Marketing Education
Eastern Michigan University
Ypsilanti, Michigan

Kathleen R. Allen, Ph.D.
Associate Professor of Entrepreneurship
The Entrepreneur Program
University of Southern California
Los Angeles, California

Glencoe
McGraw-Hill

New York, New York   Columbus, Ohio   Woodland Hills, California   Peoria, Illinois

ABOUT THE AUTHORS

Dr. Earl C. Meyer has extensive experience in both business and education. Currently the teacher educator of marketing and entrepreneurship at Eastern Michigan University, he has served as base coordinator and faculty member for Southern Illinois University and was also a high school marketing education teacher-coordinator. At the secondary level, he taught entrepreneurship for 8 years. For 16 years prior to moving into education, he was involved in advertising sales, retail, and financial services management—and owned and operated his own golf enterprise.

Meyer has been the project director and principal writer for curriculum guides that address three stages of entrepreneurship education. He also authors articles, makes state and national presentations, and holds workshops on teaching entrepreneurship. In addition, he represents Michigan in the International Consortium for Entrepreneurship Education for which he has served as president and executive board member. He was also the co-founding chair of the Entrepreneurship Professional Interest Category (PIC) of the national Marketing Education Association.

Meyer holds a B.A. in Marketing Education from the University of South Florida. His M.Ed. and Ph.D. in Vocational and Career Development (with an emphasis in Marketing Education) are from Georgia State University.

Dr. Kathleen R. Allen is a recognized authority on entrepreneurship and small business technology. Allen is the author of *Launching New Ventures* 2nd Ed., *Growing and Managing an Entrepreneurial Business*, and *Tips and Traps for Entrepreneurs*, and several trade books. She has also written for business magazines and newspapers and is called upon by the media for expert opinion on entrepreneurship.

As a professor of entrepreneurship at the nationally ranked Lloyd Greif Center for Entrepreneurial Studies of the Marshall School of Business at the University of Southern California, she helps hundreds of young entrepreneurs start new ventures. Allen is actively involved in academic research, most recently in the area of issues related to high tech start-up companies. She is also a founding member of the Entrepreneurship Research Consortium.

As an entrepreneur, Allen has been involved in commercial real estate development for the past ten years, having co-founded a development firm and a brokerage—American Pacific Investments—which she sold. She is presently the co-founder and CFO of Gentech Corporation.

Allen holds a B.A. in music and foreign language from the California State University. She holds Masters Degrees in Business Administration (MBA) and Spanish from UCLA, and a Ph.D. with a research emphasis in entrepreneurship from the University of Southern California.

Glencoe/McGraw-Hill

A Division of The **McGraw-Hill** *Companies*

Printed in the United States of America.

Send all inquiries to:
Glencoe/McGraw-Hill
21600 Oxnard Street, Suite 500
Woodland Hills, California 91367

ISBN 0-02-644068-7 (Student Text)
ISBN 0-02-644069-5 (Teacher's Annotated Edition)

4 5 6 7 8 9 052 05 04 03 02 01

ACKNOWLEDGMENTS

Dr. Meyer wishes to thank his graduate assistants, Melissa Carey and Sonia Marshall, for their research work on the text.

Dr. Allen thanks the faculty and students of the Lloyd Greif Center for Entrepreneurial Studies at the University of Southern California, and Steve Mariotti of the National Foundation for Teaching Entrepreneurship (NFTE) for their support, encouragement, and inspiration.

EDUCATIONAL CONSULTANTS

Dr. Richard Clodfelter
Associate Professor
College of Applied Professional Sciences
University of South Carolina
Columbia, SC

Diane Culpepper
Senior Administrator for Vocational/Technical Programs
Department of Workforce Education
Orange County Public Schools
Orlando, FL

REVIEWERS

Deborah Ballou
Instructor/Coordinator
Camden County High School
Kingsland, GA

Michael Cardin
Marketing Education Coordinator
Ottumwa High School
Ottumwa, IA

Dr. Tena B. Crews
Assistant Professor
Department of Management and Business Systems
State University of West Georgia College of Business
Carrollton, GA

Michael Foley
Marketing Education Instructor
Osbourn Park High School
Manassas, VA

Jennie Griffin
Marketing Education Instructor/Coordinator
Robert E. Lee High School
San Antonio, TX

Vicki Hillsman
Marketing Education Instructor
El Dorado Springs High School
El Dorado Springs, MO

Sherry Huggins
Instructor
LaFayette High School
LaFayette, GA

Craig P. Kosinsky
Marketing Education Instructor
Southington High School
Southington, CT

Lynore Levenhagen
Marketing Education Instructor
Lyman High School
Longwood, FL

Kay Masonbrink
Business Education Instructor
Rancho Bernardo High School
San Diego, CA

Dr. Melinda McCannon
Assistant Professor
Department of Information Systems and Communications
Georgia College and State University
Milledgeville, GA

Tommie Montoya
Instructor/Coordinator
Cibola High School
Albuquerque, NM

Joyce Robinson
Marketing Teacher Coordinator
Northeast High School
Macon, GA

Maureen Todd
Marketing Education Instructor
Rancho Bernardo High School
San Diego, CA

Jennie Voyles
Marketing Coordinator
Lithia Springs Comprehensive High School
Lithia Springs, GA

TABLE OF CONTENTS

UNIT 1
Going into Business for Yourself

CHAPTER 1 What Is Entrepreneurship? 2

CHAPTER 2 Your Potential as an Entrepreneur 18

UNIT 2

Researching and Planning Your Venture

LEMONADE
35¢ SMALL
50¢ LARGE

■ UNIT 3 ■

MANAGING MARKETING STRATEGIES

Mobil
Mob

■ UNIT 4 ■

MANAGING YOUR BUSINESS PROCESSES

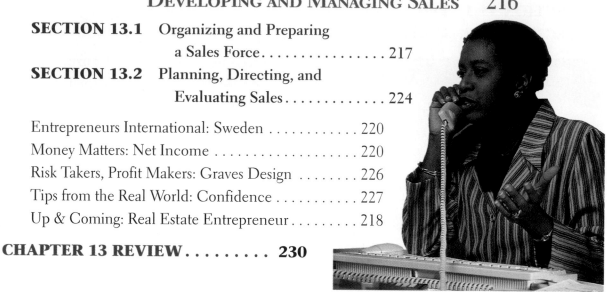

CHAPTER 15 Managing Purchasing and Inventory 252

CHAPTER 16 Production Management and Distribution 268

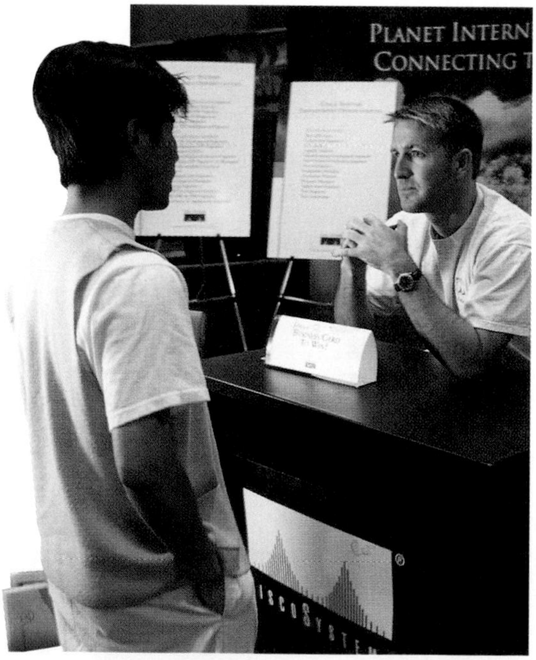
PLANET INTERN
CONNECTING T

UNIT 5
Managing the Finances of Your Business

UNIT 6

GROWING YOUR BUSINESS

UNIT 1 GOING INTO BUSINESS FOR YOURSELF

UNIT OVERVIEW

Chances are that at one time or another, you'll consider going into business for yourself. It can be a challenging, exciting, and rewarding way to make a living. You can do what you enjoy, exercise your creativity, make the best use of your abilities, and be your own boss. Starting your own business puts you in charge.

However, before you start designing your business card, consider what it takes to be an entrepreneur. Be aware of all the options in pursuing your own business. The more you know, the better able you will be to make the right choices for your venture. Solid research will help you recognize the best ideas and find the best opportunities.

Entrepreneurship: What It Takes

What do you know about starting your own business?

1. What is entrepreneurship?
2. How can you become an effective entrepreneur?
3. What are the rewards and risks of having your own business?
4. What characteristics contribute to an entrepreneur's success?
5. How can you recognize opportunity?
6. What new trends affect small businesses?
7. Where can you get business ideas?
8. What is the role of technology in today's businesses?
9. Where can you locate global opportunities?
10. How can you locate the best market for your business?

CHAPTER 1

What Is Entrepreneurship?

Learning Objectives

When you have completed this chapter, you will be able to:

- **Explain** the role of entrepreneurship in the economy
- **Discuss** the laws of supply and demand
- **List** what entrepreneurs contribute to the economy
- **Describe** the entrepreneurial process

You're the Boss!

Understanding Entrepreneurship

As the owner of a casual clothing company, you have just been selected to host an exchange student from Russia. You look forward to teaching your guest about your venture and the role of entrepreneurs in the American economy. Maybe you can teach him something that will help him start a business in Russia.

What Will You Do?
What subjects will you cover to help this student understand entrepreneurship?

SECTION 1.1

Entrepreneurship and the Economy

THE ROLE OF SMALL BUSINESS AND ENTREPRENEURSHIP IN THE ECONOMY

Have you ever considered going into business for yourself? Then you have thought about becoming an *entrepreneur.* An entrepreneur is an individual who undertakes the creation, organization, and ownership of a business. He or she accepts the risks and responsibilities to gain profits and personal satisfaction.

To create and run a successful venture, a business undertaking involving risk, requires a variety of skills and knowledge. This book will provide you with exercises and information to help you prepare for it. Even if you don't become an entrepreneur, the processes and skills you learn can help you in any job.

What you'll learn

- How small business and entrepreneurship contribute to the economy
- How the laws of supply and demand in the free enterprise system affect entrepreneurship
- The ways in which entrepreneurs contribute to our free enterprise system

Why it's important

Understanding how the economy works is essential to business survival. The free market system allows entrepreneurs to compete and succeed.

KEY TERMS

entrepreneur
venture
entrepreneurship
entrepreneurial
economics
free enterprise system
profit
services
factors of production
scarcity
demand
elastic
inelastic
diminishing marginal utility
equilibrium

Knowing more about the businesses you patronize will also benefit you as a consumer.

In this book, we will use the terms *entrepreneurship* and *entrepreneurial*. Entrepreneurship is the process of getting into and operating one's own business. Entrepreneurial means of or having to do with an entrepreneur or entrepreneurs. We will start with the role of entrepreneurship in the economy and the kinds of business entrepreneurs start.

Money Matters

THE BUSINESS

When starting your own business, make sure it is the right one for you. Norm Brodsky, entrepreneur and magazine columnist, warns:

"*People think, 'If it is successful and I'm going to make money doing it, I'll be happy.' But if you don't like the business . . . your new venture could become a nightmare.*"

Entrepreneurship Today

You might know someone who is an entrepreneur. About one in three households is involved with a new or small business. In fact, the number of home-based businesses has grown from 12 million in the early 1990s to 16 million in the mid-1990s. More than 90 percent of all businesses are small businesses with fewer than 100 employees.

Owning and operating a business today is much different than it was ten years ago. The global marketplace has resulted in new resources, markets, and ideas. Information technology allows people to communicate instantly and keep records more efficiently. Customers demand that business transactions and communication take place quickly, and they expect new products to come out often. The pressure is great for businesses to come up with better service and to make more choices available.

To really understand how entrepreneurs and customers interact in the economy, you need to start with *economics*. Economics is the study of the decisions or choices that go into making, distributing, and consuming products.

The Free Enterprise System

Most democratic nations have a *free enterprise system*. In a free enterprise system, the right to make economic choices is most important:

- People can choose what products to buy.
- People can choose to own private property.
- People can choose to start a business and compete with other businesses.

This is also called *capitalism* or a *market economy*.

The Profit Motive. Profit is money that is left after all the expenses of running a business have been deducted from the income. Making a profit is a primary incentive of free enterprise. It is one way of measuring success in a free enterprise system.

However, there is also a risk of failure. This risk serves a positive function in a free enterprise system. It encourages the production of quality products that truly meet the needs of consumers.

The Role of Competition. Competition between similar businesses is a key element in a market economy. It forces companies to become more efficient. It also keeps prices down and quality up.

Businesses compete on the basis of price and non-price factors. In a mature industry such as appliance manufacturing, the focus is on lowering prices. An established firm can do this with its large plants and an experienced work force. A small firm setting up its first production line most likely cannot. Revenues lost to lower prices can be made up through higher volume (a larger number of sales). The success of discount stores is based on this principle.

In other industries, non-price factors such as quality, service, and reputation are more important. The auto industry provides an example of this approach. For most people, a car is a long-term purchase requiring regular after-sale service. This is why people are often willing to pay more for a make or model that has a good repair history or a better warranty.

Start-up resources that a new business requires include capital, skilled labor, advisors, and customers. ***Why are customers so important?***

Economics: Making Choices

Economics is the study of the decisions (or choices) that go into making, distributing, and consuming products. To understand the entrepreneur's role in the economy, you need to know some basic economics. If that sounds intimidating to you, it shouldn't. You're already familiar with many of the concepts that will be discussed in your every-day role as a consumer.

Goods and Services. Goods and services are the products that our economic system produces to satisfy our wants. Goods are tangible (or physical) products, such as toothpaste or a bicycle tire. Services are intangible (or conceptual) products. Barbers, plumbers, and Web designers run service businesses.

Factors of Production. The resources that businesses use to produce the goods and services that people want are the

Figure 1–1

Factors of Production

There are four factors of production:

1. Land.

In economic terms, land is all the natural resources upon and beneath the Earth's surface. It includes not only geographic territory but also air, water, trees, minerals, and crude oil.

2. Labor.

Labor refers to the human effort used to produce goods and services. Labor comprises full- and part-time workers as well as management.

3. Entrepreneurship.

This factor consists of the ideas and decisions of the business owner, or entrepreneur. He or she is the initiator, the one who brings together all the other factors of production to create value in the economy.

4. Capital.

Capital consists of the equipment, factories, tools, and other goods needed to produce a product. It also includes money used to pay all the expenses.

factors of production . These factors are described in **Figure 1–1.**

Scarcity. When wants are greater than resources, you have scarcity . Land, labor, and capital are all scarce, so entrepreneurs must sometimes give up one thing to get another. For example, the owner of a new restaurant may forego a costly decor to have more money to put into staff or kitchen equipment.

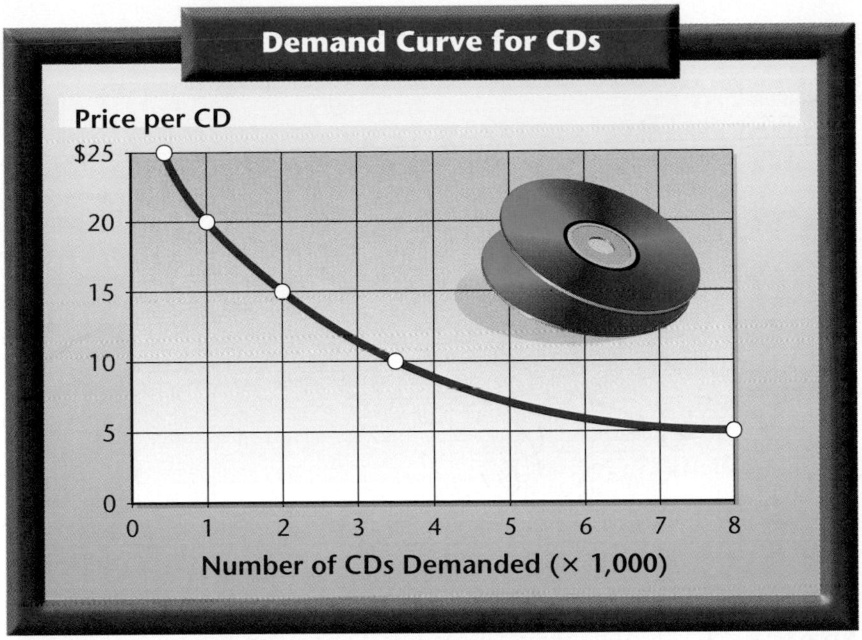

Figure 1–2
This curve shows that fewer items will be purchased at higher prices than at lower ones. ***Which price increment reduces demand the most?***

THE LAWS OF SUPPLY AND DEMAND

In a free enterprise system, the price of a product is determined in the marketplace. There, consumers and producers interact in response to the laws of supply and demand.

Demand

Demand is the amount or quantity of goods or services that consumers are willing and able to buy. According to the law of demand, price is inversely related to demand. In other words, as price goes up, the quantity demanded goes down.

The demand curve in **Figure 1–2** shows the number of CDs that would be purchased at specific prices. Notice that more CDs would be bought at $15 than at $25. This is because more people could afford the discs at the lower price.

Some products respond more readily to the law of demand than others. If a small change in the price of an item causes a significant change in the quantity demanded, the demand for the item is elastic. If a change in price has little or no effect on the quantity demanded, demand for the item is inelastic.

In general, demand tends to be inelastic in these circumstances:

- No acceptable substitutes are available.
- The price change is small relative to buyer income.
- The product is a necessity.

Figure 1–3
This curve reveals a direct relationship between price and the number of items produced. ***Describe the effect on supply of tripling the selling price from $5 to $15.***

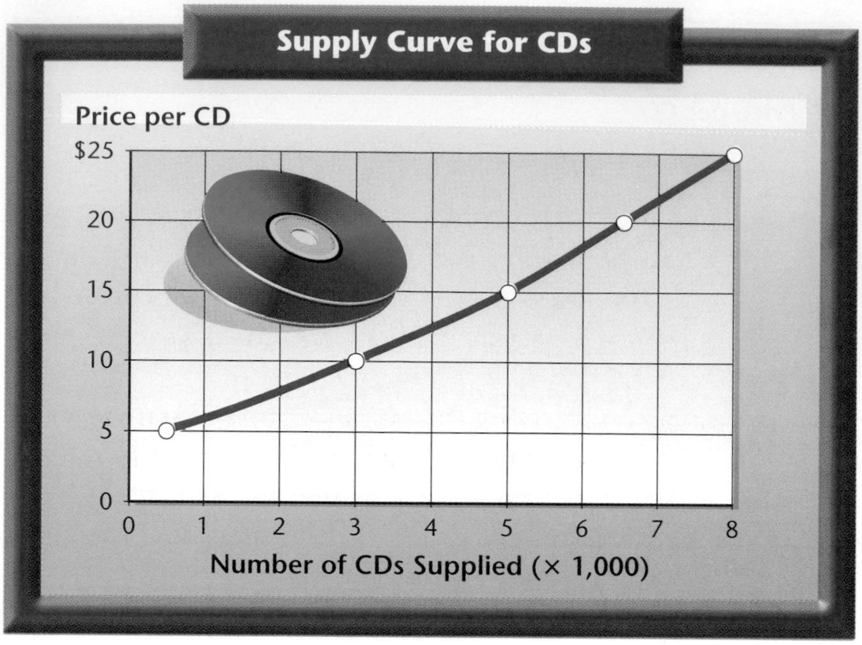

Thus, demand for butter tends to be elastic because a lower-priced substitute, margarine, is available. There is no substitute for milk, on the other hand. Demand for it tends to be inelastic.

If a product's price is low, that does not mean that people will keep buying it indefinitely. They will not, for example, buy more than they can reasonably use. This effect is known as the principle of diminishing marginal utility. It establishes that price alone does not determine demand. Other factors (like income, taste, and the amount of product already owned) play a role as well.

Supply

The amount of a good or service that producers are willing to provide is called *supply*. Producers are more willing to supply products in greater amounts when prices are high. They are less willing to do so when prices are low.

Figure 1–3 depicts a supply curve for CDs. Notice that as price goes up, the quantity supplied goes up.

Surplus, Shortage, and Equilibrium

Supply and demand are dynamic in the marketplace—that is, they are continually shifting. This creates surpluses, shortages, and *equilibrium*. Equilibrium is the point at which consumers buy all of a product that is supplied, leaving neither a surplus nor a shortage.

Consider the CD example that we've been using. On the release of a new CD, fans flock to music outlets. They buy up every copy at the high initial price and still ask for more. A shortage develops. Stores have waiting lists of customers for their next shipments. Eventually, the excitement passes. Soon those same stores find that they have more copies of the CD on hand than fans will buy at the marked price. In other words, they have a surplus. To solve this problem, they reduce the album's price. In a short time a modest discount of 20 percent clears the excess copies from their shelves. They have achieved equilibrium.

The principles underlying this situation are illustrated in **Figure 1–4.** It shows the demand and supply curves we've been studying in the same graph. The point at which the two curves meet represents the equilibrium price. It is the price at which consumers will buy all that is supplied.

Supply and demand graphs can be a bit misleading. They seem to suggest that where demand exists supply just follows—that the two just spring into existence and interact. It's not that simple.

For businesses to respond to consumer demand, they must know about it. For consumers to make purchases, they must be aware of what is available. How do businesses learn what consumers want? How do consumers find out what businesses have to offer? The answer in both cases is the same—marketing. Marketing is discussed in Unit 3.

Tips from the Real World

INTO YOUR OWN

In the 21st century, companies will continue to downsize, forcing people to think like entrepreneurs even if they aren't. George Gendron, editor-in-chief of *Inc.* magazine, notes:

“'Get a job,' has been replaced with the more complex and bewildering mandate, 'Go out and create a job for yourself.'”

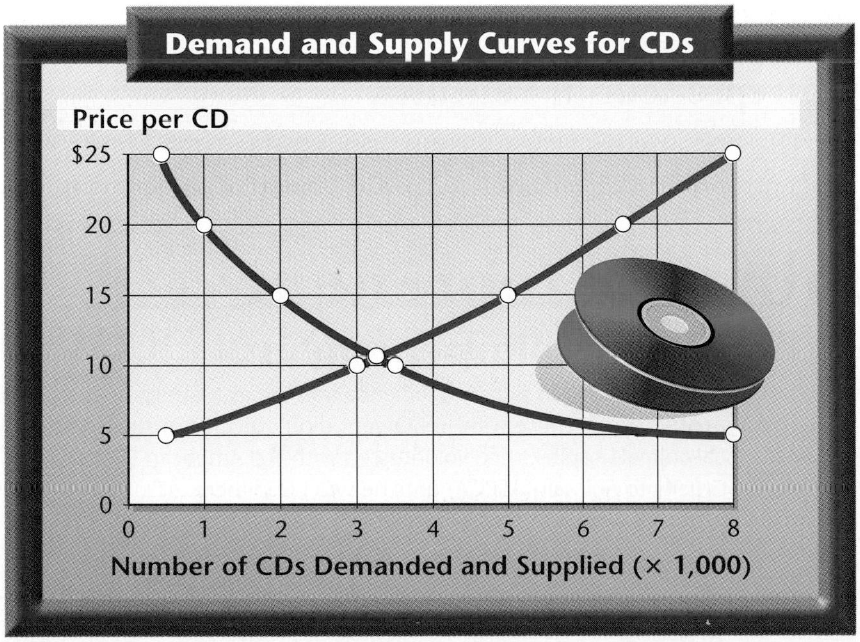

Figure 1–4
Merging the supply and demand curves into a single graph allows you to locate the equilibrium point or price. ***What is the equilibrium price for CDs? At that price approximately how many will consumers demand?***

WHAT ENTREPRENEURS CONTRIBUTE

Consider the contributions of entrepreneurs to the economy in the light of what you have learned in this chapter:

- *Entrepreneurs are the mechanism by which our economy turns demand into supply.* They recognize consumer wants and see the economic opportunities in satisfying them.
- *Entrepreneurs are a principal source of venture capital.* As part of the process of planning and setting up a new business, entrepreneurs gather resources. Money is one of the most important of these. Entrepreneurs usually start with their own funds and then seek out contributions from private investors.
- *Entrepreneurs provide jobs.* To produce goods and services, they spend capital on setting up a place of business and hiring workers. When they do this, they provide for their own financial security and for the financial security of others.
- *The most successful entrepreneurs change society.* In 1976, Steven Jobs and Steven Wozniak set out to create Apple, the first personal computer. In less than five years, they had created a whole industry comprising hundreds of related businesses and thousands of new jobs. Today it is hard to imagine a workplace without at least one personal computer.

Entrepreneurs start by responding to society's wants and end up changing that society and creating even more wants. As a result, entrepreneurs are not merely one of the driving forces in our economy. They are the initiators in the cycle of progress.

Small Businesses versus Entrepreneurial Ventures

This book makes a clear distinction between small businesses and entrepreneurial ventures. While it's true that most businesses

Up & Coming Entrepreneur

Obedience Training Entrepreneur

When Dennis Owens first decided to pursue obedience training as a career, he couldn't even find a mentor to apprentice with. Yet Owens didn't give up. Instead, he found work at a local animal hospital, then volunteered with the American Society for the Prevention of Cruelty to Animals (ASPCA) until he was hired there. His determination paid off, and he now runs Owensdale Dog Training Inc.

Analyze **How might Owens' volunteer work with ASPCA have helped him in getting his start?**

start small, not all businesses stay small. There are many reasons for this, but the principal reason is the intentions, motives, and goals of the founders of the business.

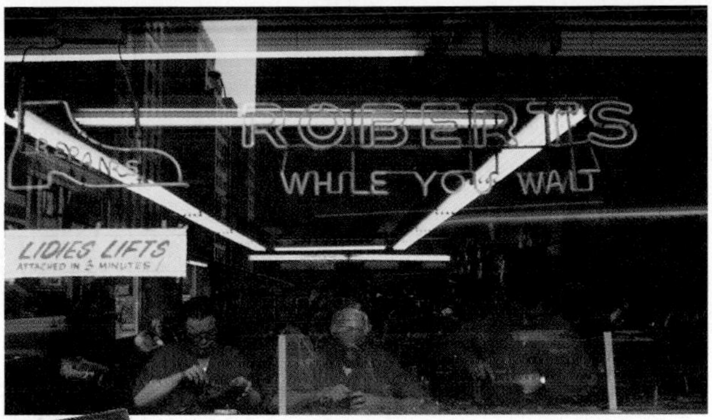

Many consumers choose to support mom and pop businesses. ***What advantages do such businesses offer?***

Small Businesses. Small business owners who start what are sometimes referred to as "mom and pop" businesses generally start them to create jobs for themselves and lifestyles that are satisfying. The shoe repair shop in the shopping center near your home may be one such small business. An accountant or lawyer may be another.

Entrepreneurial Ventures. Founders of entrepreneurial ventures have different motives for starting a business. Their principal goals are to innovate, grow the venture, and create value that can be harvested when they leave the business. Domino's Pizza, Blockbuster Entertainment, Netscape, and The Gap clothing stores are some examples of entrepreneurial ventures.

Chapter 2 will help you decide which type of business is most suited to your personality, goals, and desires.

CHECK YOUR UNDERSTANDING

SECTION 1.1

Reviewing Key Terms and Concepts

1. What roles do the profit motive and competition play in the free enterprise system?
2. What are two ways that entrepreneurs affect the economy?
3. What are some examples of elastic and inelastic goods and how do they differ?

Critical Thinking Activity

Go to a market and find examples of seemingly good items that demonstrate the principle of diminishing marginal utility? Make a chart that lists examples and reasons.

Extension Lab – Teaching Others

Who's Got Game? Working in teams of three or four, create a game for elementary school children. The game should teach, in the simplest terms, at least one of the basic economic concepts: supply and demand, equilibrium, profit, competition, or the free enterprise system.

Presentation

- Test the game with other members of your group.
- Present your idea to the class.
- Gather comments from your peers.

The Entrepreneurial Process

What you'll learn

- The process of entrepreneurship
- The components of a new venture organization
- How businesses succeed

Why it's important

Understanding the entrepreneurial process will help you build a more effective business that creates value. Learning the facts about business success and failure will help you make wiser business decisions.

KEY TERMS

environment
enterprise zones
opportunity
start-up resources
new venture organization
business failure
discontinuance

THE ENTREPRENEURIAL START-UP

The entrepreneurial start-up process includes five key components:

- The entrepreneur
- The environment
- The opportunity
- Start-up resources
- The new venture organization

In this section you'll see how these pieces fit together to create a new business. In later chapters each of these components will be discussed in more detail.

The Entrepreneur

The entrepreneur is the driving force that recognizes opportunity, pulls together the resources to exploit that opportunity, and creates a company to execute that opportunity in the marketplace. The entrepreneur brings to the process all the behaviors and experience from his or her life to that point.

The Environment

A new business environment includes all those variables that affect it that are not controlled by the entrepreneur. In general, four categories of environmental variables affect a new venture's ability to start and grow:

1. The nature of the environment, whether it's uncertain, fast-changing, stable, highly competitive, and so forth
2. The availability of resources such as skilled labor, start-up capital, and sources of assistance
3. Ways to realize value such as favorable taxes, good markets, and supportive governmental policies
4. Incentives to create new businesses such as enterprise zones, which are specially designated areas of a community that

provide tax benefits to new businesses locating there and grants for new product development

The Opportunity

An opportunity is an idea that has commercial value. An idea for a new product only has value if there are customers ready and willing to buy it. An idea plus a market equals an opportunity. New businesses are founded on recognized opportunities in the environment. In Chapter 2 you'll learn how to recognize opportunity.

Start-up Resources

To execute a concept for a new business, an entrepreneur must use his or her creative talent to pull together the necessary people and capital. The start-up resources an entrepreneur needs to start a business include capital, skilled labor, management expertise, legal and financial advice, a facility, equipment, and most important, customers.

The New Venture Organization

All the components of the new venture process come together in the organization of a company to execute the new business. The new venture organization is the shell that surrounds all the products, processes, and services that are part of the new business. Through the new venture organization or company, the entrepreneur is able to create value for him or herself, for the employees, the customers, and the economy at large.

HOW BUSINESSES SUCCEED

There is a common myth that most new businesses fail. This is simply not true. In fact, the reporting firm of Dun & Bradstreet

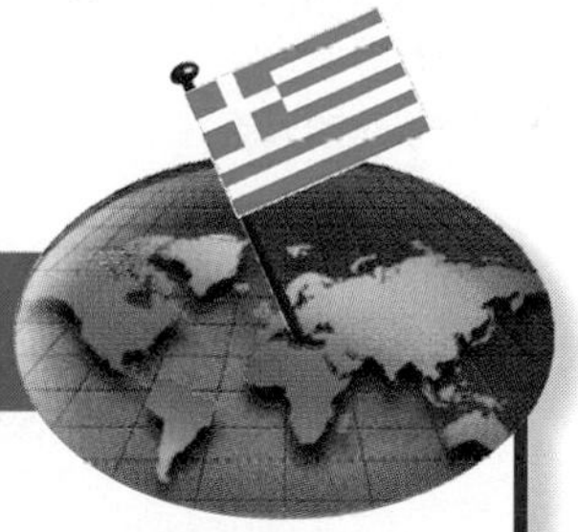

ENTREPRENEURS INTERNATIONAL

Greece

Athansio Nikoleta, a specialized and experienced crystal carver, established Studio N24 in Greece in 1962. Studio N24 quickly became the largest source of crystal glass manufacturing and engraving in his country. Nikoleta imports high-quality crystal from Germany, Slovakia, Italy, and the USA to his factory in Athens. Studio N24 distributes its high-quality products throughout the world.

Apply **Athansio Nikoleta is considered an artist and a businessperson. What are some other occupations that combine art and business?**

RISK TAKERS PROFIT MAKERS

Name: Jennifer Gilbert
Company: Save the Date
City, State: New York, New York

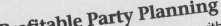

Profitable Party Planning

At 17, Jennifer Gilbert came up with an innovative way to earn money for a prom dress. She planned a party to help her peers celebrate their completion of the SAT. At the event, members of her high school football team collected money and the marching band played music. She recalls, "The proceeds . . . paid for dresses, limousines, and a memorable night."

Since high school, Jennifer has developed her flair for party planning into a business called Save the Date. Realizing that many corporations and people are reluctant to pay party planners, Jennifer created a business that coordinates events free of charge to clients. Florists, DJs, locations, and caterers pay her to gather business for them. Jennifer's innovation has paid off again. Save the Date earns more than ten million dollars annually.

Thinking Critically

What kinds of services or goods could you successfully market to your peers?

studied thousands of companies and determined that many more businesses succeed than fail. Of all businesses that were started in the mid-1980s, D&B found that 69.7 percent were still in business ten years later. D&B also discovered that the problem with most reports on business failure is that they don't define failure properly.

What Is Business Failure?

A business that files Chapter 7 bankruptcy and loses money for creditors, the people who lent them money, and their investors is considered a business failure. The business no longer appears on the tax rolls or other lists where operating businesses are found. Such businesses are rightfully counted as failures.

Businesses that disappear from public lists are not always failures. Some are *discontinuances*. A discontinuance might be a business that is operating under a new name or a business that has been purposely discontinued to start a new one. These are certainly not failures, because they are planned and cause no harm to creditors. Another way that failure is mistakenly reported is when an entrepreneur changes the legal status of the business, such as going from a sole proprietorship to a corporation.

How Can Entrepreneurs Succeed?

The bottom line is that the chances of a new business succeeding are good with effective planning. Some businesses will fail, but the number-one cause of business failure is poor management. Those people starting and running the business aren't doing what it takes to be successful. Entrepreneurs who prepare themselves by learning how to build successful new businesses and assemble a team that has the expertise they need will improve their chances of success.

This book will help you prepare for success. Chapters 3 and 5 in particular will show you how to recognize opportunity and then test that opportunity in the marketplace.

CHECK YOUR UNDERSTANDING

SECTION 1.2

Reviewing Key Terms and Concepts

1 What are the five components of the process of new venture creation?
2 How does an enterprise zone encourage new businesses?
3 Why shouldn't discontinuances be counted as business failure?

Critical Thinking Activity

Select three advertisements in newspapers or magazines and determine how they demonstrate each business' commercial value. Using this information, develop your own advertisement that shows the commercial value of each business.

Extension Lab – Individual Responsibility

Tourist Trap You started a business as a tour guide. Each week a new group arrives, and it is your job to take them to local attractions and shopping for souvenirs. You usually take them to the store where your friend works, so your friend can earn a commission that she splits with you.

Role Play In groups of three or four, play out the roles of the tour guide, the store clerk, and the tourist(s) in the event of the situation coming to light. Base your discussions upon the following questions:

- Is this illegal? Why or why not?
- Is this ethical? Explain.
- Describe a similar situation that happened to you.

CHAPTER 1 REVIEW

CHAPTER SUMMARY

- The process of becoming an entrepreneur begins when you put your thoughts of self-employment into action.
- Business ownership is the principle vehicle for creating wealth in our economy.
- Fundamental to the free enterprise system is the right of economic choice. People can choose what products to buy. They can choose to own private property. They can start a business and compete with others.
- Free enterprise is the economic system most characteristic of democratic nations. Its primary incentive is profit.
- Supply and demand are continually shifting. This creates surpluses, shortages, and equilibrium.
- Entrepreneurs respond to society's wants, change society, and create more wants.
- Entrepreneurs start businesses through a process that includes five key components: the entrepreneur, the environment, the opportunity, the resources to start the business, and the new venture organization.
- Entrepreneurs can avoid failure by planning and managing effectively.

RECALL KEY TERMS

Working in teams of two or three students, prepare an oral presentation explaining entrepreneurship and the role it plays in a free enterprise system. Use the following terms in your presentation, and be prepared to share your presentation with the class.

entrepreneur
venture
entrepreneurship
entrepreneurial
economics
free enterprise system
profit
services
factors of production
scarcity
demand
elastic
inelastic
diminishing marginal utility
equilibrium
environment
enterprise zones
opportunity
start-up resources
new venture organization
business failure
discontinuance

RECALL KEY CONCEPTS

On a separate sheet of paper, tell whether each item below is true or false. Rewrite any false statements to make them true.

1. Fundamental to the free enterprise system is the right of economic choice.
2. Large corporations are the major vehicles for providing wealth in our country and in our individual lives.
3. Profit is the primary incentive of a free enterprise system.
4. Demand is elastic when no acceptable substitutes for the product are available.
5. Equilibrium occurs when consumers will buy all the products supplied, leaving neither a surplus nor a shortage.
6. Entrepreneurs respond to society's wants but rarely change society or create wants.
7. The terms *small business* and *entrepreneurial venture* can be used interchangeably.

CHAPTER 1 REVIEW

8. New businesses are founded on recognized opportunities in the environment.
9. Most new businesses fail.

THINK CRITICALLY

Using complete sentences, answer each of the questions below on a separate sheet of paper.

1. What new opportunities might be available to you as an entrepreneur because of rapidly changing technology and the global marketplace?
2. When there are many choices in the marketplace, why do customers demand more from businesses? Give an example.
3. How has the principle of diminishing marginal utility affected a product you have purchased?
4. How have environmental factors affected a small business in your community?
5. What are some methods entrepreneurs can use to help determine consumer wants?

CONNECT ACADEMICS TO THE WORKPLACE

Math

1. In the city of Orange, 187 new businesses opened in 1995. By 1996, 15 percent of businesses were no longer in operation. How many were open in 1996? One year later, another 12 percent were considered discontinued. How many businesses were still open in 1997?

Select Equipment and Tools

2. You and a friend are starting a business repairing motorcycles. Create a list of technologies that you will need to run your business. Share the list with a classmate and make revisions.

WORK IN YOUR COMMUNITY

Working with three or four students in your class, brainstorm a list of 10–20 businesses that the team might like to start. Consider the interests and skills of the group members to help narrow down the list.

Write a short description of one of the businesses. Include the product or service you would provide and the type of resources you will need to begin.

LINK SCHOOL TO CAREER

Interview an entrepreneur or small business owner in your community. Find out the process he or she used to start the business. Ask about resources available for entrepreneurs. Report your findings to the class and create a class log of all the available resources. Write a letter thanking the person you interviewed.

*inter*NET CONNECTION

Web Page Woes

Your friend wants to begin doing business on the Internet. He knows how to create a Web page. Now he has asked you to help decide what kind of business to open. Using the Internet, research different virtual businesses.

Connect

Using a variety of search engines, search for three examples of entrepreneurial ventures. Answer the following questions about each business:

- Is the price of the product clearly defined?
- Are delivery dates mentioned?
- What process is used to place orders?
- How are the sites similar or different? Share your findings with the class.

CHAPTER 2 YOUR POTENTIAL AS AN ENTREPRENEUR

Learning Objectives

When you have completed this chapter, you will be able to:

- **Explain** the rewards and risks of being an entrepreneur
- **Identify** common characteristics and skills of entrepreneurs
- **Determine** how to get the most out of your own entrepreneurial potential
- **Identify** ways to improve your entrepreneurial skills

You're the Boss!

Improving Your Potential as an Entrepreneur

You've decided that starting a business of your own sounds appealing. However, you've read statistical lists of traits that many entrepreneurs share and inventories of skills that are needed to run a business. The problem is that you're not even close to rating 100 percent in any of these tests.

What Will You Do?

What steps can you take to increase your chances as an entrepreneur?

SECTION 2.1

Why Be An Entrepreneur?

ENTREPRENEURIAL REWARDS

Do you envision yourself as an entrepreneur? If you become your own boss, you can enjoy great benefits. However, you should be aware of the costs as well.

Rewards of Entrepreneurship

As an entrepreneur, you enjoy many rewards. For many entrepreneurs the greatest rewards are independence, personal satisfaction, and prestige.

Being Your Own Boss. Do you enjoy making decisions? Do you like to control your fate? Being the boss is a benefit that most entrepreneurs put at the top of their lists. As a business owner, you will have the freedom to make your own business decisions. You can set your own business hours, decide what products or services to offer, and what new directions to take.

Doing Something You Enjoy. What interest do you have that might lead to a successful business? Start with a business or personal activity you enjoy. If enjoy cooking, start a catering business. If you like to in-line skate or mountain bike, give

What you'll learn

- The rewards of starting your own business
- The risks involved in starting your own business
- How capital and investment are required to start an enterprise

Why it's important

You should know what to expect when you are considering going into business for yourself. Specifically, you should understand the advantages and disadvantages of self-employment.

KEY TERMS

competition
investment
capital
enterprise

Entrepreneurs have to handle tedious tasks and long hours. ***Why do they do it?***

lessons and sell equipment. You will achieve great satisfaction from creating and developing a business around your interests.

Having The Opportunity to Be Creative. Do you enjoy thinking of new ways to do things? As an entrepreneur, your ideas will directly affect your business. Would you rather create procedures or follow them? Entrepreneurs can shape their businesses in ways that employees cannot.

Freedom to Set Your Own Schedule. Are you self-motivated? The demands on you, as an entrepreneur, will be great. However, you would have the flexibility to determine your own hours. You would also have the option of working at home or at your business.

Controlling Your Salary. Would you like to have more control over how much money you can earn? As an entrepreneur your earnings are limited only by the potential of your business.

Contributing to the Community. In addition to providing goods or services that the people need, business owners generate jobs and create income for the community.

ENTREPRENEURIAL RISKS

The Costs and Risks of Entrepreneurship

If being an entrepreneur is so wonderful, you might ask, why doesn't everyone do it? Clearly, the rewards tell only one side of the

Up & Coming Entrepreneur

Fresh Juice Entrepreneur

In 1993, Arden Zinn started making fresh fruit juices in her home with the help of her children, Leslie and Ed. Today, Arden's Garden can be found everywhere from supermarkets to health clubs and cafés, and the Zinns have their own juice processing facility along with two retail stores in Atlanta. Ed Zinn attributes this success to being part of a health conscious family. "Fresh juice is a product we believe in," he says.

Analyze **Why is it important to believe in what you are promoting?**

RISK TAKERS PROFIT MAKERS

Name: Jerry Maher
Company: Portable X-Ray, Inc.
City, State: Des Moines, IA

X-Rays on Wheels

After Jerry Maher received certification as a Radiological Technician from a two-year community college, he found work with a mobile x-ray company. He would travel to nursing homes to take x-rays, which could actually help patients save money related to health costs. Business really started to boom when Medicare, a form of medical insurance provided by the federal government, discovered the advantages of mobile x-rays, and began reimbursing for this service.

As a favor to his boss, Maher moved to Dallas and expanded the business by starting up a new office. Maher learned exactly how to open, manage and grow a mobile x-ray business. In a few years, he returned to his home state of Iowa and went into the same type of business for himself. Since Maher's own Portable X-Ray, Inc.'s inception, he has seen a steady annual 10 percent growth rate.

Thinking Critically

List some business ideas that are made possible as a result of recent federal or state legislation.

story. In an economy where two or more businesses are in competition, striving for the same customer or market, an entrepreneur faces many costs and risks.

Working Long Hours. Are you willing to work long hours? As an entrepreneur, you will work long hours, especially during the start-up period of your business. During start-up, survival often depends on daily decisions, and there is little in the way of paid help. Most entrepreneurs respond by devoting most of their waking hours to their endeavor, often working seven days a week.

Having an Uncertain Income. As a rule, owners make more money than employees—but only when business is good. When business is bad, earnings can be low or even nonexistent. Business owners do not get a regular paycheck and, in the beginning, they may not be able to afford good health insurance or vacations.

Being Fully Responsible. The owner of a business is responsible for more than just decision making. He or she must see that everything gets done—from sweeping the floors to paying the bills to making repairs. Ultimately, there is no one else to take responsibility for these things. The success or failure of the venture in all its aspects, large and small, rests entirely on the owner.

Risking One's Investment. Undoubtedly, the biggest risk of being in business for oneself is the possibility of losing one's *investment.* Investment is the amount of money one puts into a business as *capital.* (Capital includes the buildings, equipment, tools, and other goods needed to produce a product, or the money used to buy these things.) To reach the stage where the earnings potential of a business is unlimited, an entrepreneur must first get his or her *enterprise* up and running. An enterprise is a company that is organized for commercial purposes. An entrepreneur who fails to do this can lose all the money he or she put into the endeavor, not to mention the lost time and work.

CHECK YOUR UNDERSTANDING

SECTION 2.1

Reviewing Key Terms and Concepts

1 What do you consider to be the greatest reward of starting your own business? Why?
2 What is the difference between investment and capital?
3 What do you consider to be the greatest risk of starting your own business? Why?

Critical Thinking Activity

In your community, find three examples of competition between entrepreneurs. In a chart, show their differences and similarities.

Extension Lab—Speaking Skills

Do I Have What It Takes? You work for an entrepreneur. She has suggested that you might have the potential to start and run your own successful business. After talking with teachers, guidance counselors, and other businesspeople in your community, you think she may be right.

Presentation Explain why you think you have what it takes to become a successful entrepreneur. Be sure to include:

- Why you want to become an entrepreneur
- The risks you are willing to take as an entrepreneur
- The personal characteristics and skills you have that will provide the opportunity for success

SECTION 2.2

What Does It Take to Be an Entrepreneur?

What you'll learn

- The background of entrepreneurs
- What characteristics are found in most entrepreneurs
- What skills are needed by entrepreneurs
- How to strengthen your entrepreneurial characteristics
- How to develop your entrepreneurial skills

Why it's important

Before starting your own business, you will need to consider what characteristics and skills will help you. Developing them will increase your chances of success.

KEY TERMS

role model
foundational skills
Internet
profile

WHO ARE ENTREPRENEURS?

Because entrepreneurs are so important to our nation's economy, there is a great deal of interest in what makes them tick. They are featured in magazine and newspaper articles. Best-sellers are written about them. Some have become celebrities. They are guests on talk shows and build ad campaigns around themselves to promote their products.

There has been research done to determine if entrepreneurs have any traits, experiences, or skills in common. The object of such studies has been to learn whether entrepreneurs are born or made. The answer is unclear, but it is definite that entrepreneurs prosper with proper skills and knowledge.

Background

A surprising variety of people become entrepreneurs. Research reveals a wide span of ages, educational backgrounds, and personal

histories. It also reveals a few common life experiences that may incline people toward entrepreneurship:

- Nearly half (47 percent) of entrepreneurs are under age 35 when they start their businesses; 16 percent are under age 25.
- Forty percent of entrepreneurs have only a high school diploma or less.
- Twenty-seven percent of entrepreneurs had some college; 33 percent have completed a college degree.
- Many entrepreneurs were independent from an early age.
- Frequently they had work experience when they were young (paper routes, yard-care services, baby-sitting, etc.).
- Sixty-two percent had parents or close relatives who owned a business.
- Many entrepreneurs were influenced early in life by a role model, a person whose attitudes and achievements they tried to emulate.

Characteristics

Studies have also been done to pinpoint personal characteristics of entrepreneurs. These are distinctive traits and qualities

Money Matters

ROAD TESTS

Your work experience is a great preparation for entrepreneurship. Fran Lent of Fran's Healthy Helpings recalls:

"*Everything I did in my corporate career I did to help me start my own company . . . It made me work even harder because I was using [that career] as a training ground.*"

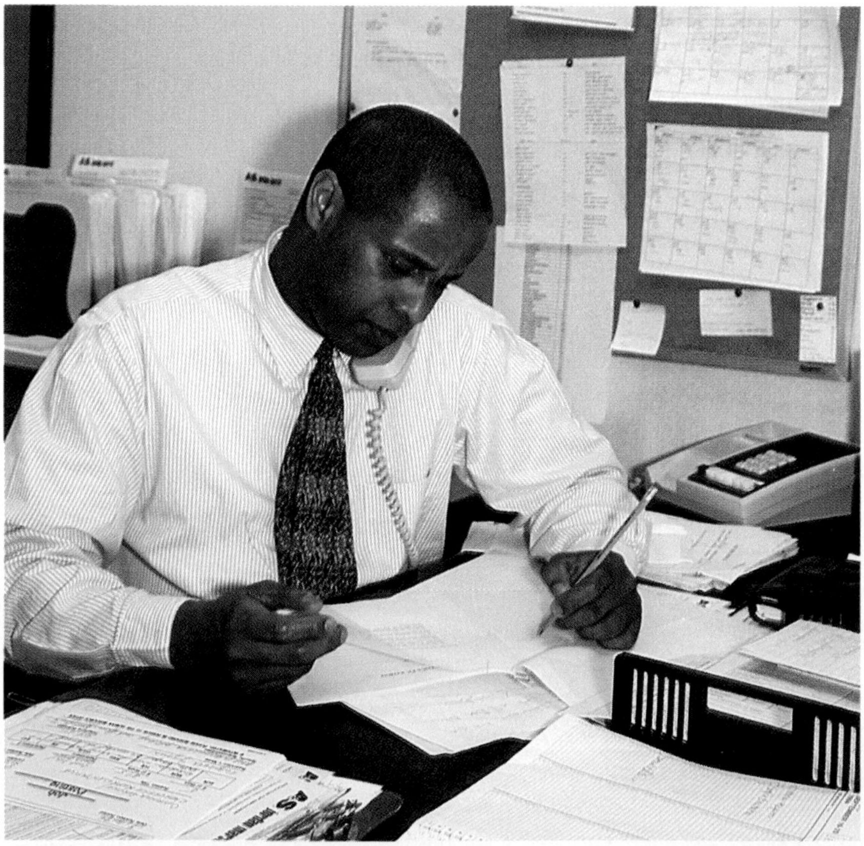

Successful small business owners are usually goal-oriented. ***Why is it important for entrepreneurs to be able to set their own goals?***

needed to set up an owner-operated business and run it successfully. Listings vary but usually include these 12 items.

1. *Persistent.* Entrepreneurs are willing to work until a job is done, no matter how long it takes. They are tenacious in overcoming obstacles and pursuing their goals.
2. *Creative.* Entrepreneurs continually look for new ways to solve old problems.
3. *Responsible.* Entrepreneurs do not "pass the buck." They take responsibility for their decisions and actions.
4. *Inquisitive.* Entrepreneurs want to know as much as possible about anything that might affect their ventures. They conduct research and ask questions to solve problems.
5. *Goal-oriented.* Entrepreneurs decide where they want to go and then set out to get there.
6. *Independent.* Entrepreneurs want to set their own agendas and schedules. They want to make their own decisions.
7. *Self-demanding.* Entrepreneurs have high expectations of themselves.
8. *Self-confident.* Entrepreneurs believe in themselves and act accordingly.
9. *Risk-taking.* Entrepreneurs like to take risks, but they are not reckless. They seek opportunities that offer both a challenge and a reasonable chance of success.
10. *Restless.* Once entrepreneurs achieve their goals, they begin looking for new challenges.
11. *Action-oriented.* Entrepreneurs are doers as opposed to spectators. They make decisions and act on them.

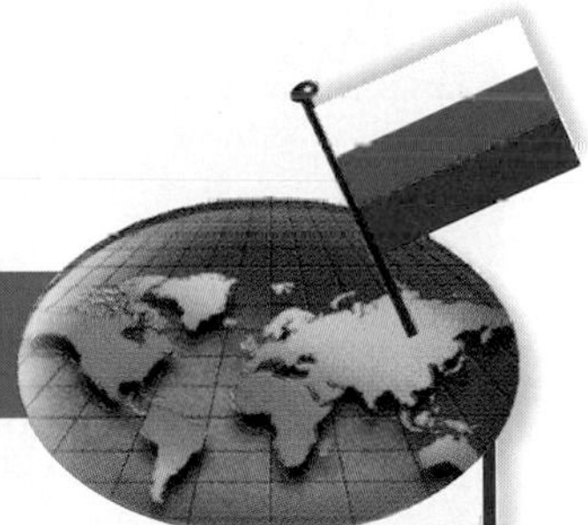

ENTREPRENEURS INTERNATIONAL

Russia

After Andrey Bazyrovich Tsyrendashiyev was trained in Oregon's Pacific Northwest timber business, he returned to his hometown of Ulan-Ude, Russia. This East Siberian village happens to be in the center of a vast coniferous tree forest expanding for a thousand miles to the north, west, and east. "Due to economic reforms, the huge concerns have disintegrated and dozens of small exporters have emerged," says Tsyrendashiyev. His C & C Exchange Center is currently exporting red pine and larch logs to Japan and China.

Apply **Tsyrendashiyev implies that small business has benefited from Russia's unstable economic climate. List some possible explanations.**

12. *Enthusiastic.* Entrepreneurs are energetic and passionate about their pursuits.

Skills

While you may have the desire and characteristics to be an entrepreneur, you also need some foundational skills. **Foundational skills** are math, communication, and decision-making skills that entrepreneurs use regularly in setting up and running a business. These skills are essential to the process of creating a business. The research has identified the following skills needed by entrepreneurs:

- *Communication skills.* How well do you communicate with others? Entrepreneurs need person-to-person, telephone, and written communication skills to gather the information necessary to organize and run their businesses.
- *Human relations skills.* Do you get along well with others? Do you enjoy meeting and talking to people? Entrepreneurs need the skills to get along with people, get cooperation, and persuade others to their way of thinking. These skills are particularly important, coupled with communication skills, in carrying out the negotiations necessary to run the business.

Entrepreneurial skills can be learned and developed. ***What skill is this person practicing?***

- *Math skills.* Are you prepared to maintain the necessary business records required to run a business? The entrepreneur needs basic arithmetic and knowledge of standard business record keeping. These are the tools needed to make initial purchase decisions, calculate potential profit, and put together financial statements.
- *Problem-solving and decision-making skills.* Do others turn to you to solve problems or for help in making decisions? Entrepreneurs must be able to make decisions to establish their business. They must also be able to use techniques for solving problems. Some will call for logical solutions and some will require creative solutions.
- *Technical skills.* Skills in the processes and technology of the business being created are important to the entrepreneur. In some instances they can be acquired quickly; in others training is needed. Computer skills are almost essential in any business. Knowing how to use word-processing, spreadsheet, database, and/E-mail programs will enhance your business operation. One valuable research tool for many entrepreneurs is the *Internet*. The Internet is a large computer network linking smaller computer networks worldwide.
- *Basic business skills.* Do you have a basic understanding of how the economy works? Your city's newspaper probably has a business section. If you're not already doing so, read it on a daily basis to learn more about the economy and the business world. You'll also need to know the fundamental concepts of finance, marketing, and management to create a successful business. Your school offers courses in these areas. Take advantage of them!

Tips from the Real World

LOOKING AHEAD

The days of large corporations are coming to an end, and we must adjust to the changes. Children's book publisher, Robert Schaen, observes:

"People are going to have to create their own lives, their own careers and their own successes. . . there is only one message there: You're now in business for yourself."

BUILDING YOUR ENTREPRENEURIAL SKILLS

If you didn't score 100 on each characteristic and skill, don't worry. You can build them up.

Don't Worry About Your Background

The more background *profile* experiences you share with the typical entrepreneur, the more likely you are to start your own business. A profile is a set of characteristics or qualities that identify a type or a category of person. However, if you did not fit the profile, you should not be discouraged from pursuing your entrepreneurial aspirations.

What the research really shows is that everyone has potential to become an entrepreneur. Entrepreneurs come from all economic circumstances. They have varying levels of education and begin their enterprises at virtually any point in their lives. What this means is that background isn't everything. A *can-do attitude* and a genuine desire to go into business for yourself are far more important.

Strengthening Your Entrepreneurial Characteristics

The personal characteristics described on pages 25–26, on the other hand, are essential to people who are going to set up and run their own enterprises. Persistence, creativity, independence, self-confidence—these are what it takes to get the job done.

You should understand that everyone has these traits. True, they are stronger in some individuals than in others. Even a small measure of a trait, however, is enough to build on. It just takes commitment and a willingness to work at strengthening those characteristics that need to be developed.

Three Steps To Follow. The following steps can help you develop your entrepreneurial skills:

1. *Determine the current strength of your entrepreneurial characteristics.* You can use the Entrepreneurial Characteristics Assessment shown in **Figure 2–1** to do a self-evaluation.

2. *Make a conscious effort to think of entrepreneurial characteristics as habits that can be changed.* You could eat less junk food, watch less television, or get up earlier each morning—if you want to. These are all things within your control. You can change them. Entrepreneurial traits are no different; you can change them, too.
3. *Developing the characteristics in which you feel weak.* How? Practice. Throughout each day, concentrate on acting as if you have the traits you want to develop. After a while, you will find that those traits become part of your makeup. You won't be acting, and you won't have to concentrate. Being entrepreneurial will come naturally.

According to research conducted by Harvard's David C. McClelland, humans have three psychological needs. People have a

Entrepreneurial Characteristics Assessment

Directions: Each of the statements below represents a characteristic helpful to entrepreneurs. Read through the list, and on a separate sheet of paper record your reactions. If you feel a particular statement describes you very accurately, write 5. If you feel it doesn't describe you at all, write 1. If you feel only partially describes you, place yourself somewhere between these two extremes by writing a number from 2 to 4.

1 2 3 4 5	1. You stay with a task despite difficulties.
1 2 3 4 5	2. You're creative.
1 2 3 4 5	3. You take responsibility for your actions.
1 2 3 4 5	4. You want to know about things.
1 2 3 4 5	5. You set goals for yourself and work toward them.
1 2 3 4 5	6. You like to work on your own schedule.
1 2 3 4 5	7. You set high standards for yourself.
1 2 3 4 5	8. You believe in yourself and in what you're doing.
1 2 3 4 5	9. You like a challenge, but you're not a gambler.
1 2 3 4 5	10. You're never completely content.

Figure 2–1
The circled numbers are a scale representing the strength of each characteristic. ***If you had to use words instead of numbers to describe each level, what terms would you use?***

need for affiliation, a need for power, and a need for achievement. Every person has each of these needs in different amounts. The entrepreneurial characteristics described in **Figure 2–1** are related most to one's need for achievement.

To become more achievement-oriented, McClelland recommends four strategies. These techniques can help increase your need for achievement:

1. Think like an achiever. Create worthwhile goals and hold high standards. Think of ways to improve what you do and how you do it.
2. Use the language of achievement. Use positive language, seeing adversity as opportunities to excel, grow, and shine.
3. Plan for achievement. Putting your short-term and long-term goals in writing will help you focus your goals and give you tools for measurement.
4. Act positive. Maintain a positive self-image and act with confidence. See the big picture and don't get discouraged by minor setbacks.

Surrounding yourself with people who demonstrate these actions will reinforce your need for achievement. You can also look

Figure 2–2

Strengthen Your Entrepreneurial Characteristics

You can strengthen your entrepreneurial characteristics with certain activities:

1. Reading.

Read articles and books about entrepreneurs and entrepreneurial activities.

2. Writing.

Write about individuals who overcame obstacles to achieve success.

3. Watching

Watch films about businesspeople, athletes, or others who are achievement-oriented.

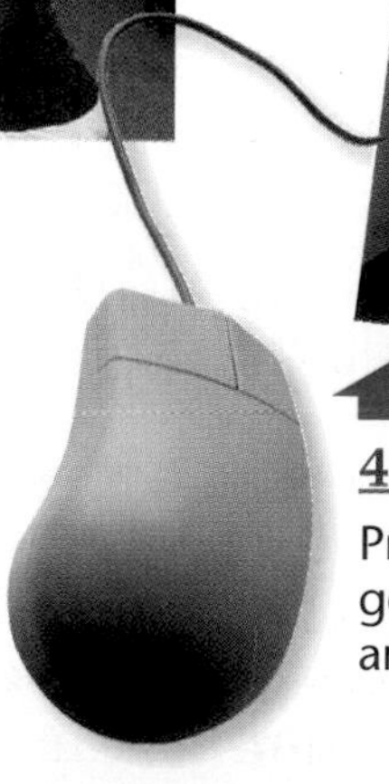

4. Practicing.

Practice case studies that involve goal-oriented behavior, creativity, and moderate risk taking.

for examples of these actions in successful small business owners.

You can also strengthen your entrepreneurial characteristics by performing certain activities. Examples are shown in **Figure 2–2**.

Turning uncharacteristic skills and behaviors into habits will take time and practice. Repetition is the key. It can make entrepreneurial behaviors a part of any person's makeup.

Developing Your Entrepreneurial Skills

Like characteristics, it is essential that entrepreneurs also develop the skills discussed in this chapter. They do not have to be experts, but they must develop as much competence as necessary to set up and run a successful operation.

CHECK YOUR UNDERSTANDING

SECTION 2.2

Reviewing Key Terms and Concepts

1. What does the research on entrepreneurs' backgrounds mean to you personally?
2. What are 12 frequently identified characteristics of successful entrepreneurs?
3. What are the steps in the process for becoming more entrepreneurial?

Critical Thinking Activity

Looking at your class schedule, identify at least three ways that each course can strengthen your entrepreneurial characteristics or improve your entrepreneurial skills.

Extension Lab—Reasoning Skills

Just a Dream? You are discussing plans to go into business for yourself with a potential investor. She makes it clear that she doubts you are the entrepreneurial type, but you are determined to make your dream become reality.

Role Play Choose one of the following tactics to convince the investor that you have what it takes to succeed:

- Talk to an entrepreneur in a business you are interested in; get his/her advice and opinion.
- Prepare a presentation of your preliminary plans for the investor.
- Make an appointment with a loan officer at a local bank to discuss your business ideas.

CHAPTER 2 REVIEW

CHAPTER SUMMARY

- An entrepreneur enjoys many rewards, such as independence, personal satisfaction, and prestige.
- An entrepreneur also faces many costs and risks including the possibility of losing his or her investment.
- Research shows that a wide variety of people become entrepreneurs. Many were influenced early in life by role models, people they tried to emulate.
- There are 12 distinctive characteristics needed to be a successful entrepreneur. However, they can be strengthened and developed through commitment and a willingness to work.
- Foundational skills such as math, communication, and decision-making skills are also needed by entrepreneurs to set up and run a business.
- Although everyone has the potential to become an entrepreneur, the more background profile you share with the typical entrepreneur, the more likely you are to start your own business.

RECALL KEY TERMS

Using your own words, write a definition for each of the following terms. In addition, find a synonym for each term. Use context clues from the chapter or a thesaurus.

competition	**role model**
investment	**foundational skills**
capital	**Internet**
enterprise	**profile**

RECALL KEY CONCEPTS

1. What do many entrepreneurs consider to be the greatest rewards of being in business for themselves?
2. What is the biggest risk of owning your own business?
3. What percentage of entrepreneurs are under the age of 25?
4. List the 12 personal characteristics of entrepreneurs. How can you strengthen and build on them?
5. What foundation skills do entrepreneurs need to set up and run their businesses?
6. What steps can you take to help develop your entrepreneurial skills?
7. List four activities you can do to strengthen your own entrepreneurial characteristics.

THINK CRITICALLY

1. Compare the rewards of being an entrepreneur with the costs and risks of owning your own business.
2. Describe how a role model has influenced your life.
3. Of the 12 personal characteristics needed by an entrepreneur, which three do you feel are your strongest? Explain why.
4. Explain how each of the following foundational skills: math, communications, and decision making, can help you be a successful entrepreneur.
5. Do you agree with the concept that everyone has the potential to become an entrepreneur? Why or why not?

CHAPTER 2 REVIEW

CONNECT ACADEMICS TO THE WORKPLACE

Math

1. After calling the local chamber of commerce, Keela found out that there were 1,677 entrepreneurs in her town. Refer to the research summary on the background of entrepreneurs (pages 24–27) and calculate the following based on Keela's findings:
   - The number of entrepreneurs who are under age 35 when they started their businesses
   - The number under age 25
   - The number with a high school diploma or less

Speaking

2. Read a magazine article or book on a biography of a successful entrepreneur. As you read, note incidents or observations that illustrate entrepreneurial characteristics and skills. Prepare an oral report to the class and focus on these traits.

   As a class, determine the traits that successful entrepreneurs have in common.

WORK IN YOUR COMMUNITY

Working in groups of two or three students, identify a business that you think would be successful in your community.

- Create a newspaper advertisement seeking a person to start the business.
- Name the characteristics and skills necessary for success as an entrepreneur.
- Develop a list of questions you would use to interview the applicants for the position. Center your questions around the traits that you advertised for.

LINK SCHOOL TO CAREER

Interview your principal or another administrator at your school.

- Share the characteristics of successful entrepreneurs that you learned about in this chapter. Ask the administrator you interviewed which traits he or she has.
- Ask about the skills and characteristics needed to be a successful administrator.
- Ask him or her to compare being a school administrator with an entrepreneur.
- Communicate your findings with the class.

*inter*NET CONNECTION

Custom Card Club

You and several of your friends decide to open a business creating and producing custom greeting cards for special occasions. The investment needed is approximately $15,000 for the computer hardware, software, and supplies.

Connect

Using a variety of Web search engines, search the Internet and prepare a business report on the following topics:

- Tips for financing the business
- Sources of start-up capital
- Potential investors for the business

CHAPTER 3 RECOGNIZING OPPORTUNITY

Learning Objectives

When you have completed this chapter, you will be able to:

- **Discuss** current entrepreneurial trends
- **List** ways to think creatively about opportunity
- **Identify** sources of ideas and how turn your own experiences into opportunities
- **Locate** business opportunities
- **Compare and contrast** buying a business and starting a business

You're the Boss!

Recognizing Opportunities

You know that it's important to be creative when you think about starting and running a business, but you've never considered yourself to be very imaginative. Unfortunately, it seems that all the good ideas have been taken.

What Will You Do?

What are some ways to exercise your creativity and apply it to your new business?

SECTION 3.1

Understanding Entrepreneurial Trends

What you'll learn

- Current trends that provide opportunity for entrepreneurs
- Where to look for business ideas
- How to recognize opportunity

Why it's important

Business owners must constantly look for new products and services to satisfy their customers. They must also find new ways to stay ahead of the competition. The ability to recognize new opportunities and to think creatively is essential for success in today's market.

KEY TERMS

outsource
strategic alliances
innovation
demographics
trade magazines
specialty magazines
trade shows

LOOKING AT TRENDS

Are you ready to begin the entrepreneurial process? This process involves taking the steps to recognize an opportunity and create a business for profit. These steps include planning, gathering information, and making decisions about a whole range of topics. First you need to identify a business opportunity.

Some Current Entrepreneurial Trends

The business trends that are sweeping our country provide a great opportunity for the creation of new businesses. Some of the major trends you can see include the growth of home-based businesses, a focus on information, increased emphasis on outsourcing, and new kinds of strategic alliances.

More Home-based Businesses. The number of businesses that start in the home has been growing rapidly. In the mid-1980s it was estimated that there were 6 million home offices. In the late 1990s estimates suggested that over 41 million businesses were being conducted from home.

The Department of Labor predicted that the number of home-based businesses would double in ten years.

Working at home can save time and money. ***What are some restrictions to working at home?***

Many home-based businesses begin as a result of downsizing in a corporation. Many people choose to work from their home in the field where they were once employed instead of finding a job with another company. Corporate tax consultant, business-plan writer, desktop video producer, and employee trainer are just a few examples of home-based businesses.

In the mid-1990s, *Money* magazine reported that about 20 percent of all entrepreneurs operating from home had business earnings of between $100,000 and $500,000. The average income of the entrepreneur in a home-based business is $50,000 to $60,000 annually. Some opportunities are shown in **Figure 3-1**.

Focus on Technology. An increased reliance on technology is the main trend that affects business today. Technology provides a strong competitive advantage for a business owner. It will continue to be important. Entrepreneurs must know how to use a computer. They must be able to use the Internet and word processing, spreadsheet, database, E-mail, and electronic publishing programs.

Technology offers potential opportunity to entrepreneurs. Many small business owners use the Internet to compete with much larger companies. A Web page on the Internet allows them

Up&Coming Entrepreneur

Auto Maintenance Entrepreneur

Before Brad Klein started Oil Valet in 1997, he was already running two small businesses. As somebody always on the go, Klein came up with the idea to bring his oil-change equipment and mechanics to office buildings in Houston. "We're in a society where everything is instant. There's drive-through food, E-mail, and faxes and everyone's putting in longer days. Speaking for myself, I don't have time to waste a Saturday in a garage waiting for an oil change," says Klein.

Analyze **Many of today's ventures are selling based on an idea of convenience. Can you list some other "convenience" based businesses?**

Figure 3–1

Business Opportunities from Popular Trends

Today you can find business opportunities in traditional industries as well as new industries that didn't exist five years ago. The secret to finding a good business opportunity is the ability to see these opportunities before everyone else does.

1. Fitness and Health

Many people are interested in extending their life expectancy, health, and well-being. One major difference between the trend today and the fitness trend of the 1980s is that today people are concerned about healing both their bodies and their minds.

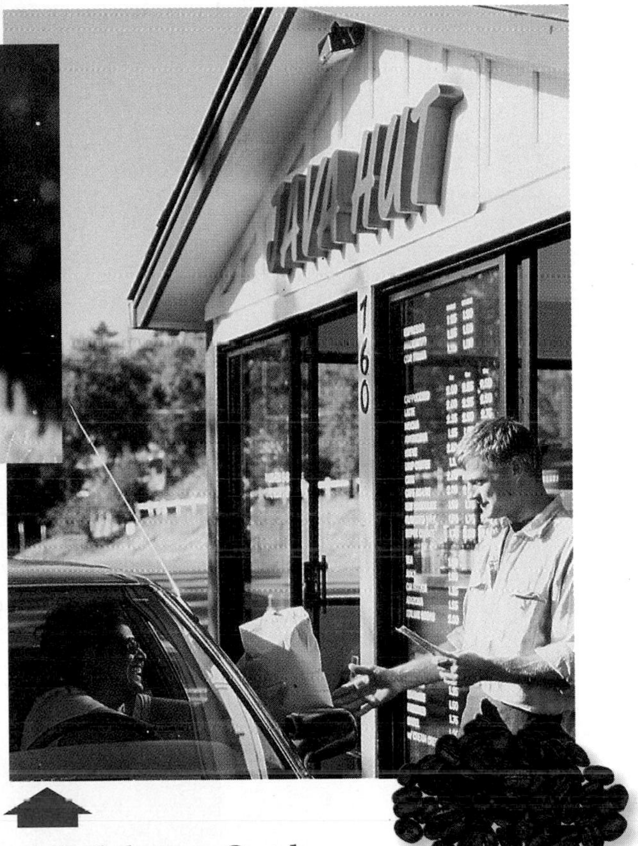

2. Indulgence Goods

People are busy. There are so many choices and so little time that there is a trend toward indulging yourself on little luxuries like expensive chocolates, gourmet coffee, unusual salsas, specialty juices, and vitamin supplements. Luxury services like pet sitting and errand services abound.

3. Ethnic Products

We are a multicultural nation. Entrepreneurs can find many opportunities to serve the special needs of particular ethnic groups with foods, hair-care products, cosmetics, and other products and services.

Money Matters

REVENUE

Be creative in managing your resources. The herbal tea company, Celestial Seasonings, was started with $500 in 1970. Co-founder, Mo Siegel, explains how:

"*My partner sold his Datsun 240Z . . . I rented a little A-frame cabin on the side of a mountain . . . and picked the herbs we used . . . for free.*"

to advertise in the same way large companies do. The Sharper Image, a retailer of toys for adults, reports millions of dollars in Internet sales. Fitscape, an on-line fitness resource started by high school and college students, can compete with larger competitors on the Internet.

Outsourcing. Many entrepreneurs outsource, or contract with other companies for services. For example, suppose you have invented a new board game. You can pay a manufacturer to produce your game. Then you can contract a distributor to find retail outlets for your game. You can outsource almost any activity of your business.

Outsourcing provides opportunities for entrepreneurs to supply services to other companies. Employee leasing companies are one example of a service that "rents" employees to companies.

Strategic Alliances. One step beyond outsourcing is forming a partnership with another company. This partnership is known as a strategic alliance. Your small company may form an alliance with a larger company to supply them with a product or service.

For example, 3M, the manufacturer of adhesive products like Scotch™ Brand Tape, looks to small companies for complementary products like tape dispensers. They form a strategic alliance. The small company provides them with all the tape dispensers they need to package with their adhesive tape.

Altering everyday activities can be a good way to trigger new ideas. ***How can being in a nonbusinesslike setting help inspire new ideas?***

LEARNING TO RECOGNIZE OPPORTUNITY

You may wonder where ideas come from. How do people come up with great ideas? Is creativity something you're born with? Not necessarily. Can you learn to be creative? Absolutely!

How do creative ideas turn into opportunities? Creativity is the activity that results in **innovation**, which is finding new ways of doing things. Innovation is a key aspect of entrepreneurship. In a global marketplace that is highly competitive, it's important that entrepreneurs find new and exciting products and services.

Thinking Creatively about Opportunity

Creativity requires you to be aware of your surroundings. Fortunately, there are many ways to activate your creativity.

1. *Thinking outside of the square.* Getting yourself to look at an ordinary item in a new way is an excellent stimulus for creativity. Find a simple item and figure out how many new products or uses you can find for it. The more you practice, the better you'll get at seeing things in a different light.
2. *Go from here to there.* When you find yourself perplexed by a problem, think about how to get from here to there—a solution. Have you ever used a flat-head screwdriver to pry something open instead of to screw something? That's finding a creative solution to a problem.
3. *Work with unrelated items.* Ask a friend to put together a tray of different items chosen at random. Then try to come up with a new product from the items you've been given. This forces you to look at things in a new way.

Creative Sources of Ideas

Ideas can come to you from anywhere, and sometimes in the strangest of moments. Research has found that some of the greatest ideas have come to people when they're brushing their teeth, driving, or sleeping. Here are some idea sources:

- *Start people watching.* Find places in your community where you'll be able to observe people. In a hotel lobby or a shopping mall, you can learn a lot about what people want and need. That's how Mary Naylor learned that people who work in office buildings wanted the same kind of concierge service offered in hotels. She formed Capitol Concierge to do just that.

Tips from the Real World

GENDER BLIND

The business world has traditionally been dominated by men, but many new industries are now breaking out of this mode. As Cheryl Thompson-Draper, head of Warren Electric Telecom & Utilities, comments:

"*The telecommunications industry is very blind to which (gender) they're dealing with, and they really don't care.*"

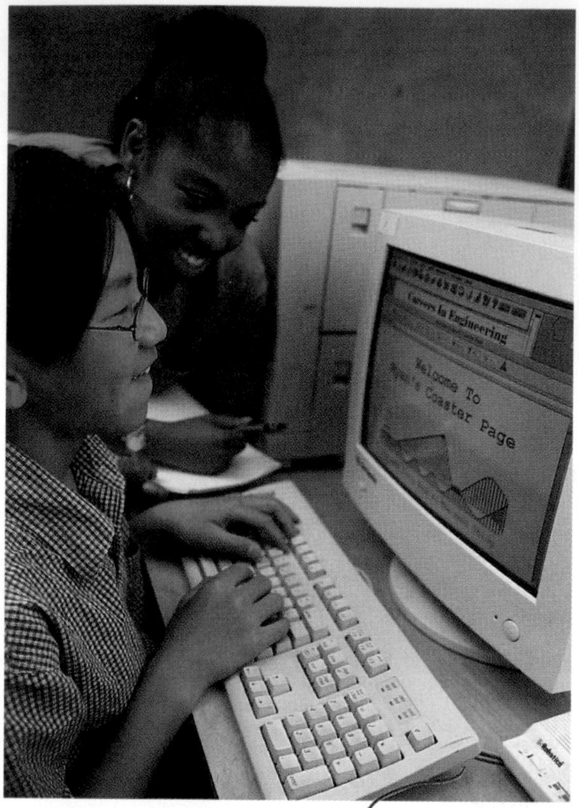

New technology can result in new commercial opportunities. ***What are some businesses that have stemmed from the growth of the Internet?***

Her business handles special services such as arranging for theater tickets or making dinner reservations.

- *Watch for demographic changes.* **Demographics** are the characteristics of human populations and population segments, especially when used to identify consumer markets. Demographic changes occur on a continuing basis. Such changes in the number of births or deaths, age distribution, levels of education, occupations, and geographic concentration can affect your business. The study mentioned in Chapter 2 showed that people under the age of 35 start about 47 percent of all new businesses. Those young business owners have unique needs that Jennifer Kushell recognized. She established *The International Directory of Young Entrepreneurs* on the Internet.
- *Become an insatiable reader.* Most successful entrepreneurs stay on top of what's going on in business and the world by reading newspapers, magazines, and books. Don't read just in your area of interest. Sometimes reading about an unrelated field will spark an idea that you can apply to your field. For example, observing the spiny burr in nature was the inspiration for Velcro, the unique fastening tape found on outdoor equipment and clothing.

Consider Your Own Experiences

Self-employment options within your own experience are the easiest to identify and are excellent sources of opportunity. Look for opportunities in your hobbies and in your work.

Hobbies. Many hobbies can be turned into successful ventures. Developing Web sites, restoring cars, playing a sport, making music—these are just a few pastimes that have potential. Try to evaluate your own favorite pastime in terms of its business potential. What equipment, supplies, or special arrangements does your hobby require? What kinds of problems or inconveniences do you face? Are there any changes on the horizon that might affect your pastime? Answers to these questions can lead to a business.

Work. If you work after school, you have another source of ideas for business opportunities. Look at it from another perspective. Ask yourself: Is there room in the market for a similar business, possibly in a different niche? Are there any gaps in the company's network of suppliers? Are the company or its customers in need of services that aren't being provided?

Consult Outside Sources

Look at people, places, and things in the business community for business ideas, but don't lose sight of your goal. Constantly ask yourself, "What self-employment opportunities does this present to someone with my interests?"

- *Trade magazines.* Trade magazines are periodicals published for specific types of businesses or industries. For example, *Presstime Online* is a monthly magazine covering the newspaper industry. *Progressive Grocer* covers the supermarket industry. *Cleaner* is a trade publication and product guide for industrial cleaning contractors. Trade magazines often contain articles, ads, and ideas on new products, services, or business concepts. You may be able to obtain copies from businesspeople, vocational instructors, or the Internet.
- *Specialty magazines.* Specialty magazines target people with special interests in sports, camping, fashion, and a variety of other areas. They can also provide ideas for new business ventures. Articles in such specialty magazines can help identify interests and needs of potential consumers.
- *Newspapers.* Newspapers provide an ongoing source of ideas for businesses. Many have business sections which, like other business publications, report on trends and innovations.

Trade shows are a rich source of information for entrepreneurs. ***What can trade shows offer that trade journals cannot?***

Beyond the business pages, other sections can be a source of ideas.

- *Trade shows and exhibitions.* Nearly every field has national or regional trade shows. The purpose of these events is to allow vendors and manufacturers to introduce new items and promote established products and services. These shows can be a source of spin-off ideas. Contact your local chamber of commerce or search the Internet for times and dates of shows and exhibitions.
- *Internet.* The Internet can be a source for opportunities. Many sites, such as the Small Business Administration site, can offer ideas for entrepreneurs. You can use a search engine to research other opportunities.
- *Government agencies.* Information regarding specific opportunities as well as trend information can also be obtained from federal agencies. The U.S. Patent Office, for example, can provide information on patents that are available for public use. Names and addresses of organizations that can provide information on any topic are available through the National Referral Service in the Library of Congress. The Bureau of Economic Analysis in the Department of Commerce publishes a survey of current business conditions. You can also contact federal agencies on the Internet.

CHECK YOUR UNDERSTANDING

SECTION 3.1

Reviewing Key Terms and Concepts

1. List two current trends that offer opportunities for entrepreneurs.
2. Discuss three ways to recognize opportunity in your community.
3. What are demographics and how do they affect your business?

Critical Thinking Activity

Look in your community for a need that is not being met. List at least three services and products related to this need that offer a business opportunity and present them to your class.

Extension Lab—Communicating Information

Back to the Future You have just graduated from college with a degree in business and have gone to work for a company that forecasts business trends. Your first assignment is to make a presentation to the boss on the entrepreneurial trends you see sweeping our country.

Role Play Explain the trends and how they will affect business in the United States and the world. Be sure to include:

- Examples of businesses that might develop as a result of the specific trend
- Predictions of future trends and how they create new businesses

SECTION 3.2

Starting Versus Buying a Business

SHOULD YOU ENTER AN EXISTING BUSINESS?

Being creative and opportunistic does not always mean that you must start a business from scratch. You may also enter a family business or buy an existing business.

Entering the Family Business

If your family owns a business, chances are you've had the opportunity to work there during the summers or after school. Perhaps you have thought about taking over the business one day. This is one way to become an entrepreneur. Such enterprises are an important part of the U.S. economy. They are not generally high-growth businesses, but some have become very large, successful companies, like Mattel Toys.

What you'll learn

- The challenges of entering a family business.
- The benefits and drawbacks of buying a business.
- The responsibilities of starting your own business.

Why it's important

Many people think that to be an entrepreneur you must start a business from scratch. However, many successful entrepreneurs find opportunity in buying an existing business. Then they make it better.

KEY TERMS

goodwill
franchise
franchisee
franchiser
business broker

The Up Side—and the Down of Family Businesses. Family businesses have great potential for success. Unfortunately, only about one-third of family-run businesses survive to the second generation. The reason so many family businesses fail lies in the dynamics of the family itself. The very advantages that family businesses have can often destroy them.

The greatest advantage of a family business is the trust and togetherness that family members share. Because they feel close, a family working as a team can often achieve more than its individual members can. This is a real asset in running a business.

One of the greatest disadvantages of a family enterprise is that its owners can never get away from the business. They may have difficulty viewing the venture and its problems objectively.

To prevent some of the problems that family businesses face, do the following:

- Establish clear lines of responsibility.
- Try to be objective about family members' qualifications.
- Keep decisions unaffected by personal emotions, if possible.
- Respect individual family members' needs.

These practices can minimize family conflicts.

Questions to Ask. Before entering a family business, ask yourself the following questions:

- Do I have the ability to work for a member of my family?
- Do I get along well with the family members who will be involved in the business?
- Do we share the same goals for the business?
- Do we share the same general goals for our personal lives?

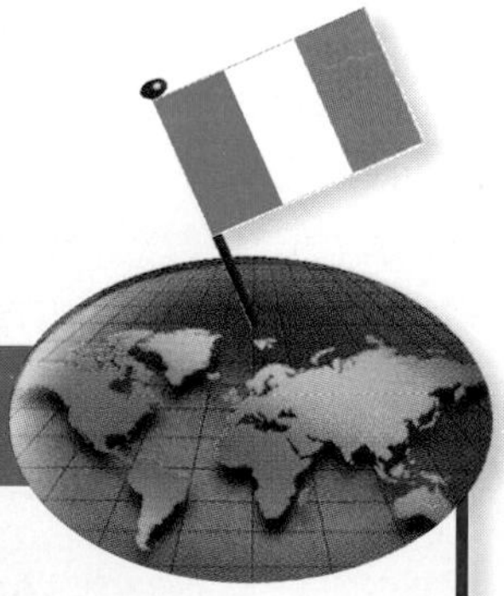

ENTREPRENEURS INTERNATIONAL

Ireland

Alan Johnston, Seamus Gallagher, and Hugh Maguire worked for a leading American manufacturer of low vision aids in Ireland until its Dublin-based operation was downsized. Now, they design and manufacture products on their own. Since September 1994 Ash Technologies has exported products to the United States, the United Kingdom, and mainland Europe.

Apply **Write a paragraph on why Ash Technologies is a good example of benefiting from a job layoff.**

- Can I leave business problems at work when I go home each night?

If you answered no to any one of these questions, you have identified a potential area of conflict. However, if the benefits are substantial, it might be worth your while to resolve the conflict.

Franchised businesses have certain elements in common. ***When a customer enters a restaurant franchise, what can he or she expect?***

Buying a Business

Another way to acquire a business is to buy one. In some cases, buying a business is less risky than starting one from scratch. It may also be an attractive alternative if you do not have a great deal of business experience. Buying a business was the route taken by Ray Kroc. He acquired a hamburger stand from the McDonald brothers, and decided to offer food items without the usual serving services. Kroc's venture redefined the fast-food industry.

Kinds of Businesses Available. Ray Kroc's example highlights one of two purchase options. You can buy an existing business or the right to set up a new business patterned on an existing model.

An existing business already has a location and a physical plant. It may even have experienced employees and regular customers. Customers are especially important. Their continued business after you take over increases your chances of success. Such loyalty, called goodwill , is an extremely valuable business asset.

Goodwill does not attach just to an existing business. It can also attach to a business concept. Millions of people, for example, eat regularly at McDonald's—any McDonald's. The name itself stands for a certain type of food prepared quickly and served in a clean environment.

McDonald's is an example of a franchise . A franchise is a legal agreement to begin a new business in the name of a recognized company. Home Depot, Jiffy Lube®, and Kinko's® are also examples of franchises. The buyers of these franchises pay a percentage of profits annually to the owner of the franchise. Chevrolet, Ford, and Honda dealerships are examples of automobile franchises.

The buyer of a franchise is called the franchisee . The seller is the franchiser . The franchisee is buying a way of operating a

RISK TAKERS PROFIT MAKERS

Name: Anna Maria Arias
Company: Latina Style, Inc.
City, State: Washington, D.C.

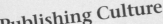

Publishing Culture

Anna Maria Arias would stand in front of news racks bewildered. "I saw zillions of magazines, but nothing for me," Arias asserts. "I founded *Latina Style* to give Hispanic women a platform to profile the success stories of Hispanics in the U.S."

Arias began the business from a hospital bed in 1994, when she was being treated for a blood disorder. She put together a prototype magazine just as Corporate America began to realize they had underestimated the Hispanic market. *Latina Style* was geared toward successful female decision-makers. Her original advertisers knew it and paid for a full year of ad space up front! *Latina Style* now has a circulation of 150,000 readers and is projected to earn $100,000 on revenues of $1 million.

Thinking Critically

List some advantages to operating a culturally segmented business.

business—and a product with name recognition. The franchiser is selling its planning and management expertise.

If you buy a McDonald's franchise, you will be trained in methods of operation. You will learn how to prepare McDonald's products. You will be supplied through McDonald's distribution channels. You will have the benefit of the company's national advertising efforts. All of these things reduce the risk of failure.

A Good Deal or a Bad One? Acquiring an existing business has advantages, such as location, goodwill, staff, and plant. An existing business may have established procedures in place. There may be substantial inventory and established trade credit. The owner may even offer his or her expertise during the transitional period. If you are buying a franchise, these benefits are probably part of the package.

There are also pitfalls. Many businesses are put up for sale because they are not successful. They may be losing money or have a poor reputation. It is difficult to maintain a good reputation, but it can be impossible to repair a bad one. Inventory may be dated and equipment or facilities may need repairs. Employees may lack the skills needed to keep the business competitive.

What can you do to prevent yourself from purchasing a business burdened with such problems? Start with research. Investigate the company and the industry very carefully. Don't rely just on what the seller tells you. The value of a retail business can be determined by verifying the value of its inventory, accounts receivable, and assets. Hire an accountant to advise you.

If you are considering a franchise, you face a different set of challenges. The first is cost. You get a package of benefits, but you pay for it. Purchase prices can be very high. You may also have to pay a fee for advertising and a percentage of your sales annually.

A second negative is lack of freedom. The prepackaged system may inspire confidence in the beginning, but it can become confining. The franchiser may limit how you can run the business.

Where to Find a Business

People find businesses in many ways. The simplest way is to look in the newspaper. Businesses that are for sale are listed in local papers as well as national business publications like *The Wall Street Journal*. One effective way to locate a business is to network with people in the community. Accountants, attorneys, bankers, and local government administrators are good sources. Let them know what kind of business you are looking for. Then keep in touch with them.

Starting a business from scratch requires high levels of research and risk. ***What are the benefits?***

You can also hire a business broker. This is someone whose job it is to bring buyers and sellers together. You can find business brokers in the telephone book.

Questions to Ask Yourself. Before purchasing a business, ask yourself the following questions:

- *Is the business interesting to me and to others?* If you do purchase the business, you will be devoting a tremendous amount of time and effort to making it grow and succeed. Make sure that you really enjoy it.

- *Why is the owner selling?* Owners sell for many reasons—retirement, lack of interest, illness, need for cash. You will want to know if the owner is selling because the business is not doing well or the industry is in decline. Check the firm's financial statements against information from suppliers and competitors.
- *What is the business's potential for growth?* Once businesses are born, they go through a life cycle of growth, maturity, and eventually, decline. Determine where the business you are considering is in this life cycle. It is probably best to avoid a declining business or industry. It is possible to turn an enterprise around, but you probably can't reverse an economic trend.

STARTING YOUR OWN BUSINESS

Suppose your family doesn't own a business and you can't find or don't want to buy an existing business. You may choose to start your own. This was the route chosen by Mo Siegel of Celestial Seasonings. In his geographic area (Colorado), there were no herbal tea companies or related businesses, so he decided to start his own.

What You Gain, What You Lose

Starting a new business entails more time and effort than the other options we have discussed. Think of what you have to do before you can even open the doors. After you determine that your venture is sound, you have to prepare a business plan to convince others. Then you have to find accountants, lawyers, public relations consultants, and other advisors. You will need to lease facilities, purchase equipment, and hire employees. You will have to initiate relationships with suppliers, set up distribution channels, and establish name recognition. The list goes on.

There are also benefits. The principal one is that you can do things your own way. By starting your own business, you avoid someone else's bad organization, poor marketing, and weak management. You can build your company with fresh ideas and enthusiasm.

Questions to Ask Yourself

Before you start your own business, ask yourself these questions:

- Do I have the motivation to start from nothing?
- Do I have sufficient knowledge of basic operations to undertake the business?
- Do I have enough financial resources to start from scratch?

Your answers will help balance your expectations with your resources. To capitalize on opportunities, you will have to take personal risks, especially when starting a business from scratch.

The Creativity Factor

Whether you choose to enter a family business, buy an existing business, or create one from scratch, you will need to think creatively about every aspect of the business. You'll also constantly need to be on the lookout for opportunity.

As an entrepreneur, you'll be responsible for gathering and processing information about your field. You'll be the one who reacts to changes and adjustments. Only you can execute plans once they're made.

CHECK YOUR UNDERSTANDING

SECTION 3.2

Reviewing Key Terms and Concepts

1 What are three questions you should ask yourself before buying an existing business?
2 Why would you start your own business instead of buying an existing one?
3 What are three questions you should ask yourself before starting a business?

Critical Thinking Activity

Talk to a franchise owner in your community and find out the pros and cons of owning a franchise.

Extension Lab—Acquire and Evaluate Data

Strategic Speedy Sir Speedy Inc., the world's largest franchise printing network, and Prontaprint Limited, a Great Britain based, quick-printing franchiser, have formed a strategic partnership that builds the Sir Speedy Global Digital Network to more than 1,200 locations worldwide.

The Sir Speedy Global Digital Network is located in more than 24 countries and has the technology in place for its customers to communicate and transfer printing and copying jobs 24 hours a day, seven days a week.

Research Research the impact that this strategic partnership has had on the rest of the printing industry in the world. Write a report on your findings.

CHAPTER 3 REVIEW

CHAPTER SUMMARY

- The ability to recognize new opportunities and think creatively is essential for success in today's market.
- Some major entrepreneurial trends include the growth of home-based businesses, a focus on information, outsourcing, and new kinds of strategic alliances.
- Creative sources of ideas can come from anywhere and at anytime.
- Many ideas for self-employment lie within an entrepreneur's own experience.
- Self-employment opportunities can also be found by consulting outside sources in the business community.
- You can become an entrepreneur by entering a family business, buying an existing business or franchise, or starting your own enterprise from scratch.
- The ties that are a family business's advantage can also be its downfall.
- Buying an existing business is often less risky for an entrepreneur, especially if you don't have a great deal of business experience.
- Starting your own business demands more time and effort than other options but allows you to do things your own way, avoiding others' mistakes.

RECALL KEY TERMS

Write an article for your school newspaper describing how important it is to be creative when thinking about starting and running a business. Use the following key terms:

outsource
strategic alliances
innovation
demographics
trade magazines
specialty magazines
trade shows
goodwill
franchise
franchisee
franchiser
business broker

RECALL KEY CONCEPTS

1. Contracting with others for services is:
   (a) creativity (b) outsourcing
   (c) developing alliances
2. Forming a partnership with another company is called a(n):
   (a) strategic alliance (b) outside source
   (c) creative alliance
3. The characteristics of human populations are called:
   (a) demographics (b) personalities
   (c) human behaviors
4. Outside sources to consult when generating business ideas include:
   (a) trade shows and exhibits
   (b) government agencies (c) both a and b
5. Which of the following is a disadvantage of entering a family-owned business?
   (a) The owners can never get away from the business.
   (b) Decisions are made without emotion.
   (c) Family members always have the same goals.
6. Which of the following is an advantage of buying a franchise?
   (a) There is no risk of failure.
   (b) You have increased freedom to run the business.
   (c) You receive planning and management expertise.

7. The main trend that affects business today is:
   (a) changing demographics
   (b) technology (including the Internet)
   (c) creativity and innovation

THINK CRITICALLY

1. Describe an entrepreneurial opportunity that might be available for each of the current trends discussed in the chapter.
2. Select an ordinary item in your classroom (chalk, computer, podium, etc.). By thinking outside of the square, develop a list of new uses for the item.
3. Would you rather enter a family-owned business or buy a business? Why or why not?
4. Compare and contrast buying an existing business and buying a franchise.
5. If you were going into business for yourself, would it be important that you enjoy what you were doing? Why or why not?

CONNECT ACADEMICS TO THE WORKPLACE

Math

1. After doing some research on the age demographics of the residents in his hometown, Antwoin learned the following:

0-5 years of age	960 residents
6 -11	1,840
12–18	4,500
19–35	8,225
36–60	5,150
Over 60	2,960

Construct a bar graph to present this information. Use computer software if possible.

Creative Thinking

2. Working in teams of two or three students, create a poster showcasing the wide variety of outside sources available to would-be entrepreneurs. Target your poster to teenagers.

WORK IN YOUR COMMUNITY

Consider the hobbies and activities that interest you. What types of businesses in your community support these hobbies and activities? Prepare a list to share with the class.

LINK SCHOOL TO CAREER

Working in teams, prepare a list of franchises in your town. As a class, compile the lists and assign each team a different franchise to research. Be sure to find out the cost of the franchise, the planning, training and management expertise offered, and the national advertising available. Each team should prepare an oral presentation of the franchise to the class.

interNET CONNECTION

Food Finding Fast

You are considering opening your own restaurant. Use the Internet to conduct research on franchise options.

Connect

Use a variety of Web search engines to locate the following information on at least three restaurant franchises:

- Initial investment
- Location and storefront requirements
- Training and management expertise

Make a selection and explain your decision.

CHAPTER 4

Global Opportunities

Learning Objectives

When you have completed this chapter, you will be able to:

- **Compare and contrast** importing with exporting
- **Discuss** why the global marketplace is important and where there are opportunities
- **List** key points to remember when doing business with another country
- **Create** a plan for finding the best market for your product or service

You're the Boss!

Exploring Exports

You have a successful business selling sporting goods in the United States. Your partner has just approached you with a new idea for your business. His uncle in Mexico City would like to import your products to supplement the stock in his store, where he sells soccer gear. This could be a great opportunity for your business to expand, but neither of you knows anything about exporting.

What Will You Do? How will you learn more about exporting?

SECTION 4.1

Global Entrepreneurship

What you'll learn

- why entrepreneurs are going global
- where the global opportunities are
- key elements of international business

Why it's important

Technological advances have made faraway markets accessible to every business. It's important for business owners to understand the global marketplace and the many opportunities and challenges it provides.

KEY TERMS

global economy
exporting
importing
trade barriers
tariffs
gross domestic product (GDP)

WHY ARE ENTREPRENEURS GOING GLOBAL?

Take a look at some of the things you own—your bike, your CD player, even your favorite pair of jeans. Chances are they were made in a country other than the United States, even if they have an American brand name or label. Businesses sell and buy goods and services to and from other countries to survive and expand. In this section, you'll learn about the global challenges and opportunities that face entrepreneurs today.

We Live in a Global Economy

A **global economy** means that the economies of countries are linked in the marketplace. The selling and shipping of products to another country is called **exporting**. When you purchase a CD player that was made in Japan and sold in the United States, Japan benefits from a bigger market for its goods. The U.S. company that purchased the CD player from Japan and sold it to you benefits

Deliveries can be made overnight to many parts of the world. ***What factors determine rates?***

from being able to offer a wider variety of products to its customers. You benefit by buying high-quality equipment at a competitive price. Businesses that buy goods from other countries to sell in their own country are importing.

If you are a business owner today, it is possible that you will purchase and sell goods or services to other countries, manufacture in other countries, or have competitors in other countries. Two of the main reasons for this global economy are the changes in trade barriers and technology.

1. **Trade Barriers Have Fallen.** In some parts of the world, the elimination or lessening of trade barriers (taxes, quotas, and other restrictions on goods entering or leaving a country) has increased the flow of goods among countries. The North American Free Trade Agreement (NAFTA) eliminates trade barriers among the United States, Mexico, and Canada. The General Agreement on Tariffs and Trade (GATT) reduces or eliminates tariffs among 117 countries around the world. Tariffs are taxes imposed by a government on imported or exported goods.

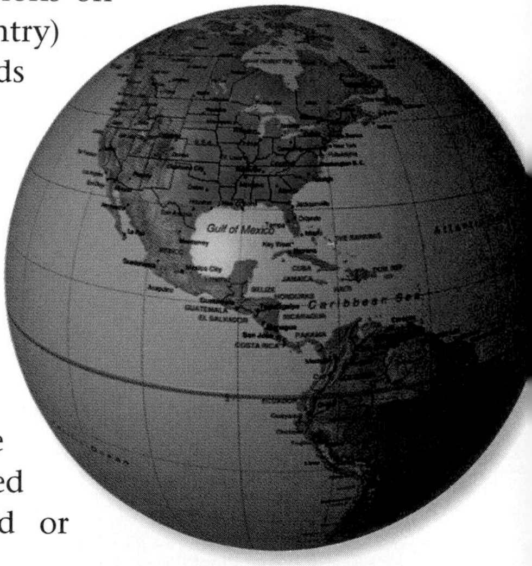

2. **Technology Has Made the World Smaller.** Today it's easier than ever to communicate with people in other countries on the phone, through facsimile machines, with E-mail, and over the Internet. Small businesses can quickly set up shop on the Internet and reach customers anywhere in the world as easily and as inexpensively as a large company. That's what Jennifer Kushell did when she founded *The International Directory of Young Entrepreneurs*, which enables young

entrepreneurs from all over the world to share ideas and information. Putting her business on the Internet made it easy for young entrepreneurs to find her no matter where they live.

Opportunities Abroad Have Never Been Greater

If you consider the fact that the international market is more than four times the size of the U.S. market, you can understand why it holds many opportunities for growing businesses. The U.S. Department of Commerce has selected the top ten countries for exporting U.S. goods. You will find them in **Figure 4–1**. Today these ten countries make up 25 percent of the world's *gross domestic product.* Gross domestic product (GDP) is the total value of all goods produced during the year. These same countries are expected to make up to half of the world's GDP by the year 2010.

Although opportunities are great in the global market, there are risks. To be successful in the global market you must be able to offer a product or service at a competitive price. You must also be able to make your product stand out in a crowded marketplace.

Dealing in the global market is often complex and expensive. The time to do it is when you know your business has survived start-up and is ready to grow.

Tips from the Real World

CULTURAL RESPECT

In your international dealings, don't expect all countries to do business the American task-oriented way. As Julia Sloan, founder of an intercultural training firm, points out:

"[Some cultures are] relationship-oriented... [where] people simply can't hear what you have to share with them in terms of business until they get to know you as a person."

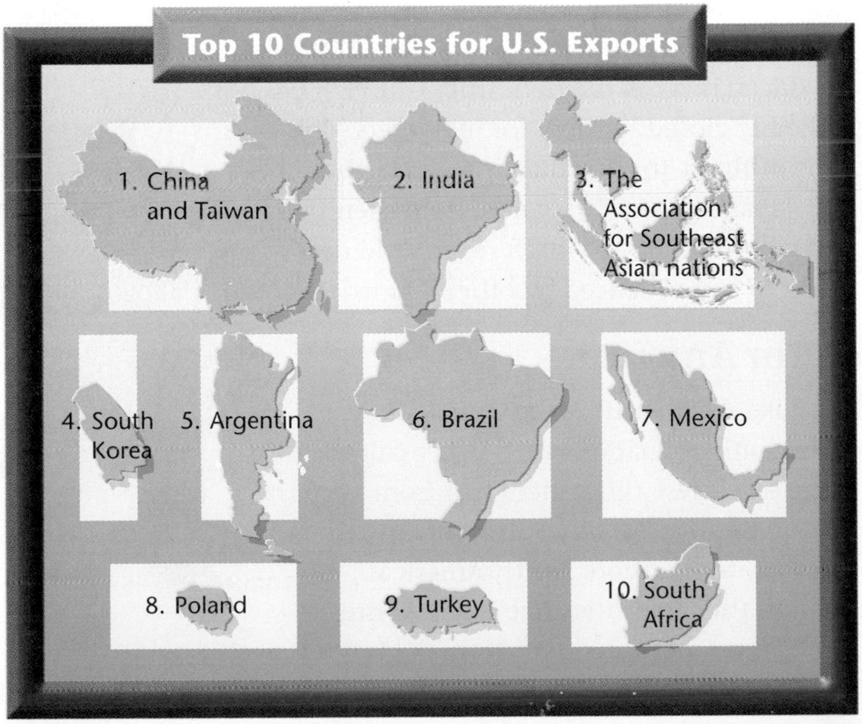

Figure 4–1
Finding out which countries import American goods and services is a good start for your export business. ***Countries from what continent import the most American goods?***

Money Matters

GLOBAL INCOME

International business is the way of the future. Michael Zey, professor of management at Montclair State University, makes a prediction about the twenty-first century:

"*Your source of labor will be international; your source of financial support will be international; your market will be international.*"

WHERE ARE THE GLOBAL OPPORTUNITIES?

As you learned in Chapter 3, opportunity can be found anywhere. In a global market, the possibilities are endless. However, cultural differences mean you have to study each country before attempting to do business there.

Asia

Asia is an enormous and diverse continent that ranges from the sophisticated market of Singapore to the unique Japanese market and the newly emerging and powerful Chinese market. It is also a growing source of products and services.

In China, the government controls business. Laws and regulations are strict. Poverty among its millions of peasants is a severe problem. These factors make China a difficult place to do business. Still, the U.S. Chamber of Commerce says there are more than 200 small U.S. companies doing business in China and the number is growing. One man from Florida who offers English classes to Chinese government officials and businesspeople says that China today is like the Wild West. It's a new market frontier. China is the fastest growing economy in the world. It is looking for new products and services from other countries that will help it grow. Some successful strategies are shown in **Figure 4–2.**

Japan is much different from China. It has been called a "closed" society for marketers. This means it is difficult to introduce products that are not Japanese. Many Japanese hold their traditional culture in very high regard and don't want to be influenced by other countries.

Latin America

Like Asia, Latin America is a diverse community of nations with many cultural differences. These differences run from very traditional cultures, as in the Mayan tribes of Mexico, to the more North American, as seen in the large cities like Buenos Aires.

Latin Americans tend to make buying decisions based on their family's needs rather than one person's individual

Figure 4–2

Finding Success in Asia

To be profitable in Asian countries, follow the examples of big companies. There seem to be three approaches that are successful there.

1. Direct marketing to the customer.

Avon partnered with the Guangzhou Cosmetics Factory to sell its cosmetics directly to Chinese women. The system is similar to the one Avon uses in the United States.

2. Collaborating with a local company.

Procter and Gamble sells its brand-name shampoos as well as a local brand, Jiejua, in a partnership with Hutchison China Trade Co.

3. Discovering a luxury niche or corner of the market.

Coca-Cola discovered that cola drinks are a luxury in China. It catered to the Chinese desire for luxury goods by marketing Coke as an upscale drink.

needs. So, they tend to choose products that will benefit the family. Latin American consumers more often look at the merits of the products and do comparison shopping before they buy.

In some countries, like Mexico, consumers prefer U.S. goods. This presents a good opportunity for an entrepreneur to meet their needs with a great product or service.

Europe

It is only recently that Europeans have begun to encourage entrepreneurship. Some say the reason is that risk taking and business failure are not accepted in Europe as they are in other parts of the world. However, that is changing with the success of entrepreneurs such as Richard Branson, who founded Virgin Atlantic Airways and Virgin Records.

Europe is a difficult market to define because there is no common European culture. The conversion of European currency to the Euro in 2002 will make commerce easier, but there are still cultural differences. For example, Italy is very different from France. French people are more likely to eat in restaurants than Italians are. Also, the French are very protective of their culture. When the Walt Disney Company placed Euro-Disney in France, it was initially viewed as an intrusion.

The important thing for entrepreneurs to understand about Europe is that cultural differences among some countries are huge,

Certain American products are highly sought after in other countries. ***What are some foreign goods that have gained good reputations in the United States?***

as in the case of France and Italy. Products that do well in one country may not do well in the other.

Regions in Transition

Developing countries, often with unstable governments, provide a risky form of opportunity for entrepreneurs. There are many barriers and little support for business owners. Some examples are Russia, the eastern European countries, Africa, and parts of the Middle East.

When doing business in these countries, it's wise to partner with a local company and to research the culture and business practices very carefully. In addition, you may not be able to take your profits out of the business in U.S. dollars. Many companies, however, have found creative ways to take their profits out of the country. For example, you might find a local product in that country that would sell well in the United States. Then you could use your profits to purchase that product in bulk.

CHECK YOUR UNDERSTANDING

SECTION 4.1

Reviewing Key Terms and Concepts

1 Discuss two reasons for the global economy today.

2 What are trade barriers?

3 Compare and contrast two global markets.

Critical Thinking Activity

Make a list of ten products you use every day. Find out what countries make them and combine your list with other students' lists to make a master list.

Extension Lab—Teach Others

A Lesson in Culture Your employer has transferred you to Latin America for one year. Your co-worker, who will be going as well, does not seem to appreciate the importance of understanding the Latin culture and doing business accordingly.

Role Play Write and present a skit that will emphasize how to be a successful international businessperson. Be sure to include:

- The cultural differences between the United States and Latin America
- Ways you can show respect and understanding for their culture
- Tips on becoming internationally savvy

SECTION 4.2

Ways to Enter the Global Market

What you'll learn

- how international business is different from U.S. business
- how to find the best international market for your product
- differences between importing and exporting

Why it's important

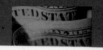

The keys to succeeding in another country are to understand its culture and find a product or service that meets its citizens' needs.

KEY TERMS

interpreter
Standard Industrial Trade Classification (SITC) codes
International Business Exchange (IBEX)
trade missions
"best prospect" list
disposable income
export management company
freight forwarder
joint venture

UNDERSTANDING INTERNATIONAL BUSINESS

Understanding how other countries conduct business is important to your success as an entrepreneur. In this section you'll learn about some of the differences between American business customs and those of other countries. You'll also learn how to prepare yourself for these differences.

Culture Shock

It's unfortunate that many people believe everyone must do business as it's done in America. For example, American business owners often go to Japan in a hurry to close a deal. They allow themselves just four days for this trip, and they're eager to get it taken care of quickly and go back home. The Japanese, by contrast, do not feel this same time pressure. They have

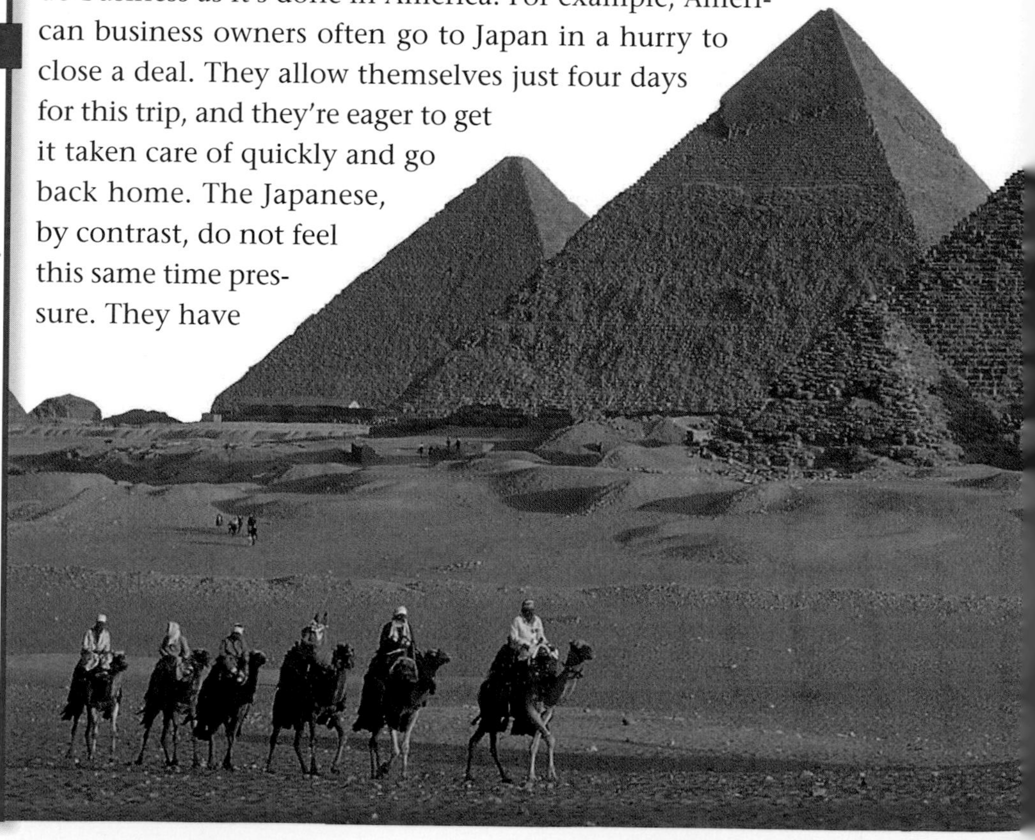

RISK TAKERS PROFIT MAKERS

Name: Dave Kappell
Business: Magnetic Poetry Inc.
City, State: Minneapolis, MN

Stuck on Magnets

"It all started five years ago as a tool I made for myself to help my songwriting." Recounting the origin of Magnetic Poetry Inc. Dave Kappell says, "I'd cut out the words and move them around until it looked more interesting. It worked great until I sneezed." Kappell later applied the words to magnets and used his refrigerator as a composition board. He couldn't help but notice his friends' interest in this idea. Kappell interviewed local retailers and gathered sales and marketing information. The same retailers took his first Magnetic Poetry Kits and were pleased to report they were selling well. Kappell hired independent sales representatives and began mass producing his kits. Today Magnetic Poetry Inc. offers 50 different products in five languages, with annual sales of nearly $6.5 million.

Thinking Critically

What are some strategies to help a product like Magnetic Poetry in the global market?

a longer-term view of things and want to get to know the *person* they're dealing with before they strike a business deal.

When in Rome. Imagine you're on your first trip to Indonesia. On the first night, your potential Indonesian business partners hold a dinner party. Since you are the honored guest, they offer you the traditional fish eye to eat. Are you surprised? You wouldn't be if you had prepared yourself by studying the country's culture. Steve Snyder, who started 21st Century Laboratories, did just that. He was prepared for the fish eye. He took the time to understand the culture and the way business is conducted. As a result, today he exports his vitamin supplements to 40 countries.

Some Important International Tips. Here are a few ways that you can show respect and understanding for the cultures of the international people with whom you do business.

- *Always accept a business card with respect.* Look at it and put it carefully into a cardholder. Don't ever write on it! In Asia, that's considered an insult.
- *Dress conservatively in dark colors.* In the Far East, for example, white is a symbol of mourning, and loud colors are taboo.
- *Be punctual.* With the possible exception of the Arab and Latin worlds, most cultures respect being on time. Don't be late to an important business meeting.
- *Don't comment on food except to praise it.* People in other countries might not want to hear about our low-fat, no-sugar diets. Respect their different taste in food.
- *Don't correct their English.* Instead, make an effort to learn a few key words in their language. You'll gain their respect for your effort.
- *Talk in terms of their currency, not U.S. dollars.* Be clear about whose currency you refer to in your negotiations. Using the other person's currency is a sign of respect.
- *Be prepared to remove your shoes in a temple, mosque (a place of worship), or in some homes.* This is a sign of respect, so wear good-looking socks!

Do Business the Way They Do. The way business is conducted in most of the world is not the same as it is in the United States. In general, Americans are far more casual. For example, Americans tend to use first names from the moment they meet someone. This is not acceptable in most other countries. It would be considered rude. Use a person's first name only after he or she has asked you to.

In the United States we also tend to be more in a hurry and are often called "pushy." Here are some things to remember that will help you become an internationally savvy businessperson.

Up&Coming Entrepreneur

Internet Entrepreneur

Rajib Momen started his on-line consulting business, The World's Greatest BBS, when he was 12. With business guidance from the National Foundation for Teaching Entrepreneurship, he has expanded into computer repair and sales, Web site design and hosting, and Internet access. After accomplishing all this in high school, what's next? "I would like to make it a self-running business with employees," the young Bostonian says. That way when he goes to college, he can let others run the business.

Analyze How can Web sites help foster international business?

- *Do your homework before the first meeting.* You should know something about the country and its culture. It is also important to learn a few key words in the other language. Doing your homework shows respect for the other person and his or her country.
- *Build a relationship before you do business.* That may mean carrying on a conversation about sports or something going on in that country, perhaps a special event. It's best to stay away from politics and religion. The goal is to build trust with your potential business partner.
- *Don't set time limits on the meeting.* Remember that other countries are much less driven by the clock than Americans are. Try to keep things as open-ended as possible. This will also give you more power when you need to negotiate something.
- *Bring your own* interpreter. This person will translate the other person's language into English for you. It's best to be represented by someone you know and trust.

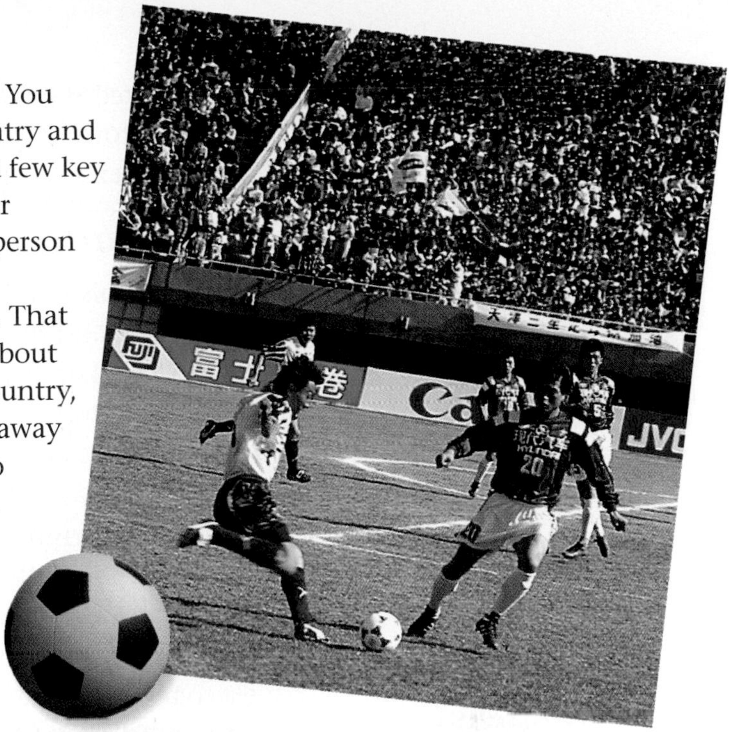

When doing business in another country, it's important to show an interest in and respect for its culture. ***What are some ways to do this?***

FINDING THE BEST INTERNATIONAL MARKET

The world market is a big place. How do you find the best place to conduct business? This section will help you find an international market for your product or service.

Sources for Finding the Best Market

There are many sources to help you locate the best market for your product or service. Start by going to your library and consulting the *International Trade Statistics Yearbook of the United States*. This book is organized by the Standard Industrial Trade Classification (SITC) codes.

Find your product or service and, in addition to the SITC codes, you will find a great deal of information about how well your type of product or service does in the different marketplaces. Suppose you're planning to export a toy. In the *Yearbook* you can find out how many toys are sold in different countries every year. You would look for a country that imports more toys than the average. The country should also have a history of importing goods from the United States. Generally, American goods should be about 5 percent of total imports in that country. A country that meets these two criteria is a good bet as an export candidate.

Other Sources of Help

You might also want to contact the International Trade Administration office and the Department of Commerce in Washington, D.C. The U.S. Chamber of Commerce has an electronic commerce system called the International Business Exchange (IBEX). It lets you sell products and services online anywhere in the world. It's also a good way to find trading partners.

The U.S. government and private agencies also offer small businesses the opportunity to go on trade missions. Trade missions give small business owners the ability to meet and talk with foreign agents, distributors, or potential business partners. The participants have a chance to make valuable contacts in other countries by traveling there. To participate in a trade mission, you will need to have a product that is on the government's "best prospect" list. That means it is a product that other countries are looking to purchase. You will also need to have a good business plan, which will show how you plan to market your product in that country. You'll learn about business plans in Chapter 5.

IMPORTING AND EXPORTING

What is the difference between importing and exporting products between countries? How do you decide on a product? What are some things you should consider before

ENTREPRENEURS INTERNATIONAL

Israel

Two brothers, Shmuel and Uzi Cohen, have forged their small factory into a major force in Israel's steel industry. Cohen Metal Works markets a wide range of steel commodities. They recently expanded their business by supplying raw materials, including cement and ceiling tiles, to the building industry. With the lowering of tension in the Middle East, Shmuel Cohen has been in contact with neighboring countries about supplying large quantities of steel to Arab companies. In 1997 sales reached over $100 million.

Apply **Find an article in the paper about international politics. Write a paragraph on how these politics concern business opportunities.**

attempting to import or export? As an entrepreneur, you'll need to know the answers to these questions before going global.

The Differences between Importing and Exporting

You already learned that exporting means selling and shipping goods to another country. Maarten Voogd, the owner of Water Ventures Inc., a California company, sells resort equipment made in the United States to other countries. In contrast, importing means buying products from other countries to resell in your own country. For example, you might import custom bicycles from France to sell in your community.

Deciding on a Product

The U.S. Department of Commerce reports that the hottest products for exporting are paper products, electronic equipment, chemical products, apparel, industrial machinery, computers, and agricultural products. It's important to know this because you will be successful as an exporter only if you sell products that other countries want. Actually, the United States is the largest exporter of merchandise and services in the world. It is followed by Canada, Japan, Mexico, the United Kingdom, South Korea, and Germany.

If you are going to export consumer products, you will also need to find a country where people have enough disposable income, that is, money to spend after necessary expenses are paid. This is because the types of products you will export are not typically necessities. In some countries, they may even be considered luxuries, such as Coca-Cola in China.

Also remember that exporting or importing is a long-term commitment. It takes time to develop a good relationship with another country. Don't expect to make money immediately.

Where to Find Import Opportunities

The United States imports a vast number of goods from other countries. One reason is the low labor costs in the other countries. Lower production costs result in products that can sell more cheaply than those produced in America. Other products are imported because they can only be found in other countries. Coffee is an example.

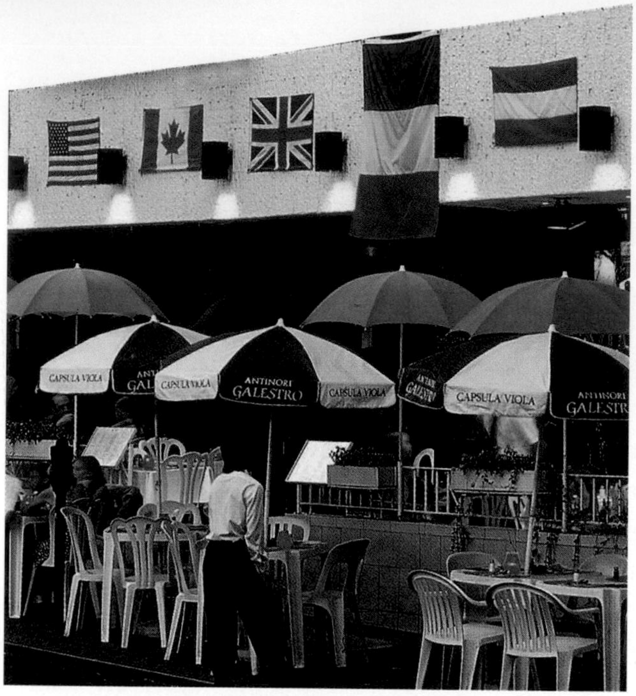

Importers are often people who have friends, relatives, or contacts in other countries. *What are some advantages they have?*

To find opportunities in importing, attend trade shows where representatives from other countries display their products and services. You can also read trade publications and catalogues that show international products available for importing. This will give you an idea of what is available, but it will not tell you if people want those products. To answer that question, you'll have to research the market. Talk to potential customers to find out what they're looking for.

What to Consider before You Import or Export

When you think about going global, make sure there is demand for the product and that you are ready for the challenge. Ask yourself four questions:

1. **Do you have solutions?** Anyone can supply a product or a service. However, can you solve a problem that people in a particular country are facing? To do this you'll need to study the country and its people very carefully.
2. **Do you have a new idea?** Ideas don't have to be completely new. They can also be improvements on something that exists. However, it must be an improvement that has value for the customer and stands out from the crowd.
3. **How good are you at handling risk and frustration?** Every country has different ways of doing business. Every group of customers has different needs and desires. You must be prepared to go through a trial-and-error process.
4. **Do you have any good contacts in other countries?** Just like doing business in your own country, you need to develop contacts with people who can help you. Start by talking to students at your own school who may have family from the country you're interested in. You might also contact your local Chamber of Commerce or Small Business Administration (SBA) office. They often have international trade experts who can help you.

Where to Find Export Opportunities

Exporting is a way to expand your business to a new market. Exporting is more complicated than importing and it takes longer to make a profit. One way to start is to use an export management company. These companies can handle all the tasks related to exporting for a manufacturer. They usually receive a commission (a percentage of sales) for their efforts. Another method is to hire a freight forwarder, who will handle overseas shipments for a fee. This method costs less than using an export management company because you handle all the work except shipping. Finally, you may be able to form a *joint venture* with a company in the country to which you're exporting. A partnership created by two or more companies for a specific purpose over a set period of time is called joint venture. If you have a joint-venture partner in the other country that understands the cultural and business differences, it will make getting your products into that market much easier.

The global market makes this an exciting time to be a business owner. Opportunities are plentiful. You will enjoy dealing in the global market if you take the time to learn about potential markets to ensure success.

CHECK YOUR UNDERSTANDING — SECTION 4.2

Reviewing Key Terms and Concepts

1. List two sources of information on international markets.
2. What is the difference between importing and exporting?
3. What are four questions you need to consider before going global?

Critical Thinking Activity

Interview someone from another country to find out what products his or her country imports. Combine your lists with your classmates to make a master list.

Extension Lab—Decision-Making Skills

Bribes for Buttons The success of your business, "Buttons by Betsy," leads you to consider expanding it into the international market. From your research, you learn that in some countries, offering and taking bribes are acceptable ways of doing business. What should you do when faced with a bribe?

Research Ask a business lawyer and a business owner the following questions, then compare their answers.

- Is taking a bribe unethical when you are a business owner?
- Is offering a bribe in order to do business in another country ethical when it is an acceptable way of doing business in that country?
- As a business owner, would you have one policy regarding bribes for yourself and a different policy for your employees?

CHAPTER 4 REVIEW

CHAPTER SUMMARY

- Technological advances and changes in trade barriers have created a global economy.
- Exporting is the selling and shipping of products to another country. Importing is the buying of goods from other countries to sell in your own country.
- Global opportunities are available in Asia, Latin America, Europe, and in developing countries like the Middle East and Russia.
- The international market, which is more than four times the size of the U.S. market, holds opportunities for businesses.
- It's important to study a country's culture before attempting to do business there.
- To succeed in international business, one must conduct business based on the customs of the other country.
- Ways to locate the best market for your product or service include governmental publications, the International Business Exchange, and the opportunity to go to trade fairs.
- By hiring an export management company, a freight forwarder, or forming a joint venture, entrepreneurs are able to knowledgeably expand their businesses to new markets.

RECALL KEY TERMS

You are working for an entrepreneur who handles international business. Your job is to prepare a reference manual that includes the following terms and their definitions.

global economy
exporting
importing
trade barriers
tariffs
gross domestic product (GDP)
interpreter
Standard Industrial Trade Classification (SITC) codes
International Business Exchange (IBEX)
trade missions
"best prospect" list
disposable income
export management company
freight forwarder
joint venture

RECALL KEY CONCEPTS

Indicate if the following is true or false.

1. Businesses that buy products from other countries to sell in their own country are exporting.
2. Trade barriers are taxes, quotas, and other restrictions on goods entering or leaving a country.
3. The top ten countries for exporting U.S. goods make up most of the world's GDP.
4. The countries that make up the Asian markets have very similar cultures.
5. Only recently has entrepreneurship been encouraged in Europe .
6. Key tips for succeeding in international business include learning about the country before you go and building relationships before doing business.
7. Most products exported from the U.S. are necessities for those who are receiving them.

THINK CRITICALLY

1. Discuss the opportunities and the risks in today's global market.

2. Are there advantages to importing a product or products from other countries to the United States? Why or why not?
3. What world region do you think holds the greatest business opportunity? Explain.
4. Why should you understand the culture of the people with whom you do business?
5. If you had the opportunity to go on a trade mission to Russia, how would you prepare?
6. Compare and contrast the following: an export management company, a freight forwarder, and a joint venture.

CONNECT ACADEMICS TO THE WORKPLACE

Math

1. The GDP (gross domestic product) for 1996 was $7,818,000,000 and for 1997 it was $8,254,000,000. What was the percentage increase from 1996 to 1997?

Organize and Maintain Files

2. Keep a folder with the newest products and trends in the domestic and foreign computer industry. Clip articles from newspapers and magazines to present to the class. For the remainder of the course, when you see or hear something on radio or television, make a note of it for your folder. Each month, share a trend with the class.

WORK IN THE COMMUNITY

Using the yellow pages, identify businesses within a two-mile radius of your school.

- Which businesses sell products made outside the United States?
- Are there more businesses selling imported products than products made in the United States?

As a class, note on a large world map the countries from which products are exported to your local businesses.

LINK SCHOOL TO CAREER

Locate a business in your community that imports or exports products. Interview the person involved with the buying and selling of goods. Ask about:

- The preparation needed to enter the global market
- The benefits of importing and exporting
- Future trends and global opportunities
- The differences between international business and U.S. business

Share the results of your interview with the class. Combine your results with other students and determine similarities and differences.

interNET CONNECTION

Global Gathering

You wish to export a line of casual clothing. Use the Internet to determine a possible international market for your product.

Connect

Use a variety of Web search engines to research a country with which you might conduct business. Answer the following:

- What are the country's demographics?
- What is the average disposable income in the country?
- Does the country export products to the United States? If so, which ones?

Include background information about the country and report your findings.

UNIT 1 LAB

Business Plan Basics

IDENTIFYING OPPORTUNITIES

OVERVIEW

New business opportunities are all around. You may recognize new business ideas as you examine existing products and businesses. What can be changed to make them better? You may also identify new business ideas as you think about current trends. What types of businesses or products will best satisfy customer needs as these trends develop? This unit lab will take you through steps that help you identify opportunities for a new business.

TOOLS

- Consumer magazines
- Newspapers
- Internet (optional)
- Word processor or graph paper

PROCEDURES

STEP A

Every new product provides opportunities for other new products or businesses.

1. Identify three new business opportunities that resulted from the invention of the following products:
   - compact discs
   - computers
   - microwave ovens
2. Then identify businesses or products that were negatively affected by these products.
3. Individually or in a small group, collect three advertisements from newspapers and magazines. These ads should announce new products or the opening of new businesses.
4. Identify the problems solved by these new products or businesses and the benefits they provide customers.
5. Organize the problems and benefits in a table, using the Unit 1 worksheet, graph paper, or the table feature of a word processor.

STEP B

You can also get ideas for new business ventures by studying existing products and businesses.

1. Individually or in your small group, identify changes or improvements that you could make to three existing products or businesses.
2. Organize these changes or improvements in a table. Use the Unit 1 worksheet, graph paper, or the table feature of a word processor.

STEP C

Examining market trends can also help you identify new business opportunities.

1. Individually or in your group, identify three trends in the marketplace. Examples may include current concerns over germs or people living longer.
2. For each of the trends, identify a new business opportunity. Organize these in a table. Use the Unit 1 worksheet, graph paper, or the table feature of a word processor.

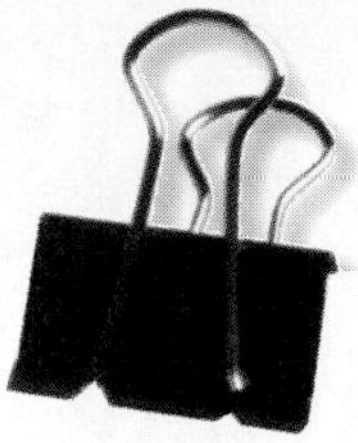

LAB REPORT

STEP D

Select a type of business that you are interested in starting. Through research at the library, interviews with local business owners, or searches on the Internet, complete the following steps:

1. Identify existing businesses of the type in which you are interested in starting. Describe how you could change or improve the businesses to better satisfy customer needs.
2. What are some trends in the market that will affect this type of business? Make a table on graph paper or use the table function of a word processor to show positive and negative trends that will affect this business.
3. Describe the innovative and creative features of your new business venture.
4. Using a word processor, write a one-page report describing your new business idea. Explain how it will meet customer wants and needs. Refer to your tables from steps A, B, C, and D to show the results of your research. Attach the tables to your report.

UNIT 2
RESEARCHING AND PLANNING YOUR VENTURE

UNIT OVERVIEW

Once you decide to launch your own business, there will be many other decisions to make. Marketing, location, and the law are only a few of the issues that an entrepreneur must consider. It can be overwhelming. As your own boss, where and how do you find the answers?

Research and planning are necessary in every step of your decision-making process. Creating a business plan will help you address and organize your venture's concerns. It can also show your venture's worth to potential investors. A good business plan and a solid understanding of your market, the law, and how your business site functions will help you turn your vision into reality.

Entrepreneurship: What It Takes

What do you know about starting your own business?

1. Where can you go for help in planning your business?
2. What is a business plan?
3. What are the parts of a business plan?
4. Who are your customers?
5. How can you reach your customers?
6. How do you analyze your market?
7. What type of business ownership is best suited to you?
8. What laws, codes, and requirements should you know about?
9. How should you choose your business location?
10. How should you lay out your business?

CHAPTER 5

Feasibility and Business Planning

Learning Objectives

When you have completed this chapter, you will be able to:

- **Develop** a business concept for a new business
- **Test** the concept in the marketplace with a feasibility study
- **Explain** the value of preparing a business plan
- **List** the parts of a business plan
- **Discuss** a strategy for creating a business plan

You're the Boss!

Developing Your Business Concept

You've made some extra money by helping friends choose computer systems, install software, and troubleshoot problems. Now you've decided to go into business. Your accountant advises you to create a business plan, but you're not sure you need to make one.

What Will You Do?

How can you be sure that your business idea will succeed?

SECTION 5.1

Feasibility Analysis: Testing an Opportunity

What you'll learn

- how to turn your idea into a business concept
- how to test your concept in the marketplace with a feasibility study
- how to make a competition grid

Why it's important

Not every idea can become a good business. Ideas must be tested before they are put in the marketplace.

KEY TERMS

business concept
feature
benefit
feasibility analysis
target customers
competitive grid

DEVELOPING A BUSINESS CONCEPT

Once you've got an idea for your new business, you need to turn it into a business concept. A **business concept** is an idea for a new business that can be tested.

The Business Concept

Frank Almeda wanted to open a sporting goods store in the Lower East Side of Manhattan in New York City. It was a good idea, but he needed to develop it further to find out if it could actually work. To build his business concept statement, Frank answered four questions.

1. *What is the product or service being offered?* Frank wants to offer sporting goods and clothing. He also plans to supply local teams with uniforms and supplies.

2. *Who is the customer?* The customer is the person who pays for your product or service. Frank's customers are the local sports teams and people who are interested in playing sports.
3. *What is the benefit you are providing?* Don't confuse product or service features with benefits. A feature is a distinctive aspect, quality, or characteristic of the product or service. For example, Frank will offer a store located in the neighborhood. A benefit is something that promotes or enhances the value of the product or service to the customer. In this case, the benefit Frank is providing his customers is the *convenience* of buying sporting equipment and apparel right in their own neighborhood.
4. *How will you get the product or service to the customer?* Businesses have many ways to deliver their products and services. Some of the choices for delivery are by retail store, wholesalers, mail order, the Internet, or door-to-door. Frank chose to deliver the product to the customer with a retail store.

Write a Concept Statement. After answering the four questions, Frank could write the following concept statement: *Eastside Sports provides sporting equipment and apparel to local teams and people who play sports. It provides the convenience of one-stop shopping at a retail outlet in the customer's own neighborhood.*

Some businesses specialize in selling to large, organized groups. ***What are some advantages and disadvantages?***

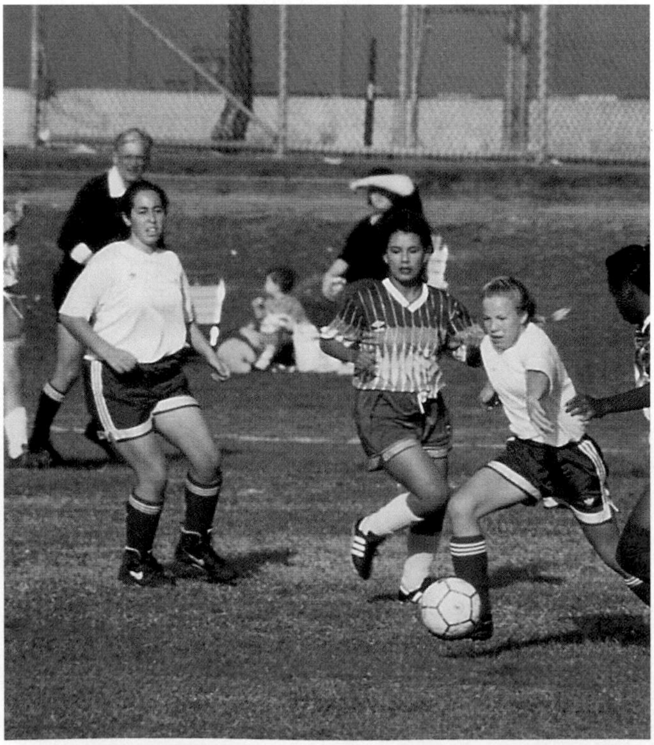

TESTING THE CONCEPT IN THE MARKET

The process used to test a business concept is called a *feasibility analysis*. A feasibility analysis determines if an idea for a new business is practical. It answers two questions.

1. Are there customers who want what you have to offer?
2. What conditions must be present for you to decide to go forward with the business?

The analysis will show if there is enough demand for your product or service. Once you have determined that you have a good business concept, you can create a business plan to put that concept into place.

Testing Product or Service Requirements

Is your product or service unique enough in the marketplace to capture attention? Research the industry. Information to gather includes trends, barriers to entry, and profit margins. The main question is: *Will the industry support your new business?*

Talking to Customers

Talk with potential customers to measure the interest in your product. For Frank Almeda's business, local sports teams are the target customers, those most likely to buy his products and services. Frank will want to learn as much as he can about their needs.

Studying the Competition

An easy way to study your competitors is to create a grid. A competitive grid allows you to organize important information about the competition. You can get this information on your competitors by reading about them, talking to them, and visiting their places of business. You can also talk to their customers and suppliers. Fill in your grid as shown in **Figure 5–1.**

Figure 5–1
Making a competitive grid can help you organize your research. ***Where can you find the information to fill your own grid?***

Competitive Grid

Competitor	Customer	Benefits	Distribution	Strengths/ Weaknesses
Local sports store	Neighborhood teams and sports enthusiasts	Convenience of shopping locally. Know the store owner.	Retail outlet in neighborhood	Owner knows his customers. Understands the neighborhood needs. Not able to stock as much variety.
NikeTown	Sports enthusiasts and tourists	Huge selection and exciting environment	Retail outlet in major commercial area	Huge selection. Don't know their customers by name. Impersonal.
Catalogue Sales	Sports enthusiast who doesn't like to shop	Quick and easy. Don't have to leave home.	Mail order	Lower costs. Can discount prices more. No personal contact with customer.

Money Matters

BE REALISTIC

Take into account the possibility of failure when planning your business, but don't let it overwhelm you. Remember you can learn from mistakes. Mark Pincus, co-founder of the defunct off-line browser, FreeLoader, says:

"Taking risks is reward, even if you have an utter failure."

The Competitive Grid

1. *The competition.* In the first column, list your direct and indirect competitors. Direct competitors are in the same or nearly the same business as you. Indirect competitors include other ways your customers receive the same benefits. (For Frank Almeda, another sporting goods store in the neighborhood would be a direct competitor. Mail-order catalogs or the Internet are indirect competitors.)
2. *Customers.* The second column should list the primary customer or target customer for each of your competitors. These may overlap.
3. *Benefits.* In the third column, list the benefits the customers receive from each of the competitors and your company. Be sure to think in terms of benefits to the customer, and not features of the product or service.
4. *Distribution.* The fourth column lists the way the company distributes its product or service to the customer. This is usually by selling directly to the customer (as many services do). Product companies often sell to a distributor, who in turn finds retail outlets.
5. *Strengths and weaknesses.* The fifth column gives your opinion on the strengths and weaknesses of your competitors. List your company's strengths and weaknesses as well.

Looking at Start-up Resource Needs

A feasibility study will help you determine a business idea's potential and profitability. Jeffrey Bezos knew when he started Amazon.com that the Internet bookstore wouldn't turn a profit

Up & Coming Entrepreneur

Skateboarding Entrepreneurs

With their knowledge in art, skating, and retail clothing sales, Catherine Lyons, Elska Sandor, and Jung Kwak founded Rookie Skateboards in New York. Competing in a male-dominated industry, making skateboards and skater clothing, sure isn't easy, especially since the three women didn't have experience doing business. Yet they've managed to double their sales every season. "Rookie fills a void and we like what we're doing," says Lyons. "It's not like we want to sell our line at Bloomingdale's."

Analyze **How might not distributing to Bloomingdale's actually be of advantage to Rookie's business plan?**

for a long time. However, Bezos was able to raise money to start the business because he could show strong financial projections.

For a feasibility study, you will need to calculate how much money it takes to do the following:

- Purchase or lease equipment and facility.
- Pay any employees you hire.
- Finish product development.
- Carry the company's expenses until you have enough sales for the business to operate on its own.

You will also want to calculate how long it will take for the business to reach a positive cash flow. When will your sales cover your expenses?

The information you gather for the feasibility study may not turn out to be favorable. If you determine that your idea cannot work, stop and pursue another idea. That's a main advantage of conducting a feasibility study. It allows you to test your idea with very little risk.

CHECK YOUR UNDERSTANDING

SECTION 5.1

Reviewing Key Terms and Concepts

1 What is the purpose of a business concept?
2 List the four components of an effective business concept.
3 Discuss two things a feasibility analysis will accomplish.

Critical Thinking Activity

Pick an idea you have for a new business. Then develop a business concept by answering the four questions on pages 75–76 and write a concept statement.

Extension Lab—Reasoning Skills

Flower Power After months of work, your business plan is ready. Your concept statement reads, "Flower Power provides floral arrangements and bouquets to people who buy flowers for patients. It provides the convenience of one-stop shopping at the hospital."

Oral Presentation Prepare an oral presentation that will convince your local banker to help finance your business. Be sure to include:

- Detailed information about the product being offered
- Who the target customers are
- The features and benefits of the product
- The delivery method

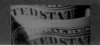

What you'll learn

- why it's important to do a business plan
- what are the parts of a business plan
- how to make a business plan

Why it's important

Once a feasible business concept has been developed, it's important to make a business plan. A business plan will help turn a concept into a business, rather than just a product or service.

KEY TERMS

business plan
vision
executive summary
distribution channel
direct channel
indirect channel
Small Business Administration (SBA)
trade associations

The Business Plan

THE PURPOSE OF THE BUSINESS PLAN

A business plan is a document that describes a new business. It explains to lenders and investors why the new business deserves financial support.

Why Make a Business Plan?

Many people think that business plans are for the banker's benefit and not the entrepreneur's. This feeling reflects the typical entrepreneur's preference for action over paperwork. However, entrepreneurs need business plans for many reasons, including financing.

- *To obtain financing.* A business plan is important because bankers and other financing sources require it. If you need a sizeable amount of money to start up your business (and most entrepreneurs do), you are going to have to raise investment capital. Prospective lenders and investors will need to know specifically what you plan to do and how you plan to do it.

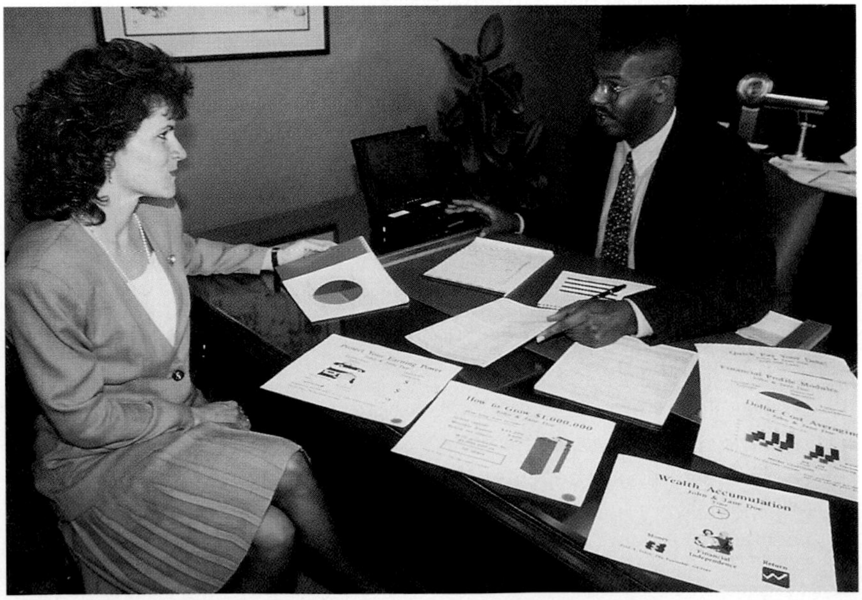

Then they can estimate the potential for repayment of any loan or investment.

- *To serve as a living guide to the business.* Making a business plan will help you organize and analyze critical data. It's possible to record your research findings in loose notes or even to carry them around in your head, but a formal business plan helps to ensure that all aspects of your business's operations are covered. It will help you to remember all the details.
- *To provide a start-up blueprint.* Sometimes things left to chance turn out well. Most people, however, don't leave important things to chance. If you value your time, effort, and money, you will plan. You will make a blueprint and follow it as you get your venture under way. That "blueprint" is your business plan. It contains all that you learned by reading, interviewing, organizing, and thinking about your enterprise. It is the best guide to making your business both a reality and a success.

Convey Your Vision for the Company in the Business Plan

It's often said, "If you can't see where you're going, how will you know when you get there?" Vision is the main concept you have for your business. This body of ideas includes what your business is, what it will become, and how you should run it. Based on your value system, vision is what you believe to be true. Very often, it is also your vision that gives you the direction you need. Walt Disney's vision for his company was "to bring happiness to millions." That vision has guided the company's decision making since it began. When Disney executives decided to move into films geared more toward adults, they formed another company rather than change their vision.

As you think about your company's vision, remember:

1. Keep the vision broad enough to last through changing times.
2. If your vision changes when something happens, then it's not really a vision.
3. Don't confuse your vision with a mission. A mission is an allotted or self-imposed duty or task.

For example, suppose you want to have 50 customers for your sporting goods business by the end of the first year. This is a mission, an achievable goal. Your vision might be "to bring the world of sports to disadvantaged kids." This broad vision lets you take

Tips from the Real World

GROWING PAINS

Many new businesses start at home, but some will eventually outgrow their location. Ricka Robb Kohnstamm, co-owner of a public relations firm, comments:

"*Juggling the needs of more than a dozen clients over the hum of the washing machine results in an all-consuming, hectic work life.*"

RISK TAKERS PROFIT MAKERS

Name: Daymond John
Business: Fubu
City, State: New York, New York

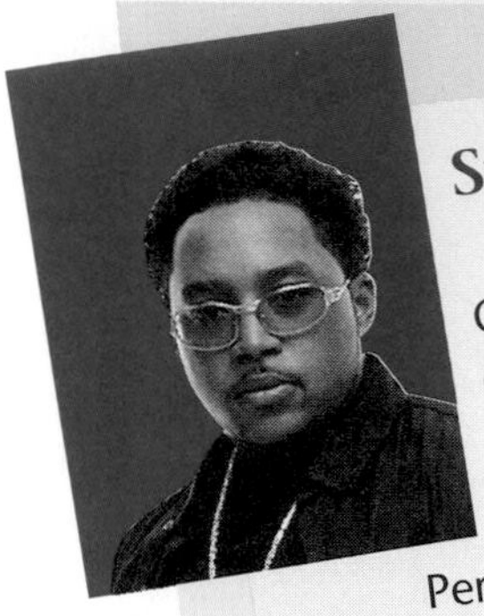

Star Power

In 1992 Daymond John was making hats at his home in Queens, New York and selling them on the streets of New York City. Encouraged by his initial success, John remortgaged his home for $100,000 and expanded his business into coats and shirts. With help from longtime friends and new partners Keith Perrin, Carl Brown, and J. Alexander Martin, he launched Fubu, which stands for "for us, by us."

One key to Fubu's success has been promotion. Fubu doesn't have to hire supermodels or sponsor athletes, which could cost millions. Instead, celebrity musicians and actors come to Fubu, asking to wear the products because they admire the label's fashion and respect its integrity. As a result of this exposure, Fubu shirts, sweats, denim, innerwear, outerwear, and footwear can now be found at large department and sporting goods stores around the world.

Thinking Critically

Imagine asking your family, friends, or a banker for a loan. What steps could you take to assure the lender you could repay it?

your business in many directions. It allows you to do many things without changing your vision.

THE PARTS OF THE BUSINESS PLAN

Formulating a business plan involves a great deal of research. Drawing so much information from so many different sources can be overwhelming. Learning the parts is a good first step.

Getting Started

There is no correct format for a business plan. They can be long, complex, and detailed or short and simple. Anticipate who will be reading your business plan and add the appropriate pieces. Certain lenders or investors may require specific information. To appeal to them, you may have to add documents or sections to your plan.

How do you know what to include in your plan? Among all the different types of business plans, there are some common features. (These are covered in greater detail in later chapters.)

- *Executive summary.* The executive summary is a brief recounting of the key points contained in a business plan. Investors and lenders may read many business plans every day. To save time, they rely on the executive summary to help them decide if the concept interests them. If the executive summary creates excitement for the concept, they'll go ahead and read the entire plan. The executive summary should be no longer than two pages. Include the most important information from each section of the plan. Persuade the reader that this business is going to be a success.
- *Product/service plan.* In this section of the business plan, you'll present the product or service you're offering. The nature of your business should be clear to the reader. It's also important to note the unique features of the product/service and any possible spin-offs. Spin-offs are additional products or services that you might do later when the business is more established.
- *Management team plan.* In this section, you'll present your qualifications and those of any partners you'll have. You will also analyze the expertise you're missing and how you will solve that problem. This section will also describe the advisory board that will help you get started.
- *Industry/market analysis.* This section presents your research into the industry and market. It will analyze your customers, competition, and industry. This section should also contain information about the prospective location's geographic, economic, and demographic data.
- *Operational plan.* The operational plan includes all the processes that take place in the business so that the product or service is produced and delivered to the customer. If you are manufacturing a product, you'll want to discuss the status of your product development. How much

Business plans reflect the varying needs of different types of businesses. ***What are some special needs that a manufacturing business might have that a retail business might not?***

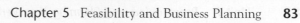

time and money will it take to get the product ready to market? You'll also want to explain the distribution of your product or service. A **distribution channel** is the means for supplying the product to the customer. If you are building Web sites, a service, you will probably have a **direct channel**. That is, you will be delivering the service directly to the customer. On the other hand, if you're manufacturing a computer game, you may have an **indirect channel**. This means you will sell your game to a wholesaler who finds retail stores to carry your product.

- *Organizational plan.* The organizational plan looks at the people aspects of the business. It discusses such things as the management philosophy, the legal form of the company, key management personnel, and key employment policies.
- *Marketing plan.* A marketing plan involves how a company makes its customers aware of its products or services. It includes such features as the market niche that is being served, the pricing policy, the company image, the marketing tactics used to reach the customer, a media plan, and a marketing budget.
- *Financial Plan.* The financial plan presents the forecasts for the future of the business. It also explains the assumptions made when calculating your forecast figures. Usually, this information is in the form of financial statements. This part of the business plan shows that the new business will be financially healthy.
- *Growth Plan.* The growth plan looks at how the business will expand in the future. Investors and lenders like to know that a business has the potential and the plans to grow over its life.

How to Make a Business Plan

Between learning what goes into a business plan and actually assembling one, there are many steps. These steps are illustrated in **Figure 5–2.**

ENTREPRENEURS INTERNATIONAL

China

Linda Hong founded Elite Advertising in 1993, focusing on improving brand recognition of foreign products by Chinese consumers. Hong's "brand philosophy" style of advertising helps her clients build up leading brands in her country's fast-growing market. "A brand without philosophy is like a man without soul," says Hong. Hong works closely with her clients to develop print, broadcast, and in-store promotions. Elite's clients include Kodak, Ray-Ban, and Hewlett Packard.

Apply **Why might a foreign client wishing to expand in China contact Elite Advertising rather than an advertising agency from their local country?**

Figure 5–2

Making a Business Plan

There are four steps to making a business plan.

1. Gathering data.

Making a business plan is not just a process of filling in the blanks. The information you need does not lend itself to a straight-line approach and it's certainly not all in the library. The information you find may be incomplete. It may need to be updated, supported, or clarified.

2. Organizing your data.

Because you will be gathering information from different sources, you should try to organize it as you go. If you keep the information you gather in order throughout the process, putting the pieces together at the end will be easier.

3. Setting up a notebook.

Setting up a business plan notebook is an effective technique. The loose-leaf notebook should have a separate section and at least one folder for each part of your business plan. As you conduct research, record your findings in the appropriate section. Store literature, forms, or similar materials in the related folders.

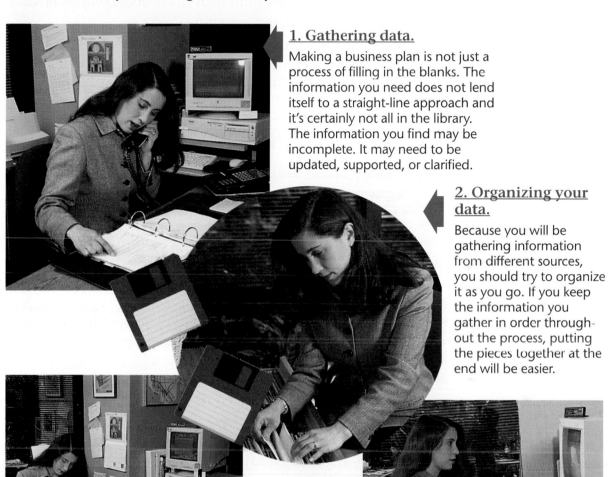

4. Writing a draft.

Only after you have finished your research will you be ready to compile a draft of your business plan. Sort out the data in your various notebook sections. Calculate your finances. Make your important decisions. Then write the plan.

Sources of Information

Where should you gather information for a business plan? First, find agencies whose primary purpose is to assist entrepreneurs. Then contact agencies and firms with whom entrepreneurs do business. The following are some examples.

Trade associations can provide information on specific industries. ***Where can you go to locate trade associations?***

- *Small Business Administration (SBA).* The Small Business Administration is a federal agency that provides services to small businesses and new entrepreneurs. The agency offers publications for a minimal charge; gives special assistance to women, minorities, and the physically challenged; and offers financial assistance.

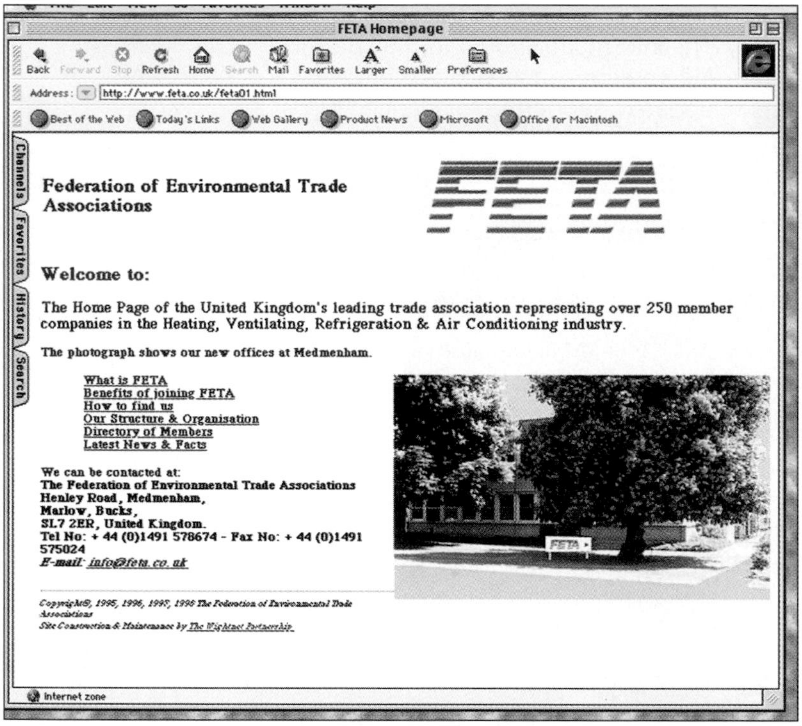

- *Service Corps of Retired Executives (SCORE).* SCORE works out of SBA district offices. Its members provide free advisory assistance to entrepreneurs.
- *Small Business Development Centers (SBDCs).* SBDCs provide counseling and management assistance. They are generally located at colleges and universities.
- *Chambers of Commerce.* Local chamber offices provide information about the local economy, business trends, and business needs. In many cities, chambers of commerce operate a small business development and assistance program.
- *Trade Associations.* A trade association offers technical and general assistance to entrepreneurs in a specific profession or industry. If can supply information such as average start-up and operating costs, trend analysis, research involving state-of-the-art technology, and supplier contacts.

PACKAGING AND PRESENTING THE BUSINESS PLAN

The appearance of a business plan is as important as its contents. To package your business plan effectively, follow these guidelines.

What to Include in the Business Plan

You already know about the main sections of the plan that will contain all the information you collected. Your business plan should convey an attractive, professional image.

Cover Page. The cover page should contain:

- the name of the company
- the words *Business Plan*
- the name of the contact person
- the address and phone number of the company

You can make your business plan stand out by using color, your business logo, or a design that shows the personality of the business. For example, if your business is a video rental store, you might include covers of the types of videos you'll carry.

Table of Contents and Headings. Just like a book, your business plan will need a table of contents. Make sure to include headings that label sections so the reader can easily find information.

Supporting Documents. The appendix of the business plan contains documents that are important for the reader. For example, you will want to include your résumé and those of any partners.

CHECK YOUR UNDERSTANDING

SECTION 5.2

Reviewing Key Terms and Concepts

1 Why should you make a business plan after you know you have a feasible concept?
2 What is the difference between the industry/market analysis and the marketing plan?
3 What are two resources you can use to prepare your business plan?

Critical Thinking Activity

Find out from an entrepreneur how he or she made a business plan.

Extension Lab—Evaluating Data

School Spirit Belinda has an idea for a store selling spirit items and novelty gifts on her school campus. The athletic department, which already operates one store selling school supplies and snacks, opposed her idea. She conducted a feasibility analysis and found that there is enough demand for the second store.

Research Develop and conduct a survey in class and use the data to answer these questions:

- Should Belinda continue to pursue her idea?
- If she continues, how could she ensure success?
- If she does not continue, what could she do instead?

CHAPTER 5 REVIEW

CHAPTER SUMMARY

- A business concept is an idea for a new business that can be tested by answering four questions: What is the product or service being offered? Who is the customer? What is the provided benefit? How will you deliver the product or service?
- A feasibility analysis will show if there is enough demand for your product or service to justify creating a business.
- By talking to potential customers and studying the competition, you should be able to determine if the industry will support your new business.
- A business plan is a document that explains to lenders and investors why a new business deserves the financial support.
- Business plans also serve as living guides to the business and as start-up blueprints.
- Business plans have common features such as an executive summary, a product/service plan, a management team plan, and an industry/market plan. They also have operational, organizational, marketing, financial, and growth plans.
- Many sources (the SBA, small business development centers, chambers of commerce, and trade associations) can help entrepreneurs gather information for creating a business plan.

RECALL KEY TERMS

Think about a business you would like to open. Write a letter to the vice president of a local bank requesting an appointment to share your idea. Use the key terms in your letter.

business concept
feature
benefit
feasibility analysis
target customers
competitive grid
business plan
vision
executive summary
distribution channel
direct channel
indirect channel
Small Business Administration (SBA)
trade associations

RECALL KEY CONCEPTS

1. Compare the terms *feature* and *benefit* regarding a product or service.
2. Why is it important to conduct a feasibility analysis of your business concept?
3. Explain the features of a business plan.
4. What is the difference between a *direct* and an *indirect* distribution channel? Which part of the business plan includes this information?
5. Describe one way to organize data you collect while researching your business plan.
6. What do the following abbreviations stand for? What do the organizations themselves do for prospective entrepreneurs?
   - SBA
   - SCORE
   - SBDC
7. Describe how to package your business plan effectively. Why is it important to do so?

THINK CRITICALLY

1. Write a concept statement for a coffee kiosk you plan to open in a large downtown office complex.

CHAPTER 5 REVIEW

2. How will you research the industry to determine whether your coffee kiosk idea is unique enough to pursue as a business?
3. Define a mission and a vision as it relates to the coffee kiosk concept.
4. Which component of a typical business plan is the most important? Explain.
5. If you had all the money you needed to start your own business, would you prepare a business plan? Why or why not?

CONNECT ACADEMICS TO THE WORKPLACE

Math

1. While conducting a feasibility study for a new product in development, you interview 387 target customers at 15 different locations. What is the average number of target customers per location?

Acquire and Evaluate Data

2. Contact a small business development center or other agency in your area that assists entrepreneurs in preparing business plans. Request a copy of an actual plan. Review and evaluate the following:

- Does the plan have all the basic features?
- How did the plan's writer handle the contents of each section of the plan?
- evaluate the business plan's completeness.
- Share your findings with the class.

WORK IN YOUR COMMUNITY

Create a business concept statement for a product or service you are interested in pursuing. Be sure to include:

- The product or service
- The customer
- The benefit you are providing
- The delivery method

Present the business concepts to the class. After all the presentations are complete, vote on which concept has the best chance for success.

LINK SCHOOL TO CAREER

As a class, divide into six groups. Each group will select one of the agencies listed in the chapter to contact.

- Inquire about the specific forms of assistance available to entrepreneurs.
- Request brochures, publications, and other materials.
- If possible, invite someone from the agency to speak to your class about their services.
- Report your findings to the class and add to the class resource log created in Chapter 1.
- Be sure to write a letter thanking the agency for its help.

interNET CONNECTION

Tag Team

Luis knows that writing a business plan for his custom license tag company is important. Using the Internet, help Luis use the Internet to find sample business plans and format procedures.

Connect

Use a variety of Web search engines to locate the following:

- Sample business plans you can review
- Web sites that offer templates for the development of a business plan
- Services that provide free help preparing or evaluating business plans
- Software that is available to create a business plan

CHAPTER 6

MARKET ANALYSIS

Learning Objectives

When you have completed this chapter, you will be able to:

- **Define** the areas in which to conduct market analysis
- **Describe** how to conduct effective market research
- **Explain** how to analyze an industry
- **Explain** how to analyze a target market

You're the Boss!

Understanding the Market

Your neighborhood's food supply seems to consist only of fast food and convenience stores. You see an opportunity to open a healthy snack food shop. It won't serve full meals, but will give an alternative to greasy fries or candy bars. To start, you plan on finding out more about the service industry.

What Will You Do?

What steps can you take to analyze the market?

SECTION 6.1

Doing Market Research

DEFINING AREAS OF ANALYSIS

If a business is to succeed and make a profit, it must satisfy its customers. Every business starts with this basic marketing concept. However, you cannot satisfy your customers (or potential customers) if you don't know who they are and what they want. To find out, you conduct market analysis.

A thorough market analysis requires that you examine your market from two entirely different perspectives. On the one hand, you will need to identify your prospective customers and determine their buying habits. On the other hand, you will need to analyze your field of endeavor, or industry, and rate your prospects for success within it. This section will help you do both.

Industry

An **industry** is a collection of businesses with a common line of products or services. It includes manufacturers, suppliers, distributors, and others who deal with businesses in that industry. You'll want to learn the state of an industry before you enter it. In

What you'll learn

- how to define an area of analysis for your research
- when to use different types of research
- how to develop an effective market research process

Why it's important

One of the biggest preventable causes of failure at start-up is not understanding the industry and the market. You need to conduct effective market research *before* you start your business to increase your chances of success.

KEY TERMS

industry
market
target market
market segments
psychographics
industrial markets
market research
exploratory research
descriptive research
historical research
secondary data
primary data

Money Matters

PRICING

It is important to know the market and the prices of similar products within the industry. According to Bob Beaubien of Merchant Direct:

“*Manufacturers often enter into negotiations with a higher price than is realistic. . . . [We] feel like they've wasted our time.*”

other words, find out its current status and where it is going. You will also want to find out who the major players are and how business is typically conducted in that industry.

Target Market and Customer

A **market** is a group of people or companies who have a demand for a product or service and are willing and able to buy it. The particular group you are interested in, the **target market**, will be the focus of all your company's efforts. You will want to know everything about them—and in as much detail as possible.

Market Segmentation. Getting the detail you need usually involves breaking down the total market into smaller groups of buyers with similar needs and interests. These are called **market segments**. Consumer markets (customers who buy for personal use) are usually segmented on the following bases:

- *Geographics*—region, state, country, city, and/or area
- *Demographics*—age, gender, family size, family life cycle, income, occupation, education, religion, race, nationality, and/or social class

Market Segment Profiles

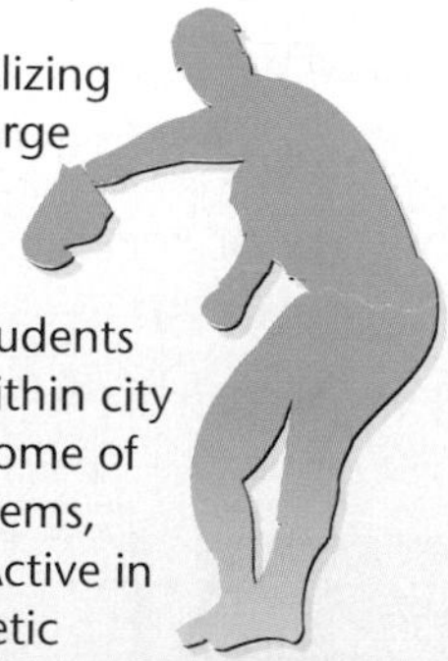

Situation: **Sporting goods operation** specializing in letter jackets and uniforms, located in a large metropolitan area with several high schools and colleges.

Profile of one market segment: High school students 15–18 years old, male and female. Reside within city and in nearby suburbs. Part-time annual income of $1200–$2000, rarely buy big-ticket sports items, dependent on parents for large purchases. Active in sports, gain feeling of importance from athletic recognition. Aware of what is "in," attitude toward where to buy influenced by peers.

Situation: **Business forms company** specializing in forms for institutions and large offices.

Profile of one market segment: Medical offices and clinics with three or more physicians. In business for over one year, provide a wide range of medical services. Office manager typically does buying with input from medical personnel. Need registration, billing, medical record, and patient instruction forms. Will remain with the same business form company as long as service is timely, pay on first billing.

Figure 6–1
Segmenting your market can make your customers' needs more clear. ***Which of the two profiles presented here is targeting an industrial market?***

- *Psychographics*—personality, opinions, and lifestyle elements, including activities and interests
- *Buying characteristics*—knowledge of actual goods or services, personal experience with them, and/or responses to them

Customers who buy goods or services for business use make up the industrial markets. They are segmented differently. Variables include type of business, size, goods or services sold, geographic location, and products needed. Businesses that cater to industrial markets must also consider the customers' individual situations and preferred contractual arrangements.

When you divide the total market, you create profiles of the customers you are considering. **Figure 6–1** shows an example of two different market segments. Notice that only variables relevant to the business are included.

Target Marketing. After all the segments within your range of consideration have been identified, you are ready to select your target market. This is the specific market segment on which you are going to concentrate your efforts. Within this segment you will find your first customer. For example, suppose the target market for your healthy snack food shop is high school students. That's a broad category that needs to be segmented into something more manageable. Here are some guidelines to use in segmenting your market:

- *The market segment should be measurable.* If you have no idea how many potential buyers there are in the market, you cannot know if it is worth pursuing. How big is the high school market?
- *The segment should be large enough to be potentially profitable.* You will have to spend money to market your product. The segment you select must be big enough to enable you to recover your costs and make a profit.
- *The segment should be reachable.* First, you must be able to reach potential customers with words. You must be able to get information about your product and its availability to interested buyers in the segment. Second, you must be able to reach potential customers physically. You must be able to deliver your product to their homes or businesses or to the places where they shop.
- *The market segment should be responsive.* You should have some indication from your research that people in the segment

Tips from the Real World

NEW SERVICE

Some experts predict that the service industry will be a fast-growing category of small businesses in the coming years. Chunka Mui of the Diamond Exchange, an executive learning forum, speculates:

"*The next wave of entrepreneurial start-ups will be those providing services to companies that are getting smaller.*"

would, in fact, be interested in your product and willing to buy it. Do they care about the healthiness of their food?

It is possible for a business to select and serve multiple market segments, but that doesn't usually happen in the start-up stage. If you have identified more than one target market—for example, the preteen set, you will need to decide which market will be the easiest to enter first. In which market will you find it easiest to make sales? Those "easy" sales will give you the foundation you need to explore other markets as your company grows.

CONDUCTING MARKET RESEARCH

Once you know the areas of the market you need to analyze, you are ready to begin investigating them. That process is called market research. The steps involved in the process are the same whether you are doing research for an existing business or a new venture.

A focus group can help you learn which features and benefits are important to customers. ***What would you do to make this focus group a success?***

Define the Research Question

The first step is extremely important because it helps you focus your research. It reduces the chances that you will spend time gathering information you won't use. For example, if high school students in your area have never been exposed to healthy snacks, you will want to see if the industry will support a business of this type. You will want to find data to support customer acceptance of the new product or service.

Types of Market Research

Once you have defined your problem, you can select a research approach. There are several basic ways to structure your research. These are called research designs. The kind and amount of information you require will determine which design you use.

- *Exploratory research.* Exploratory research is used when you know little about a subject. A good place to start might be government or industry publications. You might also talk to people who are knowledgeable about your field or organize focus groups. These are interviews with small groups of potential customers or businesspeople in your field.

RISK TAKERS PROFIT MAKERS

Name: Dineh Mohajer
Company: Hard Candy, Inc.
City, State: Beverly Hills, CA

Hitting it on the Nail

Dineh Mohajer wanted nail polish colors that matched the latest fashions, so the 22-year-old mixed a bit of white polish and blue dye. When she brought her creation to a boutique where she had once worked, the owner asked Mohajer for 200 more bottles! Hard Candy was born.

Mohajer delivered polish in pale shades of yellow, blue, violet, and green. Its look caught on with celebrities, made appearances in magazines, and soared in popularity.

As business boomed, Mohajer hired a business manager and returned to creating new products. Now sold in Bloomingdale's, Nordstrom, Neiman-Marcus, and other well-known stores, Hard Candy sees annual sales of nearly $20 million.

Thinking Critically

How might realizing your limitations actually help grow a small business?

- *Descriptive research.* Descriptive research is done when you want to determine the status of something. You might want to find out the age, gender, occupation, income, or buying habits of potential customers. Such information can be collected through questionnaires, interviews, or observation.
- *Historical research.* Historical research involves studying the past. The idea is that patterns from the past can be used to explain present circumstances and predict future trends. Trade associations and trade publications are two sources of useful historical data. Owners in similar businesses can also provide you with historical information. You can use these findings to help you predict your business's potential.

The Research Process

To successfully research your industry and market, it's important to have a plan of attack. An effective plan will include the following five steps.

Primary data is information obtained for the first time and used specifically for your study. ***What are some ways this person can obtain primary data?***

Step 1: Look at Your Information Needs. Before you collect data on your market, find out what you need. For example, before opening a healthy snack shop, you need to find out what customers want. Survey your target market. Gather information about the competitors. Do you provide for a need that they can't meet? Their deficiencies are your opportunities.

Step 2: Start with Secondary Resources. Information that has already been collected is called secondary data. It is easily obtained and inexpensive. Government and community organizations are good sources. Also refer to trade associations, trade publications, and commercial research agencies.

A good place to begin your search is the Internet. Good sites include the *Wall Street Journal,* Thomas Register, Securities and Exchange Commission, the Department of Commerce, and CNN's financial news. Check the sources you find carefully. Just because information is on a Web page doesn't mean it's true.

Step 3: Collect Primary Data. Primary data is information obtained for the first time and used specifically for your study. It is the most important data you can collect because it's current and relates most directly to what you're looking for. The most commonly used methods of gathering such data about customers are observation, interviews, and surveys. For your snack shop, you might go to a convenience store and observe the kinds of food people buy. Ask them questions. Note what people eat while they are walking, driving, or watching movies.

ENTREPRENEURS INTERNATIONAL

Zimbabwe

Doreen Sibanda was trained in art in England and Russia and has worked on the Permanent Collection of Zimbabwe's National Gallery. She has published, exhibited, and participated in art projects both locally and internationally. Her experiences have made her an authority in African Art and led her to open Gallery Mutupo. "Our works define their authors, beyond mere sales representation. Mutupo Gallery will give you an authentic artistic experience," says Sibanda.

Apply **Why was it important that Doreen Sibanda gain worldwide experience in art before opening Gallery Mutupo?**

In surveys, individuals answer questions in person, by telephone, or through the mail. Focus groups, the group discussions described earlier, can also be used. Whichever data you collect, use several reputable sources. Relying on only one source is not wise.

Step 4: Organize Your Data. Collect primary and secondary data. Then set up charts and record results in report form. The results will help you assess your venture's feasibility.

If you decide to start your venture, put your market analysis in the marketing section of your business plan. As you continue the entrepreneurial process, you can refer to this information or add to it. This data will help you refine your market analysis and can eventually serve as the basis for a marketing plan.

Step 5: Analyze your data. Now that your information has been organized, ask yourself some basic questions.

1. Is there a market for your product or service?
2. How big is that market?
3. Will the industry support a business like yours?

The answers to these questions will help you judge your potential for having a successful business.

CHECK YOUR UNDERSTANDING

SECTION 6.1

Reviewing Key Terms and Concepts

1 Why is it important to study your industry before developing your business concept?

2 What kinds of information do you need to know about your target market?

3 What are the five steps in market research?

Critical Thinking Activity

Using an idea you have for a business, create a questionnaire and survey 12 potential customers. Be sure you ask questions that address demographics and customer needs.

Extension Lab—Acquiring and Evaluating Data

Teddy Bear Phones Ericsson, an Australian cellular phone company, is producing a stuffed teddy bear with a mobile phone tucked inside. This new toy will allow children to receive calls from working parents, who can now check on them throughout the day.

Research Through information gathered from current business journals and/or the Internet, answer the following questions:

- What steps should Ericsson take to research the market before trying to sell the teddy bear phone in the United States?
- What industry trends should Ericsson consider?
- Who are Ericsson's competitors for this product?

Industry and Market Analysis

What you'll learn

- how to research an industry
- what obstacles typically block a new venture's success
- how to study a target market

Why it's important

Studying your company's industry and market will help you create a product or service that people want. It will also help you understand your chances for success.

KEY TERMS

- sales potential
- barriers to entry
- economies of scale
- brand loyalty
- proprietary technology
- market share
- niche
- customer profile
- customer needs analysis

LOOKING AT THE INDUSTRY

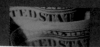

Once you have identified your market, it's time to evaluate your prospects for success in it. Those prospects will depend largely on two factors—the sales potential of your product and your competition. To find this information, do industry research. This section will help you look at the trends and patterns of change in the industry. It will also show you how to look at the demographics of the industry and the competition.

Trends and Patterns of Change

Opportunity in an industry is found by looking at trends and patterns of change. For example, is it becoming more difficult for new companies to enter the industry? Has the rate of sales growth slowed? Does the government heavily regulate the industry? How volatile is the industry? Volatility refers to how quickly things change in the industry. The high-tech industry (computer components, software, and accessories) changes rapidly, so its companies need to design products quickly and move rapidly in the marketplace. Understanding where

the industry is headed and how it works will help you determine your entry strategy.

Your Company and the Industry

How will your products and services compare to others in the industry? How much of your product can you realistically expect to sell? The answer —the projected or estimated figure—is called sales potential . You can determine sales potential by considering three variables.

1. The Nature of Your Product. What you sell influences how much you can sell. Products and services that are well matched to their markets have potential for success. Also, relatively new products and services are resistant to the ups and downs of the economy. Old ones that are given a new look can be winners, too.

Even the most successful products and services are often updated or repackaged. *How does this help sales?*

2. Industry Trends. Identifying trends can also help you predict your product or service's sales potential. Look for projected sales figures for your industry. Past and current sales levels, if graphed or charted, can help as well. They can be visually or mathematically extended to provide a basis for prediction. Try to project current trends 3–5 years into the future.

3. Sources of Supply. Your suppliers will have an impact on your sales. You must have access to affordable sources of inventory, raw materials, and goods. Otherwise, you will not be able to offer your product or service at prices that will generate interest or sales. You should also consider where your suppliers are located, the trade discounts they offer, and the availability of alternate sources. These can affect your costs, your pricing, and sales.

Demographics

Each industry has basic characteristics, or demographics. These include the number of companies and amount of revenue produced annually. Demographics also include the average size of the companies by number of employees and annual revenues. These facts indicate if the industry is growing, shrinking, or remaining stable.

Figure 6–2

Barriers to Entry

New businesses face many obstacles, including the following:

1. Economies of Scale.

As businesses grow bigger, they can churn out products more cheaply and quickly. This phenomenon is known as economies of scale. It is difficult for a small new business to compete with an efficient big business. Finding a niche that no one else serves is one way to overcome economies of scale.

2. Brand Loyalty.

Customers who like to purchase products and services from companies they know demonstrate brand loyalty. To overcome this barrier, a new business needs to increase brand awareness. This requires money to advertise.

3. Access to Distribution Channels.

New businesses often have a hard time getting into an industry's distribution channels. To persuade distributors that customers accept products and services from a new business can be costly.

4. Proprietary Technology.

Any new company that wants to start dealing in PC software may have to make arrangements with Microsoft first. This is because Microsoft has proprietary technology, know-how that is owned and often protected by patents.

Barriers to Entry

Barriers to entry keep new businesses either from entering an industry or succeeding in that industry. Several of these barriers are illustrated in **Figure 6–2.**

The Competition

Outstanding sales potential for your product does not guarantee success. Products are seldom offered to consumers in a vacuum. Usually there are competing products already established in the market. To succeed, you must be able to capture market share from other companies in the field. Market share is simply a portion of the total sales generated by all the competing companies in a given market. Most entrepreneurial companies choose to succeed by defining a niche in the market. A niche is simply a small segment of the market, usually based on customer needs that you've discovered in your market research.

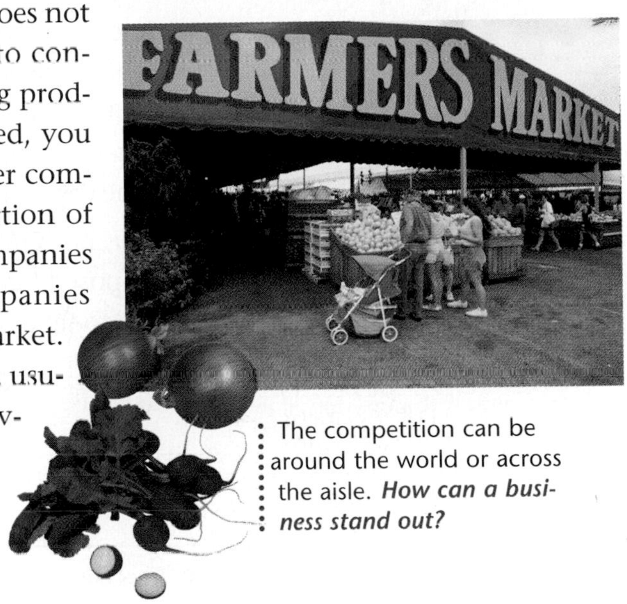

The competition can be around the world or across the aisle. ***How can a business stand out?***

To succeed in the face of competition, you must do a thorough analysis of your competition. Here are some areas to research.

- *Identity of competitors.* Determine the names and locations of your direct and indirect competitors. Direct competitors are those with products or services like yours. Using the healthy snack food example, this might be a local farmers' market. Indirect competitors are products and services that may not be like yours but compete for the same dollars from customers. A good example would be a doughnut shop.

Up&Coming Entrepreneur

Career Building Entrepreneur

Twenty-seven-year-old Tammie Chestnut helped out college students by typing up resumes and giving advice on how best to market their skills. "Some kids paid and some didn't. I wanted them all to pay, so I opened my own business," says Chestnut. Today her Resume Shop is a one-stop resume preparation company.

Analyze **What other products and services could Tammie Chestnut sell at her company to help grow her business?**

- *Strengths and weaknesses of competitors.* Obtain information on your competitors' products, prices, quality, selection, advertising, personnel, customer service, and distribution methods. You can get some of this information by actually buying their goods or services. You can also ask customers about them. Evaluate each of the companies on the basis of their strengths and weaknesses in these areas. If possible, try to determine their responsiveness to changing market conditions. In other words, can they respond quickly when the tastes and preferences of customers change? It's also a good idea to make note of similar companies that have recently gone out of business, and try to determine why.
- *Your competitive advantage.* Identify those things about your proposed business that are clearly unique and would enable you to take business away from your competitors. For example, you develop a recipe for a mango bar that no one else has.

One way to conduct research is to put yourself in the place of the customer. ***What can this aspiring restaurant owner look for?***

LOOKING AT THE TARGET CUSTOMER

No matter how large the target market, it's important that you know your customer. As a provider of a good or service, you have to meet your customers' needs.

What Do We Want to Know about the Customer?

A customer profile is a complete picture of a venture's prospective customers. It includes geographic, demographic, and psychographic data. This profile will help you make decisions about your product or service. When you are creating your customer profile, ask yourself four questions:

1. Who are my customers?
2. What do they generally buy and how do they hear about it?
3. How often do they buy?
4. How can my business meet their needs?

If you do a thorough job of studying your customer, you ought to be able to describe that customer in detail. For example: *My typical customer is a 14- to 17-year-old high school student who has a part-time job or allowance. This person buys ready-to-eat foods almost every day after school, basing decisions on low price as well as quality. Advertising and word-of-mouth are equally effective factors.* Once you have the demographics in place, you can move on to look at customer needs.

What Do My Customers Need?

A customer needs analysis is a way to pinpoint exactly which features and benefits of your goods or services your customers value. Suppose you're proposing to sell a new type of cookie. What kinds of features and benefits do your customers prefer? Perhaps you learn that more students like crunchy cookies than soft ones. Because they are hungry right after school, they want food that is easily accessible. The first is a feature of the product, while the second is a benefit to the customer. You want to be sure that you're providing the features and benefits the customers want so they'll choose your product or service over the competition.

CHECK YOUR UNDERSTANDING — SECTION 6.2

Reviewing Key Terms and Concepts

1 Why should you study trends and patterns of change in an industry?
2 Discuss three barriers to entry for new businesses in an industry.
3 What are the four key questions you should ask about your target customer?

Critical Thinking Activity

Pick an industry that interests you and research the trends and patterns of changes. Project where it will be in 10 years.

Extension Lab—Decision-Making Skills

Bagel Bonanza You and your friend work in a bagel shop in town. Since bagels seem to be increasingly popular, you are thinking about opening your own store. Your friend has cautioned you to consider the barriers to entry that might keep you from being successful.

Role Play With a partner, role play a discussion you might have with your friend regarding these barriers. One of you should support and the other should oppose the idea. Be sure to consider:

- Specific examples of the barriers to entry
- Possible ways to overcome the barriers
- Whether or not you could be successful

CHAPTER 6 REVIEW

CHAPTER SUMMARY

- A market analysis examines your prospective customers and the state of the industry before you enter it.
- Consumer market segmentation is based on geographics, demographics, psychographics, and buying characteristics. Industrial market segmentation involves business type, size, goods or services sold, geographic location, and products needed.
- The target market segment for your product or service should be measurable, profitable, reachable, and responsive.
- Market research is the process used to collect and evaluate market data. It involves defining the research question; selecting a research approach; and gathering, organizing, and analyzing information.
- Industry research identifies your product's sales potential and your competition.
- Barriers to entry keep new business from either entering or succeeding in an industry. Examples include economies of scale, brand loyalty, access to distribution channels, and proprietary technology.
- Research your competitors, their strengths and weaknesses, and your own competitive advantage to determine your ability to capture market share from other companies in the field.

RECALL KEY TERMS

Imagine you own your own marketing research firm. Write a job description for yourself using the following key terms:

industry
market
target market
market segments
psychographics
industrial markets
market research
exploratory research
descriptive research
historical research
secondary data
primary data
sales potential
barriers to entry
economies of scale
brand loyalty
proprietary technology
market share
niche
customer profile
customer needs analysis

RECALL KEY CONCEPTS

1. Consumer and industrial markets are segmented based on what variables?
2. What guidelines would you use to select a target market?
3. Define the steps involved in conducting market research.
4. When would you use primary rather than secondary data in doing market research?
5. When and where will you use the results of your market research?
6. Name at least three trends you might consider when looking for opportunity in an industry.
7. What is a customer profile and why do you need to create one?

THINK CRITICALLY

1. Review the sample profile in **Figure 6–1** on page 92. For each business situation, describe another market segment.
2. When segmenting consumer markets is most important, which variable is used?

3. Can target market selection be done before market segmentation? Why or why not?
4. Give an example of a product you purchase based on the brand. Is brand loyalty important to you? Why or why not?
5. Design a plan to capture market share for the new mango bar you developed.

CONNECT ACADEMICS TO THE WORKPLACE

Math

1. According to projections, total market sales for the health food industry should be $4 million for your first year of operation, $6 million your second, and $9 million your third. You have estimated your healthy snack food shop will have total sales of $200,000 in your first year, $450,000 in your second, and $900,000 in your third. What would be your market share percentage in each of the three years?

Sociability

2. You have been asked to conduct descriptive research to find out the age, gender, occupation, income, and buying habits of potential customers. You will be interviewing and questioning hundreds of people. Develop a list of strategies to help you feel comfortable asking questions of strangers.

WORK IN YOUR COMMUNITY

Working in teams of three or four students, select a business concept you created from an earlier chapter or develop a new one.

Survey and identify potential competitors. Do the following:

- List the companies by name and location.
- Determine (as closely as possible) the market share percentage for each company and estimate its sales.
- Estimate how much each company would lose in sales if you entered the market.
- Create a chart that summarizes the information you have gathered.

LINK SCHOOL TO CAREER

Invite a marketing specialist from a local company to speak to your class about the company's target market.

- Find out how the company conducts its market research.
- Ask about the demographics of its target customers.
- Ask about what its competitive advantage might be.

*inter*NET CONNECTION

Arts and Crafts

Laticia and Jorge are hoping to start a small arts and crafts school in your hometown. Before they decide on the specifics of the curriculum, they have come to you to help them access the Internet to find demographic information.

Connect

Use a variety of Web search engines to locate the following information.

- Average age
- Percentages of gender
- Average income and education
- Ethnicity
- Occupation information

CHAPTER 7

Types of Business Ownership

Learning Objectives

When you have completed this chapter, you will be able to:

- **Contrast** sole proprietorships, partnerships, and corporations
- **List** the different types of partnerships
- **Define** the different types of corporations

You're the Boss!

Forms of Business Ownership

You and a co-worker have decided to start your own book publishing company. You've identified the target market and have conducted research into starting your own business. The only question mark is how you will arrange your partnership.

What Will You Do?

How will you decide which form of ownership is best suited for your new company?

SECTION 7.1

Sole Proprietorships and Partnerships

SOLE PROPRIETORSHIP

The easiest and most popular form of business to create is the *sole proprietorship.* In a sole proprietorship, the owner is the only one responsible for the business's activities. Nearly 76 percent of all businesses in the United States are sole proprietorships.

What you'll learn

- the pros and cons of forming a sole proprietorship
- the advantages and disadvantages of partnerships
- the differences between types of partnerships

Why it's important

The easiest businesses to form are sole proprietorships and partnerships. You should know the advantages and disadvantages of each before choosing either.

KEY TERMS

sole proprietorship
liability
unlimited liability
partnership
general partners
limited partners

Tips from the Real World

R-E-S-P-E-C-T

There are many rewards to having your own business, one of which is respect. For Josie Natori, founder of Natori Lingerie:

"Respect is the result of passion. You cannot expect to get respectful reactions from people if what you are doing doesn't originate from deep within your soul."

What Is a Sole Proprietorship?

The owner of a sole proprietorship is the only one who receives profits. He or she is also the only one responsible for liability, or money owed to others. Most businesses start as sole proprietorships. They're easy to start quickly. However, most entrepreneurs switch to a form that affords more personal financial protection as the business grows. To decide whether a sole proprietorship is right for you, ask yourself the following questions.

1. How much liability protection do you need?
2. What are your business's operating requirements?
3. What effect will the business have on your tax status?

Consider these questions as you examine the advantages and disadvantages of the sole proprietorship.

Advantages. The sole proprietorship is easy and inexpensive to create. It also allows the owner to have complete authority over all the business's activities and to receive all the profits. It is the least regulated form of ownership. In addition, the business itself pays no taxes because it is not separate from the owner. Instead, the income from the business is taxed at the personal rate of the owner. The personal tax rate is often lower than other forms of ownership.

Disadvantages. The principal disadvantage of a sole proprietorship is financial. To start, the owner has unlimited liability for all debts and actions of the business. The debts incurred by the firm may have to be paid from the owner's personal assets. In other words, the owner's home, car, and bank account could all be at risk. In addition, it is more difficult to raise capital for sole proprietorships. This is because the owner by him- or herself may not have sufficient assets to qualify for a loan.

Other disadvantages center on the owner as a person. A sole proprietorship can be limited by its total reliance on the abilities and skills of the owner. These simply may not be sufficient to keep the enterprise going. Finally, the death of the owner automatically dissolves the business.

How to Set Up a Sole Proprietorship

To operate as a sole proprietor, first decide on a business name. Will you use your own name for the company or create a new name? If you make up a name, you will need to apply for a Certificate of Doing Business Under an Assumed Name. This is often called a DBA (for "doing business as"). You can get a DBA from the government offices in the area where your business will operate. In filing for the certificate, you ensure that you are the only business in the area using the name that you have chosen.

If you are going to hire employees, you will also need an Employer Identification Number (EIN). This number, which comes from the Internal Revenue Service, is used for tax purposes. It is used to track federal income tax withheld and federal income tax returns.

If your business name is different from your legal name, you have to apply for a Certificate of Doing Business Under an Assumed Name. ***What are some benefits?***

PARTNERSHIPS

In a **partnership**, more than one person shares the business decisions and outcomes. Partners must make several considerations.

What Is a Partnership?

A partnership is a sole proprietorship with more than one owner. Two or more people own a business and share the assets, liabilities, and profits. As a legal form of ownership, the partnership compensates for some of the shortcomings of a sole proprietorship. For example, partners share liability.

General vs. Limited Partners. A partnership may be set up so that all of the partners are **general partners**. This means that they all have unlimited personal liability and take full responsibility for the management of the business. The law requires that all partnerships have at least one general partner.

ENTREPRENEURS INTERNATIONAL

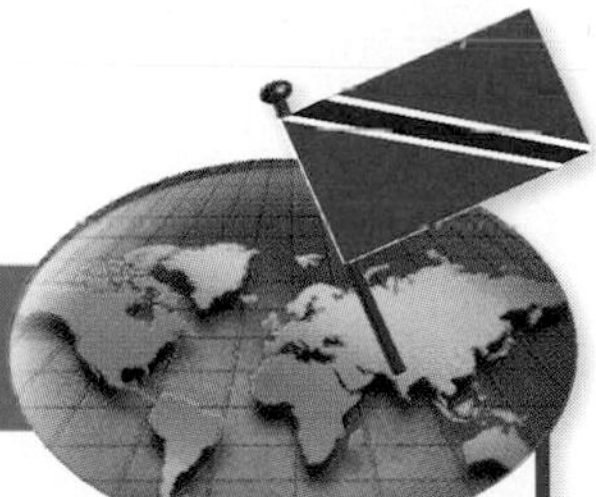

Trinidad and Tobago

In 1986, Veronica and Shane Collens began Cupboard Love to showcase their furniture designs. The married couple are both experienced professionals. Shane has a background in the arts. Veronica has experience in advertising and public relations. "The will to experiment and go beyond the conventional has given way to our innovative thinking. Subsequently it shows in our furniture," says Veronica Collens. Cupboard Love furniture is made from tropical hardwoods by skilled cabinetmakers.

Apply **What advantages do partners like Shane and Veronica Collens have in working together? Are there any disadvantages?**

Money Matters

FAMILY

Sometimes the most cost-efficient and trustworthy staff is drawn from family members. Cheryl Woodward, co-founder of *PC Magazine*, recalls from 1981:

“*My sister was the bookkeeper. . . my partner's wife took over production, and my brother-in-law handled distribution. No one but family would ever have worked so hard.*”

Partners do not have to share a business equally. Sometimes businesses have limited partners, whose liability is limited to their investment. If a limited partner invests $10,000 in a business, the most he or she can lose if the business fails is $10,000. Limited partners cannot be actively involved in managing the business. If they become involved, they lose their limited liability status.

Other types of partnerships. A *joint venture* is a type of partnership where two companies join to complete a specific project. They act like partners for a specified period of time and then the partnership ends. For example, many real estate developers make a joint venture with a financial source to design and build a construction project.

A *strategic alliance* is a partnership in which two businesses work together for mutual benefit. For example, you may form a strategic alliance with a manufacturer that agrees to produce your new product for you. You don't have to set up a manufacturing plant. The manufacturer gets your continued business.

Advantages. The advantages of a partnership are similar to those of a sole proprietorship. This form of business is inexpensive to create, and the general partners have complete control. Partnerships have other benefits. They can share ideas and secure investment capital more easily and in greater amounts.

If you form a partnership, it's important to choose your partner carefully. ***What are some qualities that you would look for?***

Disadvantages. In spite of these advantages the partnership may not be a preferred form of ownership. Why? At best it's a fragile entity. For example, it is very difficult to dissolve one partner's interest in the business without dissolving the partnership. In other words, if one of the partners wants to pull out or dies, that ends the busi-

RISK TAKERS PROFIT MAKERS

Name: Mary Ann McKenzie
Company: McKenzie Equipment
City, State: Houston, TX

Fresh Air

When Mary Ann McKenzie went into the family air systems business following the deaths of her father and grandfather in 1992, she had a difficult road ahead of her. McKenzie Equipment Company was near bankruptcy and its corporate culture was outdated. "We were just getting into computers when I arrived," McKenzie says, referring to the antiquated operations. Through a lot of hard work, McKenzie was able to implement major technological and professional advancements. Some of the changes were not easy. "We had 78 employees when I arrived and we had to cut back to 53 to survive. We're back to 66 employees," says McKenzie.

McKenzie's efforts have paid off. Today, her multimillion dollar business packages and installs air systems and compressors for a variety of business applications from offshore drilling to food processing.

Thinking Critically

What are the pros and cons of laying off employees, especially for a family business?

ness. Only if provisions to the contrary have been placed in the partnership agreement is the business likely to survive.

The major threat that partnerships face is personality conflicts. This factor results in more partnership breakups than any other. Problems often start as disagreements about authority. Problems become complicated when roles are not clearly defined.

There are more technical disadvantages, too. Partners are bound by the laws of agency. This means that they can be held liable for each other's actions. Thus, if one partner signs a contract agreeing to buy all the business's raw materials from one supplier, the other partner must honor this arrangement. Otherwise, the business can be sued for breach of contract.

Making a Partnership Work

Partnerships start with the best of intentions. However, disagreements are bound to occur. It is important for partners to consider each other's needs before committing to the partnership. It is even more important that they plan for disagreements.

In general, your partnership has the greatest chance of surviving if you and your partner(s) do the following:

- Share business responsibilities.
- Put things in writing.
- Always be honest about how the business is doing.

Also, be sure to establish a partnership agreement in advance. The law does not require a partnership to be based on a written agreement. It is still a good idea to have one. Partnership agreements are usually drawn up by attorneys and based on the Uniform Partnership Act. They answer questions about profit sharing among partners, business responsibilities, and what happens if one of the partners dies or quits. A well-constructed partnership agreement can prevent many problems when disagreements occur.

CHECK YOUR UNDERSTANDING

SECTION 7.1

Reviewing Key Terms and Concepts

1 Why is the sole proprietorship the most popular form of legal organization?
2 If you form a partnership, why should you draft a partnership agreement?
3 What is the difference between general and limited partners?

Critical Thinking Activity

Contact a sole proprietorship and a partnership. Ask the owners why they chose their particular type of ownership. Then compare and contrast your results.

Extension Lab—Creative-Thinking Skills

Cycle Center You are the sole proprietor of a bicycle shop. You sell a variety of bikes, accessories, clothing, and parts. Although your prices are a bit higher than the competition, you pride yourself on the individual attention you provide your customers.

Creative Project Working in groups of five or six, write a 30-second television commercial about your business.

- Emphasize the advantages of your sole proprietorship as they relate to the customer.
- Assign parts and videotape the commercial.
- Evaluate the results. Do you think your ad would be effective and increase sales?

SECTION 7.2

Corporations

CORPORATE FORMS

Neither sole proprietorships nor partnerships protect business owners from liability for the actions of the company. In this section you will see how the corporate form gives owners protection from liability.

What Is a Corporation?

A **corporation** is a business that is chartered, or registered, by a state. It legally operates apart from its owner or owners. A corporation lives on after the owners have sold their interests or pass away. There are three major types of corporations: the

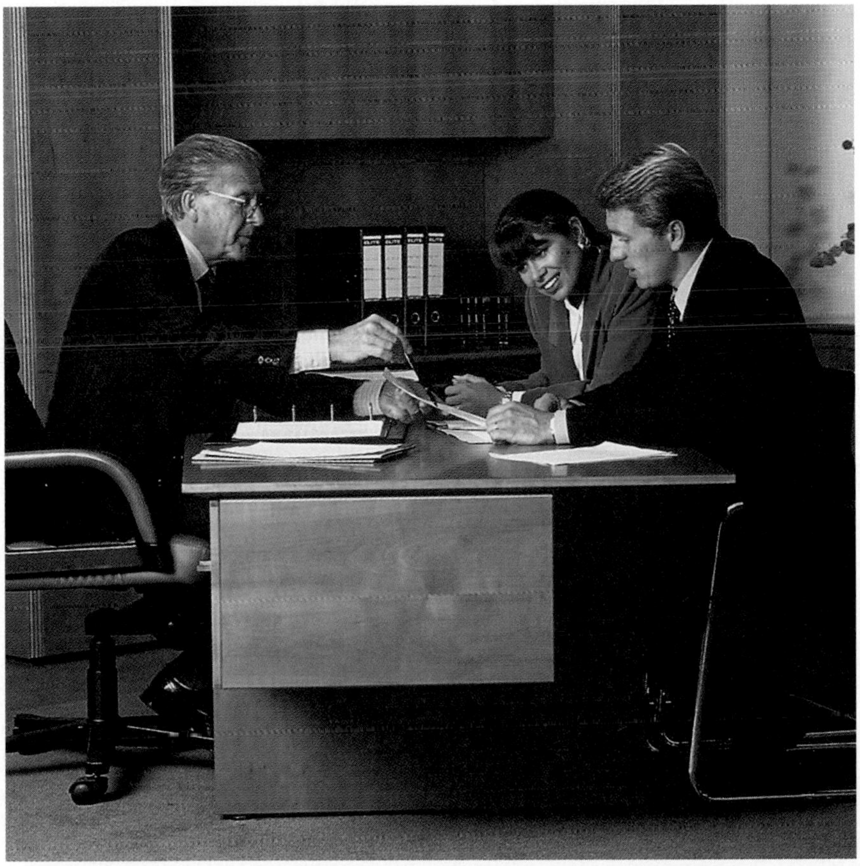

What you'll learn

- the benefits and costs of setting up a corporation
- the difference between a C-corporation and a Subchapter S corporation
- how a Limited Liability Company works

Why it's important

In a corporation the owner or owners of the business are protected from liability for the actions of the company.

KEY TERMS

corporation
C-corporation
limited liability
Subchapter S corporation
nonprofit corporation
Limited Liability Company

C-corporation, the Subchapter S corporation, and the nonprofit corporation. **Figure 7–1** compares sole proprietorship, partnerships, and corporations.

C-Corporation

The C-corporation is the most common corporate form. It protects the entrepreneur from being sued for actions and debts of the corporation. Corporations can be complex to create and operate.

Ask an attorney to guide you through the incorporation process. This includes filing a Certificate of Incorporation with the state and issuing stock. Stock certificates indicate the amount of

Figure 7–1
Each form of ownership has benefits and drawbacks. ***Which form is best suited for your business?***

Legal Forms of Ownership—A Comparison

	Sole Proprietorship	Partnerships	Corporations
Start-up costs	Filing fees for DBA and business license	Attorney's fees for partnership agreement, filing fees for DBA	Attorney's fees for incorporation documents, filing fees, taxes and state fees
Liability	Owner liable for all actions of business	All partners liable for actions of business, but limited partners liable only to amount invested	Shareholders liable only to amount invested; officers may be personally liable for full amounts owed
Continuity of business	Dissolves on death of owner	Dissolves on death of general partner, unless partnership agreement states otherwise; not so on death of limited partner	Not affected by death of shareholders
Control of business	Rests entirely with owner	Shared equally by general partners	Rests with shareholders who own majority of stock*
Distribution of profits	All to owner	Shared as specified in partnership agreement	Paid to shareholders according to amount invested
Transfer of interest	Owner can sell business at any time	General partner requires consent of other general partners to sell interest; limited partner's ability to sell depends on partnership agreement	Shareholders free to sell at any time unless restricted by agreement

*Day-to-day control rests with management hired by board of directors

equity, or ownership, each investor has in the business. Corporations are also required to have a board of directors. The board meets periodically to make policy decisions and select officers.

Advantages. The corporation has advantages over sole proprietorships and partnerships. It can raise money by issuing shares of stock. It may issue common stock, which has voting rights, or it may issue *preferred stock*. Owners of preferred stock are the first to receive their investment back in case of business failure.

A corporation also offers its owners, or shareholders, limited liability. The owners are liable only up to the amount of their individual investments. However, some banks and creditors require new corporations to have officers who will personally guarantee any debt.

Finally, corporations enjoy more status than the other kinds of businesses. Corporate owners can create pension and retirement funds. They can also offer profit sharing plans to their employees.

Disadvantages. The corporate form of business does pose some financial problems. It is expensive to set up. It may cost between $500 and $2,500 in fees to create a corporation. Its income is more heavily taxed. The corporation pays taxes on its profits. From these profits, it pays its stockholders earnings, or dividends. The stockholders must pay income taxes on their dividends.

Subchapter S Corporation

You can avoid the double taxation of a C-corporation by setting up a Subchapter S corporation. The Subchapter S corporation is taxed like a sole proprietorship or partnership. Profits pass through the corporation and are taxed only once.

Up&Coming Entrepreneur

Golf Car Entrepreneur

For years, Bob Stredwick was employed by a small motor repair shop in Alaska where he learned how to dismantle and replace all makes and models of engines. When he decided to go into business for himself, he contacted Yamaha and was awarded a regional golf car distributorship in Oregon in 1993. Today, Stredwick's Keystone Golf Cars sells, repairs, and rents new and used golf cars throughout Oregon.

Analyze **How is Keystone Golf Cars actually a partner with Yamaha?**

Figure 7–2

Nonprofit Corporations

Nonprofit corporations must fall within one of four categories:

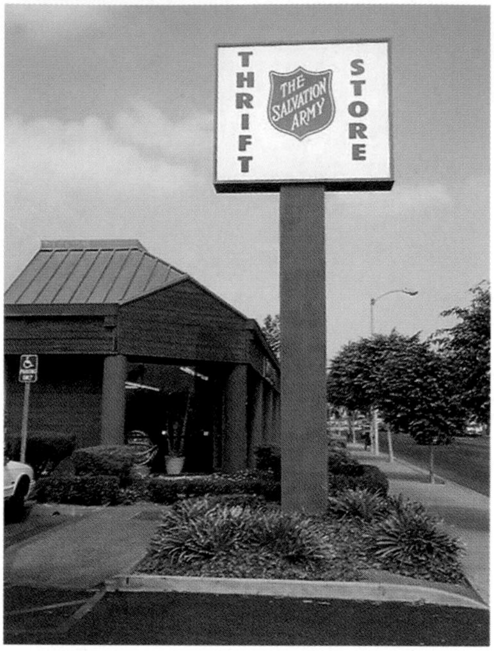

1. Charity.
Charitable causes include feeding the hungry and providing job training for the unemployed.

2. Public benefit.
Many foundations are created to advance science, education, and the arts.

3. Religion.
The money received by churches and temples goes toward paying their bills and advancing their causes.

4. Mutual benefit.
Trade associations, amateur sports leagues, and political groups are formed to benefit a specific group.

Cash businesses are often S corporations. If the business produces enough cash, the form works. Problems come if the business shows enough taxable profit, but not enough to cover taxes.

Nonprofit Corporation

Many entrepreneurs run businesses that benefit a certain cause in their communities. Nonprofit corporations are legal entities that make money for reasons other than the owners' profit. The types of nonprofit corporations are shown in **Figure 7–2**. Nonprofit businesses can make a profit. However, the profit must remain within the company.

Limited Liability Companies

The most recent form of business organization is the Limited Liability Company (LLC). The LLC combines the best of all worlds. It has the limited liability of a corporation. Its members are not liable for the company's debts. It also has the pass-through tax advantages of a partnership. Shareholders are only taxed once.

Many law and medical firms form LLCs to protect their partners. LLCs are also popular with foreign investors and family owners. Check with your state for its requirements.

CHECK YOUR UNDERSTANDING

SECTION 7.2

Reviewing Key Terms and Concepts

1. What are three reasons people chose the corporate form?
2. What is the difference between a C-corporation and a Subchapter S corporation?
3. Explain how a nonprofit business can try to make a profit.

Critical Thinking Activity

Ask the owner of a nonprofit company how he or she gives to the community. Describe how a business can benefit the owner and the community well.

Extension Lab – Teaching Others

Web Weavers You and a partner run a busy Web page design company. When you decided to hire an office assistant, your partner suggested you could save money by hiring someone who is willing to be paid in cash. That way, you could avoid reporting this employee's earnings to the federal government and paying workman's compensation.

Role Play In groups of two or three, role play a conversation based on the given situation. Consider the following:

- What should you tell your partner?
- How could you prevent this type of issue from developing in the future?

CHAPTER 7 REVIEW

CHAPTER SUMMARY

- The three basic legal forms of business ownership are the sole proprietorship, partnerships, and corporations.
- The easiest form of business to create is a sole proprietorship, where the owner is the only one responsible for the activities of the business.
- In a partnership, two or more people own a business and share the assets, liabilities, and profits.
- Joint ventures and strategic alliances are two types of partnerships that form for a specific project or mutual benefit.
- A partnership agreement, which spells out specific information regarding business responsibilities and money issues, can prevent problems when disagreements occur.
- A corporation legally operates apart from its owner or owners. There are three major types: C-corporation, Subchapter S corporation, and nonprofit corporation.
- Because of the personal, legal, and financial issues surrounding business ownership, it is wise to consult a business attorney before you begin.

RECALL KEY TERMS

Assume you are a business attorney who is being consulted by a potential entrepreneur. In one or two paragraphs, explain the legal forms of ownership to your client. Be sure to include the following terms:

sole proprietorship
liability
unlimited liability
partnership
general partners
limited partners
corporation
C-corporation
Subchapter S corporation
limited liability
nonprofit corporation
Limited Liability Company

RECALL KEY CONCEPTS

1. What is the most popular form of business ownership in the United States?
2. Discuss the advantages and disadvantages of a sole proprietorship.
3. What is the process you should follow when setting up a sole proprietorship?
4. What are the differences between a sole proprietorship and a partnership?
5. Contrast a general partner and a limited partner.
6. Compare a joint venture with a strategic alliance.
7. Why is a partnership agreement necessary?
8. What happens when a partner dies or leaves the business?
9. Compare the C-corporation, Subchapter S corporation, and nonprofit corporation.
10. How is starting a corporation different from starting a sole proprietorship?

THINK CRITICALLY

1. Mountain Music Company is a sole proprietorship. However, the owner is considering becoming a corporation. Is this a good idea? Why or why not?
2. Working as a team member on a class project is similar in many ways to being in a partnership. What are some advantages

and disadvantages of working together?

3. Propose an example of a joint venture or strategic alliance that might be successful in today's global economy. Explain your proposal.
4. Which type of business structure would have the easiest time obtaining financing from a bank? Explain your answer.
5. Compare a Limited Liability Company with a C-corporation.

CONNECT ACADEMICS TO THE WORKPLACE

Math

1. You are the owner of a retail craft supply store. You pay your sales associate $7.50 per hour and 1.5 times the regular rate for every hour over 40 hours per week. Last week, your associate worked 54 hours. How much did he earn?

Teach Others

2. Create a bulletin board idea showing the advantages and disadvantages of sole proprietorships, partnerships, and corporations. As a class, vote on the best idea and then actually put up the board. Use it to explain the types of business ownership to another class.

WORK IN YOUR COMMUNITY

Volunteer to work or job shadow in a nonprofit organization. (Some examples might include the Coalition for the Homeless, Goodwill, or Habitat for Humanity.)

- Find out about their organizational structure.
- Have the supervisor explain the similarities and differences between a nonprofit and for-profit corporation.
- If the organization makes a profit, who benefits?
- As a class, share your experiences and compare your findings.

LINK SCHOOL TO CAREER

Invite local businesspersons representing sole proprietorships, partnerships, a variety of corporations (C, Subchapter S, nonprofit) and an LLC to serve on a panel discussion in your class. Ask them to share:

- Pros and cons of each type of business ownership
- How they got started
- Qualities they feel are important to succeed in the particular type of business ownership they represent

Have questions ready when the panel members arrive. Be sure to thank them for their time.

*inter*NET CONNECTION

Legal Lingo

Art can't decide whether to create a partnership or a Subchapter S corporation. You suggest he use the Internet to find background information before contacting a local attorney.

Connect

Use a variety of search engines to conduct research on the following:

- What legal issues does Art face if he creates a partnership?
- What legal issues does Art face if he creates a Subchapter S corporation?
- Are there legal forms that can be downloaded from the Internet?

CHAPTER 8

The Legal Environment

Learning Objectives

When you have completed this chapter, you will be able to:

- **Suggest** ways to get legal protection for the business products you create
- **Describe** laws related to starting your business
- **List** the laws affecting the hiring of employees
- **Discuss** the laws that deal with trade issues
- **Identify** some of the taxes for which business owners are responsible

You're the Boss!

Keeping the Law on Your Side

You have just started a fast and affordable flower delivery service. You have come up with a spectacular design for your new logo and slogan, "You'll never have to say you're sorry again." A friend suggests that you protect the desirable logo and attention-grabbing slogan.

What Will You Do?

What actions could you take to protect your ideas?

SECTION 8.1

Legal Issues Facing Start-Ups

What you'll learn

- how to protect the product or service your business is offering
- the laws that affect the start up of a business
- where to get legal advice

Why it's important

There is no aspect of a business that is not affected by the law. You will save yourself time and money if you learn about these laws in advance.

KEY TERMS

patent
patent-applied-for
patent-pending
copyright
public domain
trademark
service mark
contract
consideration
capacity

PROTECTING YOUR IDEAS

Suppose you have a marketable idea for a product or service. You know you need help to put the idea into effect, but you don't want someone to steal your idea. What can you do? Depending on your product, you have several options.

What Are You Trying to Protect?

The group of laws that affects how ideas are protected is called *intellectual property law*. Before you can learn how intellectual property laws can help you protect your ideas, you need to define what it is you're trying to protect. If you want to protect an invention of some type, that falls under *patent* law. Protecting a logo for your business is a *trademark* issue. If you write music, software, or books, your protections come under the heading of *copyright* law. And if you create recipes for food, you will deal with *trade secrets*.

Patents

A **patent** is a grant to an inventor that gives him or her the exclusive right to produce and sell an invention. It lasts for a period of 21 years from

Figure 8–1

Patent and Trademark Rules

There are four rules that determine if your invention can be patented.

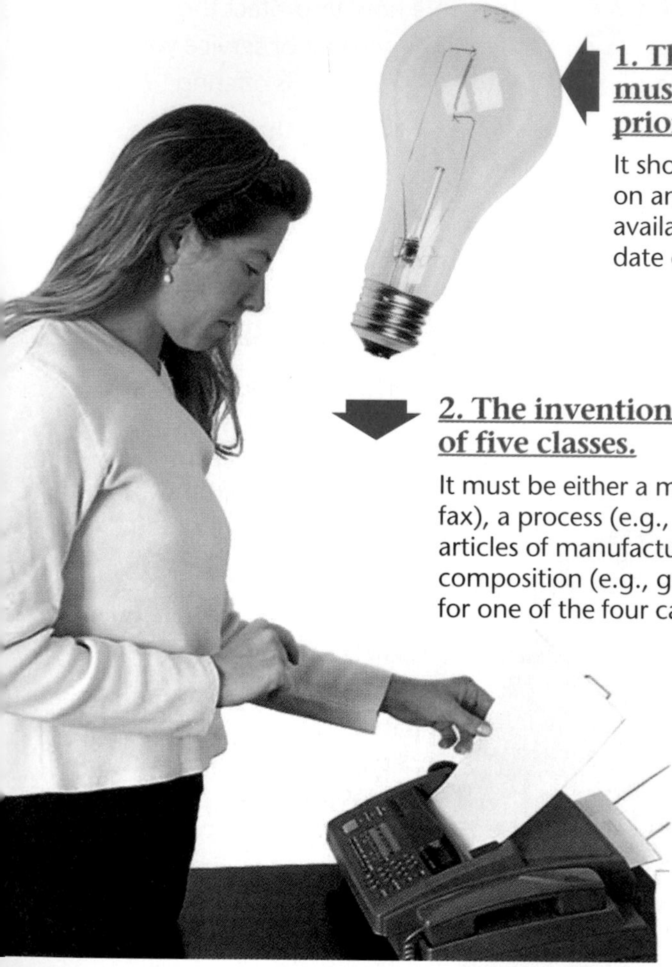

1. The invention must not contain prior art.

It shouldn't be based on anything publicly available before the date of the invention.

2. The invention must fit into one of five classes.

It must be either a machine (e.g., a rocket, fax), a process (e.g., chemical reactions), articles of manufacture (e.g., furniture), a composition (e.g., gasoline), or a new use for one of the four categories.

3. The invention must be "unobvious."

The invention must not be obvious to someone with skills in the field. It should be new and unexpected.

4. The invention must have utility.

This means it must be useful, not just whimsical or silly.

the date of application. The invention must qualify under the rules of the Patent and Trademark Office. **Figure 8–1** shows the rules that apply.

The Process. To protect your invention, you should file a disclosure document with the Patent and Trademark Office (PTO). This statement costs $25 to process. In the application, you confirm that you are the inventor of your product and describe it in detail. Within two years you must file an application with the PTO.

The Patent Search. While the PTO researches the patent application, the patent is said to be in patent-applied-for status. This means that the public can't look at the application and drawings. If the PTO decides your claims are valid, it will issue you a patent. It may, however, decide that some or all of your claims are not valid. In that case, you may revise them and resubmit your application. Once the PTO declares that your claims are accepted, your patent is in patent-pending status until the patent is actually issued. If you are marketing your product at that point, you must put the phrase *patent pending* on the product or packaging.

Copyrights

A copyright is similar to a patent, except that it protects original works of authors. These works include such things as books, movies, musical compositions, and computer software.

If you plan to publish (or make public) your work, copyright law recommends that you do two things. First, place a notice of copyright in a prominent location on the work. This notice must include the symbol © or the word *Copyright*, the year of first publication, and the name of the copyright holder. Second, register your work with the Copyright Office. The office is a branch of the Library of Congress.

Jeep is a trademarked word that has entered the common vocabulary. As a result, the manufacturers make a point to keep other makers of rugged utility vehicles from using it. ***What are some other examples of trademarked words that have entered everyday vocabulary?***

You should be aware that a copyright protects only the form in which the idea is presented. It does not protect the idea itself. For example, if you write a database software program, the program that produces the database is protected, but the idea of a database as a tool is not.

A copyright lasts for the life of the author plus 50 years. After that, the work goes into the public domain, which means that it can be used by anyone free of charge.

Trademarks

A trademark is a word, symbol, design, or combination of these that a business uses to identify itself or something it sells. Trademarks are followed by the registered trademark symbol ®. For example, a rainbow-colored apple with a bite taken out of it is the trademark of Apple Computer. It is recognized worldwide. Similarly, a design or symbol that describes a service business is called a service mark. The stylized *M* on a McDonald's sign is an example of a service mark.

Like a patent or a copyright, a trademark provides legal protection. If a business registers its trademark with the PTO, the trademark cannot be used by a competitor. However, a trademark cannot be registered with the PTO until it is actually going to be used. Like a patent applicant, a business seeking trademark status for its symbol must prove that the design is original and distinctive.

Unlike a patent, a trademark can be held indefinitely—unless it becomes common usage in the English language. Words like *aspirin*, *yo-yo*, and *thermos* were once registered trademarks. Today they are no longer used exclusively by the businesses that created them. They have become generic terms.

From the very start, a new business is affected by many government regulations and requirements. ***What laws might affect this bowling alley?***

LAWS AFFECTING STARTING UP YOUR BUSINESS

Certain legal requirements are fundamental to your ability to do business. If you cannot meet the requirements, you cannot even start up your company. There are three categories of laws you should be aware of before you start your business.

1. Permits and Licenses

Before you can officially open the doors of your business you must get a business permit from your local government. This permit allows you to do business in your community. It will most likely have to be renewed annually. You will be required to pay

Up&Coming Entrepreneur

Investment Education Entrepreneur

Fabiola Petigny first learned about mutual funds and IRAs while working for a mutual investments firm. The more she found out about these investment opportunities, the more she wished she had known about them sooner. With this in mind, and with guidance from the National Federation for Teaching Entrepreneurship, Petigny started Young Investors, a company dedicated to teaching youths aged 13–21 about investments. She currently travels to schools to educate students on mutual funds and IRAs.

Analyze **What might be some legal issues involved in teaching investment opportunities to young adults?**

periodic fees throughout the life of your business. The size of the fee is usually based on how much the business earns.

You may also have to get a license. Certain professions require you to show that you have the necessary education and training to do the job. For example, doctors, nurses, barbers, accountants, and counselors all need special licenses. Such licenses protect consumers from unskilled or unqualified business operators. Licensing requirements vary from one state or locality to another.

Be sure you have the necessary licenses before you start your business. Check with your local government or your state department of licensing and regulation for information.

2. Contracts

A **contract** is a binding legal agreement between two or more persons or parties. As an entrepreneur, you will sign contracts to start and run your business. Some contracts will be with vendors or landlords, others with clients, and still others with government agencies.

Most people fulfill the requirements of the contracts they sign. However, when one of the parties fails to meet his or her obligations, the other party may be entitled to monetary damages. The right to these damages is usually determined in court. This is why it is important to draw up a legally binding contract that clearly states the intentions of all the parties. To be a valid legal contract, a document must contain certain elements.

- *Agreement.* Agreement occurs when one party to a contract makes an offer or promises to do something and the other party accepts. For example, suppose a vendor offers to sell your business a fax machine. There is no agreement until you have either sent the vendor a purchase order or a check signifying that you accept the offer. If you change any of the terms of the vendor's offer, you have created what is called a counteroffer. This is a new offer that now requires the acceptance of the vendor to form a new contract.
- *Consideration.* **Consideration** is what is exchanged for the promise. The money you pay to the vendor for the fax machine is valuable *consideration* and causes the contract to be binding.

Tips from the Real World

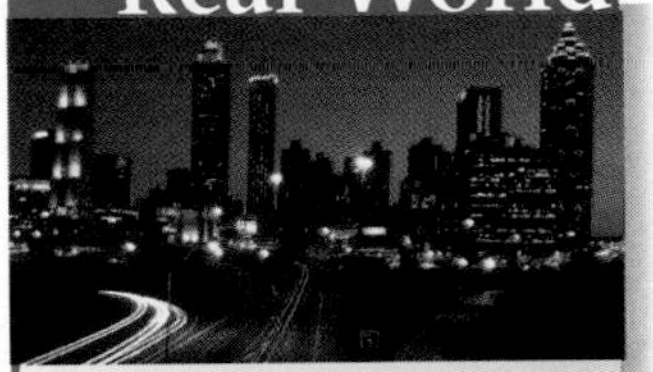

PARTNERSHIP

Between business partners, deciding up front how the business will be evaluated, sold, or divided saves a lot of anger if things don't work out. Independent management consultant Sam Lane advises:

"It's kind of like your roll bar. You hope you never have to use it, but you want it in there."

- *Capacity.* Capacity means that you are legally able to enter into a binding agreement. By law, minors, intoxicated persons, and insane persons cannot enter into valid contracts. If they do sign such a contract, the agreement can be considered void. This means that the contract never existed.
- *Legality.* The final contract element is legality. For a contract to be valid, it must be legal. In other words, it cannot have any provisions that are illegal or would result in illegal activities.

3. Choosing a Location

Before you start your business, you need to decide where to locate it. The type of business, need for foot traffic, and location of competition are factors. The law also affects where you place the business.

Zoning Laws and Building Codes. If you build a new facility or locate your business in an existing building, you will need to conform to local zoning laws. Cities typically designate particular areas, or zones, for certain uses. Zones are usually specified as residential, commercial, industrial, or public. For example, you cannot locate a tire manufacturing plant in the middle of a residential neighborhood.

Zoning laws also address environmental issues. They may restrict such things as the disposal of toxic waste, noise and air pollution, and incompatible building styles. For example, a residential neighborhood might permit office buildings, but only those that are low-rise and fit in with the residential architecture. Zoning laws may also define the type and style of signs that businesses can use and the appearance of the buildings.

In addition to restrictions on use and appearance, you need to check the laws that relate to the actual construction of your facility. These are called *building codes*. Building codes set standards for construction or modification of buildings. These standards include such things as the strength of concrete, the amount of insulation, and other structural requirements.

Local governments employ inspectors to verify that building code requirements are met at each stage of construction. How can you to meet the requirements?

Licensed building contractors or architects should be familiar with local

It's important to inspect a space carefully before leasing it. ***Why should you hire an expert to check it out?***

building codes. You can assure that your facility is built to code by hiring such a person to supervise your project.

Leasing. Most entrepreneurs start with few resources and little money. Therefore, prudent entrepreneurs will usually *lease* buildings and equipment rather than buy them. A lease is a contract to use a facility or equipment for a specified period of time. The lessee (the person who is leasing the building or equipment) has no ownership rights. Those belong to the lessor (the person who owns the building or equipment).

Leasing usually does not require spending a large amount of money up front. The money saved can be used for purchasing inventory and supplies and hiring employees. This can be a definite advantage for a new business. Another advantage is that some lease expenses are tax deductible. This can reduce the tax liability of the company.

Nevertheless, leasing could also bring on its own set of troubles. For example, the lease contract itself is a very complex document. It states the terms: the length of the lease, the monthly rent, the penalty for failing to pay, and the procedure for termination. Because a lease is a long-term contract, an entrepreneur should consult with an attorney before signing one.

CHECK YOUR UNDERSTANDING

SECTION 8.1

Reviewing Key Terms and Concepts

1 What is the first document you should file in the patent process? Why?
2 How can you protect the use of your business logo?
3 What are the four elements of a binding contract?

Critical Thinking Activity

Walk the commercial area near your home. What kinds of businesses are located there? Then call your city government offices to find out what the zoning is for that area. What kinds of businesses can locate there?

Extension Lab—Negotiation Skills

The Case of the Fired Employee You manage a human resources department. A recently fired employee has filed a lawsuit against your company suggesting wrongful termination. Your boss says that this employee was regularly late to work and consistently refused to make up the time. The ex-employee insists that he couldn't help it if his car was unreliable. You decide to seek advice from an attorney.

Role Play With a partner, enact a dialog between you and your attorney. Be sure to include:

- The information you kept in the file regarding the employee's violations
- The procedure you used to fire the employee
- What you might do to prevent future lawsuits

SECTION 8.2

Handling Government Regulation

What you'll learn

- the laws that affect the hiring of employees
- the laws dealing with trade issues
- the laws dealing with taxes

Why it's important

Handling government regulation is an ongoing expense for a small business. You can prevent a lot of problems by learning these regulations as part of your business research.

KEY TERMS

Equal Opportunity Employment Commission
wrongful termination
price discrimination
Uniform Commercial Code
warranty of merchantability
bait-and-switch
FICA

HIRING YOUR EMPLOYEES

Businesses, both large and small, are affected on a daily basis by the laws of federal, state, and local governments. We can't discuss all of the laws that affect business here, but this section will touch on some of the major ones. It will give you a better sense of what you need to know before starting your own business. **Figure 8–2** provides an overview of the areas that will be covered.

Laws that Affect Your Employees

If you start a business, you will probably hire employees. There are many laws that affect the hiring, firing, and paying of employees.

Laws Against Discrimination in Hiring. The Equal Employment Opportunity Commission (EEOC) is charged with protecting the rights of employees. It ensures that employers do not discriminate against employees because of age, race, color or national origin, religion, gender, or physical challenge.

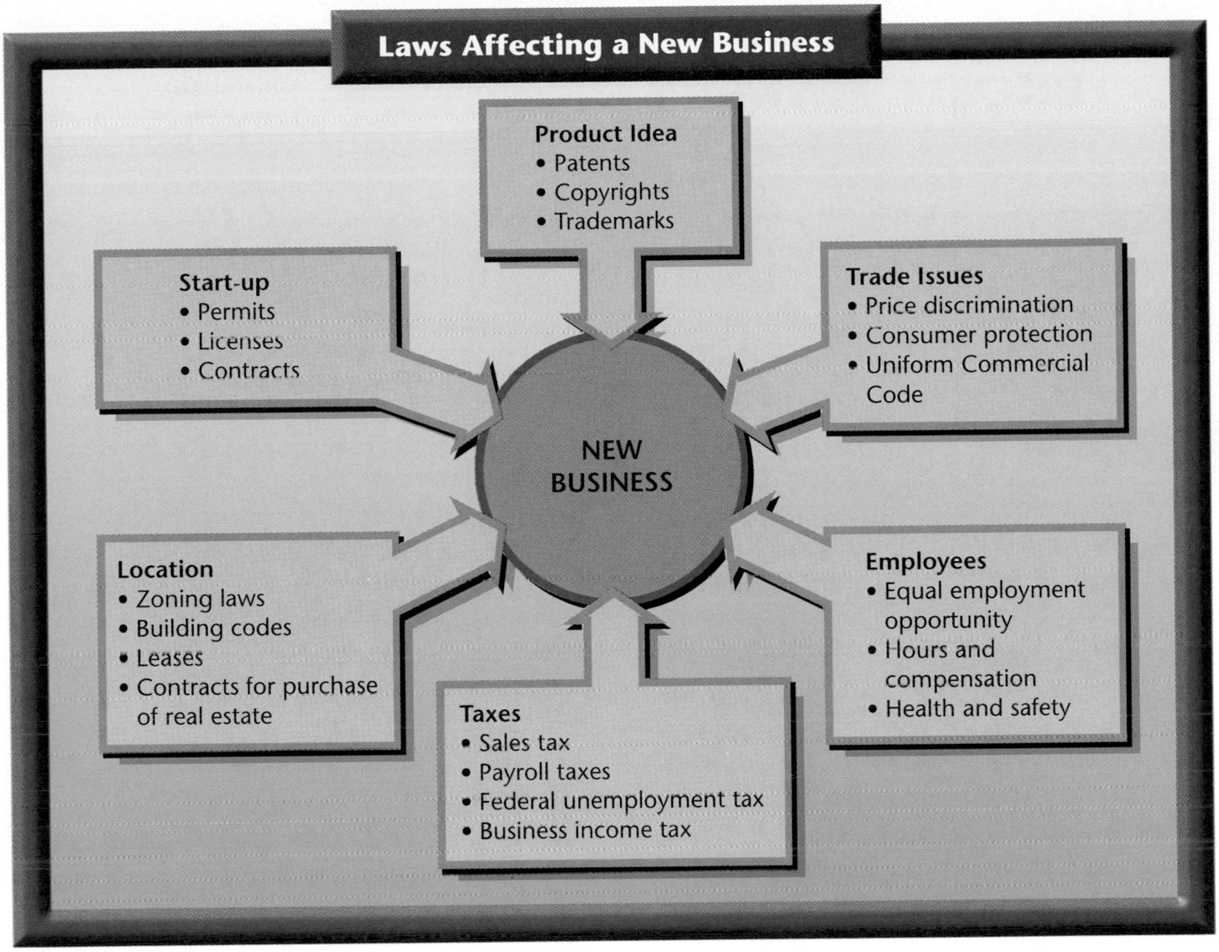

Figure 8–2
Every business is affected by government regulations and requirements. ***How might these laws protect a new business?***

An employer cannot refuse to hire, promote, or give pay increases to an employee based on any of these characteristics. If you give any tests or use any screening devices to check out potential employees, the U.S. Department of Labor states they must be related directly to the job.

Wrongful Termination. When an employee is fired for wrongful reasons, it is called wrongful termination. As a business owner you should be very careful about important events related to each employee. Notify employees who violate rules in writing. Then get a receipt from the employee saying that he or she was notified of the violation. Taking care in keeping good records will help prevent unwanted lawsuits.

Equal Pay Act of 1963. This act says that all employers must pay men and women the same wage for the same work. *Same work* involves similar skills, responsibility, and effort.

RISK TAKERS PROFIT MAKERS

Name: Crissy Barnett
Company: Peerless Hotel
City, State: Ashland, OR

Inn Style

Crissy Barnett wasn't certain how to keep busy when her husband was transferred from Honolulu to the small town of Ashland, Oregon. Then she noticed a dilapidated building in the city's Railroad District. Barnett inquired and found it was built in 1900 as a boarding house for the Southern Pacific Railroad workers. It was overpriced. When the bankrupt owners had to sell the building at a discount of 50 percent, Barnett made her offer.

Barnett had her work cut out for her. It took her 18 months to petition for zoning permits, a place in the National Historic Register, and a Federal Tax Rehabilitation Credit. Construction began and Barnett acted as her own general contractor for a year. In 1994, the Peerless Hotel opened as a beautifully restored showpiece. It took three years to increase the occupancy rates enough to result in a steady business, but now business is booming. In fact, Barnett just added a restaurant next door!

Thinking Critically

One person's junk is another person's treasure. Can you list some business opportunities that might exist in your city's vacant buildings?

Fair Labor Standards Act. The Fair Labor Standards Act was passed in 1938. This law established a minimum wage and maximum working hours. It also ensured that children under the age of 16 could not be employed full-time except by their parents.

Occupational Safety and Health Act. The Occupational Safety and Health Act of 1970 was passed to ensure safe and healthy working conditions for employees. You have probably heard of the agency that was created by this Act—OSHA, the Occupational Safety and Health Administration.

OSHA requires employers to look for hazardous areas in their workplace. Employers must maintain health and safety records, provide safety training, keep up-to-date on new OSHA standards, and take care of violations promptly.

OSHA frequently comes under fire from businesspeople for the stiff rules and regulations it enforces. The agency also requires that a large amount of paperwork be done and charges heavy fines on companies that don't follow its rules.

DEALING WITH TRADE ISSUES

In general, the American government allows businesses to compete in the marketplace with relative freedom. However, since the early 1800s, many laws have been enacted that regulate and restrict business practices. These key trade laws were created to preserve competition and fairness in the marketplace.

Price Discrimination

The Clayton Act of 1914 and the Robinson-Patman Act of 1936 are aimed to prohibit *price discrimination*. Price discrimination occurs when a business sells the same product to different people at different prices. Businesses must justify giving one customer a lower price than another. They must show that the favored customer bought more, bought lower-quality goods, or benefited from cost savings. This means that entrepreneurs must to be fair to all customers when setting prices.

Consumer Protection

Most laws pertaining to trade are designed to protect the consumer. These laws protect against the following:

- Unscrupulous sellers
- Unreasonable credit terms
- Unsafe products
- Mislabeling of products

ENTREPRENEURS INTERNATIONAL

Egypt

Blue Bubbles Diving Safari arranges unforgettable underwater safaris. "The most beautiful dive sites are in the Red Sea," says founder Ahmed Moharram. Blue Bubbles arranges for airport transfers, hotels, meals, boats, a diving staff, and all the necessary equipment. "We provide a personal touch you might miss with larger companies," says Moharram. Clients not certified to dive can discover the abundant underwater wildlife of the Red Sea on Blue Bubbles's snorkeling trips.

Apply **Safety is a major legal concern for Blue Bubbles Diving Safari and many other types of business. How can a company assure safety to its clients?**

There are also many federal agencies involved in regulating trade. Many of them function to protect the consumer as well. A list of some major federal trade regulators is shown in **Figure 8–3.**

The Food and Drug Administration (FDA). One of the largest federal agencies monitoring product safety is the FDA. It is responsible for researching and testing new products and inspecting the operations of food and drug manufacturers. If your new product idea is a cosmetic, drug, food item, or even suntan lotion, you will need to have approval of the FDA to market it.

The Consumer Product Safety Commission (CPSC). This commission serves as the watchdog for consumers

Figure 8–3
Many of the agencies that have the greatest impact on small businesses are part of the federal government. ***Which ones will directly affect you when you start your own business?***

Federal Trade Regulators

Agency	Function
Consumer Product Safety Commission	Establishes product safety standards and recalls products
Environmental Protection Agency	Creates and enforces standards for the environment, regulating air, water, and noise pollution as well as toxic waste
Equal Employment Opportunity Commission	Establishes the rules relating to discrimination in the workplace
Federal Communications Commission	Licenses the operation of television, radio, telephone, and telegraph operations
Federal Trade Commission	Enforces the antitrust, truth-in-lending, and labeling laws
Food and Drug Administration	Creates the standards for foods and drugs and approves any new drugs
Internal Revenue Service	Enforces the tax statutes and resolves disputes
Interstate Commerce Commission	Determines the trade practices, rates, and routes for interstate railroads, bus companies, and pipelines
Justice Department	Enforces the laws to maintain free trade
National Labor Relations Board	Monitors and governs the relationship between employers and unions
Occupational Safety and Health Administration	Establishes and regulates safety and health standards for employees
Patent and Trademark Office	Issues patents and trademarks for new products

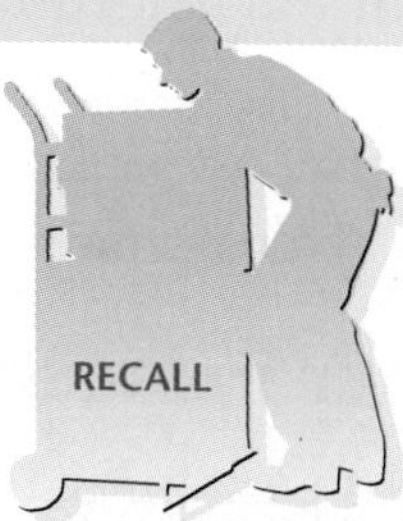

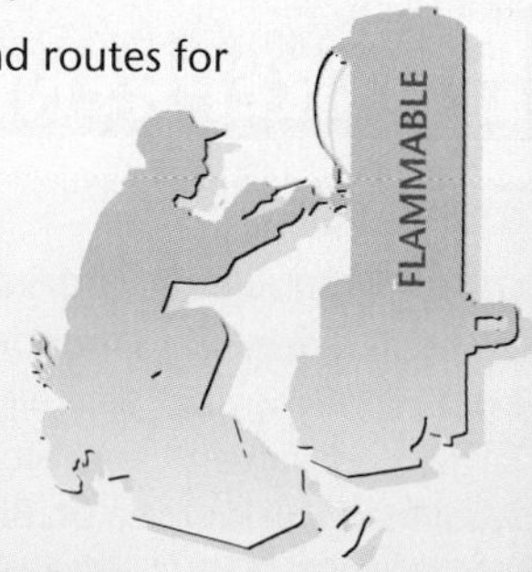

over products that may be hazardous. It also creates safety standards for products such as toys for children under the age of five.

The Fair Packaging and Labeling Act. The act requires that manufacturer labels truthfully list all raw materials used in the production of products. The act also requires that the size and weight of the product be on the label.

If you are manufacturing products for the public, you will need to become familiar with consumer protection laws. That way you can avoid possible recalls of your product and potential lawsuits.

The Uniform Commercial Code

The Uniform Commercial Code (UCC) is a group of laws that covers everything from sales to bank deposits and investment securities. The UCC has been adopted by all states. Since it applies to sales transactions between merchants, its provisions are likely to affect you as an entrepreneur.

Formation of Contracts. As we discussed earlier, when you enter into an agreement to sell a product, you create a valid contract. This means that you must abide by contract laws. However, as a merchant, you must also abide by the requirements of the UCC. In some cases, the two are not the same.

For example, in a valid contract, all the terms of price, place, delivery date, and quantity should be present. Suppose you are a manufacturer who has ordered some parts from a supplier, but you have not asked the price. When the parts arrive, you find they cost more than you expected. Do you have a contract despite the confusion about price?

The UCC says yes, but assigns a price that is reasonable at the time of delivery. The code assumes the parties intended to form a contract and knew the consequences of any ambiguity. Why? Because both are merchants—professionals who understand the business. Different rules, the UCC rules, apply to them than would apply to nonmerchants.

Warranties and Product Liability. Have you ever heard the term *caveat emptor*—let the buyer beware? That used to be a basic principle of the U.S. marketplace. Today, however, many believe the emphasis has shifted to the point where it is the seller who must beware. The law looks after the safety and economic interests of buyers. It also regulates sales warranties. Many of these laws and legal principles have been made part of the UCC.

Money Matters

ESTATES

Entrepreneurs need to make plans for their estates. Michael F. Rogers, attorney and CPA with Kauffman, Freeman & Rogers P.C., says:

"*Proper planning means . . . families won't have a 'fire sale' mentality upon the death of one of the owners, which could result in a quick and unwise sale of the company.*"

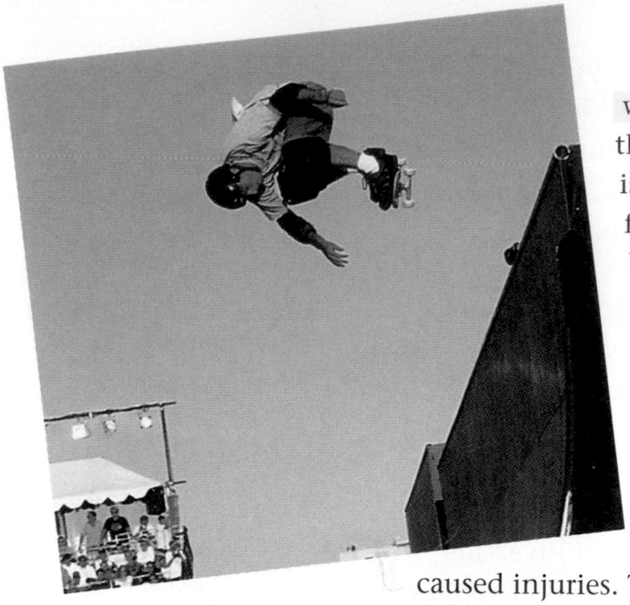

It's important for all manufacturers to include clear instructions for their products' use. ***What are some instructions that might come with sporting goods?***

When a merchant sells goods, he or she gives a warranty of merchantability. The warranty assures the buyer that the product he or she is purchasing is of at least average quality and fit for the purpose for which it was intended. The warranty is implied by law. Even if the merchant does not express it in words, it can be assumed by the customer.

You have probably seen or heard news stories about product liability. This is the legal theory that manufacturers are responsible for injuries caused by their products. For example, automobiles can be recalled because of defects. Manufacturers can also be sued if their products have caused injuries. The costs of product liability have boosted insurance costs for manufacturers. This raises prices for consumers. For example, about 25 percent of the cost of a football helmet pays for insurance.

If you are going to manufacture a product for sale to consumers, you must be very careful. Be sure to include clear instructions for the product's use. Also, give clear warnings of any potential dangers involved. This protects you and your consumer.

Truth in Lending

Those involved in retail businesses must familiarize themselves with the Consumer Credit Protection Act. This act requires those who give credit to reveal all the terms and conditions of their credit agreements. As a result, it is called the Truth-in-Lending Act. Like price discrimination laws, it is enforced by the Federal Trade Commission. The Truth-in-Lending Act applies to anything purchased over a period of time greater than four months.

Truth in Advertising

The Federal Trade Commission is also concerned about protecting customers from false and misleading advertising. The laws that address this trade issue are sometimes called truth-in-advertising laws. Regardless of your business, when you advertise, you should be aware of the following rules:

- *Misleading ads.* Your advertising should not mislead customers about what your product can do. It should not claim that the product can do something that it cannot.

- *Sale prices.* You cannot offer a reduced price on your product unless it has been offered to the public at the regular price for a period of time.
- *Price comparisons.* You cannot use list price as your comparison-selling price unless your product has actually been sold for that amount. The list price is commonly the manufacturer's suggested retail price (MSRP). Also, you must have proof that your prices are lower than your competitors' if you intend to use that fact in your advertising.
- *Bait-and-switch.* Bait-and-switch advertising uses a bargain-priced item to lure potential customers into a store. Then a salesperson tries to sell them higher-priced merchandise.

PAYING TAXES

A number of taxes apply to every business. ***What are taxes that apply to this restaurant?***

All business owners whose goal is to make a profit are responsible for certain taxes. These may include sales tax, payroll taxes, unemployment tax, and income tax.

Sales Tax

Sales tax is a percentage of the price of an item that goes to a state or local government. The percentage varies from state to state. Retailers collect sales tax from their customers and send it to the appropriate government agency. Usually this is the State Board of Equalization. Most retailers make payments every three months.

Payroll Taxes

If you hire employees, you need to deduct certain payroll taxes from their earnings. One payroll tax deducted from employee earnings is the FICA, or Social Security, tax. (FICA stands for *Federal Insurance Contribution Act.*) The tax is figured as a percentage of an employee's income. As an employer, you are required by law to contribute an amount equal to that deducted from each employee's paycheck. If you deducted $20.27 from an employee's paycheck for FICA, you, the employer, would have to match that amount. You would send a total of $40.54 to the Internal Revenue Service. There is a ceiling on the amount of wages subject to the FICA tax. Wages above that ceiling are not taxed.

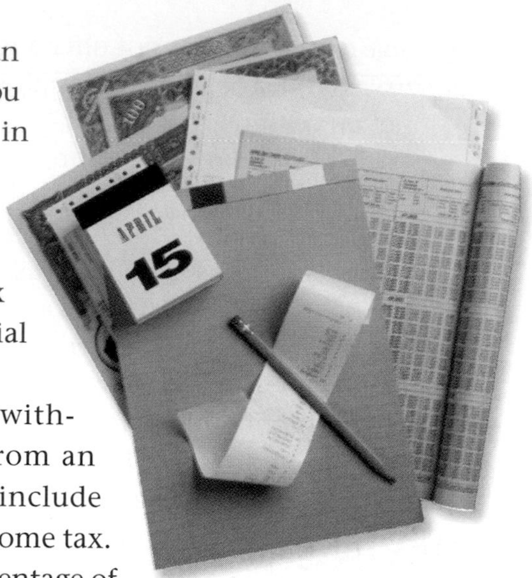

Withholding these taxes can be complex. As an employer you must be aware of any changes in the FICA tax rate or in the amount of wages subject to it. You can obtain information on the current FICA tax rate and ceiling from the Social Security Administration.

You are also required to withhold certain income taxes from an employee's paycheck. These include federal and, usually, a state income tax. These taxes are based on a percentage of gross pay. Contact your local and state governments and the IRS for information about these deductions.

Federal Unemployment Tax

As an employer, you are required to make contributions under the Federal Unemployment Tax Act (FUTA). The act was designed to provide help to workers who are temporarily unemployed. You may also be responsible for state unemployment taxes. However, they are usually credited against the federal taxes paid.

Business Income Taxes

Your business is also legally responsible for paying federal and possibly state and local taxes on the income it earns. If you are a sole proprietor or a partner in a partnership, the income your business earns is considered your personal income. As a result, the business income is taxed at your personal tax rate.

Let's say you are the sole owner of a catering business. Based on your income statement, your business's net income before taxes is $32,500. You would use that amount as your personal income when paying taxes to your state and the IRS. As a self-employed business owner, you also pay a FICA tax. It is exactly double what an employee pays because you are considered both employer and employee. The ceiling on the amount taxed is the same.

If your business is a corporation, the income tax situation is much different. The business will pay a corporate income tax. You will pay personal income tax based on the salary you earn and any other income derived from the business. In addition, the shareholders will pay personal income tax on salaries or dividends.

There are severe penalties for failure to file and pay income taxes. Therefore, it is a good idea to consult an accountant who will help you learn how to plan for taxes.

Getting Legal Advice

At every stage of developing a new business, you will probably need to seek some kind of legal advice. However, you can research a great deal of information on your own. There are many sources that you can use to find an attorney or get up-to-date information on your legal obligations as a business owner. They include the American Bar Association, the National Resource Center for Consumers of Legal Services, and the Commissioner of Patents and Trademarks. Also, the IRS can be of special help in tax matters. It often holds workshops and seminars to make business owners aware of their tax obligations.

If your business is involved in areas regulated by government, you should consult the appropriate agencies. You can find contact information at your local library or on the Internet. You can also consult an attorney who specializes in regulatory matters.

CHECK YOUR UNDERSTANDING

SECTION 8.2

Reviewing Key Terms and Concepts

1. What are the three main areas of business operations that the government regulates?
2. What is the purpose of OSHA?
3. What is the difference between general business contracts and contracts that fall under the Uniform Commercial code?

Critical Thinking Activity

From the IRS or Small Business Administration, find out the current taxes and tax rates that business owners must pay. (Hint: look up these agencies in a phone book or on the Internet.)

Extension Lab—Problem-Solving

I've Been Framed You open a new business selling picture frames that reflect light and appear to change colors. After one month of business, your customers complain that the frames don't do what you claim, and the Federal Trade Commission files charges against you for running misleading ads.

Research Contact one or two consumer agencies in your area for suggestions on these topics:

- What could you do to satisfy your complaining customers?
- How could you appeal to the FTC?
- What can you do to save your business?
- What should you have done to prevent this situation from occurring?

CHAPTER 8 REVIEW

CHAPTER SUMMARY

- To protect your business ideas or products, you can use patents, copyrights, and trademarks.
- Before you start your business, you need to understand three categories of laws: permits and licenses, contracts, and laws relating to your location.
- To be a valid, legal contract, a document must contain four elements: parties who have the legal capacity to enter into a contract, agreement among those parties, consideration, and legality of provisions.
- In hiring and compensating employees, a business may not discriminate on the basis of age, race, color, national origin, religion, gender, or physical challenge.
- Federal laws protect consumers against price discrimination, unscrupulous sellers, unreasonable credit terms, and unsafe and mislabeled products.
- Businesses are responsible for collecting and paying sales taxes; payroll taxes; unemployment taxes; and federal, state, and local income taxes.

RECALL KEY TERMS

An attorney who specializes in business law asks you to prepare a presentation for a new client on today's legal environment and how it affects the start-up of a new business. Use the following key terms in your presentation.

patent
patent-applied-for
patent pending
copyright
public domain
trademark
service mark
contract
consideration
capacity
Equal Opportunity Employment Commission
wrongful termination
price discrimination
Uniform Commercial Code
warranty of merchantability
bait-and-switch
FICA

RECALL KEY CONCEPTS

1. How long does a patent last? a copyright? a trademark?
2. List at least three professions that require a special license.
3. Describe what issues zoning laws address.
4. What is the purpose of the Equal Employment Opportunity Commission?
5. Why was OSHA established?
6. What is the Uniform Commercial Code and how does it affect entrepreneurs?
7. What does the Truth-in-Lending Act require retail businesses to do?
8. Contrast FICA and FUTA.
9. What agency or department would you contact if you had questions about the following?
   - Patents
   - Federal income taxes
   - Firing an employee

THINK CRITICALLY

1. Suppose you have an idea for a new kind of applicator that takes the mess out of applying suntan lotion. What steps would you need to take to protect your invention?
2. If you owned a trademark for a product, how would you protect that trademark

from becoming a generic term in the English language?

3. Compare leasing versus buying a building for your business. Include cost, ownership rights, need for an attorney, and contract terms.
4. As a business owner, what would you do to make sure you have complied with all the laws affecting the hiring, firing, and safety of your employees?
5. Should trade laws be designed to protect the buyer or the seller? Explain.

CONNECT ACADEMICS TO THE WORKPLACE

Math

1. Suppose that one of your employees earns $1,500 this month. The current FICA deduction is 7.5%. How much in FICA contributions will you deposit with the IRS in the employee's name?

Serve Customers

2. You work as a customer care representative for a retail stereo store. Last Sunday, a stereo system was advertised for only $89. This week, you've received telephone calls from customers who tried to buy the system and felt pressured to purchase a higher-priced stereo. The customers are complaining of bait-and-switch tactics. How do you handle this situation? What should you tell your boss? What do you think the store should do to satisfy the unhappy customers?

WORK IN YOUR COMMUNITY

Choose a business you would like to launch. As part of the start-up process, research the following:

- Necessary business permits and fees
- Required licenses
- Laws that will affect your business
- Sales, payroll, and business income tax forms you will need

Summarize your findings in a business report to the class.

LINK SCHOOL TO CAREER

Interview a member of the local zoning board or commission in your community.

- Ask about the differences among residential, commercial, industrial, and public zones in your town.
- Find out about any restrictions regarding environmental issues.
- Ask how the local building codes are developed and enforced.

Report to the class what you have learned.

interNET CONNECTION

Jazz Fest

Murphie has just written a trumpet solo that she will play in the National Youth Jazz Festival. Since she plans to publish the piece, she needs your help.

Connect

Using a variety of Web search engines, find out about copyrighting music.

- What is the procedure necessary to copyright a piece of music?
- How do you register your work with the Copyright Office?
- What specific laws protect the original works of authors?

CHAPTER 9

Site Selection and Layout Planning

Learning Objectives

When you have completed this chapter, you will be able to:

- **Apply** the process used to select a community and site in which to start your business
- **List** the factors that enter into selecting a business site
- **Contrast** the steps in laying out different types of businesses
- **Design** the interior and exterior layout plan of a business

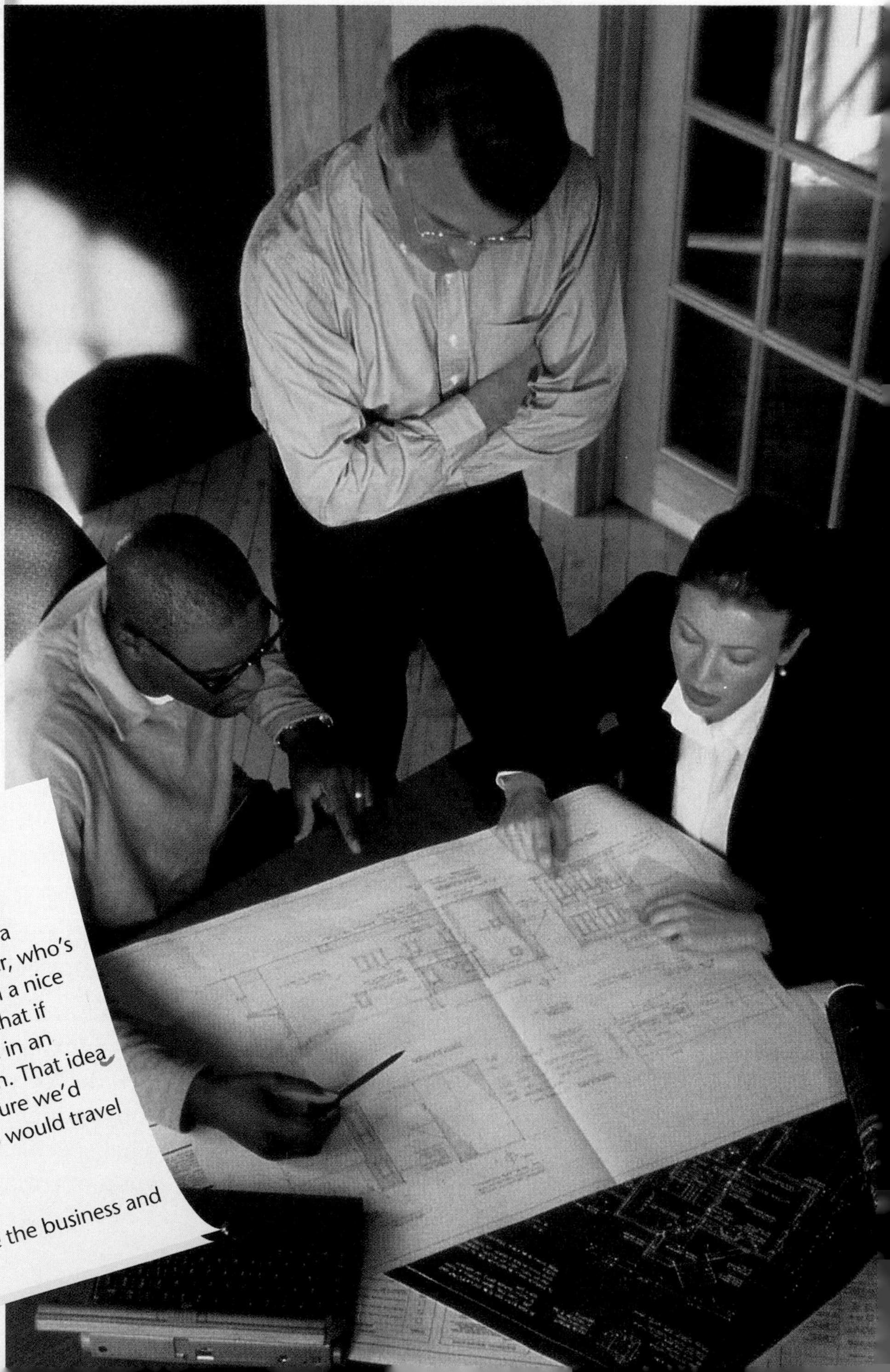

You're the Boss!

Locating Your Business

You and two partners are starting a design services business. One partner, who's big on impressions, wants it to be in a nice office building. The other believes that if work is done well you could locate in an industrial park at the edge of town. That idea makes the first partner cringe. "Sure we'd save money," he says, "but who would travel that far for a design job?"

What Will You Do?

Where should you locate the business and how will you lay it out?

SECTION 9.1

Site Selection

What you'll learn

- how to determine a community for your business site
- the criteria to apply when selecting a business site
- the factors in location analysis and decision making
- the advantages of starting a business at home

Why it's important

Location affects the visibility and accessibility of a business. After investing in land, a building, fixtures, or heavy equipment, it may be difficult or impossible to move.

KEY TERMS

economic base
incentives
Standard Metropolitan Statistical Areas
census tracts
trade area
industrial parks

FACTORS IN SITE SELECTION

Your own community is not always the best place to start a business. Sometimes neighboring or even distant communities are better. You may also want to locate in another country, or base your services in the Internet. No matter where you decide to settle, there are certain questions to consider.

Is the Economic Base Favorable?

First, study a community's main source of income, or economic base . Government reports label economic bases as "primarily industrial," "primarily service-oriented," or other categories that indicate the main source of income. Find an economic base that matches your business. Is it growing or shrinking?

A growing economic base has more money coming into it than leaving it. For example, an agricultural city may make most of its money in farming. However, the residents go shopping elsewhere. If the residents make more money farming than they spend in other cities' malls, the economic base grows. If they spend more money in different cities than they make, the economic base shrinks. New business should look for a growing economic base that has money to help fuel new ventures and grow established ones.

Are There Financial Incentives?

To attract new enterprises, many communities offer *incentives.* Incentives are advantages that help businesses, such as lower taxes, cheaper land, and employee training programs. Also, states can establish enterprise zones that give tax-favored status to new businesses. Local economic development offices can tell you if such programs are available.

What Is the Makeup of the Population?

Is the community's population aging as young people move away? Is it getting younger as families with children settle into the area? Such trends affect who spends how much on what type of products or services. A local economic development office or chamber of commerce can provide this information.

Every ten years the Census Bureau surveys American citizens to track changes in population size and demographics. Demographics include characteristics such as general age, education, gender, race, religion, and income. This information can show if a location matches your target market.

Look in the Census Bureau's *Census Basics* for Standard Metropolitan Statistical Areas (SMSA) that interest you. SMSAs are geographic areas that usually include a metropolitan area such as Chicago or Atlanta. Narrow your search to census tracts, subdivisions of SMSAs containing 4,000-5,000 people. An example is shown in **Figure 9–1**.

Does the Labor Supply Match Your Needs?

When considering a community, you must consider your labor needs and how well the local labor pool can meet them. Ask yourself: How many employees will I need? Is there a sufficient labor pool to meet my needs? Does the available pool have the appropriate skills to help my business? Local workforce agencies can tell you the skill levels and training needed by the unemployed in the community.

Figure 9–1
Here is a sample of the kind of data the Census Bureau makes available for every census tract in the nation. ***If you were planning to open an art gallery, would this area be a promising location? Why or why not?***

Demographic Data for Census Tract 6204*

Population by Age	
13 and under	663
14–24	518
25–39	1,430
40–54	1,073
55–69	701
70 and over	241

Household Income (1989)	
Less than $9,999	47
$10,000–$19,999	49
$20,000–$34,999	267
$35,000–$49,999	205
$50,000–$74,999	430
$75,000 or more	915

Educational Attainment (Persons 25 and Over)	
Less than 9th grade	37
High school graduate	579
Associate's degree	287
Bachelor's degree	1,207
Graduate/professional degree	599

Workers per Household (1989)	
None	106
1	361
2	668
3 or more	177

*California, Los Angeles County
Source: U.S. Bureau of the Census, 1990 Census of Population and Housing

CRITERIA FOR SITE SELECTION

Once you have determined that a community is suitable for your business, you can begin looking for sites within it. The criteria used to judge sites vary with the type of business.

Using a map can help you visualize and organize your search. ***What other tools can be used?***

Retail Business Considerations

If you start a retail business, you will be selling directly to consumers. Therefore, you will need to be accessible to your target market. You will need to determine your trade area, the region or section of the community from which you can expect to draw your customers.

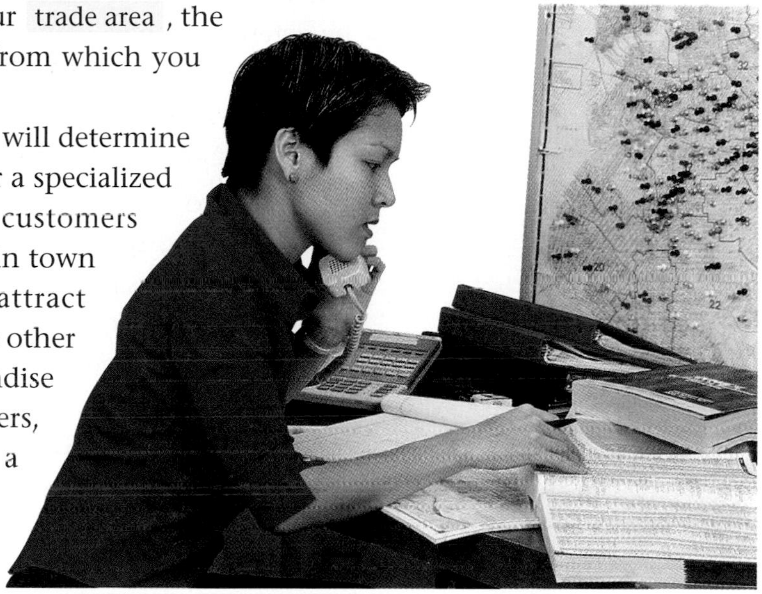

The type and size of your business will determine the size of your trade area. If you offer a specialized line of merchandise, you may draw customers from a great distance. The only store in town that sells phonograph needles will attract record collectors from far away. On the other hand, one that offers general merchandise solely for the convenience of customers, like a 7-Eleven store, will draw from a much smaller area.

Once you have pinpointed the area of the community you wish to serve, you can begin locating potential sites within it. At this point, a local city map is especially helpful. Mark critical data on it as you investigate each site.

Up & Coming Entrepreneur

Decorating Entrepreneur

In her spare time from work, Barbara Douglass designed and sold curtains and other fabric creations. When Douglass saw an opportunity to get into full-time decorating in 1996, she took it. "I moved out to Los Angeles and worked for a decorator, where I learned the basics of design and basically how not to run a business," says Douglass. She now runs three jobs simultaneously and has designed home and office interiors across the Atlantic seaboard.

Analyze **Why might you consider moving from one state to another state to pursue an opportunity?**

Begin by drawing a circle delineating the trade area around each site you are considering. Then, within each trade area, you will need to examine and note four additional features:

1. Number and Size of Competing Businesses. You should first mark all potential competitors. Calculating the number, size, and location of stores that will compete either directly or indirectly with your business will give you a sense of where customers go to shop. It will also tell you how large your trade area is. Look for clusters of stores and low vacancy rates. Vacancy rate can be determined by a simple walk through, count, and calculation. (Vacancy rate = amount of vacant space/total space available).

2. Nature of the Competition. If your business is similar in size and merchandise to its competitors, you may want to locate near them to encourage comparison shopping. That's why it's not uncommon to see an entire block of furniture shops, clothing stores, or auto dealers. On the other hand, if your operation will be significantly larger and you will be able to offer a greater variety of products, you may be able to generate your own drawing power and on that basis locate away from your competitors.

3. Character of the Area. Look carefully at the character of the area. Is it attractive and inviting? Does it have the appearance of success? In general, consumers like to shop in attractive, safe, thriving environments. Individual businesses or blocks that counter this impression are potential problems. You should mark them on your map.

4. Accessibility and Traffic. Identify the highways, streets, and public transportation routes that lead to the site. If you find that there is no convenient route to your business or if the site is difficult to locate, customers are not going to reach you.

You can get ideas for laying out your business by surveying your competitors and talking to experts. *Where else can you go for ideas?*

RISK TAKERS PROFIT MAKERS

Name: Johnny Johnson
Business: Community Pride
City, State: Richmond, VA

Changing the City

After working at grocery stores for more than 13 years, Johnny Johnson was ready to start his own in 1992. As an entrepreneur, he could earn money, be independent, and benefit his hometown of Richmond, Virginia.

In the middle of rough neighborhoods, Johnson's chain of Community Pride Food Stores is clean and well managed. It offers high quality products at affordable prices and provides more than 500 jobs for residents. Customers can get a free ride home after they shop, and Johnson has developed a program that encourages students to be successful in academics.

Giving to the community has also paid dividends to the business. Johnson's chain has increased from four to seven stores and now earns 47 million dollars annually.

Thinking Critically

How much of a difference can one entrepreneur make in his or her community?

Both foot and car traffic are important to a retail business. Entrepreneurs often stand at a potential site and count the cars and pedestrians passing by. If you use this technique, it is important to study different times of day and days of the week.

Service/Wholesale Business Considerations

Some service and wholesale businesses have the same needs as retail businesses. This is true when customers come to a restaurant, dry cleaner, or wholesale outlet. If this describes your service or wholesale business, all the factors relevant to a retail site apply.

Many service and wholesale businesses do not have customers or clients coming to their business sites. Exterminators and plumbers go to their customers' homes. Distributors serve manufacturers and retailers through sales representatives and purchase orders. Many do business exclusively through catalogs or the Internet. They don't need expensive, high-profile locations.

Money Matters

WWW.COM

The Internet provides great possibilities as well as challenges for entrepreneurs with limited resources. William J. Weiner of Precision Auto Designs remarks:

"A lot of small companies don't understand the intricacies of hosting a Web site. And if they don't have someone they can count on, they won't succeed."

Manufacturing/Extraction Business Considerations

If you start a manufacturing or extraction business, your location will largely be predetermined by the nature of your business. An extraction business must be near whatever it is extracting—ore, fish, trees. A manufacturing firm can locate only where local zoning laws allow. Most communities have set aside certain areas for industrial uses, sometimes called industrial parks.

The location decisions faced by manufacturers and extractors are very different from those of other entrepreneurs. For example, they are not concerned with pedestrian access. Rather, they need access to sources of supply and major transportation routes. Being close to sources of supply can cut transportation costs and shipping times.

LOCATING POTENTIAL SITES

Knowing what to look for is one thing. Finding it is another. There are a number of practical resources available for your search:

- *Newspapers.* When property owners want to rent or sell space, they often advertise in newspapers.
- *Realtors.* Realtors who specialize in business property emphasize that specialty in display ads in the Yellow Pages.
- *Internet.* Realtors and owners also list their offerings on the Internet. The Internet itself may be a site of business.
- *Visual surveys.* A drive through the community in which you plan to locate will enable you to visually identify vacant facilities and get a sense of their suitability.
- *Contacts.* Personal or business contacts may have firsthand knowledge of available facilities.

SITE ANALYSIS AND DECISION MAKING

Once you have identified possible sites for your business, you must consider three areas. The three areas you should look at in your analysis are the surrounding area, the building, and the costs of buying, building, or leasing.

Surrounding Area Analysis

The criteria you examined earlier addressed site area considerations for your type of business. Each of the potential sites you identify should be evaluated on the basis of those criteria.

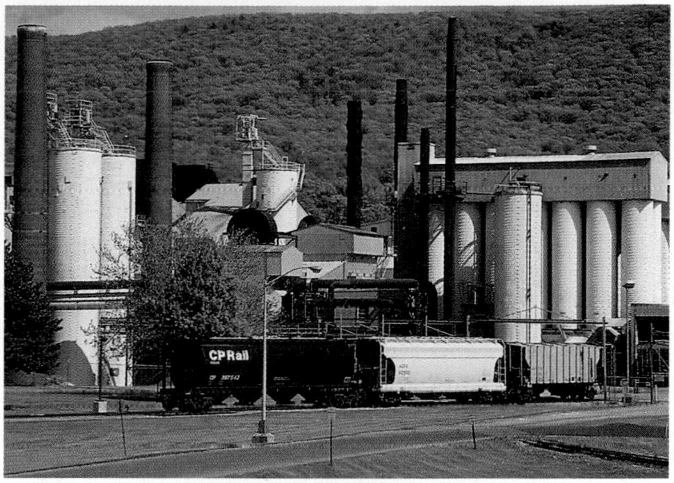

This manufacturing plant is strategically located by train tracks. ***What are some other ways that a manufacturing plant can save money on shipping?***

Building Evaluation

The building must be big enough to take care of present needs and to allow for expansion. All businesses need room for customers, storage, inventory, an office, and rest rooms. It is far less costly to pay for more room at the outset than to pay for a move later.

Exterior. You should begin your evaluation of the building by considering its construction. It may be worthwhile to hire a professional—perhaps a contractor, inspector, or appraiser—to examine the building for structural soundness.

You should be able to judge the building's looks. Customers and clients may get their first impression of your business from the front of your building.

Check the signage on the building. Most communities have regulations limiting the number, type, and size of signs you may have on or in front of your building. Make sure your signs are easy to read, attractive, and correct.

Finally, don't forget parking for your customers, your staff, or both. Your community will probably have building code requirements demanding a specific number of parking spaces, depending on the type of business using the site.

Interior. Next you should check the building's interior. Look at the walls, floors, and ceilings. Are they functional, attractive, and easy to care for? Are there a sufficient number of lighting fixtures and outlets? Do you have enough power to run your equipment? How efficient are the heating and cooling units?

Entrepreneurs International

Haiti

Mario Percy is a gifted sculptor living in Haiti who employs about ten other artists and runs a gift shop. Percy cuts used oil drums and then paints them to make decorative and useful handicrafts. Percy has recently been invited by an American businessperson to perform his craft in front of a Haitian handicraft shop in Tarpon Springs, Florida.

Apply **Why is the Haitian shop in Florida a good site for Percy to visit?**

Some zones have codes that regulate signage. *What are the benefits and drawbacks of such codes?*

Lease, Buy, or Build

Another factor you will have to consider is whether to lease, buy, or build your facility. For most new businesses, the advantages of leasing outweigh the other options. Specifically:

1. *A large cash outlay is avoided.* The money saved by leasing can be used for inventory, supplies, and other expenses.
2. *Risk is reduced.* Leasing requires less investment and a shorter commitment than buying or building.
3. *Lease expenses are tax deductible.* Such a reduction in your tax liability can save you money.

If you decide to lease, you need to compare certain terms of each potential property. Those terms include monthly rent, length of the lease, and provisions for termination. You will also have to consider who is responsible for insuring against various risks, remodeling costs, and repairs.

If you decide to buy or build, you will have to gather similar information. Both of these routes are typically more complex. They require applying for financing, and will take more time.

Regardless of whether you lease, buy, or build, it is important that you carefully study, and have an attorney review, any lease or contract before you sign it. You should discuss and arrive at the best terms possible before completing the deal.

Making Your Decision

When your location analysis is complete, examine and compare the alternatives. Consider the variables listed below:

- *Cost comparison.* What is the initial cost and monthly expense? What are the other expenses such as utilities and water?
- *Advantages and disadvantages.* What are the advantages and disadvantages of each option? Consider the physical environment, the exterior, and the interior.
- *Desirability.* Intangibles will enter into a final decision. Atmosphere, character, convenience, and personal preferences all make a difference.

HOME BUSINESS OPTION

Why not start your business in your home? It worked for Debbie Fields of Mrs. Fields Cookies and for Steven Jobs and Steve Wozniak of Apple Computers. It could work for you, too.

The main advantage of working from home is financial. There is no rent to pay. You may also be able to save money on your taxes by working from home.

This arrangement can work for many types of businesses. For example, a Web site design service is well suited for the home because it doesn't require a large facility or large amounts of clients visiting. Work is done on a personal computer and jobs can be sent or sampled though the Internet. In general, enterprises involving little personal contact with customers or where work is picked up and dropped off when completed are possibilities.

Whether or not you decide to start your business at home will depend on factors such as the type of business, the space and equipment you have at home, and the effect on others living in your home. You must also consider the laws that exist in your community. Generally, if your enterprise doesn't create traffic, noise, or pollution, it won't be a problem.

CHECK YOUR UNDERSTANDING

SECTION 9.1

Reviewing Key Terms and Concepts

1 What are the factors to consider in selecting a community for your business?
2 What are the criteria that apply to selecting a site for your business?
3 Which of the resources for locating business sites will give you specific information the quickest?
4 What are the advantages to leasing a building instead of buying or constructing your own?

Critical Thinking Activity

What are some examples of businesses that can easily be started at home?

Extension Lab—Teach Others

Place Setting You work in a restaurant. A co-worker plans to establish a new quick-serve restaurant, thinking it will be easy to succeed no matter where it is located if the cooking is good.

Role Play Explain the importance of location to your co-worker, emphasizing why it is especially important in the restaurant business. Be sure to include:

- What to consider when selecting a community
- Criteria for selecting a site
- Factors for selecting a building
- Layout considerations

SECTION 9.2

Physical Layout

What you'll learn

- the steps in layout planning
- layout requirements and possibilities for different kinds of businesses
- considerations in planning for office space
- factors to consider in interior and exterior design

Why it's important

A well-planned layout can mean a more efficient operation, a more appealing sales floor, or greater convenience for customers. A poorly planned layout can mean just the opposite.

KEY TERMS

layout
interrelationships
workstation
façade
appointments

LAYOUT PLANNING

Once you have a site in mind for your enterprise, you are ready to plan the *layout*. A layout is a floor plan or map that shows how you intend to use the space in your site to conduct your business. An interior layout might include features such as display cases, lighting fixtures, and the traffic pattern for customers or production processes. An exterior layout might show landscaping, parking spaces, and the traffic pattern for both pedestrians and vehicles.

Regulations must also be followed. All cities have standards that relate to safety and zoning, for example. Also, the Americans with Disabilities Act requires certain businesses to provide access for people with physical, hearing, or visual impairments.

The basic steps in layout planning are the same for all types of businesses. There are six of them:

1. Define the objectives of the facility.
2. Identify the primary and supporting activities that will take place in the facility.
3. Determine the interrelationships—access, arrangement, and flow—among all the activities.
4. Determine the space requirements for all activities.
5. Design alternative layouts for the facility.
6. Evaluate the various layouts and choose one.

LAYOUT NEEDS AND POSSIBILITIES

The steps in layout planning are the same for all businesses. The options and considerations that enter into them are not. Different types of businesses have different operational needs.

This section describes layout factors and plans for all types of businesses. As you go through the steps involved in layout planning, you will want to focus on the considerations and layout options relevant to your type of business.

Manufacturing Businesses

If your proposed business involves manufacturing goods, your key layout concern will be the placement of machinery. You will want to maximize the efficiency of your operation.

What to Consider. The following groups of questions will help you formulate your specific layout needs:

- *Production processes.* What kind of manufacturing processes will you be involved in? Will you be breaking down raw materials into products? Will you be assembling products from parts? Will you be converting raw materials into products?
- *Production sequence.* Does your operation call for mass-producing standardized goods in assembly-line sequence? Or will you manufacture your products one at a time or in batches? Will you use a combination of these two approaches?
- *Materials flow.* What is the most efficient flow of materials? **Figure 9–2** shows your options. Will materials come in one end of your building and finished goods leave the other? (That's an *I* flow.) Will materials enter and finished products leave from the same end? (That's a *U* flow.) What do you do when space is limited? (That's when you use an *S* flow.)
- *Control.* What is the best arrangement for managing your operation? What is best for inventory control?
- *Environmental needs.* Are there chemical, water treatment, or other special processes that must be provided for? Are temperatures, noise, or fumes likely to be problems?

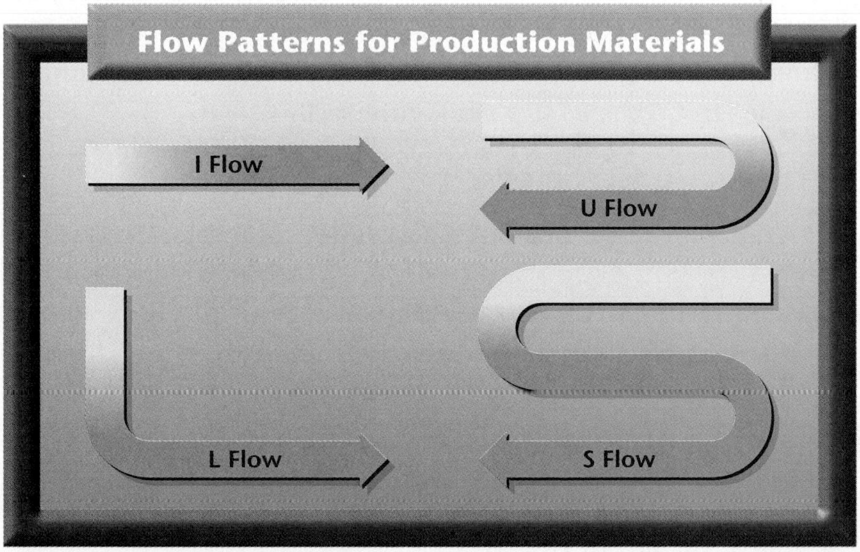

Figure 9–2
In most business operations, the flow of production materials is determined by the placement of entrances and exits and the total amounts of space available. ***By this standard, when would you use an L flow?***

Tips from the Real World

HOME OFFICE

Modern communication technology allows some small businesses to operate at home even as they grow. Sandy Wineberg, professor of Entrepreneurship at Muhlenberg College notes:

> *"The home office used to be simply a stage in growth for many businesses. Now there's less of a need for many to ever move out of the home."*

- *Space requirements.* How much space will you need for the placement and travel of equipment? What are your specific needs for machine maintenance, plant service, and storage? What is your anticipated production capacity?

Types of Layouts. The layout you use for a manufacturing business will be heavily influenced by your production process and sequence. There are three general types:

- *Product layout.* In this layout, machines and supporting activities are arranged along a product flow line. As products come down the line, something is done to them at specific areas with equipment for a single worker, or workstations .
- *Fixed-product layout.* This layout is used when the product is too heavy or bulky to be moved. Parts are brought to the job and workers come to the product.
- *Process layout.* This type of layout involves the grouping of machines and equipment by function. Products are then moved from one area to another, with a specific function being performed on them at each location.

Of course, these three basic layouts can be modified to suit the needs of a particular operation. They can also be used in combination.

There are secondary areas to map out as well. Inside, these include areas for shipping, receiving, storage, warehousing, maintenance services, and office space. Outside, they include storage yards for materials, repair areas, loading docks, and parking.

Retail Businesses

The arrangement of a retail layout has a great effect on sales and profits. Merchandise and aisles should "pull" customers through the store. Most of the options center on merchandise placement. They are shown in **Figure 9–3**.

Wholesale Businesses

Wholesale operations can take a variety of forms. However, in warehousing facilities used by wholesalers who take possession of goods, there are two primary goals involved in planning warehouse layouts: cost-effective storage and efficient movement of products in and out of the facility.

Types of Layouts. Most modern wholesale operations are housed in single-story buildings. This makes controlling and

Figure 9–3

Types of Layouts

Retail layouts generally contain three types of floor space—selling space, storage space, and customer space. What distinguishes one plan from another is the way these three kinds of space are configured. Different arrangements can produce different selling effects. Most store layouts fall into one of four categories:

1. Right-angle grid.

The pattern of crossing aisles of this supermarket provides a highly structured system for facilitating the flow of traffic. The layout reduces security concerns and lends itself to self-service operations.

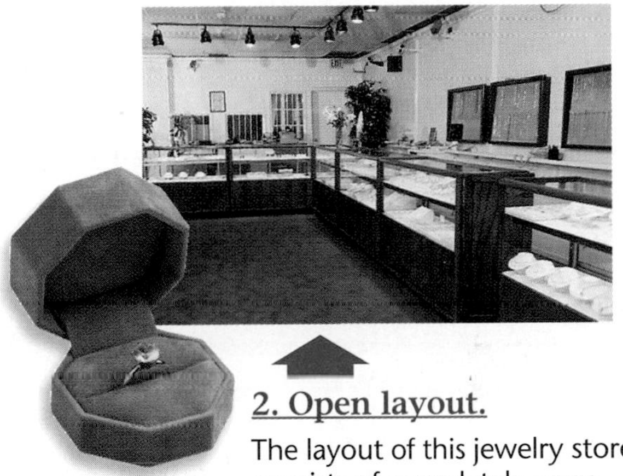

2. Open layout.

The layout of this jewelry store consists of completely open sales space bounded by outside walls. It enhances visibility of merchandise, sales coverage, and security.

3. Landscaped layout.

The landscaped layout of this store combines elements of the open and enclosed layouts. It improves customer and sales staff interaction and creative displays.

4. Enclosed layout.

The layout of this department store organizes types of merchandise into separate operations. Walls are placed between these units to create shopping environments.

moving stock easier. Arrange receiving, storage, order assembly, and shipping areas so that goods can be moved quickly and easily.

Interior layout plans should include office space and, if necessary, showroom areas. Exterior plans might show loading and vehicle storage areas.

Figure 9–4
The service businesses listed in the top half of the table have customers that come to them. Those in the bottom half either go to their customers or send a product with them. ***What effect does this have on the considerations listed in the last column?***

Service Businesses

The physical layout of a service business depends largely on the specific service it provides. However, it is possible to categorize service businesses into some very general types. These types are identified in **Figure 9–4.**

Layout Considerations for Different Types of Service Businesses

Business Type	Examples	Things to Consider
■ Customers come to facility to use equipment	■ Driving range ■ Amusement park ■ Laundromat	■ Customer appeal ■ Equipment to engage in service ■ Space to engage in service ■ Pay station ■ Safety
■ Customers come to facility for assistance	■ Copy service ■ Car repair ■ Dry cleaner	■ Customer appeal ■ Ease of access ■ Waiting area ■ Customer contact station ■ Equipment and/or service area ■ Supply storage
■ Customers come to facility for care	■ Day care center ■ Doctor's office ■ Beauty salon	■ Customer appeal ■ Ease of access (drop-off and pickup) ■ Waiting area ■ Ease of contact with service provider ■ Rest rooms ■ Areas for performing service ■ Office space ■ Supply and equipment storage
■ Business operator goes to customer to provide service	■ Exterminator ■ Painting contractor ■ Interior designer ■ Taxicab service	■ Office space with telephone ■ Storage areas for equipment, supplies, and vehicles
■ Business operator brings customer and equipment together	■ Car rental ■ Video rental	■ Customer appeal ■ Display area ■ Storage area ■ Pay and return stations
■ Business operator brings customer and service together	■ Employment agency ■ Real estate agency ■ Tax preparation	■ Customer appeal ■ Office space (private and general use) ■ Conference room ■ Waiting area

Extraction Businesses

Extraction firms have unique layouts because they must adapt to the particular environment in which the extraction takes place. However, all extraction layouts include an office area, storage areas for equipment and supplies, and the extraction site itself.

FINISHING TOUCHES

Once you have settled on a particular layout for your business, you can begin filling in the final details. These include at least minimal office space, interior design features, and alterations or improvements in the façade, or face of your building.

Every business owner needs a place to take care of paperwork and administrative tasks. If cost, limited space, employee supervision, or access to files and equipment are important, an *open-office* layout is probably best. Such an arrangement often uses partitions to divide workspace. If privacy and noise reduction are concerns, then plan for *closed offices*. Closed offices are contained by walls.

If your operation involves multiple offices, they may be divided by corridors or aisles. They can also be defined by appointments, interior design equipment and furnishings such as fish tanks and planters.

CHECK YOUR UNDERSTANDING

SECTION 9.2

Reviewing Key Terms and Concepts

1. What are the different layout needs of manufacturing and service businesses?
2. What are the different layout needs of retail and wholesale businesses?
3. Why is location critically important to an extraction business?

Critical Thinking Activity

Decide on a type of extraction business and follow the six steps in determining layout.

Extension Lab—Acquiring Data

Uncarbonated Nation When the Coca-Cola Company tried to enter the Indonesian soft-drink market, it faced a dilemma. The favorite beverages in the country were tea and tropical fruit juices. Currently, Coca-Cola is introducing strawberry-, banana-, and pineapple-flavored soft drinks and is using the phased-in marketing approach to develop the Indonesians' taste for carbonation.

Research Using newspapers, magazines, and/or Internet articles, answer the following questions.

- Did Coca-Cola study the community (Indonesia) before they tried to market their product?
- How does Coca-Cola sell their products in Indonesia? Do they sell retail? Do they manufacture there?

CHAPTER 9 REVIEW

CHAPTER SUMMARY

- When selecting a community in which to start your business, examine the economic base, financial incentives, and relevant population data.
- When choosing a site for a retail business, consider the competing businesses, the character of the area, and the site's accessibility to customers.
- Wholesale and service firms base their site decisions on whether or not customers will be coming to their places of business.
- Manufacturers and extraction businesses look for sites with easy access to transportation, suppliers, and raw materials.
- Resources available to help you locate a site include newspapers, realtors, the Internet, visual surveys, and contacts.
- A building should be chosen based on its suitability for the intended use, whether you will buy or lease, and costs.
- Starting your new business at home can save you money in overhead expenses.
- The specific steps in layout planning are (1) define facility objectives, (2) define primary and supporting activities, (3) determine activity interrelationships, (4) determine space requirements, (5) design alternative layouts, and (6) select the final layout.
- Layout considerations and plans are different for each type of business.

RECALL KEY TERMS

Describe the ideal location for a business of your choice. Devote paragraphs to community, site, building and layout. Use the following terms:

economic base
incentives
Standard Metropolitan Statistical Areas
census tracts
trade area
industrial parks
layout
interrelationships
workstation
façade
appointments

RECALL KEY CONCEPTS

1. Describe in economic terms the ideal community in which to start up a business.
2. Name two financial incentives a community might offer a new business.
3. What kinds of population trends will you look for when considering a community?
4. What determines the trade size of a business?
5. Why might a service business require a different type of location from the type needed by a retail business?
6. Why should a manufacturing business locate near a transportation network?
7. What are the advantages of leasing, rather than buying, a building for a business?
8. What should you consider when planning the layout for a manufacturing business? A retail business? A service business?

THINK CRITICALLY

1. Why should you consider demographics before locating a business?
2. If you were starting up an ice cream manufacturing business, what site and layout considerations would you give high priority? Explain your answer.

CHAPTER 9 REVIEW

3. Describe how the following entrepreneurs might choose a location. Include community, site, and building considerations.
    - Owner of an exclusive boutique
    - Caterer
    - Manufacturer of security systems
4. Are you the type of person who could locate a new business at home? Why or why not?
5. Think of a service business that you might like to start. Discuss the finishing touches you would include in your location and explain why they would be needed.

CONNECT ACADEMICS TO THE WORKPLACE

Math

1. Suppose you are opening a 1,000 square-foot baseball card store. Your lease calls for a flat monthly rent of $1.75 per square foot, plus 5 percent of your gross annual sales. What is the total rent you will pay in one year if you have sales of $85,000?

Listening and Speaking

2. You just finished interviewing a successful entrepreneur for a school project. She told you that her site location happened by chance, that she did no research, and it is a waste of time to do so. How would you respond?

WORK IN YOUR COMMUNITY

Choose a site for your business. As part of your decision-making process, do the following:

- Using population, demographic, and zoning data, select two or more potential sites.
- Visit each of your potential sites. Note potential competitors and available buildings in the area.
- On a map, mark trade areas, potential competitors, and transportation routes for your potential sites.
- Compare your site possibilities. Summarize your findings in written or table form and make a final choice.

LINK SCHOOL TO CAREER

Interview two entrepreneurs.

- Ask them how they selected their sites.
- Find out what skills helped them in the process.
- Have them explain the pros and cons of the various sites they considered.

Report to the class about what you have learned.

*inter*NET CONNECTION

Virtual Shoe Store

Your friend wants to open a shoe business in your area, but hasn't determined a location. You have been asked to show your friend how to use the Internet to conduct research.

Connect

Use a variety of Web browsers to research potential competitors in your area.

- Locate other shoe stores to determine your trade area.
- Determine what types of shoes are sold at the competitors' locations.
- Find out what other shoe-related services are being offered.

Present your data to the class and explain how you found the information.

UNIT 2 LAB

Business Plan Basics

Analyzing a Market and Choosing a Site

OVERVIEW

Deciding on a location is one of the most important decisions an entrepreneur can make. A bad location can cause him or her to fail even if all other decisions are made wisely. This unit lab will take you through the steps of analyzing a market and choosing a site for a new business.

TOOLS

- Map of local community
- Information sheets on local community
- The Internet (optional)
- Graph paper, rulers, and colored pens or illustrator software
- Word processor

PROCEDURES

STEP A Individually or in a small group, develop a profile of your community.

1. Conduct research on the Internet or obtain brochures describing other communities.
2. Interview government officials or talk to representatives of planning agencies like the Chamber of Commerce. Find out the following information about your community:
   - types of businesses and jobs
   - average wages
   - demographic characteristics
   - types of businesses moving in or out
   - spending patterns of consumers
3. Organize the information using the Unit 2 worksheet, graph paper, or the table feature of a word processor.
4. From your results, develop a brief profile describing your community's economic and market conditions.
5. On a map of your area, identify the locations of key businesses and industries. Mark the areas with concentrations of specific types of consumers, such as high- or low-income levels.

STEP B

What types of businesses (that are not already located there) would be successful in your community?

1. Identify three new businesses that you feel could succeed in your community.
2. Identify reasons why they aren't there.
3. Organize the business types and reasons on a chart. Use the Unit 2 worksheet, graph paper, or the table feature of a word processor.

STEP C

Individually or in your group, study three grocery stores.

1. Locate the three stores on the map.
2. Identify benefits and weaknesses of each location. Which grocery store has the best location? Why?
3. Expand your analysis. In your community, identify one location for the following:
   - Warehouse
   - Department store
   - Fast food restaurant
   - Dry cleaners
   - Doctor's office
   - Manufacturing plant
4. How does each location fit or not fit the certain type of business?
5. Organize your findings using the Unit 2 worksheet, graph paper, or the table feature of a word processor.

LAB REPORT

STEP D

Select one of the following types of businesses: ice cream shop, lawyer's office, small manufacturing plant for pens, or another type of business that you might be interested in starting in the future.

1. Survey your community for vacant lots, empty commercial buildings, and vacant businesses. Make a list of at least three possible locations that would be suitable for the business type you selected. Identify benefits and drawbacks of each.
2. Select the best location. On a graph paper or using an illustration program, draw a map of this location. Show roads, other businesses, competitors, and any other relevant information.
3. Using a word processor, write a one-page letter explaining why the location you selected would be the most suitable for the type of business you selected. Address it to a potential lender. Refer to your research, analysis, and map. Cite and attach the information you gathered in Steps A, B, C, and D. Be sure to use the following:

- Complete sentences
- Proper grammar
- Correct spelling

UNIT 3
MANAGING MARKET STRATEGIES

UNIT OVERVIEW

Some of an entrepreneur's most important business decisions involve marketing. No matter how good your product or service, marketing will determine whether or not it sells.

Successful marketing starts with research and planning. Objectives must be set and factors must be considered. Pricing, promotion and sales management are only a few of the vital issues you will face. Understanding these will help you develop your strategies. It will also help you adjust to and take advantage of changes as they occur in the marketplace.

Entrepreneurship: What It Takes

What do you know about starting your own business?

1. Why should you develop marketing objectives?
2. What considerations go into a marketing plan?
3. What is product strategy?
4. How does distribution affect sales?
5. What factors go into pricing?
6. How do price adjustments affect your profit?
7. What are the objectives of a promotional plan?
8. How do you budget your promotional expenses?
9. What are the steps in the selling process?
10. What does it take to direct sales operation?

CHAPTER 10

The Marketing Plan

Learning Objectives

When you have completed this chapter, you will be able to:

- **Recognize** the role of marketing objectives in a marketing plan
- **Identify** the four marketing strategies that make up the marketing mix
- **Describe** the product and place strategies
- **Explain** the process of updating the marketing plan and mix

You're the Boss!

Improving on Your Marketing Mix

You thought your plan for a denim shop was pretty good. However, yesterday you received a mixed reaction from a counselor at the small business development center. She said there was a large enough population of the 16- to 24-year-olds you were trying to reach in the area, but that you need to develop a more precise marketing mix.

What Will You Do?
What steps can you take to develop a better marketing mix?

SECTION 10.1

Developing the Marketing Mix

MARKET PLANNING

After completing your market analysis and identifying your target market, you are ready to take the next step in planning your business. You must identify what you want to do with your marketing efforts. You must define your **marketing objectives**. Most businesses objectives relate to sales, market share, growth, and profit.

Short-term marketing objectives are for one year. Long-range marketing objectives might reflect what you hope to achieve in three to five years. These are sometimes called goals. When objectives are clearly written, they provide a blueprint for developing your individual marketing strategies and your overall marketing plan. They also help you measure your success.

Next, you must create an appropriate *marketing plan.* The **marketing plan** consists of four strategies—*product, place, price,* and *promotion.* To reach your marketing objectives, all four P's must be mixed appropriately. They must be directed toward the target market. The combination of product, price, place, and promotion strategies that you use to reach your market is the **marketing mix**. This chapter will help you develop your marketing objectives, marketing strategies, and marketing mix. It will also show the importance of periodically evaluating and updating them.

THE PRODUCT STRATEGY

The product strategy deals with goods or services. Product decisions are crucial to the success of your business. Products that don't match up with customer needs or expectations will not sell. While conducting market analysis, you have probably already gathered some product information and made some product decisions. Now you must address such considerations thoroughly and systematically.

What you'll learn

- the steps in market planning
- the role of marketing objectives
- the relationship between marketing objectives, the marketing plan, and the marketing mix
- factors to consider in developing your product and place strategies

Why it's important

To succeed and grow, a business must have the proper mix of the four P's of marketing and realistic marketing objectives.

KEY TERMS

marketing objectives
marketing plan
marketing mix
brand
package
label
product positioning
product mix
channel of distribution
intensive distribution
selective distribution
exclusive distribution
intermediaries

Product Features. Think about your product as a package of features or benefits for the customer. Goods such as cars, appliances, or clothing include physical features. They have style, color, quality, and options. Also consider intangibles such as warranties, service contracts, delivery, installation, and instructions. Service businesses, such as financial institutions and video arcades, offer intangible benefits. They include convenience, health, a sense of well-being, and entertainment. What will your product offer?

Branding, Packaging, and Labeling. How will you identify your product? How can it stand out from the competition? Part of the answer lies in branding, packaging, and labeling. A brand is the name, symbol, or design used to identify a product. A package is the physical container or wrapper that holds it. The label is the part of the package used to present information. All three contribute something to the product and, in the process, become part of it. For example, when you buy Puma footwear, you expect a certain quality of athletic shoe in a specific type of box with a clearly marked label.

Product Selection. What products will you sell? Are you going to manufacture them or resell them? Developing and manufacturing new products to sell involves several steps. First you generate product ideas and sort out the good ones from the bad. Then you study the product's potential costs and revenues. You develop the product and test-market it. Finally, if everything looks promising, you introduce it.

In contrast, choosing products for resale is largely a matter of gathering information. First you study consumer demands and product availability, then make decisions to bring the two together. If you begin selling more than one item, consider how well the new product might fit in with the other items you sell.

Product Positioning. Product positioning refers to how consumers see your product. Luxury cars such as Mercedes-Benz and Cadillac are positioned as the most prestigious. Economy cars are positioned as the best bargain. How you position your product depends on your marketing goals. Who is your target customer? You can position your product through its quality, availability, pricing, and uses. Branding, packaging, and labeling also affect your product's image and positioning.

Product Mix. Finally, you will need to consider your product mix. This term refers to all the products a company makes or sells. If you are going to offer multiple products, you should think about how they relate to each other. If you want to reach a single market, you may decide to include only products that complement each other. Alpine concentrates on car stereo equipment. If you try to reach multiple markets, you may decide on a more diversified mix. Sony sells audio equipment of all kinds, as well as video, computer, and home appliances. What you sell will depend on the image you want to project and the market you are targeting.

Product Decisions. As you consider the product strategy for your marketing plan, ask yourself the following questions, keeping your target market in mind.

- What products should I manufacture or sell?
- At what quality level should I make my goods?
- How much inventory should I maintain?
- How will my products be better than my competitors'?
- How will I position my products?
- What will my customer service policy be?
- Will the physical layout of my business encourage sales?
- Do my hours of operation match the times that my target market prefers to do business?

Money Matters

CUSTOMER SERVICE

Repeat customers may be one source of ongoing financial strength for a business. Chrysler Corporation is relearning this lesson, says President Thomas T. Stallkamp:

"*[Customer contact] used to end when the customer bought his car. Now . . . we want him to be as happy when he's ready to move into another product as when he first bought.*"

THE PLACE STRATEGY

Place strategy involves how you will deliver your goods and services to your customers. Where will customers buy your product? When will they buy it? Will your product actually be there, ready and available for sale? Note that all these questions involve movement of your product—to your location and to your customers. Therefore, this part of the marketing mix is also known as the *distribution strategy*.

You have already considered some aspects of distribution. As you conducted market analysis, you noted how your competitors operate. What can you learn from their distribution? How can you do better? Likewise, as you investigated potential sites, you identified the suitability of loading and storage areas. You also checked the sites' proximity to distribution systems. Examining the following areas will help you finalize your strategy.

Channels of Distribution. To formulate your place strategy, you need to understand the possible *channels of distribution.* A channel of distribution is the path a product takes from producer (or manufacturer) to final user (or consumer). As shown in **Figure 10–1** and **Figure 10–2**, consumer and industrial markets have different channel members. However, there are only two basic types of channels—direct and indirect.

A *direct channel* moves a product from producer to customer with no one in between. Service businesses are typical examples. If you give an H & R Block tax preparer your financial records, he or she will return to you a finished tax return a few days later. No one else is involved.

In contrast, an *indirect channel* employs intermediaries . These are people or businesses that move products between producers and final users. They include wholesalers and retailers (who sell in the consumer market), distributors (who sell in the industrial market), and agents (who arrange sales). For example, a clothing designer might use an agent to contact wholesalers and retailers. This way, he or she can reach a large market without having to

Figure 10–1
The path your product takes to reach the consumer can be either direct or indirect. ***How many of the channels of distribution shown here are indirect?***

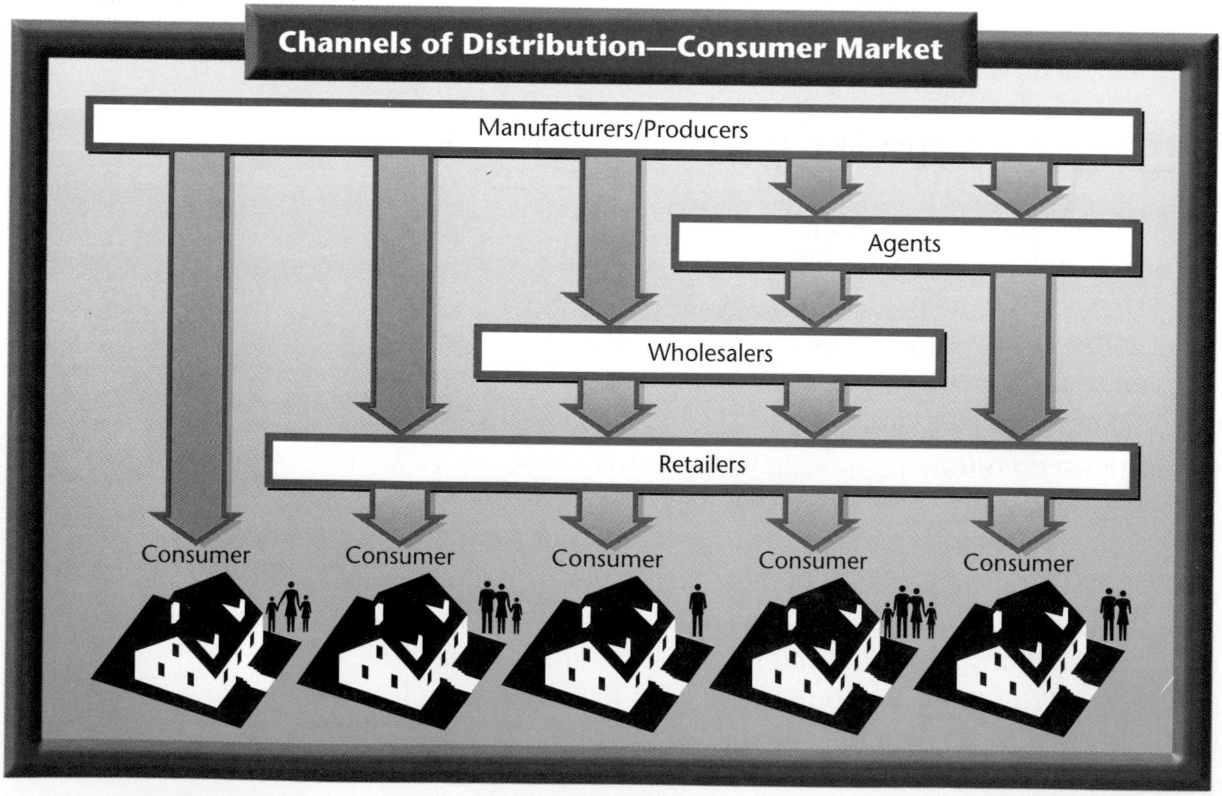

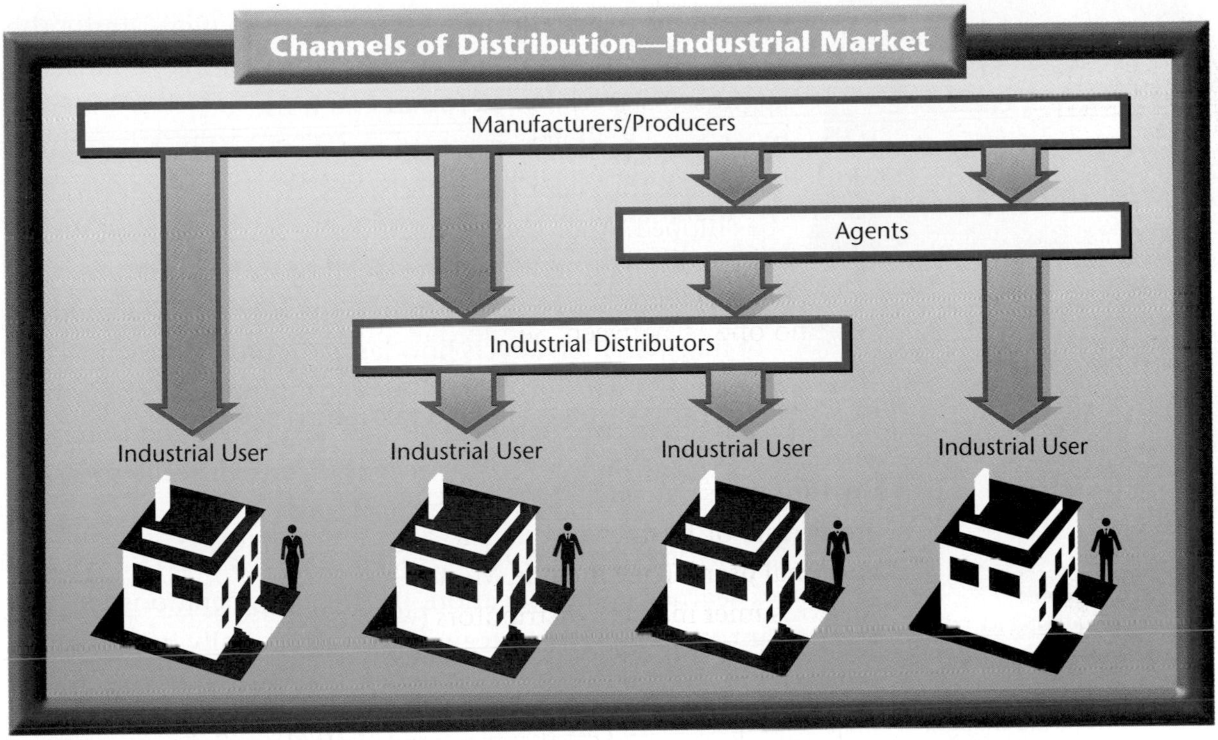

Figure 10–2
Channels of distribution for industrial products differ from those for consumer products. ***How?***

worry about maintaining a sales staff or store. This allows the designer to concentrate on what he or she does best—designing.

The type of business you have will determine where you fit in your channel of distribution. If you are a producer, you will be concerned with sending products through a channel. If you are a retailer, you will be concerned with receiving them. If you are a wholesaler, you will be concerned with both. You may also use or be involved in more than one channel.

The channel of distribution you choose can affect your product in many ways. It can raise or lower your product's cost. It can affect the potential for loss or damage to your product in transit. Most important, it can determine how quickly your product reaches your customers. If you can find a channel that is more efficient than the ones similar businesses are using, you can gain a competitive edge.

Intensity of Distribution. How broadly will you distribute your product? You have three choices. Intensive distribution involves placement of a product in all suitable sales outlets. For example, you can find best-selling paperbacks in bookstores, supermarkets, and magazine stands. Selective distribution limits the number of sales outlets in an area. For example, textbooks are

There are many ways to deliver your product. ***What types of items are suitable for the method pictured above?***

only found near schools. Exclusive distribution limits the number of outlets to one per area. For example, a museum might sell a special book for an exhibit.

Transportation. The physical movement of goods will also enter into your place decisions. How will your product be shipped? Your choices include by truck, train, airplane, ship, or pipeline. If you are dealing in information, you might be able to send it through the Internet. The method of transportation affects how fast your product reaches consumers. It will also determine your shipping costs. Generally, air transportation is the most expensive and waterway is the cheapest. Finally, it will dictate in some measure how your product will be packaged.

Location, Layout, and Availability. As you learned earlier, location, or site, considerations are also important to your place strategy. They are especially important to retail and service businesses that depend on customers to come to them. If yours is such a business, you can increase customer access and encourage sales by selecting a location near transportation routes. You might decide to have entrances on different sides of your site. You might also favor evening over morning hours of operation. What do these options have in common? They are designed to match the needs and opportunities of your potential customers. In other words, they are designed to make it easy for people to do business with you.

Place Decisions. When you make your place decisions, keep your target market in mind and ask yourself the following questions:

Up & Coming Entrepreneur

Musical Entrepreneur

Rand Moore has been around music all his life. His grandfather was a mandolin player, his father is a guitarist, and Moore is a percussionist. After attending the Berklee College of Music, Moore had stints with Disney World and Ringling Bros. and Barnum & Bailey. Then in 1993, he founded Drums n' Moore, which carries everything for a drummer's needs and offers lessons, rentals, and professional drum clinics. "The Madison Symphony called just yesterday to rent some chimes," Moore happily reports.

Analyze **How might Drums n' Moore's decision to offer lessons affect future business?**

- How will my product be sold and distributed?
- Will my product go directly from producer to user, or will it go through an intermediary?
- Can I use more efficient channels of distribution?
- What are the channel members I will use to obtain my products?
- What are the channel members I will use to distribute my products?
- How intensively will I distribute my products?
- Is my location appropriate for my target market (or markets)?
- Will the physical layout of my business encourage or discourage sales?
- Do my hours of operation match the times that my target market prefers to do business?

CHECK YOUR UNDERSTANDING — SECTION 10.1

Reviewing Key Terms and Concepts

1 What is the difference between the marketing plan and the marketing mix?

2 Describe the four strategies of the marketing mix.

3 What questions should you ask yourself as you put together your product and place strategies?

Critical Thinking Activity

Prepare preliminary drafts of the product and place strategies for a proposed business.

Extension Lab—Communicating Information

Bridal Basics Patricia works in the marketing department of a nationally franchised bridal shop. Her boss asked her to prepare a presentation for the board of directors, explaining the positioning of their bridal gowns in the market.

Oral Presentation Be sure to include answers to the following questions:

- What are your marketing goals?
- Who are your customers?
- What is the quality of your product?
- What is the availability of your product?
- How does the branding and labeling of the product affect the positioning?

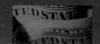

What you'll learn

- the importance of ongoing market research in keeping your business profitable
- the factors to consider for possible changes in product strategy
- the factors to consider for possible changes in place strategy
- general considerations in determining price and promotion strategy changes
- the process involved in revising the marketing mix and plan

Why it's important

The target markets, customer demands, and competition of a business change over time. Making constant adjustments in one's marketing plan is necessary for a business to succeed.

KEY TERMS

private brand
guarantee
diversification

Reviewing and Revising the Marketing Plan

CONTINUING YOUR MARKET RESEARCH

In business, change is constant. Technology makes products obsolete. Clothing styles go forward from season to season. A sport that is popular now will be replaced by a new one next year. How can you measure change? How can you predict it and prepare for it? Such adjustments are made according to market research.

Suppose you own and manage a CD store. The releases that are selling well this week may not even be on the charts next month. To stay profitable, you must keep up with what's going on in the music scene. In business terms, you must continue your market research. Steps are shown in **Figure 10–3**.

Figure 10–3

Marketing Research

Once you've started a business, your marketing research is not over.

1. You now have another source of primary information—your customers.

Gather information from current and former customers. Conduct surveys by mail, on the phone, over the Internet, in personal interviews, and through focus groups.

2. Secondary information is available through your operation itself.

Accounting records and sales receipts indicate your expenses. They also show which products are moving and which ones aren't.

4. Make market research an ongoing priority. You can rely on informal research for much of your information gathering, but at some point you may want more sophisticated methods. If so, consider hiring a professional market researcher.

3. Collect information that affects your operation.

Read newspaper, magazine, Internet, and trade publications. Clip articles that pertain to your business and make a file.

Tips from the Real World

PROMOTION

Giving away free merchandise may not seem like good business, but such exposure and word-of-mouth publicity can do wonders for a new product. Ava DeMarco, cofounder of Little Earth Productions, suggests:

"Donating products is great because it gets your company's name out and it can be expensed."

REVIEWING YOUR MARKETING MIX

Ever wonder why cereal boxes undergo face-lifts every now and then? Market research provides information a business needs to make such adjustments to the marketing plan. By being aware of what's happening in your market, you can make changes in your marketing strategies (the four P's) as needed to meet your marketing objectives. In this section, we will look at the kinds of changes businesses often have to consider in their product and place strategies. We will also overview price and promotion considerations.

Possible Product Changes

Concerns about product strategy are the same for both start-up and ongoing businesses; what goods or services should you offer? How will your products be different from your competitors' products? What can you do to make sure customers can identify your products? The only difference is that now you will be making decisions about existing products rather than projected ones.

A change in any one of your products could affect your other products. A change might stimulate sales through increased traffic or cause a loss of sales through negative consumer reaction. For example, when Volkswagen reintroduced the Beetle in 1998, the increase in traffic benefited all Volkswagen models in the showroom. In contrast, if a car model gets a bad reputation, the entire image of a manufacturer can suffer.

Adding Products. Before adding products to your line or adding lines, ask yourself these questions:

- *Is there sufficient demand to add the new product?* A few people may have expressed interest, but you've got to sell enough to break even.
- *Is the product consistent with your current business?* It may be a good idea for somebody's operation but not for yours.
- *Will it compete with your current products?* It may sell very well, but what if it takes away an equal amount in current sales?
- *Is it the best use and application of your economic resources?* Can your money, labor, and facilities be better used by putting them to work in connection with another product line or another part of your marketing mix?

Eliminating Products. One reason to eliminate a product is that it isn't selling. Sometimes businesspeople are slow to take such action, thinking they can make the item sell. Not cutting the product can lead to a build-up of inventory and financial losses. By not cutting it, you may be misusing sales or production efforts.

Another reason for eliminating products is to simplify your line of goods or services. This allows you to focus on the things you do well.

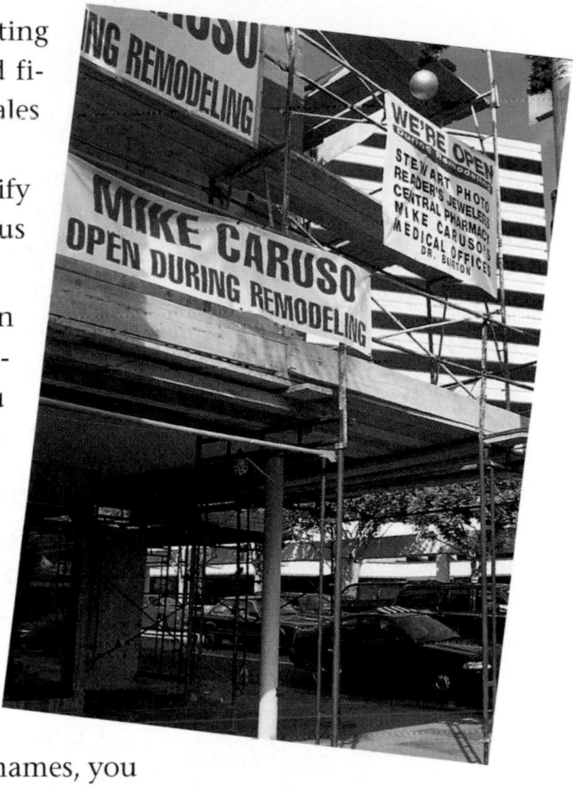

Changing the layout can improve sales for a business. *What are some of the costs?*

Changing Products. Changing the style or design of your product, if the changes are consistent with customer demands, can give you a competitive edge. You may make changes to keep in step with current fashions. You may also improve your products with the latest technology.

Changing your product may affect your prices and distribution. Timing must be considered, too. Your offerings should be up- to-date, but not ahead of the market.

Changing Brands, Packaging, or Labels. If you manufacture products under a variety of brand names, you may want to consolidate them all under one brand. This could help to build a brand preference among customers. If you carry other people's brands for resale, you may be able to sell more by offering your own private brand. Larger supermarkets often offer a variety of products on their own label.

You may want to change packaging and labels to enhance the attractiveness, interest, and salability of your products. You may also change your packaging for environmental reasons. Budget Gourmet dinners are packaged in molded paper containers. Because so many consumers are concerned about the environment, these kinds of changes could make your product more appealing.

Revising Guarantees and Service Policies. To build customer confidence and increase sales, a business can improve or add service policies and guarantees. A guarantee is an assurance of the quality of a product. Guarantees and policies can make the difference in a sale, particularly with big-ticket items. Of course, you must be able to provide the additional guaranteed services.

Possible Place Changes

When you make changes in your ongoing place strategy, they will most likely be in the areas of location, layout, and availability.

RISK TAKERS PROFIT MAKERS

Name: David Stoecklin
Business: Stoecklin Photography
City, State: Ketchum, ID

Flash! Photographer Shoots Truck

Upon completing a photography course at a two-year college, David Stoecklin traveled to the mountains of California and Colorado. He taught himself how to take action skiing photos and sold them through local papers, art galleries, and art fairs.

Today, Stoecklin Photography is a seven-person operation with its own art gallery and a ranch. Stoecklin also owns a stock photo business that sells his existing photography for commercial use. He even sells coffee-table books and calendars to consumers.

Stoecklin's popularity is growing. Lately, he has been touring the world and giving lectures to amateur photographers. Camera and film manufacturers and other professional organizations sponsor his lectures. He says, "I'm only doing actual photo shoots two to three times a week, but it seems like I'm working more than ever!"

Thinking Critically

Why might photographic equipment manufacturers sponsor David Stoecklin's lectures?

To some extent, you may also make changes in your channels of distribution.

Improving Location. As your business grows, you may look for ways to improve your location. You could extend it by using kiosks, or stands, on street corners or in malls. With some businesses, you could "take your location to the customer" through mobile units.

You might also want to consider more permanent and substantial changes. You might add outlets or branch operations. You could change your base location to be more accessible to customers. Because these are more permanent steps, however, they would have to be coordinated with your plans for growth.

Rearranging Layout. You may also want to rearrange the physical layout of your operation. For retail and some service businesses, this change can enhance sales. Adding or expanding parking or access to your business can do the same. If you are a manufacturer, wholesaler, or extractor, you might reorganize how your goods are physically distributed. This could increase your capability to serve your customers and, thus, increase sales.

Increasing Availability. Availability is generally the easiest adjustment you can make in your place strategy.

Let's say you have a video rental store. Presently it is open until 7:00 p.m. on weekdays and 9:00 p.m. on weekends. You can increase your availability and business by staying open later seven days a week. Consider another example—you supply food to restaurants. You may change your delivery schedule to match their needs better. These are both ways of increasing availability.

Providing Electronic Access. The increasing use of electronic communication, such as the Internet and fax, opens a new door to potential customers. Web sites can advertise your product as well as provide an outlet for sales. The applications of these opportunities to your business should be thoroughly explored.

Changing Channels of Distribution. The type of business you have and where you are in the channel determine the choices you have here. If you are in a manufacturing business, you have some control over channel decisions. You can continually look out for ways to improve your channel choices. For example, you could use a more direct channel with fewer intermediaries.

Businesses at other points in the channel have more limited options. If you are a retailer or wholesaler, you could look for product sources that can deliver more effectively and efficiently. You could also look for alternatives in that part of the channel where you do have some control—between you and your customers.

ENTREPRENEURS INTERNATIONAL

Monaco

At 38 years of age, Luca Bassani Antivari founded Wally Yachts in Monte Carlo. Wally Yachts doesn't actually build boats, but instead acts as a creative general contractor. They select, direct, organize, and manage the best architect, shipyard crew, interior designer, and other professionals until a finished yacht is delivered to their client. Wally Yachts creates distinctive custom sailing yachts of more than 20 meters (65 feet) featuring high performance and easy handling.

Apply **How can marketing a luxury item differ from marketing a nonluxury item? Who should Wally Yachts target as potential clients?**

Businesses can strengthen their appeal by offering complementary goods or services. ***What are the risks of offering something unrelated?***

Before you make any change in channels, you should look at the new channel, keeping in mind three questions:

- What effect will the new channel have on your sales volume and stability?
- What effect will it have on your gross profit?
- What effect will it have on your operating costs?

Possible Price and Promotion Changes

Price strategy revision possibilities are discussed in Chapter 11 along with initial price strategy. Price revision considerations include pricing for profit, reacting to market prices, and revising terms of sale.

Promotion strategy revisions will also be discussed separately. Although the promotion strategy will encompass two chapters, 12 and 13, possible changes will be examined in Chapter 12. Areas considered will be making the most of your advertising dollars, stimulating sales, and long-term planning.

Possible changes in all the marketing strategies should be considered before undertaking revisions in the marketing plan. The importance of coordinating these changes is discussed next.

REVISING YOUR MARKETING MIX AND PLAN

As you adjust each of your marketing strategies, you will probably need to make changes in your other strategies. Let's look at an example.

You are the operator of a "no-frills" driving range. You decide to upgrade your facility by covering the tee areas. This would be considered a change in product. Then you would probably consider changing your price strategy to pay for the improvement. You would certainly want to advertise to let the golfing public know about your improved facility. This change in promotion strategy could generate more business. You would now have the capability to stay open during bad weather in the summer and even in the winter. This would be a change in availability, which is part of the place strategy.

Ideally, as you change one strategy, you adjust the others. However, in reality it doesn't usually work that way. Because owners are so busy with other business activities, they do not make all the changes as quickly as would be profitable.

Reviewing and revising your marketing plan regularly can remedy this situation. It will provide an opportunity to identify and make strategy changes. It can also ensure that your strategies are consistent with your marketing objectives.

In addition, an annual review of your marketing objectives and marketing plan should be scheduled. Such a review sets the stage for longer-term market planning. Once your business is underway, this yearly review may result in expansion as well as revision decisions. You may decide to add diversification, investing in products you do not currently produce or businesses you are not currently involved in.

CHECK YOUR UNDERSTANDING — SECTION 10.2

Reviewing Key Terms and Concepts

1 What are the factors to consider for possible changes in product strategy?
2 What are the factors to consider for possible changes in place strategy?
3 Why is it important to review and revise your marketing mix regularly?

Critical Thinking Activity

Develop a review checklist for each of the marketing strategies that would be appropriate for your business.

Extension Lab—Acquiring Data

ATM Advantage The Bank of Philippine Islands, in Manila, has initiated soft-drink vending machines operated by ATM machines. The marketing manger at the bank believes that customers should be using their ATM cards for all kinds of purchases, not just expensive ones. Future plans for the bank's ATM machines include fast-food restaurants and movie theaters.

Research:

- What trends led to this decision by the bank?
- Why does the bank want people to use ATM cards for less expensive purchases?
- How long do you suppose it will take for this movement to arrive in the United States?

CHAPTER 10 REVIEW

CHAPTER SUMMARY

- The particular combination of the four P's—product, place, price, and promotion—used to reach the target market is called the marketing mix.
- Product strategy deals with goods or services and how they match up with customer needs and expectations.
- The place, or distribution, strategy deals with how to deliver goods or services to customers.
- A channel of distribution is the path a product takes from the producer to the consumer. There are two basic types—direct and indirect.
- Once your business is started, you must continue to conduct market research to keep your business successful.
- Product changes, altering the style or design of a product, changing brands, or revising guarantees, must be considered as markets change.
- When changes occur in place strategy, they often occur in the areas of location, layout, and availability.
- Reviewing and revising your marketing plan regularly will help you identify and make necessary strategy changes.

RECALL KEY TERMS

Write a short-term marketing plan for a new product you wish to sell. Be sure to use the following key terms:

marketing objectives
marketing plan
marketing mix
brand
package
label
product positioning
product mix
channel of distribution
intensive distribution
selective distribution
exclusive distribution
intermediaries
sufficient demand
private brand
guarantees
diversification

RECALL KEY CONCEPTS

1. List the four P's that make up a marketing plan.
2. What are the features of a service business?
3. Name the steps in the process of developing and manufacturing a new product.
4. Describe the difference between a direct and an indirect channel of distribution.
5. How does the choice of the channel of distribution affect the product itself?
6. Explain the differences between intensive, selective and exclusive distribution.
7. Before you decide to add a product to your line, what should you consider?
8. Why is it a good idea to review your marketing plan on a regular basis?

THINK CRITICALLY

1. Can you prepare a marketing plan before choosing a target market? Explain.
2. Would you be willing to invest in a business that did not have long-range marketing objectives? Explain.
3. Which one of the 4 P's is most critical to the success of your business? Which is the least important? Defend your answers.

CHAPTER 10 REVIEW

4. Choose a product you recently purchased. How did its features, branding, packaging, and labeling affect your decision to purchase the product?
5. Consider the product you selected in Question 4. How could the product and its packaging be changed to expand sales? Could the place strategy be improved? What about improving its availability or channel of distribution?

CONNECT ACADEMICS TO THE WORKPLACE

Math

1. Your boss has asked that you calculate the price of tennis shoes your company is planning to manufacture. Your cost to produce each pair of shoes is $40. Your related overhead and projected profit are $15. If the wholesaler's markup is 50 percent of the cost and the retailer's markup is 100 percent of its cost, what is:

- The manufacturer's price to the wholesaler?
- The wholesaler's price to the retailer?
- The retailer's price to the consumer?

Creative Thinking

2. Select a product that is marketed specifically to teenagers. Using a computer or other resources, create new packaging or labeling for the item so it will appeal to a broader market.

WORK IN YOUR COMMUNITY

Interview two business owners in your community.

- Ask them about the channels of distribution that they use to obtain products and sell products.
- Research alternative methods that might be appropriate for the particular business.
- Prepare a report for the business owners with recommendations you have for improving the way they obtain and sell their products. Include a cost analysis.

LINK SCHOOL TO CAREER

Working in teams of three or four, conduct market research on a product or service sold at school to determine whether possible product or place changes are needed.

- Create and conduct the survey.
- Compile the results.
- Make recommendations in writing to the principal based on your findings.

*inter*NET CONNECTION

Farmer's Market

You are planning to add another channel of distribution to your wholesale nursery business—the Internet. Your friends suggest you conduct some research before you begin.

Connect

Use a variety of search engines to find out:

- How to create a business presence on the Internet.
- How to develop the Web site.
- What the appropriate netiquette (net etiquette) is for doing business on the Web.

CHAPTER 11

The Price Strategy

Learning Objectives

When you have completed this chapter, you will be able to:

- **Recognize** the factors that affect price strategy
- **Identify** marketing objectives related to pricing
- **Describe** the components that go into making price strategy decisions
- **Apply** formulas used in setting prices
- **List** considerations for updating price strategy

You're the Boss!

Pricing Your Goods

Everyone has always complimented you on your woodworking. Recently, you've been thinking about turning your hobby into a furniture business. Starting small, you plan to keep working in the garage. You already have a list of acquaintances who have requested work from you. The only problem is what to charge them. You used to ask for "whatever is fair." That won't work if you want to stay in business.

What Will You Do?
How will you make your pricing decision?

SECTION 11.1

Price Strategy Considerations

FACTORS AFFECTING PRICE

Setting a price for a good or service is not easy. You have to consider costs, expenses, economic forces, customer impressions, the competition, government regulations, and technological trends. Each of these factors can affect the market price.

Costs and Expenses

To stay in business you have to make a profit. That means your prices must exceed your costs and expenses. These include fixed costs such as rent, utilities, and insurance premiums. Some expenses, such as sales commissions and delivery charges, vary with the number of units sold.

The costs of a product are also affected by the pricing structure in the distribution channel. Channel members will only handle your product if they can make a profit. If you publish magazines, your distributors and magazine vendors must make money as well. Your price will have to be low enough to allow them to make a profit.

Supply and Demand

The law of supply and demand also affects price. If the demand for your product is high and supply is low, you can command a high price. On the other hand, if the reverse is true—low demand and high supply—you'll have to set lower prices.

Some prices are not always affected by supply and demand. That is because prices reflect the sensitivity of industry demand. As discussed in Chapter 1, if customers will buy a product no matter what the price, like milk or gasoline, it is said to have *inelastic* demand. In contrast, if prices are especially sensitive to demand, such as gourmet foods or other luxury items, the demand is said to be *elastic*.

What you'll learn

- the factors that affect price strategy
- marketing objectives that can be accomplished through price strategy
- considerations in developing a price strategy

Why it's important

Setting the right prices is necessary for a business to succeed. It enables your business to make a profit, meet the competition, and establish an image.

KEY TERMS

psychological pricing
prestige pricing
odd/even pricing
price lining
promotional pricing
discount pricing
price skimming
penetration pricing

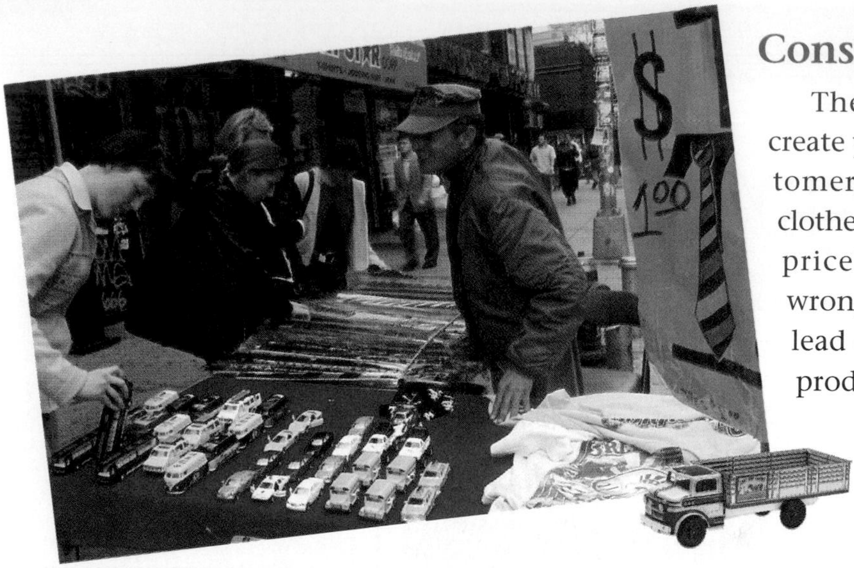

Customers can associate the price of an item with its quality. ***What would you think about this street vendor's products?***

Consumer Perceptions

The price of your products helps create your image in the minds of customers. Have you ever shopped for clothes and found an unbelievably low price? Did you wonder what was wrong with it? Prices set too low can lead customers to believe that your product lacks quality. Prices set too high may turn away customers as well. High prices, however, do convey quality and status.

Competition

The competition also affects price. Your price will have to be competitive with similar goods or services. This effect can be offset and higher prices charged by adding services. Customers will pay more for personal attention, credit, and warrantees.

Government Regulations

Your price strategy may be affected by federal and state laws. The Clayton Act and the Robinson-Patman Act are two federal laws that make it illegal for businesses to sell the same product to different customers at different prices. An auto dealer can't charge a lower price to men than to women. Businesses who do have to be able to show that certain conditions exist. For example, one customer may buy a higher volume or lesser quality of products.

Laws addressing price gouging, price fixing, resale maintenance, minimum pricing, unit pricing, and price advertising also affect pricing. If you familiarize yourself with federal and state laws and are fair to your customers, you'll be in good shape.

Technological Trends

Technological trends affect price strategy. When big bookstores like Barnes & Noble and Borders were competing with each other in the mid-1990s, Amazon.com was changing the way people buy books. Through the Internet, Amazon.com provides customers with easy access to prices, product information, and services. Also, the company saves overhead by not running a store. These

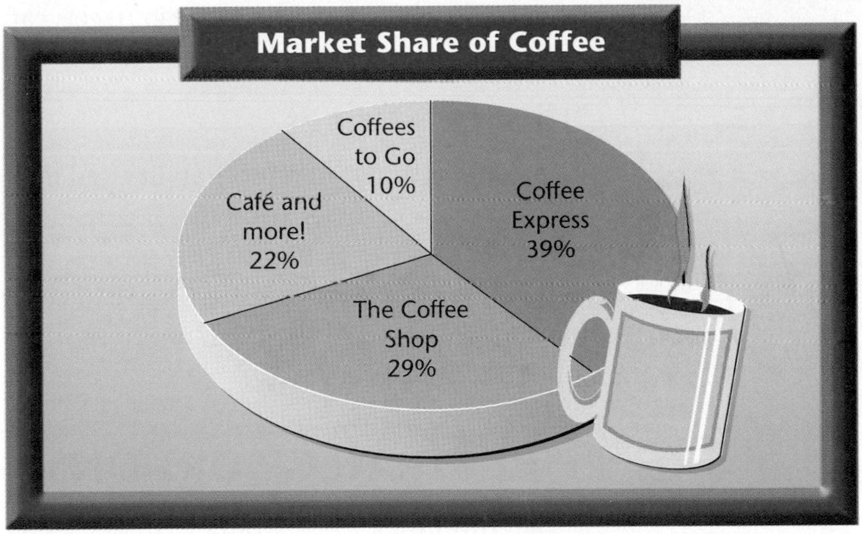

Figure 11–1
The Coffee Express shop has the largest market share of sales for the coffee shops in this community. ***What kinds of business tactics could the other shops employ to increase their market share?***

savings are passed on to the customer in the form of discount prices. Whether or not you adapt to such change can either give you a competitive edge or make you obsolete.

PRICING OBJECTIVES

For new companies, obtaining a return-on-investment and obtaining market share are the most important goals. Other objectives can be added as the company grows. Include your pricing objectives in your marketing plan and review and revise them regularly.

Obtaining a Target Return-on-Investment

The profitability objective involves pricing products to obtain a certain percentage return-on-investment. For example, a company might create a goal of 20 percent return-on-investment. *Investment* refers to what it costs to make and market the product.

Obtaining Market Share

Market share is a business's portion of the total sales generated by all of the competing companies in a given market. **Figure 11–1** shows that the Coffee Express shop has a 39 percent market share of local coffee shops. As a new business, you have to set your prices to obtain your competitors' customers. You may try to undercut them with lower prices. You may also set them higher to suggest higher quality. Besides pricing, other marketing strategies such as

Competition is a major factor that affects the prices you can charge. *If you were starting up a similar business just down the street from this one, where would you set your prices and why?*

fixing coffee makers or selling fresh bagels can also work.

Other Objectives

Objectives other than profitability and market share include social and ethical considerations, meeting the competition's prices, and establishing an image. Consider these in combination with obtaining return on investment and obtaining market share.

PRICE STRATEGY OPTIONS

Determining a price strategy involves several considerations. These include selecting a basic approach to pricing, determining your pricing policy, and identifying effective pricing tactics.

Basic Price Strategies

There are three basic price strategies you can use when pricing your product: cost-based, demand-based, and competition-based pricing. You will probably employ a combination of these strategies. If you have a range of products, you may even use all three strategies separately. In any event, the strategy or strategies you choose must be compatible with your target market and consistent with your pricing objectives.

1. Cost-Based Pricing. A cost-based strategy dictates that you consider your business costs and

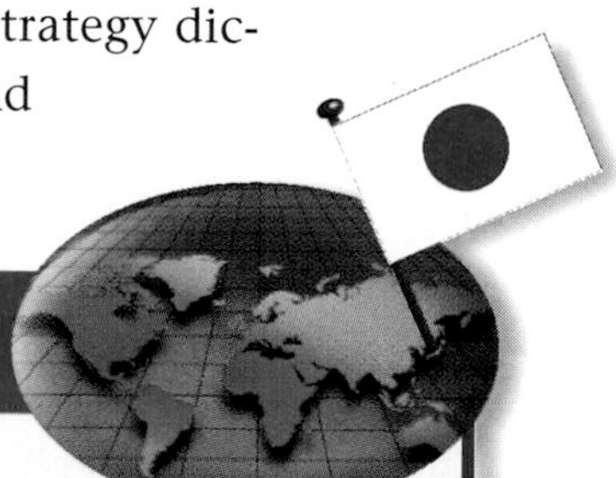

ENTREPRENEURS INTERNATIONAL

Japan

Chuck and Kelly Grafft began Foreign Buyer's Club in Japan to provide their overseas friends with American conveniences. "We didn't expect it be a full-time job or even a long-term thing," says Grafft. They developed catalogs and took orders in their living room for "convenience items" from cotton swabs to brownie mix. FBC now operates full-time out of a storefront in Kobe. Of course, they still ship direct to their clients throughout Japan.

Apply **Our everyday conveniences are often thought of as "specialty items" in other countries. Even though Japan is an extremely modern country, why is FBC a good idea?**

your profit objectives. To calculate price using this strategy, first figure your cost to make or buy your product. Then figure the related cost of doing business. Finally, add your projected profit margin to arrive at your price. The amount that you add on to your cost to ensure a profit is called your *markup*.

2. Demand-Based Pricing. This strategy requires you to find out what your customers are willing to pay for your product, and set the price accordingly. Demand-based pricing is useful only when certain conditions exist. Demand for your product has to be inelastic. Customers also have to believe your product is different or of greater value than the competition's.

3. Competition-Based Pricing. To determine prices using this strategy, you will need to find out what your competitors charge. Then decide whether it is to your advantage to price below the competition, in line with the competition, or above the competition. This strategy is concerned with being competitive.

Pricing Policies

Establishing a pricing policy frees you from making the same pricing decisions over and over again. It lets the employees and the customers know what to expect. There are two types:

1. Flexible-Price Policy. If you sell handcrafted jewelry, it may be to your benefit to allow your customers to haggle with you over the price. This type of pricing takes into account market conditions, such as increased or decreased demand, and the prices of your competitors.

Up & Coming Entrepreneur

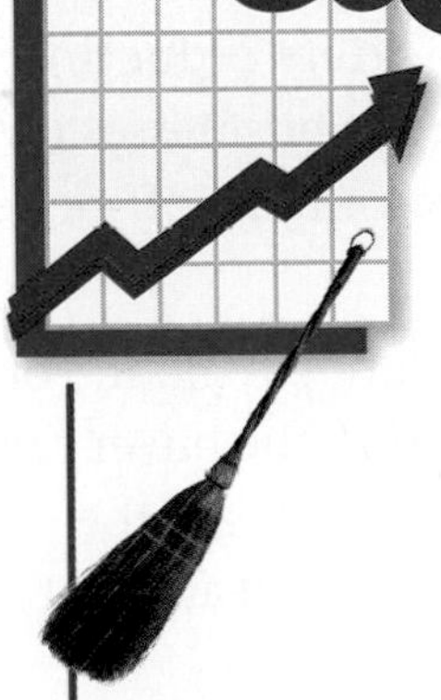

Chimney Sweeping Entrepreneur

Jim Brewer was a professional Virginia firefighter, who often saw firsthand the number of chimney-fire calls in his area. When he noticed the lack of chimney sweeps, Brewer placed an ad in the local Yellow Pages and started to run the business out of his home. Today, Brewer's company, Magic Sweep Chimney Sweeps, is located in a storefront and also offers a variety of fireplace equipment, from gas logs to tool sets. His company has now swept over 15,000 chimneys, and even rescued stray animals in the process!

Analyze **How might different seasons affect the pricing for chimney sweeps?**

Money Matters

THE COMPETITION

One of the ways to stay aware of what is happening in the market is by visiting your competitors. Says Tom Stemberg, CEO of Staples:

"You must never have the hubris to take your competition for granted, because that can come back and hurt you."

2. One-Price Policy. A one-price policy tells customers that they are treated equally. What they pay is not based on knowledge or experience with the bargaining process. The one-price policy is recommended very strongly for service businesses. If customers haggle over the value of a service, the price will invariably go down.

The Product Life Cycle

All products move through a four-stage life cycle: introduction, growth, maturity, decline. The stages are shown in **Figure 11–2**.

Pricing Techniques

Once you've introduced your new product through penetration pricing or skimming, you need to arrive at a final price. You need to find the prices that meet your needs and are most attractive to buyers. These techniques fall into two broad categories—*psychological pricing* and *discount pricing*.

1. Psychological Pricing. Psychological pricing is based on the belief that customers base perceptions of a product on price. Psychological pricing is often used by retail businesses. There are several varieties:

- Prestige pricing employs higher-than-average prices. A shirt that costs $100 suggests exclusiveness, status, and prestige.
- Odd/even pricing uses odd prices ($19.99) to suggest bargains and even prices ($20.00) to suggest higher quality.
- Price lining prices items according to category. For example, a store may sell its basic television set for $99. Its mid-range and top-of-the-line models may cost $279 and $499.
- Promotional pricing offers lower prices for a limited period to generate sales. A fast-food restaurant may promote its new burger for 99 cents "for a limited time only."

2. Discount Pricing. Discount pricing offers reductions from the regular price to customers. Many types of businesses use discounts. In some instances, they are basic percentage-off-price discounts. There are also specialized discounts:

- *Cash discounts* are given to customers for prompt payment. For example 2/10, n/30 on the invoice indicates that the buyer can reduce the bill by 2 percent by paying within 10 days of the invoice. If the bill is not paid within 10 days, the full amount (net) is due within 30 days.

Figure 11–2

Pricing in the Product Life Cycle

Each stage calls for different price considerations. As a new business owner, you may be handling products in any or all of the stages. Each affects the price strategy.

1. Introduction.
One of two methods is often used when introducing a product—*price skimming* or *penetration pricing*. Price skimming involves charging a high price to recover costs as quickly as possible. Then the price is dropped when the product is no longer unique. Penetration pricing builds sales by charging a low initial price to keep unit costs to customers as low as possible. This approach can discourage competition.

2. Growth.
In the growth stage, sales are increasing and unit costs are decreasing. If you skimmed, you would need to lower prices to appeal to price-conscious customers. If you were penetrating, very little price change would be necessary, but promotion costs would increase.

3. Maturity.
During the maturity stage, you would need to look for new markets and possibly make product improvements to hold prices.

4. Decline.
In the decline stage, you would cut prices to stimulate sales or clear inventory.

At the end of the season, certain retail stores lower prices to clear their inventory. ***What are examples of seasonal stores?***

- *Quantity discounts* encourage buyers to order large amounts. A customer who buys over $50,000 of materials within a year might be given a 10 percent discount.
- *Trade discounts* are given to distribution-channel members who provide marketing services for the manufacturer. As an example, a manufacturer might designate a discount relationship of 30-15 percent. This means that the retailer takes 30 percent of the sales price to the consumer. The wholesaler keeps 15 percent for handling, storing, and delivering merchandise to the retailer.
- *Promotional discounts* are used when manufacturers want to pay wholesalers or retailers for carrying out promotional activities for the manufacturer. The discounts can be made in the price paid for promotion goods or by a direct cash payment. They may even be actual promotional materials.
- *Seasonal discounts* are used for products that have highly seasonal demand. Heavy coats are not in demand in the middle of the summer. Manufacturers give seasonal discounts to those who buy them in the off-season. This enables a manufacturer to keep operations going throughout the year. It also enables a business to shift storage costs to other points in the channel of distribution.

CHECK YOUR UNDERSTANDING

SECTION 11.1

Reviewing Key Terms and Concepts

1 What are some factors that affect price?
2 What pricing objectives are most important to a new business?
3 Is it possible to have more than one primary pricing strategy?

Critical Thinking Activity

Draft a preliminary price strategy for your proposed business.

Extension Lab—Serving Customers

Dirty Dwellings You and a friend run a house-cleaning service. You charge $45 per house. Recently, several of your clients have tried to haggle with you over the price. One homeowner has offered $40 per cleaning, while another wants to pay only $35.

Role Play With a classmate, simulate a discussion between the partners in the scenario.

- Explain why you believe $45 is a fair price.
- Defend your one-price policy.
- Describe what you can do to ensure your clients remain happy with both your service and your price.

SECTION 11.2

Calculating and Revising Prices

What you'll learn

- how to calculate break-even point
- how to calculate markup and markdown
- how to calculate discounts
- considerations in adjusting prices
- the potential for revising terms of sale as a price adjustment
- the process for review and revision of your price strategy

Why it's important

Setting up a price strategy and revising it periodically are critical to business survival and success.

KEY TERMS

break-even point
markup
markdown
special market circumstances

BREAK-EVEN ANALYSIS

The break-even point is reached when the money from product sales equals the costs of making and distributing the product. At that point, you have covered your costs and are ready to make a profit. Finding this point will let you know how many units you will have to sell at a given price to make a profit.

To determine the number of units you need to sell to break even, you need to know three figures. You need to know fixed expenses, such as rent, utilities, and insurance payments. You need to know variable expenses, including the cost of the goods or services, salaries, and advertising expenses. You also have to know the selling price. Plug the numbers into the following formula to find out how many units you need to reach the break-even point.

$$\frac{\text{Fixed expenses}}{\text{Unit sales price} - \text{Variable expenses}} = \text{Break-even point (units)}$$

For example, a board game manufacturer is considering selling a new product for \$10 per unit. The cost per unit will be \$6.50. In order to produce the game, the manufacturer will have to buy a new piece of equipment costing \$7,000. How many units would have to be sold at \$10 for the manufacturer to break even?

$$\frac{\$7000}{\$10 - \$6.50} = 2{,}000 \text{ units}$$

Break-even analysis has other applications. For example, you can figure out how many dollars in sales it will take for a product to break even.

Tips from the Real World

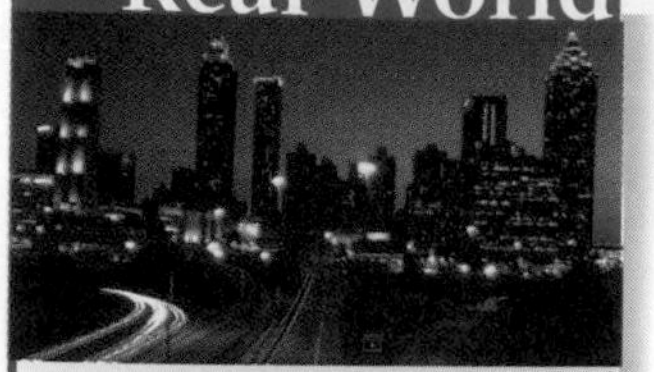

FASTER SERVICE

In some cases, the service may be more important than the price. According to Patricia Gallup, co-founder of PC Connection:

"We wanted to have the best and fastest delivery system in existence. So. . . . we instituted. . . . 'Everything Overnight.' [This program] makes us stand out from our competitors."

MARKUP

Businesses that purchase or manufacture goods for resale use *markup* pricing. A markup is the amount added to the cost of an item to cover expenses and ensure a profit.

Suppose it costs $5 to make a fancy ball-point pen ($3 for the casing and $2 for the ink refill). The manufacturer will have to charge more than $5 to make a profit. If the manufacturer marks up the cost by $2, the cost and markup are added to make a price of $7.

$$\text{Cost} + \text{Markup} = \text{Price}$$
$$\$5 + \$6.50 = \$7$$

Once you understand the relationships among these items, you can compute any one figure if you know the other two. For example, if you know the price and the markup, you can figure the cost:

$$\text{Price} - \text{Markup} = \text{Cost}$$
$$\$7 - \$2 = \$5$$

If you know the price and the cost, you can determine the markup:

$$\text{Price} - \text{Cost} = \text{Markup}$$
$$\$7 - \$5 = \$2$$

Most business owners decide on a standard percentage markup. They can use the average for their industry. They can match their competitors' markup. They can also estimate how much they will need per item sold to cover their expenses.

The pen manufacturer discussed above decided that $2 on a cost of $5 was about right. To convert that figure to a percentage, use the following formula:

$$\frac{\text{Markup}}{\text{Cost}} = \text{Percentage markup}$$

$$\frac{\$2}{\$5} = .4 \text{ or } 40 \text{ percent}$$

The $2 markup represents a 40 percent markup on cost.

Once a percentage has been decided on, it can be applied to any cost figure to arrive at a price. If the pen manufacturer has a deluxe pen that costs $10, you would find markup by multiplying $10 × 40 percent: $4. The total price would be $10 plus the markup, or $14.

MARKDOWN

To reduce their inventories, businesses sometimes mark down their merchandise. By lowering their prices a certain percentage, they tempt shoppers to buy. In other words, they have a sale.

Suppose a footwear store has a few $105 basketball shoes that are just not selling. To get them to sell, the manager decides to mark them down by 30 percent. First, she determines the markdown, the amount of money taken from the original price:

Price	**×**	**Markdown percentage**	**=**	**$ Markdown**
$105	**×**	**.30**	**=**	**$31.50**

Then she computes the sale price:

Price	**−**	**Markdown**	**=**	**sale price**
$105	**−**	**$31.50**	**=**	**$73.50**

The sale price is $73.50.

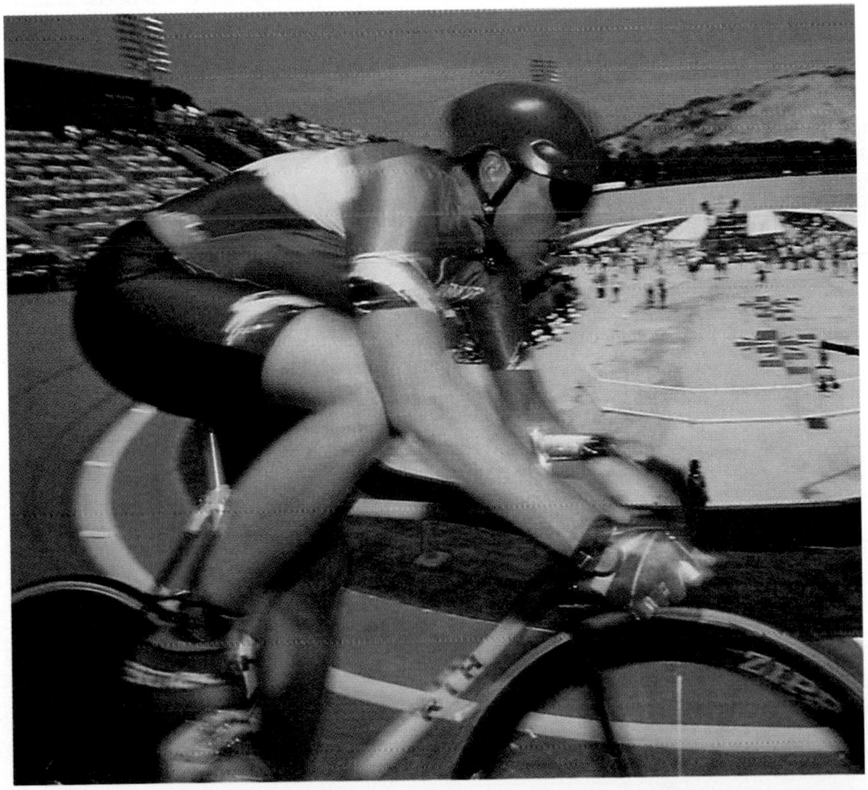

Suppose a bicycle shop has a sale in which $600 racing bikes are marked down 40 percent. ***What is the sale price?***

DISCOUNTS

A discount is a reduction in price to the customer. Your customer might be another business in the channel of distribution or it might be the final consumer. In all cases, the basic procedure requires two steps: To get the dollar amount of the discount, multiply the price by the discount percentage. Then, subtract the discount from the price to get the amount the customer will actually pay.

Assume for example, that a golf pro shop was overstocked on starter sets of clubs. In order to move the $200 sets, a 20 percent discount is implemented. The discount price can be arrived at by applying the steps:

1. **Price × Discount Percentage = Discount Dollars**
   $200 × .20 = $40
2. **Price − Discount Dollars = Discounted Price**
   $200 − $40 = $160

Although the calculation is the same, some discounts involve additional steps. Cash discounts, described earlier, are stated in terms. In our example—2/10, n/30—the only discount calculation is the first number (2%). The other numbers identify when payment is due—with discount and without. Trade discounts are often quoted in a series. In our earlier example, it was 30% and 15% for retailers and wholesalers in that order. These series of discounts are calculated in sequence.

Thus, if the manufacturer's list price was $100, in the example, the calculation would be:

Retailer's discount	**$100**	**×**	**.30**	**=**	**$30**
Cost to retailer	**$100**	**−**	**$30**	**=**	**$70**
Wholesaler's discount	**$70**	**×**	**.15**	**=**	**$10.50**
Cost to wholesaler	**$70**	**−**	**$10.50**	**=**	**$59.50**

Note that in a series discount, the wholesaler's discount is based on the retailer's discount, not the list price.

POSSIBLE PRICE CHANGES

Developing a pricing strategy is a complex process. Once the strategy has been established, it may be difficult to change prices

RISK TAKERS PROFIT MAKERS

Name: Lane Nemeth
Company: Discovery Toys
City, State: Livermore, CA

Teaching Through Toys

In 1978, Lane Nemeth founded Discovery Toys when she saw the need to provide her child and the children of other parents with the "educational toys" that were only available in schools. Nemeth attended an educational toy convention in Los Angeles and found 60 products to market. With a small loan from her grandmother, Nemeth organized her samples and recruited a friend to host the first home demonstration party for other mothers.

Nemeth's idea was simple. A demonstrator would present toys, take orders, and provide the host with a few free toys for inviting his or her friends. The idea was a success and soon, Discovery Toys became the sixteenth fastest growing company in America. Today, Nemeth employs 30,000 "educational consultants," and her home demonstrations continue to bring in $100 million annually.

Thinking Critically

Free toys for the host can be considered an incentive. Why is incentive marketing effective?

without affecting it. Nonetheless, events in the market may require you to change your price and your strategy. To protect and increase your share of the market, you will have to tend to the strategy continually.

Adjusting Prices to Maximize Profit

Whether you gain a profit or lose money is determined by the difference between your sales and your costs. To increase your profits on individual sales, you can increase prices. You can also lower prices to increase sales volume.

Before you raise or lower prices, ask yourself two questions.

1. *Are your products' prices elastic or inelastic?* If the price is elastic, a small change in price may cause a significant change in demand. If the price is inelastic, changing the price will have little or no effect on demand.

2. *What are your competitors' prices?* Whether you raise or lower your price, you'll still want it to relate to the competition's price properly.

Reacting to Market Prices

As part of your ongoing market research, keep an eye on current market prices for your products. If you are in a competitive market and prices fall, you can lose customers quickly if you don't lower your prices. If prices are on the rise, it is equally important that you raise your prices.

Occasionally, special market circumstances call for a temporary price increase. When a national convention comes to town, tourists arrive, spend money on souvenirs, and eat out often. Natural disasters also increase demand for goods and services. During floods, hurricanes, and other emergencies, people buy provisions and pay for repair work. These cases require a balance between responsibility to your business and social responsibility.

Revising Terms of Sale

Another way to change your pricing strategy is to revise the terms of sale. You can change your credit policies or introduce trade, quantity, or cash discounts. You might also offer leasing or arrange financing for customers with an outside lender. Whether or not any of these options are useful depends on the nature of your business.

Revising the Price Strategy

It's important to review your price strategy and objectives regularly. Price strategy review should focus on basic strategies, policy review, and pricing tactics. The overall effectiveness of the strategy should also be considered. Pricing objectives should be reviewed to confirm or reset sales goals. In some instances, you may want to revise, add, or even delete objectives. Changing your

It's important to keep tabs on the competition's prices. *How should this business react if a competing business lowered their prices?*

prices may affect your other marketing objectives and strategies. If changes are made, you may have to adjust your marketing plan, too.

CHECK YOUR UNDERSTANDING

SECTION 11.2

Reviewing Key Terms and Concepts

1. What is the formula for calculating break-even point?
2. What are the formulas for calculating markup and markdown?
3. What two factors should be considered before adjusting prices?

Critical Thinking Activity

Develop a list of details to consider when reviewing and revising pricing objectives and price strategy.

Extension Lab—Individual Responsibility

Storm's Brewing You own the only hardware store in town. Yesterday, the meteorologist on the local television station predicted a hurricane by the end of the week. This is the perfect opportunity for you to make a little more profit by raising the prices on items like flashlights, masking tape, and generators.

Research Speak with at least two or three local business owners, and compare their answers to the following questions.

- Is it ethical to raise prices in this type of emergency?
- Are there any laws against such practices?
- Have you ever raised prices in anticipation of a shortage? What are the consequences?

CHAPTER 11 REVIEW

CHAPTER SUMMARY

- Costs, expenses, economic forces, customer impressions, the competition, government regulation, and technological trends all affect the pricing of your product or service.
- The goals of obtaining a return-on-investment and obtaining market share are influenced by your pricing objectives.
- Pricing strategy includes selecting a basic approach to pricing, determining your pricing policy, and identifying effective pricing strategies.
- The three basic price strategies are cost-based, demand-based, and competition-based pricing.
- During the product's life cycle, the price strategy will change.
- Psychological pricing, often used by retail businesses, is based on the belief that customers base perception of a product on price.
- Discount pricing, used by many different types of businesses, offers customers reductions from the regular prices.
- A break-even analysis provides information about how many units you will have to sell at a given price to make a profit and what it takes to reach a desired profit.
- Various events in the market may require you to change your price strategy. Prices might be adjusted to maximize profit and might be raised or lowered as a reaction to special market circumstances or changes in the terms of sale.

RECALL KEY TERMS

Illustrate the terms below with real examples such as products, advertisements, and news articles.

price skimming
penetration pricing
psychological pricing
prestige pricing
odd/even pricing
price lining
promotional pricing
discount pricing
break-even point
markup
markdown
special market circumstances

RECALL KEY CONCEPTS

1. Describe the factors that affect setting the price for a product or service.
2. What pricing objectives should companies consider when developing pricing strategy?
3. Contrast cost-based, demand-based, and competition-based pricing.
4. What are the advantages of a flexible-price policy?
5. Explain the four stages in the life cycle of a product and their effects on price strategy.
6. What is the difference between markup and markdown pricing?
7. What two questions should you ask yourself before you raise or lower prices?

THINK CRITICALLY

1. Which pricing strategy is the best under what circumstances? Why?
2. Do you believe that a higher price suggests quality and prestige? Explain your answer and give examples.

3. Compare psychological pricing with discount pricing.
4. If you were going to introduce a new perfume into the market, would you use price skimming or penetration pricing as your strategy? Defend your answer.
5. How are pricing objectives related to marketing objectives?

CONNECT ACADEMICS TO THE WORKPLACE

Math

1. Otis paid $34 for a poodle he plans to sell in his pet store for $103. What is the percentage markup on the cost of this dog? Three months later, Otis still has not sold the poodle. He decides to mark it down 25 percent. What will it sell for now?

Teaching Others

2. Working in teams, create a fun lesson plan for teaching another team the basics of business math. Be sure to include:
   - How to figure break-even point
   - Markup and markdown
   - Cash discounts
   - Trade discounts

Practice the lessons on each other to reinforce the math skills. Vote as a class on the best lesson.

WORK IN YOUR COMMUNITY

Choose a product or service that you might like to sell in your community. Develop a pricing strategy and include the following:

- Which of the basic price strategies you will use
- What type of price policy you will implement
- Pricing techniques employed
- Determine the cost and break-even point

Justify your decisions.

LINK SCHOOL TO CAREER

If you are employed, choose a product sold by your company and determine the following:

- The pricing structure at each point in the channel of distribution
- The pricing strategy utilized by the company
- The stage in the life cycle of the product
- Any recent price changes and the reasons why

(Note: If you are not employed, interview a local businessperson to obtain the same kind of information for a selected product.)

*inter*NET CONNECTION

Shutterbug

You own a camera shop in your town. In addition to cameras, you are also selling accessories, film, and processing supplies. Since this is a very competitive market, you try very hard to keep an eye on current market prices and are very aware of the technological trends that might affect your business and price strategy.

Connect

Use a variety of Web browsers to find the following information:

- Competitors in your local market
- Internet competitors
- Trends in the camera industry that might affect your price strategy

CHAPTER 12

The Promotion Strategy

Learning Objectives

When you have completed this chapter, you will be able to:

- **Distinguish** among pre-opening and ongoing promotional plans
- **Select** the promotional mix for a given business
- **Determine** promotional costs for a start-up business
- **Identify** the principal approaches needed to carry out your promotional plans
- **Describe** considerations for updating the promotion strategy

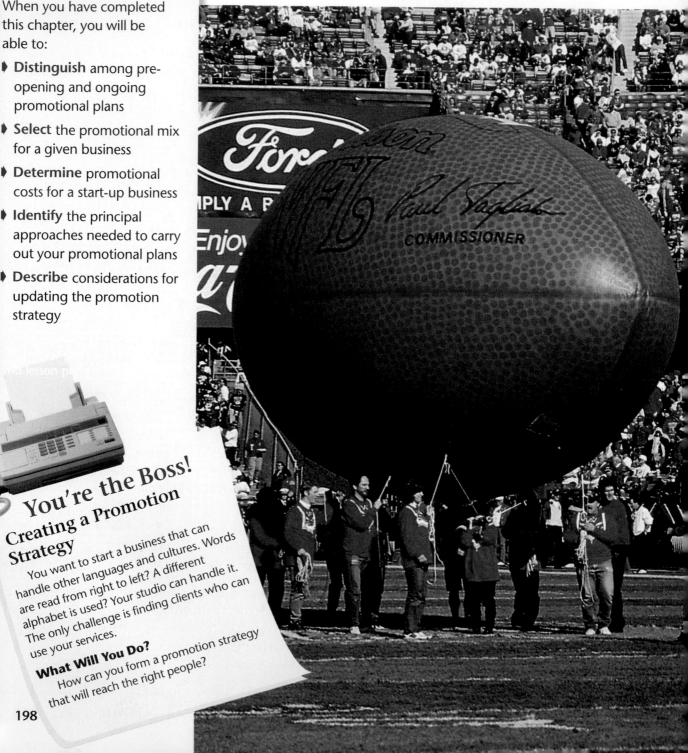

You're the Boss!

Creating a Promotion Strategy

You want to start a business that can handle other languages and cultures. Words are read from right to left? A different alphabet is used? Your studio can handle it. The only challenge is finding clients who can use your services.

What Will You Do?

How can you form a promotion strategy that will reach the right people?

SECTION 12.1

Developing a Promotional Mix

THE PROMOTION STRATEGY

Spring Clearances, White Sales, and Back-to-School Specials—have you ever wondered why department stores have so many promotions? Their promotional plans are designed to influence their target market to buy products or services. As a new business, you'll need two promotional strategies: a pre-opening plan and an ongoing plan.

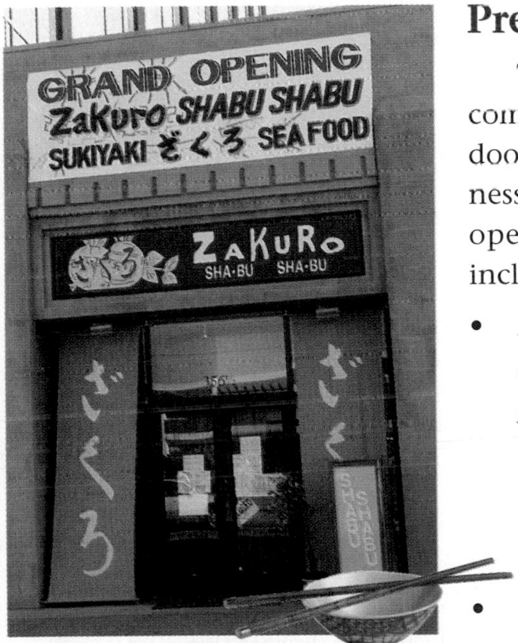

Pre-opening Plan

To ensure that you have money coming in as soon as you open your doors, you must promote your business beforehand. This is called a pre-opening plan. Such a plan usually includes the following objectives:

- *Establish a positive* **image***, or beliefs, ideas, and impressions that people have about your business.* This will set the tone for implementing your other objectives and your promotional plan.
- *Let potential customers know that you are opening for business.* Timing is an important factor in your pre-opening plan. A good rule is to begin your promotion at least six weeks prior to your opening. Promotional efforts should then intensify as you near your opening date.
- *Bring in customers, or have them contact your business.* In some types of businesses, pre-opening efforts should be capped off

What you'll learn

- how to establish pre-opening and ongoing promotional plans
- timing considerations and components of promotional plans
- types of promotion that can be used in a promotional mix

Why it's important

Potential customers rely on your promotion strategy to describe your product's characteristics, benefits, and availability. Your promotion will create your company's image and determine its chances of success.

KEY TERMS

image
preselling
campaign
promotional mix
advertising
specialty items
publicity
news releases
public relations
premiums
rebates
sweepstakes

RISK TAKERS PROFIT MAKERS

Name: Jeff Arthur
Business: Jeff Arthur Productions
City, State: Clearwater, FL

Jingle All the Way

Back in the 1970s, Jeff Arthur had his own folk-rock band, and even recorded two albums for major labels. Today, Arthur's latest recordings can be heard everyday on television. He writes advertising jingles for small businesses.

Arthur usually meets a business owner at a TV station, learns what they do and writes a jingle right there, using the offer of a free jingle as a sales tool. He tries to instill the company's main message, but gives equal consideration to the founder's ideals in his songs. He explains, "It's my job to provide the image of a well thought out professional company. That includes the ethics of its principles." Arthur estimates he has averaged over 500 jingles in one year since he began his million-dollar business in 1980!

Thinking Critically

Can you think of some ways to turn your hobby or personal interest into a business opportunity?

with a grand opening. In others, a party or reception for prospective customers would be appropriate.

- *Interest customers in your product rather than your competitors' products.* Your first three objectives should lead to this.

Ongoing Plan

Once your business has opened, what's the next step? You will need an ongoing promotional plan to help you maintain and build sales. Your new plan should be made to help you *presell* your goods or services. Preselling is influencing potential customers to buy from you before contact is actually made. However, some of the objectives from your pre-opening plan are still important. For example, you will want to keep up your business's positive image.

Objectives for ongoing promotional plans usually include:

- Explaining major features and benefits of your products.
- Communicating sales information.

- Answering customers' questions and concerns.
- Introducing new goods or services.

There are several types of promotional plans to choose from. Most businesses develop ongoing promotional plans seasonally (every six months) or quarterly. They also have monthly or weekly plans that are based on seasonal or quarterly plans.

For your new business, start with quarterly or seasonal plans. Then rough out monthly plans to estimate your promotional costs.

Promotional Plan Format

You can use the same format for both your pre-opening and ongoing plans. Both can be organized around independent or related activities or a combination of the two. A series of related promotional activities with a similar theme constitutes a **campaign**.

For each activity in your promotional plans, you should provide certain information. Include the following:

- Brief description
- Specific media placement
- Submit dates
- Scheduled date of run or release
- Number of runs, copies, or items
- Costs
- Rationale and any other pertinent notes

Apply these to pre-opening and ongoing plans.

In outdoor displays, bigger can be better. ***Why would a giant display be an effective promotion?***

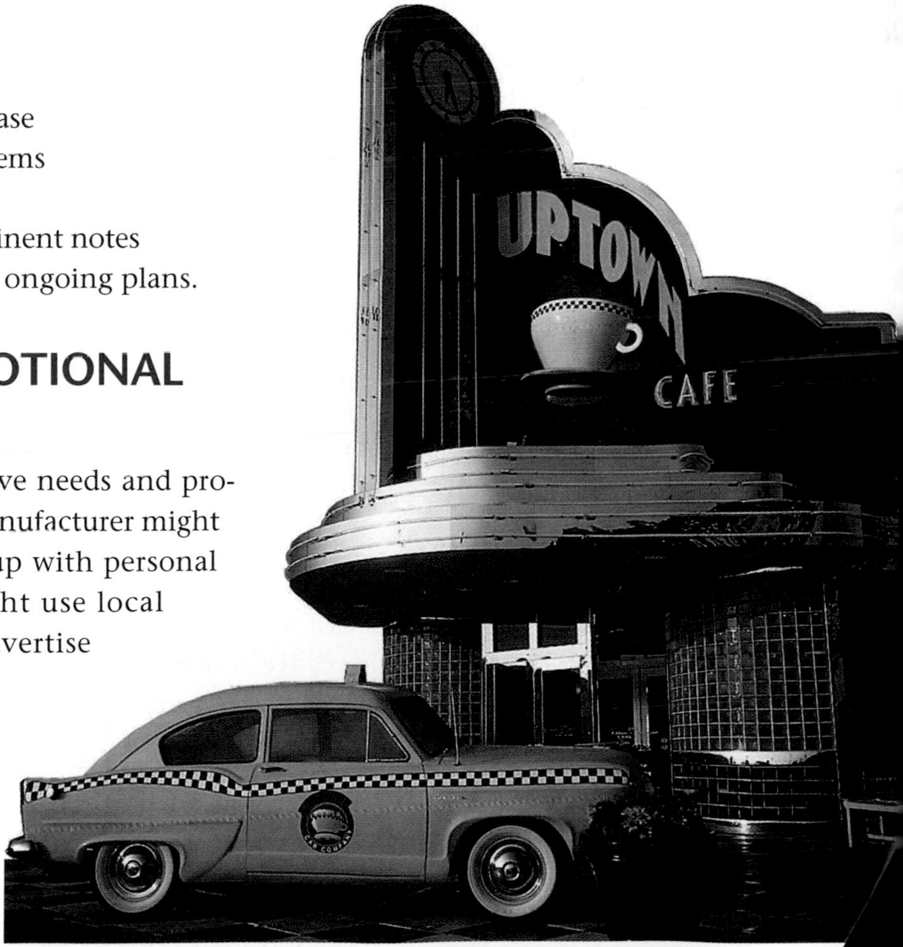

CREATING A PROMOTIONAL STRATEGY

Every business has distinctive needs and promotional strategies. A faucet manufacturer might send direct mail, then follow up with personal selling. A hardware store might use local newspapers and displays to advertise specials. A plumbing firm might rely on flyers and word-of-mouth to advertise its work.

Even in the same market, promotional strategies can vary greatly. For example, consider cosmetics.

Tips from the Real World

CREDIBILITY

A marketing plan won't sell your product if your customer doesn't trust you. Jay Conrad Levinson, author of *Guerrilla Marketing* warns us:

"Entire marketing plans fall by the wayside because inattention to seemingly unimportant details undermines prospects' confidence."

Revlon concentrates on advertising. In contrast, Avon focuses on personal selling.

When developing your promotional strategy, consider the following:

- *Target market.* Even after you've identified your target market, keep in mind that the market is always changing and evolving. Your list of potential customers may have narrowed, expanded, or changed. You may have to re-focus your promotional options to reach your customers.
- *Promotional mix.* Most businesses work with a promotional mix that includes print and broadcast media in their plans. The types of promotion you choose depend on your type of business, your target market, and your promotional budget. What's the most effective and affordable way to reach your target market?
- *Costs.* You'll need to decide what combination of activities will give you the best results for your money. These costs may be affected by seasonal or peak business times. For example, if you sell exercise equipment, your sales may increase in January when people make resolutions to get fit. Plan for your promotional budget to increase at this time.

TYPES OF PROMOTIONAL ACTIVITIES

Most businesses choose a number of promotions. Each type is designed to complement the others, but not all types used must be coordinated.

Advertising

Advertising is the paid presentation of ideas, goods, or services directed toward a mass audience by an identified sponsor. There are two types of traditional advertising media—print and broadcast. Print media include newspapers, magazines, direct mail, outdoor advertising, directories, and transit advertising. Television, radio, and the Internet are examples of broadcast media.

Newspapers. In the United States, most businesses spend about one fourth of their advertising dollars on newspaper ads. Newspaper advertising is useful for small business because it can be tailored to the local community. Newspapers can reach nearly everyone in a target area. Also, ads can be placed on short notice. They generate immediate sales. They cost relatively little.

Newspaper ads also have disadvantages. Not everyone who sees an ad will be interested in the product. Newspaper ads also have a short life span.

Magazines. By advertising in general-interest magazines such as *People, Time,* or *Life,* a business can reach an extremely large national audience. For a new business, this can be very costly. It can be less expensive to advertise in a regional edition. One might also advertise in specialty magazines. Magazines such as *Vogue, PC World,* and *Sports Illustrated* can supply you with information that describes their readers. Trade magazines provide a similar opportunity for business-to-business advertisers.

Magazine ads are usually more expensive than newspaper ads. An example of a rate sheet for a small magazine is shown in **Figure 12–1.** Ad files or artwork can be required as much as

1998/1999 Advertising Rates

South American Explorer

The quarterly magazine of the South American Explorers Club is circulated to Club members and in select retail outlets. The *South American Explorer* offers its advertisers a unique audience:

- Circulation, Autumn 1998: 8,000 copies
- 79 percent of our members earn more than $25,000 per year, 46 percent earn $50,000 per year or more
- 85 percent of our members are college educated, 42 percent have master's or doctorate degrees
- 82 percent of our members purchase goods and services advertised in the *South American Explorer*
- 57 percent of readers are professionals

DISPLAY AD RATES

Size	B&W	Color	Depth/Width
Full page	$775	$975	9 1/2" x 7 1/4"
1/2	$395	$495	7 1/4" x 4 3/4"
1/3	$275	$345	9 1/2" x 2 1/4"
1/4	$210	$265	7" x 2 1/4"
1/6	$145	N/A	4 1/2" x 2 1/4"
1/8	$110	N/A	3 1/2" x 2 1/4"
1/12	$80	N/A	2 1/4" x 2 1/4"
1/16	$60	N/A	2 1/4" x 1 3/4"
1/32	$40	N/A	2 1/4" x 1"

10% discount for multiple insertions
15% agency commission

Figure 12–1
Newspapers, magazines, and other media prepare printed summaries of their advertising rates and will mail them to prospective advertisers on request. ***According to this chart, how much would it cost you to run two 1/4-page color ads?***

6–8 weeks in advance. Advertisers will pay more and prepare their ads sooner because magazines have a longer life. Magazines are often kept for long periods of time and are passed from one person to another.

Direct Mail. Direct mail advertisements are sent directly to the homes or businesses of potential customers. Direct mail includes such items as announcements of grocery store specials, letters offering credit cards, and mail order catalogs.

This promotional method allows you to do two things at once. You can cover a wide geographic territory. It costs the same amount to send a flyer across town or to another state. At the same time, you can direct your mailings to a specific target market. A restaurant may send coupons to residents within a five-mile radius. A mail-order sports collectibles store may send catalogs to basketball fans across the country. Mailing lists of people with specific interests or backgrounds can be purchased from a variety of sources.

Direct mail does have limitations. Most significantly, these ads are often thrown away without being opened, let alone read. A second drawback is the cost of printing and postage.

Up&Coming Entrepreneur

Metal Manufacturing Entrepreneur

Dave Wehr, 31, describes his company as "a metal manufacturer specializing in promotional products." Wehr employs around 30 people at his Rhode Island factory, producing such items as golf divot tools and ball markers personalized with a company's name or message. In turn, his buyers usually give prospective clients these promotions at trade shows and other events as a gesture of goodwill. "An average order might be for a thousand or so units, but we do get orders for 70,000 units and are happy to fill them."

Analyze **List some inexpensive ways to familiarize customers with a company's name.**

Outdoor Advertising. The advantage of outdoor displays is that they expose their messages to large numbers of people. This category includes billboards, painted signs, and neon displays. It can also include the smaller, moveable signs. On the sidewalk outside the entrance, a café may put up a sign listing its specials for the day.

Unfortunately, after the first few viewings, people ignore them. In addition, some communities restrict their use. In the summer of 1998, Touchstone Pictures promoted the movie *Armageddon* by painting a hole on the side of a Los Angeles building. Within days they removed the advertisement because it was causing traffic jams.

Directories. The telephone directory is a relatively inexpensive form of advertising. It's also long lasting, since potential customers refer to their phone books for a full year. The downside is that if you change your address, telephone number, or advertising, your ad can't be updated until the next printing.

Transit Advertising. Advertising placed in public transportation has an obvious and unique advantage. It reaches a captive audience! Reading advertisements can be the only way for riders on a bus, subway, or train to pass time. Advertisements placed outside of buses serve as billboards that roam the streets of your city. Naturally, these forms of advertising are limited to areas that have public transportation.

Other Print Media. Specialty items include giveaways such as pens, caps, and T-shirts that have a business name or logo. Such items serve as a reminder of your business. For example, if your construction business gives potential customers message pads that feature your company name, address, and phone number, it will be easy for them to contact you when they have a job. If your construction workers wear T-shirts with your company's logo on it, passers-by will know who is responsible for the good job.

Television. Television is the leader in national advertising. Its main advantage is that it lets people see your product as well as hear your message. It can also be used to reach audiences of various sizes, from mass national audiences to selected major market areas. It can even be used to reach smaller, local markets through cable channels.

Cost is the biggest obstacle to the use of television advertising. Large businesses can spend millions of dollars on major ad campaigns. Buying a spot of airtime can also be expensive, especially

Money Matters

OLD CUSTOMERS

It is sometimes more profitable to keep the old customers than to attract new ones. Patrick Daly of DHL Worldwide Express explains:

"*Profits in most companies [are generated] through current customers. . . . [with whom] the 'close rate'. . . . is far higher than from new customer leads from advertising.*"

during the prime-time hours of 7–11 p.m. A spot during the Super Bowl can cost millions.

Radio. Radio is an effective and economical way to reach a lot of customers. It allows advertisers to target a geographic area and an audience. Formats include country, rock, urban, news, talk, alternative, and so on. The stations can tell you how their format and listener demographics match up with your target market.

As with television, rates for radio advertising vary according to the time of the day. Prime-time hours for radio are usually during the early morning and late afternoon.

Internet. The Internet is a rapidly growing vehicle for advertising. Companies place ads, called banners, on browsers and other people's Web sites. From there, Net users can link to the company's own site. Through the Internet, enormous amounts of product information can be provided to customers who want it. Customers can see what is available. Then they can contact sellers directly to request additional information. As computer users become more comfortable with the Internet and online transactions become more secure, ads are leading to more purchases.

Publicity

Publicity is the placement of newsworthy items about a company or product in the media. To use publicity, you have to call attention to yourself and your enterprise.

1. *Write news releases.* News releases are brief newsworthy stories that are sent to the media. **Figure 12–2** shows an example.
2. *Write feature articles.* Submit articles to newspapers, magazines, or newsletters that reach your target market.

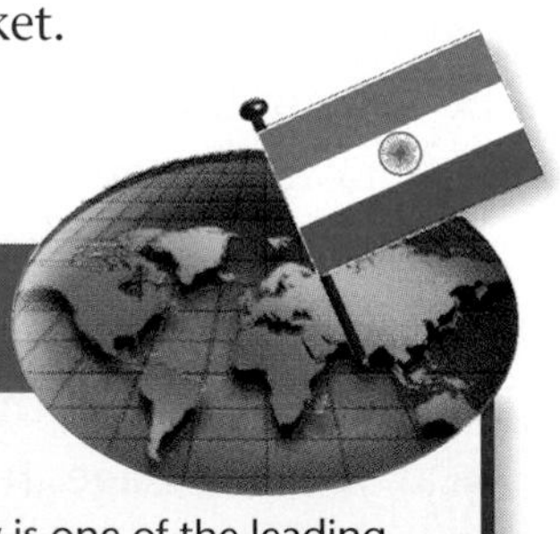

ENTREPRENEURS INTERNATIONAL

India

India is the largest producer of films in the world and the Kailash Picture Company is one of the leading production houses there. KPC makes television commercials, documentaries, music videos, and public service films. Producer/Director Kailash Surendranath has been in the business for over two decades. He has worked with the world's leading advertising agencies for such major brands and multinational companies as Procter & Gamble, Colgate-Palmolive, and Gillette.

Apply **Why is winning industry awards an important tool in marketing your business?**

3. *Submit captioned photos*. Send photos and explanations of your company's new products, facilities, or employees to the media.
4. *Call a press conference*. Make major announcements related to your company to the media.
5. *Seek interviews*. Discuss some newsworthy aspect of your business with the media. Offer your expert opinion.

Unsolicited publicity can also come from *public relations*. Public relations are activities designed to create goodwill toward a business. Some companies donate money or equipment to schools. Others participate in environmental cleanups. Such activities are often noted by the media and, eventually, consumers.

The most obvious advantage of publicity is that it is free. Also, because it is not company sponsored, people often think it is more credible than advertising.

There is a downside. As a businessperson, you have no control over publicity. You don't know when, where, how, or even if it will be printed or aired. However, you really have nothing to lose and a lot to gain.

News Release

Date: MARCH 12
To: BUSINESS EDITORS
From: YIKES! BIKES! Bicycle Shop
Earl Brown, Owner
Re: Grand Opening

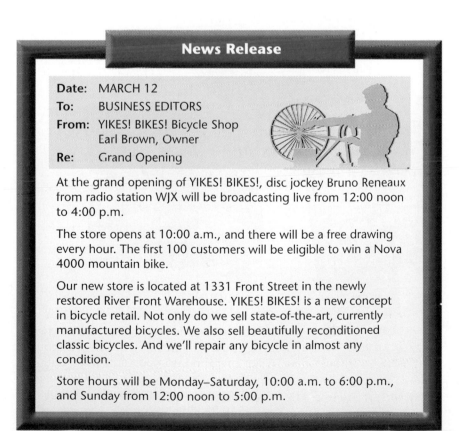

At the grand opening of YIKES! BIKES!, disc jockey Bruno Reneaux from radio station WJX will be broadcasting live from 12:00 noon to 4:00 p.m.

The store opens at 10:00 a.m., and there will be a free drawing every hour. The first 100 customers will be eligible to win a Nova 4000 mountain bike.

Our new store is located at 1331 Front Street in the newly restored River Front Warehouse. YIKES! BIKES! is a new concept in bicycle retail. Not only do we sell state-of-the-art, currently manufactured bicycles. We also sell beautifully reconditioned classic bicycles. And we'll repair any bicycle in almost any condition.

Store hours will be Monday–Saturday, 10:00 a.m. to 6:00 p.m., and Sunday from 12:00 noon to 5:00 p.m.

Figure 12–2
A news release should always answer these key questions: Who? What? Where? When? Why? ***What is missing from the above example?***

Figure 12–3

Examples of Sales Promotion

Examples of sales promotion include the following:

2. Premiums.

Premiums are anything of value that a customer receives in addition to the good or service purchased. They include coupons and gifts. Premiums can be used to attract new customers or build loyalty among existing customers.

1. Displays.

Window, showroom, point-of-purchase, and exterior displays all increase buyer awareness. While many displays are designed in-house, others are put together by manufacturers and wholesalers.

3. Rebates.

Many companies give rebates (return part of the purchase price) as an incentive for customers to purchase their products. Rebates are available for software, computers, and many other types of goods.

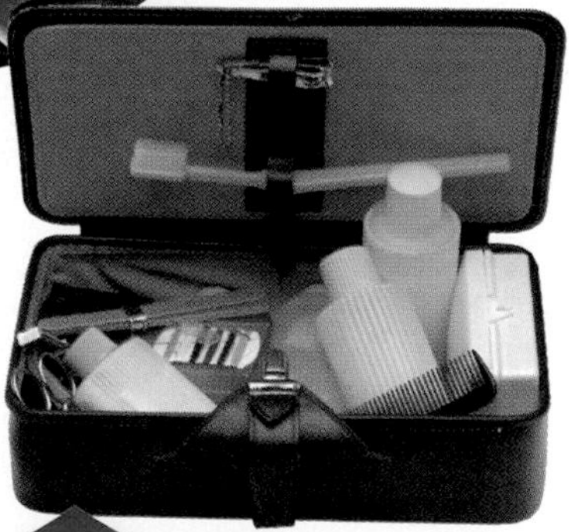

5. Sweepstakes and Contests.

Sweepstakes and contests are games used by businesses to get customers thinking and talking about what the company has to offer. Sweepstakes are simple games of chance. Contests require the customer to do something to win.

4. Samples.

Free trial-size and travel-size packages are particularly useful in introducing new products. Such samples can be distributed by mail, door-to-door, or handed out in retail stores. Soap manufacturers, pharmaceutical companies, and publishers use this technique.

Sales Promotion

Sales promotion involves the use of incentives or activities to stimulate traffic or sales. Examples are shown in **Figure 12–3**.

Personal Selling

Personal selling consists of oral presentations to one or more potential buyers with the intent of making a sale. Personal selling is most often designed to bring the sale to a close after advertising, publicity, or sales promotions have attracted the customer.

Promotional Decisions

As you make your decisions about promotions, keep your target market in mind and ask yourself the following questions.

- What will be my message or theme?
- What kind of advertising media should I use?
- What public relations efforts and publicity activities should I plan?
- What sales promotion devices and activities are appropriate?
- Will I use personal selling? How?
- How will my promotional activities be coordinated?

CHECK YOUR UNDERSTANDING — SECTION 12.1

Reviewing Key Terms and Concepts

1. What objectives can be accomplished through pre-opening promotional plans? Through ongoing plans?
2. When should pre-opening promotion begin?
3. What are five options that can be used in a promotional mix?

Critical Thinking Activity

Develop a pre-opening promotional plan for your proposed business. Then, develop a promotional plan for your first six weeks of operation.

Extension Lab—Creative Thinking Skills

Swap Shop You own a used CD shop where customers can buy and swap music CDs. As part of your promotional plan for this year, you've decided to advertise on the radio. After selecting the radio station based on the target market you wish to reach, you are ready to produce the commercial.

Role Play Working in teams of three or four, complete the following exercise.

- Create a 30-second radio commercial for the CD Swap Shop.
- In addition to the product and service you offer, be sure to include your location, phone number, hours you are open, and any other important information.
- Record and play the commercial for the class.

What you'll learn

- how to develop a promotional budget
- options for carrying out your promotional plans
- sources of assistance for implementing your promotional plans
- how to optimize your sales force
- techniques for improving the results of advertising and publicity
- advantages of sales promotion to stimulate sales
- the process of reviewing and revising your promotion strategy

Why it's important

Budgeting and promoting go hand in hand. They ensure that you don't overspend and that you get the best return on your promotional dollars.

KEY TERMS

industry average
cooperative advertising
advertising agencies
consumer pretests

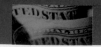

Budgeting and Implementing Promotional Plans

BUDGETING FOR PROMOTION

How can you create a promotions budget a new venture with no prior plan or sales figures? You must arrive at a budgeting estimate.

Cost Out Promotional Activities

Once you have decided on your promotional mix, you can determine the cost. You can obtain advertising rates from the media. Sales promotion items are unique. To figure out their costs you must contact whoever is going to produce the promotional pieces.

Publicity your business gets from community or other events will not cost you anything. However, the event itself probably will. Grand openings, sneak previews, or press conferences can be expensive. Figure in those costs if you are planning to use this option.

Finally, if you hire an agency or consultant to handle all or part of your promotion, you will need to budget for the fees. Personal

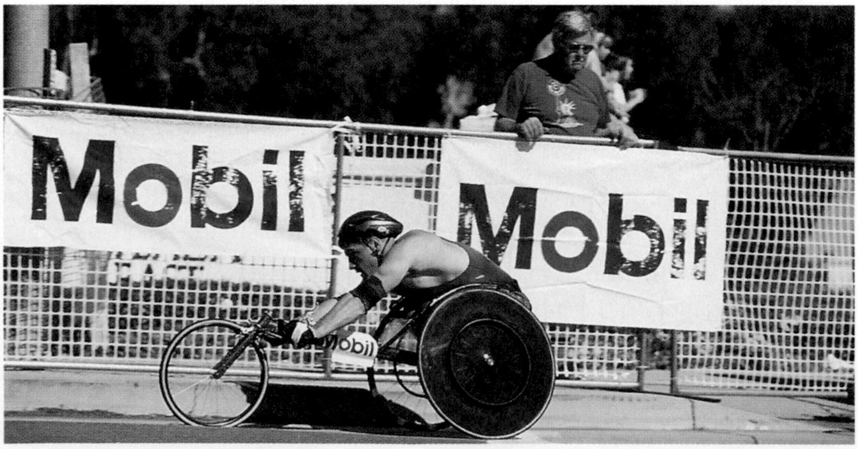

selling staff and sales training are not included in your promotional budget. These costs are part of your operating expenses.

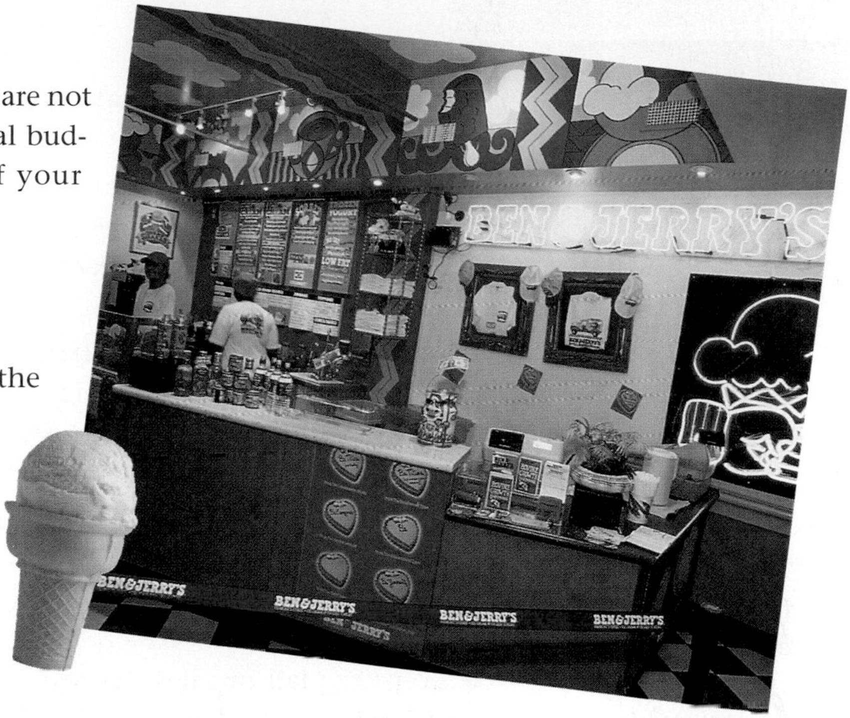

Compare Industry Averages

After you have found out the prices for all the parts in your proposed mix, you can calculate its cost. Then contact trade associations, business publications, the SBA, or business owners in the field to find out the **industry average** (the standard used to compare costs) for promotional expenses. The figure is usually expressed as a percentage of sales.

Many non–clothing-related businesses sell T-shirts to their customers. ***What are some advantages?***

Make Final Adjustments

The industry figures will help you measure your estimate. If the difference between the two figures is large, you might want to reexamine and adjust your mix. If the difference is small, you probably have a realistic budget and mix.

CARRYING OUT YOUR PLANS

When it is time to put your promotional plans into action, you—or someone you hire—will have to prepare and place ads, generate publicity, and create sales promotion pieces. If personal selling is part of your mix, you may also need sales training.

Doing It Yourself

As you complete your promotional budget, you may choose to carry out the plan yourself. With desktop publishing, it's easy for a small business to make professional-looking ads and flyers. The same is true with some commercials for the radio.

Getting Help

You can also hire professional help. The cost of professional help can vary from a no-fee arrangement to a sizeable percentage

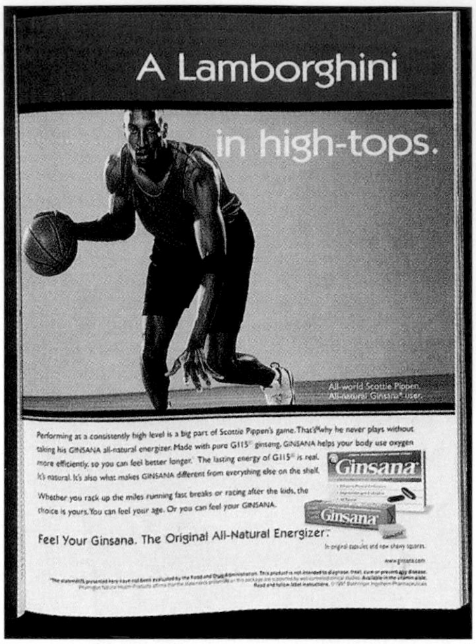

A Lamborghini
in high-tops.
All-world Scottie Pippen.
All-natural Ginsana® user.
Performing at a consistently high level is a big part of Scottie Pippen's game. That's why he never plays without taking his GINSANA all-natural energizer. Made with pure G115® ginseng, GINSANA helps your body use oxygen more efficiently, so you can feel better longer. The lasting energy of G115® is real. It's natural. It's also what makes GINSANA different from everything else on the shelf.
Whether you rack up the miles running fast breaks or racing after the kids, the choice is yours. You can feel your age. Or you can feel your GINSANA.
Ginsana
Ginsana
Feel Your Ginsana. The Original All-Natural Energizer.

Cooperative advertisements include both the manufacturer's name or brand name along with the name of a local advertiser. ***How do manufacturers and retailers benefit from such an arrangement?***

of your promotional budget. The range depends on the services.

Media. All the major advertising media—television, radio, newspapers, and magazines—have advertising departments. To encourage advertising, they will often help businesses make ads.

Manufacturers and Suppliers. In cooperative advertising, suppliers or manufacturers of goods that a business sells agree to share advertising costs.

Agencies. Advertising agencies are companies that can handle all phases of advertising. They write copy, create artwork, choose media, and produce ads or commercials. Agencies typically receive a 15 percent discount on the price of an ad.

POSSIBLE PROMOTION CHANGES

If your sales aren't meeting your goals, change your strategies. There are many ways to adjust your promotional mix.

Making the Most of Your Advertising Dollar

If a campaign isn't working, you'll want to change it as quickly as possible. Most advertising problems stem from using the wrong media or bad timing.

You can gauge your advertising's effectiveness in a number of ways. In consumer pretests, a panel of consumers evaluates an ad before it runs. You can also get feedback on your advertising from your customers. Watch for the sales results. You can also hire advertising researchers such as the Arbitron Ratings Company. These companies can provide the numbers and demographics of viewers, listeners, or readers for different media.

Capitalizing on Publicity Opportunities

Community-based activities are opportunities for publicity. Donate equipment to a trash cleanup. Sponsor a Little League team. Involvement in your community gains attention and builds customer loyalty for your business.

Stimulating Sales

No matter how well you plan your promotions, sales may not move. How can you jump-start sales? You could use sales promotions. Displays, premiums, sweepstakes, contests, rebates, and samples build interest in your products.

Good personal selling can also help. Chapter 13 will give guidelines for effectively recruiting, training, and overseeing this part of your promotion strategy.

REVISING THE PROMOTION STRATEGY

Review your promotion plan on a regular schedule. This may be as often as quarterly or semiannually. Steps include:

- Acquiring a sales forecast for the upcoming period.
- Arriving at a promotional budget.
- Deciding on a revised promotional mix.

When revising your promotional mix, look at your market research, previous plans, and recent short-term decisions.

Once you've determined your mix, revise your promotional plan. Revisions to the promotional plan should be consistent with your marketing objectives and strategies.

CHECK YOUR UNDERSTANDING

SECTION 12.2

Reviewing Key Terms and Concepts

1. What are the advantages and disadvantages of hiring an advertising agency?
2. List two ways to improve sales-force results.
3. Describe two techniques for determining if your advertising is effective.

Critical Thinking Activity

Develop a calendar and a guidesheet for reviewing and revising the promotional plan for your proposed business.

Extension Lab – Acquiring and Evaluating Data

Nike Knows Recently, the Nike swoosh has taken a nosedive. Profits are down and so are the company's stock prices. The reason: the disclosure that workers in Asian sweatshops earn as little as 80 cents per day stitching together athletic shoes for Americans to wear. In order to combat its image problem, Nike has reduced the use of the swoosh in commercials and removed it from its corporate letterhead. The swoosh is being replaced with an inconspicuous, lower-case "nike."

Research:

- What else can Nike do to try and change its image?
- Why have critics attacked Nike and avoided the competitors such as Reebok and Adidas?

CHAPTER 12 REVIEW

CHAPTER SUMMARY

- Promotional plans, whether pre-opening or ongoing, should provide the following information: a brief description; specific media placement; submit dates; scheduled date of run or release; number of runs; copies; or items, costs, and rationale.
- Promotional strategies can vary, even in the same market.
- Consider your target market, promotional mix, and costs when creating your promotional strategy.
- Advertising is the paid presentation of ideas, goods, or services directed toward a mass audience by an identified sponsor. There are two types: print and broadcast.
- Publicity is the free placement of newsworthy items about your company or product in the media.
- Examples of sales promotions include displays, premiums, sweepstakes, contests, rebates, and sample giveaways.
- You can determine the cost of your promotional activities once you have decided on your promotional mix.
- Your promotional mix might need adjusting if your advertising is not generating results, your sales need a boost, or you need to increase productivity of your existing sales force.

RECALL KEY TERMS

Create a promotional strategy for a brand new candy bar being introduced to the market. Use the following terms in your plan and be creative.

image
preselling
campaign
promotional mix
advertising
specialty items
publicity
news releases
public relations
premiums
rebates
sweepstakes
industry average
cooperative advertising
advertising agencies
consumer pretests

RECALL KEY CONCEPTS

1. Why is a pre-opening promotional plan important to a new business?
2. What are the objectives of an ongoing promotional plan?
3. Why is it important to refocus on your target market when developing your promotional strategy?
4. How are advertising and publicity similar? How are they different?
5. Is it possible to have a promotional mix that consists of one technique? Why or why not?
6. What kind of audience is the newspaper particularly effective in reaching? radio? the Internet?
7. Describe three examples of sales promotion.
8. How are budgets for promotional plans developed when the business is brand new?
9. What are the steps you should follow when reviewing your promotional plan? What resources should you use to revise that plan if necessary?

CHAPTER 12 REVIEW

THINK CRITICALLY

1. Which type of promotional activity is most cost–effective? Why?
2. Is it possible to have more than one "best" promotional mix? Explain.
3. Compare and contrast print versus broadcast advertising.
4. Can promotion done by a small business owner be as effective as promotion done by professionals? Why or why not?
5. Give an example of a product you purchased recently that was promoted by each of the following methods:
   - Television
   - Radio
   - Direct mail
   - Point-of-purchase
   - Sample

CONNECT ACADEMICS TO THE WORKPLACE

Math

1. You have created a newspaper ad whose dimensions are 1 column by 12 inches (or 12 column inches). You want the ad to run every week during your first quarter of operation. The newspaper has given you three pricing options:
   - A series of single runs at a rate of $19.69 per column inch
   - A 13-week contract requiring you run the ad 13 times in 13 weeks at a rate of $16.06 per column inch
   - A "bulk rate" contract requiring you to purchase a minimum of 150 column inches a year at $15.16 per column inch.

   Which is your best option in terms of cost?

Writing

2. Write a news release about the grand opening activities of your new business. Make the news release about one page in length. Who would you send it to? Why?

WORK IN YOUR COMMUNITY

The business you have owned for several years has reported declining sales during the last quarter. Develop a promotional plan to improve the situation. Include the following:

- Objectives
- Your promotional mix
- Budget

LINK SCHOOL TO CAREER

Contact the media (at least three) you plan to use for advertising your business. Obtain information about:

- Rates
- Services they provide

Write a summary of your results and compile your findings with those of your class.

*inter*NET CONNECTION

Banner Mania

Since your business target market uses the Internet on a regular basis, you decide to create an Internet banner to advertise your business.

Connect

Using a variety of search engines, research and develop your own banner.

- Find five banners on the Web
- Evaluate their design and effectiveness
- Design your banner. If possible, use a paint or drawing software program.

CHAPTER 13

The Promotion Strategy: Developing and Managing Sales

Learning Objectives

When you have completed this chapter, you will be able to:

- **Determine** the type of salespeople needed by your organization
- **Coordinate** training for your salespeople
- **Identify** components of sales planning for your organization
- **Explain** how to direct sales operations
- **Describe** the aspects of evaluating sales performance

You're the Boss!

Tough Beans

Last week, you completed preliminary planning for your home-made chili business. Now that you have begun to gather data on supermarkets' buying procedures, you see a dilemma. It is apparent that you are going to have to use *salespeople* to call on buyers for supermarket chains rather than sending flyers.

What Will You Do? What kind of salespeople do you hire and how will you train them?

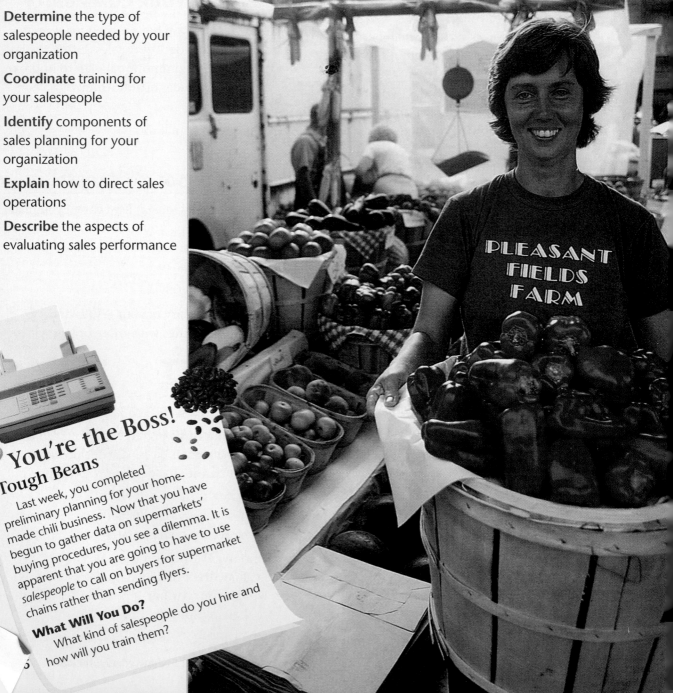

SECTION 13.1

Organizing and Preparing a Sales Force

STAFFING THE SALES FORCE

One of the most common ways that businesses sell goods or services is through *personal selling.* Personal selling is the oral presentation made by a salesperson to help a customer make a buying decision. This is most helpful when customers are purchasing something that requires detailed information. For example, most people need assistance when buying a large appliance, an item involving new technology, or real estate.

Who should do your selling? First, you have to determine what kind of salesperson you need. The types of sales jobs and the requirements to fill them vary greatly. A salesperson who calls on a group of retail stores has a very different job from a manufacturer's rep who calls on wholesalers. Both jobs are different from that of a sales clerk in a retail or service business. It's important to define a position before you fill it.

Sales are classified into two groups: *order getting* and *order taking.* Order getting is sometimes called "creative selling." It involves seeking out buyers and giving them a well-organized presentation. Getting orders is necessary when customers are not aware that they need a product. Many people will go to a vacation resort or add home improvements only when they discover what's available. Selling highly technical products or complex services also requires order getting.

Many order-getting positions involve calling on customers. Others can be found in retail stores where customers require sales assistance. For example, a family buying its first computer may seek help. They'll want to select the computer with the functions and features that are right for them.

What you'll learn

- the role of personal selling in your business
- the difference between order getting and order taking
- how to provide sales training
- the steps involved in the buying process
- the steps involved in the selling process

Why it's important

By thoroughly preparing your salespeople, you will maximize their effectiveness. This is true no matter what background and experience they bring to the job.

KEY TERMS

personal selling
order getting
order taking
customer benefits
rational buying motives
emotional buying motives
buying process
prospecting

In contrast, order taking is the completion of a sale to a customer who has sought out a product. Retail clerks who stand by cash registers and sales representatives who call on retail stores take orders. They do little creative selling. Delivery people also take orders, but their primary function is to deliver products. Their selling responsibility is secondary.

Besides determining the type of selling your people will do, you need to determine what traits you want in your sales people. Some desirable sales traits, identified by professional buyers, include the following:

- Knowledge
- Organization
- Follow-through
- Punctuality
- Energy
- Empathy
- Promptness
- Ability to solve problems
- Willingness to work hard
- Honesty

It's important to hire someone with the traits you want. You can teach skills to a person with good traits. Hiring a skilled person and trying to impart good traits is not so easy.

PROVIDING SALES TRAINING

Whether your salespeople are new or experienced, you will have to provide training. Your program must prepare them to sell and teach them the buying and selling processes for your business.

Up & Coming Entrepreneur

Real Estate Entrepreneur

"I opened my own office in 1992 because of the potential for higher profitability," says Brian Wilson, owner of Alpha Omega Real Estate. Wilson got started by making a plan and executing it. He found office space and decided to entice real estate agents to work for him by hiring them as employees and eliminating the usual commission-only pay structure. "It's more of a team environment this way. My agents have the security of a paycheck and the benefit of a bonus when they make a sale."

Analyze **Why might a salesperson's performance be affected by pay structure?**

Figure 13–1

Product Knowledge

A salesperson must be knowledgeable about his or her product on at least three levels:

1. The benefits to the customer.

Just knowing a product's features is not enough. A salesperson should be able to describe the features as benefits to the customer. Customer benefits are the advantages or personal satisfaction that customers will get from the product. People buy products for their benefits.

2. The details about the company and its products.

Sales trainees must be familiar with the goods or services they are selling. The more complex the product, the more training they will need.

3. The competition's products.

Salespeople must also be familiar with the competition. They should be able to tell customers the advantages of their products over the competition's.

Preparing to Sell

Before a salesperson is ready to sell a product, he or she must be knowledgeable about it. The individual should know the following information:

1. Company Knowledge. Sales trainees should understand a company's background, goals, organization, policy, and procedures. They must also understand its values and interests.

2. Product Knowledge. What does a salesperson need to know about your product? To be effective, he or she must be familiar with several things. These are listed in **Figure 13–1**.

Money Matters

NET INCOME

Establishing a Web site brought in new business for many entrepreneurs. Robert Atallah of Cedarlane Foods Inc. has been happy with the cyber-experience:

"The exposure we've gained from the Web site has enabled us to start distributing our products internationally."

3. Customer Knowledge. What should salespeople know about the customers? Salespeople need to know how to identify and meet the different personalities and needs of customers. They also need to be familiar with the company's typical customers and be able to figure out their buying motives.

Customers may have rational or emotional motives for making a purchase. Rational buying motives are conscious decisions for making a purchase. They are based on fact. Factors may include the following:

- Product dependability
- Time or money savings
- Convenience
- Comfort
- Safety issues
- Service
- Quality

Emotional buying motives are feelings the buyer associates with the product. Feelings may include the following:

- Social approval
- Recognition
- Power
- Prestige

Train salespeople to match the product to the customer's motivation.

Customers salespeople meet can be at varying stages of buying readiness. One may be a decided customer, who knows what he or she wants. Another may be an undecided

ENTREPRENEURS INTERNATIONAL

Sweden

Lennart Lundberg launched LINO in 1987. LINO sells games that assist the physically challenged. His products also help arthritis patients, the elderly, and those recuperating from surgery. Lundberg has developed simple items such as a box containing brightly colored pegs that can actually test a patient for strength, perception, and thinking ability. He also sells "throwing tubes" that judge hand-eye coordination, and an aquatic chair that assists with rehabilitation and provides recreation for the disabled.

Apply **How might LINO target end users, retailers and professional institutions differently when marketing its product?**

customer who is unsure. Casual lookers, or information gatherers, don't intend to buy yet.

Customers may also exhibit different dispositions during the sales contact. They can be talkative or silent. They can be impulsive or procrastinating, suspicious or trusting. Train salespeople to quickly recognize the customer's buying stage and mood.

New salespeople must also be trained to recognize your company's customers. Customers may come into your business regularly, or they may be clients who are called on by your salespeople. Each will have his or own set of interests and concerns.

4. Foundational Skills for Selling. Sales training must include a variety of foundational skills. Time management is an important skill, especially for sales representatives who are on the road. Legal knowledge is important, especially when it comes to issues of product liability and false promotion. Depending on your product, there may be a number of additional skills required.

The Buying Process

In preparation for selling, the sales trainee must also understand the *buying process*. The buying process is the series of mental steps that a customer goes through when making a purchase. Sales activities should take the customer through that process. From a sales perspective, there are four phases of buying:

- Getting the prospective buyer's attention
- Developing an interest in the product
- Creating a desire to have the product
- Getting the customer to buy the product

Certain selling jobs require foundational skills. ***What are some foundational skills needed to sell real estate?***

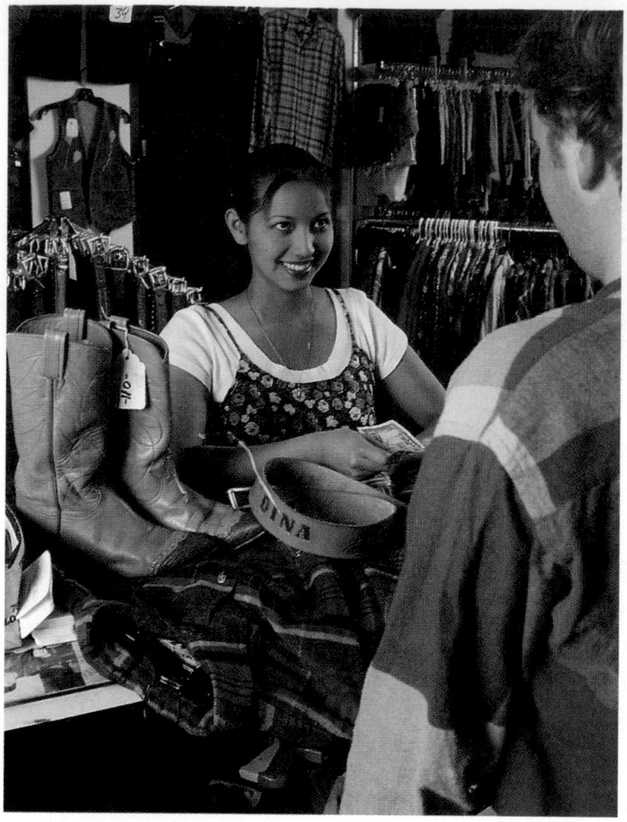

Order takers close out sales when the customer is ready to buy. ***What steps of the selling process can they take?***

The Selling Process

There are ten steps in the complete selling process. Almost every sale involves those steps. In order-getting, the salesperson usually carries out all the steps. In order taking, many of the steps will have been taken before the customer and salesperson meet. Even so, order takers will be more effective if they know the steps of the selling process:

1. *Prospecting.* Prospecting entails looking for new customers. Present customers, public records, or surveys can give referrals. Prospects can be found through "cold canvassing," making contacts without leads.
2. *Pre-approach.* Prior to the sales contact, research the potential customers. Gather information about their needs and wants. What products are they currently using? Are they satisfied? Why or why not?
3. *Approach.* This is the salesperson's first contact with the customer. The salesperson must keep several points in mind. First, he or she should make a friendly and professional impression. Second, he or she should foster open communication. Finally, credibility must be built. These steps are important, whether the customer is coming into the business or the salesperson is calling on the customer. In either case, they must be carefully planned to get the customer's attention, interest, and trust.
4. *Determining needs.* The salesperson must listen carefully and ask questions to determine the customer's wants and needs.
5. *Presentation.* This is an actual demonstration or presentation of the product to the customer. The benefits to the prospective customers, in terms of meeting their needs, are emphasized. If possible, customers should try out the product. This will enable them to feel ownership and to see how it works.
6. *Overcoming objections.* Customers may voice objections during the presentation. A good salesperson anticipates these objections. He or she will use them as opportunities to provide additional information about the product.

7. *Closing the sale.* To complete the process, the salesperson must ask for the sale. Often it is necessary to attempt a number of trial closes to get the sale. Questions such as "Will this be cash or charge?" or "When would you want delivery?" are examples of closing techniques. It's important not to be pushy.
8. *Suggestion selling.* Once it is apparent that the customer is going to buy, suggest additional items that go with the product. If a customer is buying a suit, the retail salesperson may suggest a shirt and tie that go with it.
9. *Closing techniques.* Closing mechanics vary with the sales situation. They may involve writing up the order when order-getting. When order-taking, they may involve wrapping the merchandise and ringing up the sale.
10. *Follow-up.* The sale isn't over until the salesperson is sure the customer is satisfied with the purchase. Following up might entail making sure that delivery and installation were carried out effectively. It might also include contacting the customer to make sure that he or she is happy with the purchase. Follow-up contacts can lead to additional sales. They can also lead to a long-term relationship with a customer.

CHECK YOUR UNDERSTANDING

SECTION 13.1

Reviewing Key Terms and Concepts

1. Which would be the most appropriate type of salespeople for your operation, order takers or order getters? Why?
2. What knowledge and skills do salespeople need to be able to sell?
3. What are the steps in the buying and selling processes?

Critical Thinking Activity

Write a training plan and schedule for the sales staff of your proposed business.

Extension Lab—Speaking and Listening Skills

Car Show Your uncle has just offered you a sales position in his used car dealership. During the next two weeks, you'll be attending sales training seminars where you will learn about the buying and selling process.

Role Play Practice your personal selling skills in a variety of scenarios dealing with a prospective customer who:

- Is "just looking"
- Is looking for a car that is reliable, yet inexpensive
- Doesn't trust car salespeople

Planning, Directing and Evaluating Sales

What you'll learn

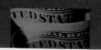

- the steps involved in sales planning
- the steps in implementing and maintaining a sales force
- how to evaluate a company's sales performance
- how to evaluate salespeople

Why it's important

Effective sales operations are developed through careful planning, directing, and controlling.

KEY TERMS

sales call reports
sales forecast
sales quota

MANAGING SALES

Before putting your new sales force to work, you must plan your sales. After that be ready to implement and direct your sales operation. Even then, you're not done: You have to evaluate your sales performance constantly to improve the process. Planning, implementing, directing, evaluating, and improving are part of managing sales.

Sales operations differ with the type of business and size of operation. As the number of people involved in your sales operation grows, the nature of your sales operation may change, too. Much of this section will apply to all sales operations. Some may apply only in order-getting situations. All of it will pertain to the sales operations that affect your business.

Directing Sales Operations

One of your jobs as a sales manager is to implement and maintain an effective sales staff. This involves five main tasks:

1. **Motivating Your Salespeople.** The most effective salespeople are the motivated ones. It's up to the manager to determine a good combination of motivators. Financial incentives are important to all salespeople. You may give bonuses to those who reach pre-set goals. Nonfinancial rewards such as plaques, pins, trophies, and certificates are important, too. Achievement-oriented salespeople will value the recognition of their accomplishments. Motivational sales meetings, contests, and just letting salespeople know when they are doing a good job can help as well.
2. **Compensating Your Sales Staff.** To attract and keep the best sales staff, design your pay plan to compete with other companies. There are three types of payment for salespeople. The first is straight salary, in which a salesperson is paid a specified amount for a certain period of time no matter how many sales he or she makes. A second is straight commission, in which payment is based on sales alone. The third is to combine the two. A salary is paid and sales are rewarded. Most plans fall into this third category. Whichever payment style you choose, make sure it is easy to understand and implement.

Companies usually pay for their salespeople's travel costs and expenses. ***What are some costs incurred doing business out of the office?***

3. **Handling Expenses and Transportation.** Typically, salespeople who are in the field (and away from their homes) are reimbursed for their food, lodging, and travel expenses. To keep track of their expenditures, they keep receipts for items such as business meals, hotel rooms, and plane fare. These expenses must be explained on paper, or itemized, to make sure the costs are reasonable.

   If travel expenses are too high, you may want to consider alternatives. For example, leasing a company car may be less expensive than paying for miles that your salespeople drive. (Companies typically pay 32¢ per mile driven for business purposes.) Making phone calls from your workplace may be

RISK TAKERS PROFIT MAKERS

Name: Michael Graves
Company: Graves Design
City, State: Princeton, NJ

Designing Profits

Michael Graves's designs are famous for their distinctive look. This renowned architect is best known for designing the Walt Disney World Swan and Dolphin Hotels and the Humana Building in Louisville, Kentucky.

Yet Graves does not restrict himself to architecture alone. He also designed a stainless steel tea kettle that has sold more than one million units since 1985. In fact, Graves has designed more than 100 household items, from tabletop kitchen items to clocks, and continues his relationship with Disney by designing numerous consumer goods. Each contains subtle hints of Mickey Mouse. He now displays these wares among 500 other products in a small retail store and mail-order catalog through his own company, Graves Designs.

Thinking Critically

What reasons might Graves have for selling his wares in both a retail store and a mail-order catalog?

less expensive and just as effective as making a sale in person. These decisions will depend on the size and nature of your operation.

4. **Supervising Your Sales Force.** The goals of sales-force supervision are to increase sales and reduce costs. Reaching those goals requires training the sales staff. It also requires setting sales policies and monitoring sales-force activities to make sure that they are consistent with sales objectives.

   You can use several techniques to supervise a sales staff. Some methods are the following:

   - *Personal contact.* When you personally visit salespeople, you can assist with sales problems and training.
   - *Client/Account reporting.* Sales call reports provide a means of monitoring and evaluating outside sales activities. On these reports, salespeople record and report information such as the number of calls made, orders

taken, miles traveled, days worked, new prospects contacted, and new accounts sold.

- *Electronic communications*. You can maintain contact with salespeople through electronic communications. The telephone conversations, facsimiles, voice mail, and E-mail provide some opportunities to maintain contact.
- *Meetings*. Motivational sales meetings mentioned earlier can also serve a supervisory purpose. They can be used for training, information dissemination, and problem solving.

5. **Maintaining Morale.** Having a high level of morale is an important factor in a sales staff's success. High morale can be brought about by the following:
   - a positive work climate
   - the salesperson's satisfaction with his or her work
   - productive interaction with other members of the sales staff

   Your job is to facilitate these conditions.

Sales Planning

Sales planning is tied directly to a company's marketing plan. Therefore, sales planning starts with determining market potential and making sales forecasts.

Sales Forecasting. When you made your marketing plan, you made a market analysis. This included an estimation of your share of the market. Your sales forecast is tied to that estimate; it is an estimate of sales for a specified period.

When you start a new business, you have to rely on your market analysis and industry information for forecasting. After you are in operation, you will have other sources. They include customers, sales staff, sales records, and your capacity to deliver.

Sales Budgeting. You need three basic budgets for your sales activities. These include the following:

- *Sales budget*. The sales budget is developed from the sales forecast. It includes expected sales of each item in the product line.
- *Selling expense budget*. This estimates the costs of personal selling activities.
- *Administrative sales costs budget*. The administrative costs for managing the operation are budgeted separately.

Combined with the sales forecast, these budgets can give you criteria for judging performance. If sales are below budget, you can

Tips from the Real World

CONFIDENCE

Confidence and honesty are the basis of a good sales presentation. Allan Gibby of Dynacom Productions recounts the sale that got his business off and running:

"*When I went into that first [sales] presentation, I was petrified . . . but I figured I was just going to be myself and not build up a scenario that was bigger than it really was.*"

determine the cause and take steps to increase them. Similarly, if costs are above budget, you can look for ways to control them.

By handling mail orders, an entrepreneur can do business in a wide area without sending out salespeople. ***What are some costs of this technique?***

Establishing Territories. If all your sales are handled from inside your workplace, sales territories are not needed. Everyone comes to you or calls you. Even if you handle sales outside, territories may not be needed if you have just a few salespeople in a local market. However, if your market covers a wide area, setting territories would be beneficial. No place will be forgotten and no place will be served more than once.

Establishing territories is a three-step process. The first step is to determine the probable areas. That might be cities, counties, states, or other divisions. The next step is to determine the sales potential or time needed to cover the proposed territories. The final step is to make adjustments and decide on the boundaries. Once territories are established, you can assign salespeople.

Setting Sales Quotas. A sales quota is a goal assigned to a salesperson for a specific period. Whether or not such goals are met will indicate the strength or weakness of your sales operation. They also provide incentives for your sales force. With a number to aim for, a salesperson can measure his or her effectiveness. He or she knows what it takes to earn a bonus—or what is unacceptable.

There are three general approaches to setting quotas for a starting business. Quotas can be set according to a territorial sales potential. For example, it's harder to sell iced tea in Alaska than in Hawaii. Quotas can also be set in relation to your company's total sales forecast. If a company has four sales reps, each should make about a quarter of the total sales. Quotas can be based on your judgment. However, you should be able to provide a reason for giving different quotas to different salespeople.

After your business is in operation, there is a final approach: to use past sales as a guide. Make quotas realistic, objective, and fair.

Evaluating Sales Performance

The final step in managing your sales operation is to evaluate sales performance. Sales performance can be seen from two perspectives. There is a company's perspective and a salesperson's perspective.

Evaluating the Company's Sales Performance. Evaluating the entire company's sales performance enables you to consider the effectiveness of your marketing plan and your operations. Two types of analysis are useful in this evaluation.

1. *Analysis of sales volume.* Compare your company's actual sales with its budgeted sales goals. Examine sales according to territory, products, and individual salespeople. Then compare your findings with industry averages.
2. *Marketing cost analysis* goes beyond sales volume analysis. How much does marketing cost compared to its results? Identify the unprofitable segments in marketing and sales.

Evaluating Individual Sales Performance. Formally evaluating individual sales can increase performance and lower selling costs. The procedure involves multiple steps:

1. *Establish guidelines.* Include who does the rating, when the ratings will be done, and how they will be used.
2. *Identify factors to be measured.* Quantitative (sales and number of customers assisted) and qualitative (quality of sales presentation and ethical standards) factors should be set.
3. *Compare each salesperson's performance to the standards.* Review your findings with the individual salespeople.

CHECK YOUR UNDERSTANDING — SECTION 13.2

Reviewing Key Terms and Concepts

1. Where does the sales planning process begin?
2. What motivational techniques are appropriate, especially for salespeople?
3. List the steps in establishing a procedure for evaluating salespeople.

Critical Thinking Activity

Design an evaluation form for salespeople in your proposed business.

Extension Lab—Exercising Integrity

Delivery Dilemma You co-own a business selling building supplies to contractors. Over the years, you have earned a reputation for being trustworthy. However, shipping problems have surfaced recently, and supplies are not being delivered on time. In order to continue making sales, your partner asked you not to reveal the shipping problems to your customers.

Role Play In groups of three or four people, role play a situation where a valued customer calls on you and your partner for a routine order. Be sure to consider the following:

- Should you tell your customers about the shipping problems, even though your partner asked you not to?
- Is it ethical for your partner to ask you to withhold critical information from your customers?

CHAPTER 13 REVIEW

CHAPTER SUMMARY

- Businesses use salespeople to help a customer make a buying decision.
- Sales are classified into two groups. Order getting is necessary when customers do not know they need a product. Order taking is the completion of the sale to a customer who has sought out a product.
- Effective salespeople have common traits such as organization, punctuality, and follow-through. They also need knowledge of the company, its products and customers, and selling skills.
- There are ten steps in the complete selling process. Even those salespeople who are order takers will be more effective if they understand the whole sales process.
- As a sales manager, you must be able to supervise and motivate your salespeople, compensate them adequately, handle sales expenses and transportation issues, and maintain high morale among your staff.
- Sales planning begins with determining the market potential and making sales forecasts. It is tied to a marketing plan.
- Evaluating the entire company's sales performance as well as the performance of individual salespeople is critical to the future success of the business.

RECALL KEY TERMS

Imagine you are a sales manager preparing an orientation workshop for your new sales force. Create a presentation using the key terms:

personal selling
order getting
order taking
customer benefits
rational buying motives
emotional buying motives
buying process
prospecting
sales call reports
sales forecast
sales quota

RECALL KEY CONCEPTS

1. Describe the difference between order getting and order taking.
2. What are the three levels of product knowledge a salesperson must have?
3. Why must a salesperson understand the differences between rational and emotional buying motives of customers?
4. List and briefly explain the ten steps in the selling process.
5. Describe some of the ways sales managers motivate their sales staff.
6. What techniques can be used to supervise a sales staff?
7. After your business is running, what sources are available to help you prepare an accurate sales forecast?
8. What are the three approaches to setting quotas for a business that is just beginning?
9. What procedures should a sales manager use to evaluate the sales performance of the company and the individual salesperson?

THINK CRITICALLY

1. Review the desirable sales traits listed on page 218. Which traits do you have? Do you have the traits to be a good salesperson? Explain.

CHAPTER 13 REVIEW

2. Name three products you might buy based on rational buying motives and three products you might buy based on emotional buying motives.
3. Choose a product you purchased recently from a retail store. Describe the steps in the selling process.
4. If you were a salesperson, which compensation method would you prefer? Why?
5. Compare the duties and responsibilities of a teacher with those of a sales manager.

CONNECT ACADEMICS TO THE WORKPLACE

Math

1. Jamara is paid a salary plus commission. Based on the following information, how much money did he make last month?

Salary:	$600 per month
Commission rate:	2% of sales
Sales:	$14,763.52

Serve Customers

2. Working in teams of two, role play a scenario between a salesperson and a customer. The salesperson should choose a product and describe its features as benefits to the customer. Change products and reverse the roles. Decide if you would buy each other's product.

WORK IN YOUR COMMUNITY

Choose a product you would like to sell. Prepare a sales presentation that will include the following:

- The benefits of the product
- How the product will meet the prospective customers' needs
- Potential objections that might be raised about the product
- Follow-up activities you might use to ensure that your customers are satisfied
- Share the presentation with the class.

LINK SCHOOL TO CAREER

If you are employed, observe and note techniques your manager (and other managers in the business) use to motivate employees.

- Which techniques are most effective?
- Which are the least effective?
- Compile a list of all the techniques.

If you are not employed, interview someone who is working and ask about the motivational techniques used in his or her business.

*inter*NET CONNECTION

Photo Plus

Trish is the sales manager for a company that sells framed photographs. Part of her job includes looking for new customers and repeat business. Trish has heard about electronic mailing lists being used to boost sales. She has asked for your help in providing her with additional information.

Connect

Using a variety of search engines, search the Internet for:

- Ways to set up an electronic mailing list
- Software and hardware needed
- Costs involved

Provide Trish with ideas for using her E-mail list to increase sales.

UNIT 3 LAB

Business Plan Basics

Examining and Planning Promotional Strategies

OVERVIEW

Promotional options for a business include advertising, publicity, sales promotion, and personal selling. Using these activities, entrepreneurs develop promotional plans for their businesses. They must select the right mix of activities, develop a budget, and determine ways to implement their plan. In this unit lab, you will examine and plan promotional strategies for a business.

TOOLS

- Consumer magazines
- TV and radio advertisements
- Word processor (optional)
- Graph paper or spreadsheet software

PROCEDURES

STEP A Individually or in a small group, study local promotions.

1. List the promotional activities that are used to promote that product brand.
2. Identify the similarities and differences among the different promotions. Were the similar messages, images, and spokespeople used?
3. Organize the similarities and differences using the Unit 3 worksheet, graph paper, or the table feature of a word processor.
4. Study a competing brand's promotions. Examine the similarities and differences between the two promotional campaigns. Consider messages, target markets, features, and benefits.
5. Organize the similarities and differences using the Unit 3 worksheet, graph paper, or the table feature of a word processor.
6. Now identify a small business in your community and the activities used to promote it. Compare the promotional activities used by a small business to those used for consumer products sold throughout the country.
7. Organize the similarities and differences using the Unit 3 worksheet, graph paper, or the table feature of a word processor.

STEP B

Identify promotional activities used by the following types of businesses:

- Self-storage warehouse
- Dentist office
- Department store
- Daycare center

You may want to visit local businesses or interview their owners or managers.

1. Explain why these promotional activities were appropriate for each type of business.
2. Describe why promotional activities must vary for these businesses.
3. Organize the businesses, their promotions, and their reasoning on the Unit 3 worksheet, graph paper, or the table feature of a word processor.

STEP C

Identify the promotional media available to small businesses in your community.

1. Through telephone inquiries or browsing the Internet, obtain rate sheets to identify the costs of these media.
2. Share your information with the class. On graph paper or using a spreadsheet program, develop an information sheet/rate card that lists the costs of various media in your community.

LAB REPORT

STEP D

Select a business that you might be interested in starting in the future. Examine the promotional activities used by a similar business in your community.

1. First, identify at least five promotional activities that could be used by this business.
2. Develop a three-month promotional plan for this business. Indicate what promotional activities you would use during the period.
3. Using the rate card your class previously developed, prepare a budget that indicates the cost for each promotional activity that you plan to use. Organize this using the table function of a word processor, a spreadsheet, or on graph paper.
4. Finally, prepare a one-page analysis describing why the plan you have prepared would be the most effective for this type of business. In your report, cite the findings shown in your tables and bar charts and attach them as references.

UNIT 4
MANAGING YOUR BUSINESS PROCESSES

UNIT OVERVIEW

Do you have a great business plan? Have you developed an exciting marketing idea? Do you have ambitious long-term goals? Have you wondered how you're going to execute all these plans at once? This is where business management comes in.

Management activities include organizing, planning, and controlling resources. Decisions to make range from purchasing and production to operations and staffing. Acquiring and improving your management skills will allow you to run your business smoothly and profitably.

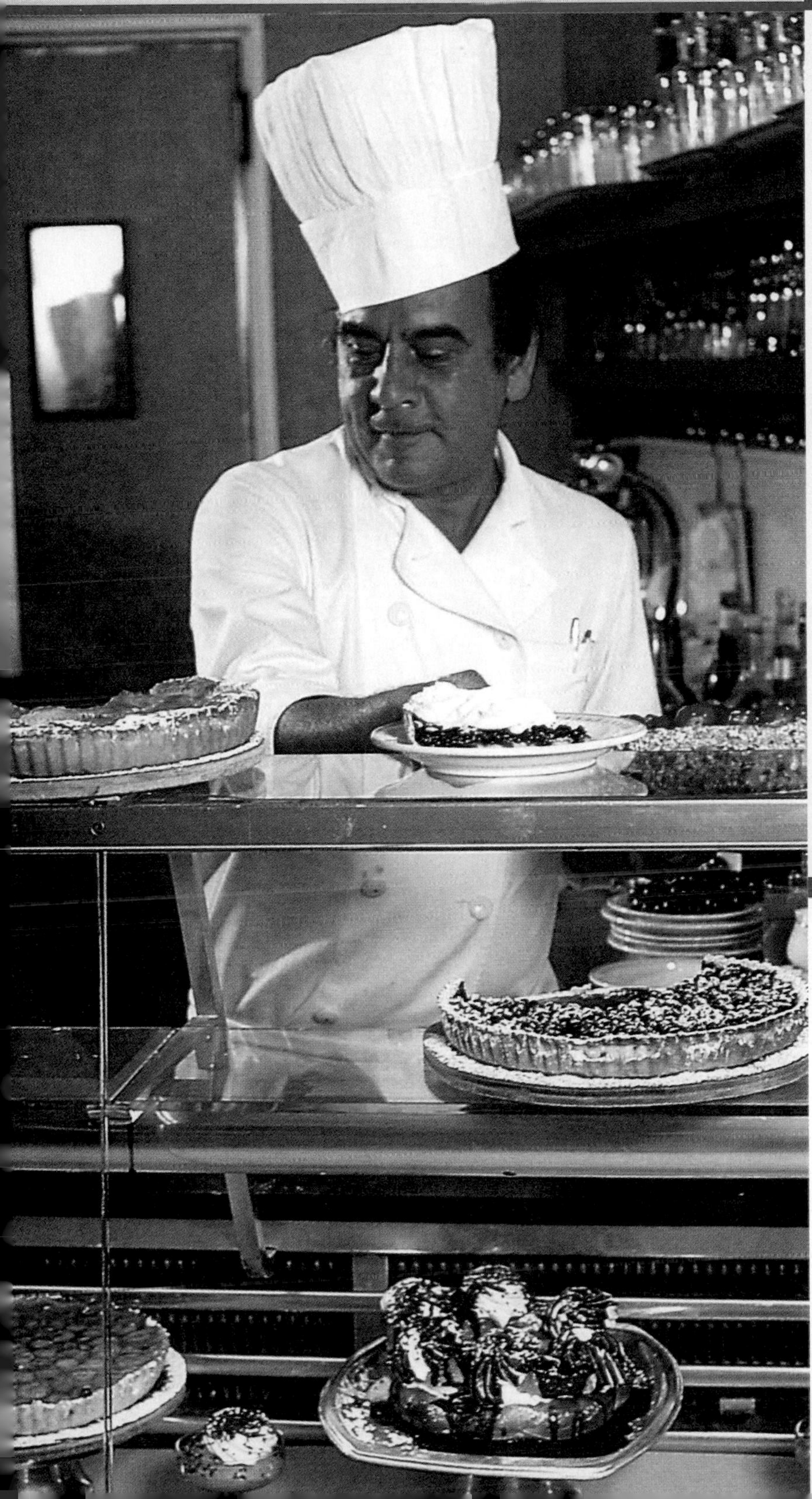

Entrepreneurship: What It Takes

What do you know about starting your own business?

1. What is a management plan?
2. What does it take to be a good manager?
3. What is purchasing management?
4. How should you keep track of inventory?
5. What steps should be taken when developing a product?
6. What is production management?
7. What operating policies do you need?
8. Where can you look for prospective employees?
9. How will you resolve employee problems?
10. What are some ways to motivate your staff?

CHAPTER 14

Preparing and Planning to Manage

Learning Objectives

When you have completed this chapter, you will be able to:

- **Distinguish** the difference between managers and entrepreneurs
- **Identify** how to manage a small business effectively
- **Choose** a leadership style option
- **Develop** office policies to keep routine business activities in check

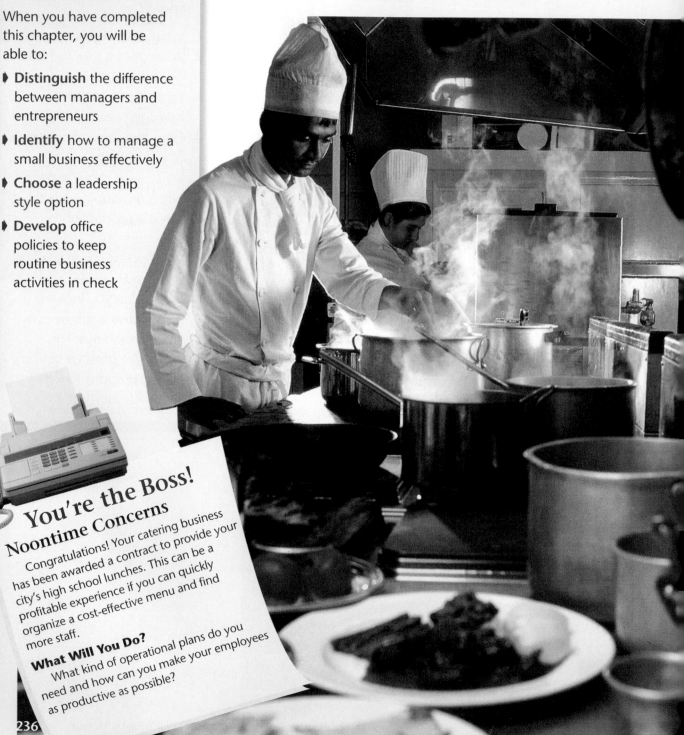

You're the Boss!

Noontime Concerns

Congratulations! Your catering business has been awarded a contract to provide your city's high school lunches. This can be a profitable experience if you can quickly organize a cost-effective menu and find more staff.

What Will You Do?

What kind of operational plans do you need and how can you make your employees as productive as possible?

SECTION 14.1

Entrepreneur or Manager?

MANAGERS, LEADERSHIP, AND TEAMWORK

As a business owner, you will look to others for assistance. The saying, *there's no I in TEAM,* means that everyone in your organization is a valuable resource. Everyone works together toward a common goal.

For example, if you are a designer, you may rely on a salesperson to let you know that your customers like short-sleeve shirts. You may rely on garment workers to create your fashions. Without an accountant, you may not know if you are making a profit.

In this section, you will look at how entrepreneurs organize their human resources and the structure of their businesses. You'll also see what it takes to be a responsible leader, an effective manager, and a respected team player.

Entrepreneur and Manager

Once you open the doors of your business, you'll be putting on a second hat. You will continue to wear the hat of the entrepreneur, but your focus will shift from starting your own business to growing and expanding it. Your second hat will be that of the *manager*. As a manager, you will coordinate on a daily basis:

- The people
- Processes
- Other resources of your operation

You will juggle these responsibilities to achieve your principal objectives—to survive and make a profit.

Even if you hire someone else to manage your business, you will still oversee the operation. For this reason, and because your operation will most likely start out small, you will probably play the role of the manager.

What you'll learn

- why an entrepreneur may also be a manager
- how to handle many different situations at the same time
- what skills are necessary to manage successfully

Why it's important

To make a profit, you'll need to coordinate the people and processes of your day-to-day operations.

KEY TERMS

manager
strategic plans
tactical plans
operational plans
quality control program
situational management
time management
conceptual skills

A manager has to handle many different kinds of situations. ***How can an entrepreneur prepare to handle so many tasks if it's his or her first business?***

Your Management Role

As a manager, you will deal with many situations, often all at once. On a given day, you might send out an order, review sales figures, revise your budget, and represent your company at a civic meeting. You might also handle a dispute between two employees, interview a job applicant, and patch up relations with a dissatisfied customer. You might spend an entire day negotiating a contract or revising short-term plans.

How do you manage so many situations and still provide your good or service? It's similar to what you now do when you hear, "Take out the garbage. Get ready for dinner. Don't forget to do your homework!" Odds are you're able to accomplish these chores when they need to get done. A good manager will develop activities, a leadership style, and skills to get through his or her tasks.

Performing Management Functions. Managers use a series of activities called management functions to achieve their goals. These functions include the following:

- Planning
- Organizing
- Directing
- Controlling

The four performing management functions are basically used in that order.

Entrepreneurs International

Argentina

Argentinean musician, Guillermo Rodriguez Pericoli, formed his PC MIDI Center in 1989. He saw that "the future of applied music technology was intimately linked to computers and MIDI," a production technique using a computer to control synthesizer output. In 1992, Pericoli opened the first commercial shop in Buenos Aires retailing MIDI equipment. Today PC MIDI Center has more than 6,500 professional and amateur musicians throughout South America as its customers.

Apply **How is Pericoli's background as a musician a particular asset in his management role as the owner of PC MIDI Center?**

Planning. The first step in managing is planning. A plan determines your business objectives or specific desired results. It also determines how you are going to reach them. There are three kinds of plans, each type narrowing broad goals into specific tasks.

- Strategic plans are *long range*. They map where you want your business to be in 3–5 years. Usually they don't include a specific target date. For example, you may want your paintball manufacturing company to be the largest in the field.
- Tactical plans are *mid-range* and focus on a period of one year or less. They consist of specific objectives with target dates. Tactical objectives help to make strategic goals a reality. You can promote your paintball company by sponsoring national contests.
- Operational plans are *short-term objectives* that help to achieve tactical plans. These routine plans also include policies, rules and regulations, and budgets for the day-to-day operation of the business. You can test the quality of your paintballs to ensure that there are no duds in any batch.

Figure 14–1 shows how these three types of planning can work together. Suppose your strategic plan is to double your paintball production capacity within the next four years. One of your tactical plans might be to complete a new paintball factory, which

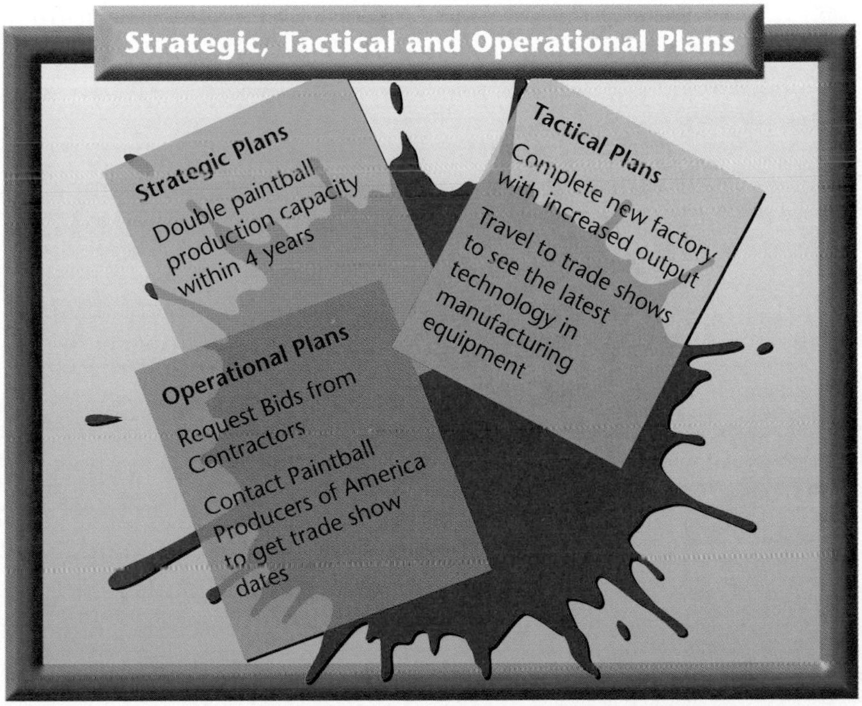

Strategic, Tactical and Operational Plans
Strategic Plans
Double paintball production capacity within 4 years
Tactical Plans
Complete new factory with increased output
Travel to trade shows to see the latest technology in manufacturing equipment
Operational Plans
Request Bids from Contractors
Contact Paintball Producers of America to get trade show dates

Figure 14–1
Strategic, tactical, and operational plans are great ways to zero in on your goals. ***How might you use these plans to assist with your studies?***

will increase output by 25 percent, by March of next year. Your operational plans would include a request for bids to be sent out to contractors for the proposed plant.

Planning is an ongoing process. Strategic and tactical plans must be reviewed at least once a year. Operational plans are done for much shorter periods, such as monthly, weekly, and daily.

Forces such as the political climate, technological advances, and the economy may require you to review your plans. For example, a new law requiring expensive safety gear may dampen your paintball company's expansion plans. Likewise, a weak economy could change your advertising campaign from party planning to low cost.

Organizing. Organizing means deciding what jobs need to get done. You will organize people to carry out your company's plans. You may hire and train new employees and assign authority and responsibility to them. Organizing also includes arranging equipment, materials, and other resources to help you reach your objectives. Setting up a chart can help you organize effectively. It can give structure to your resources.

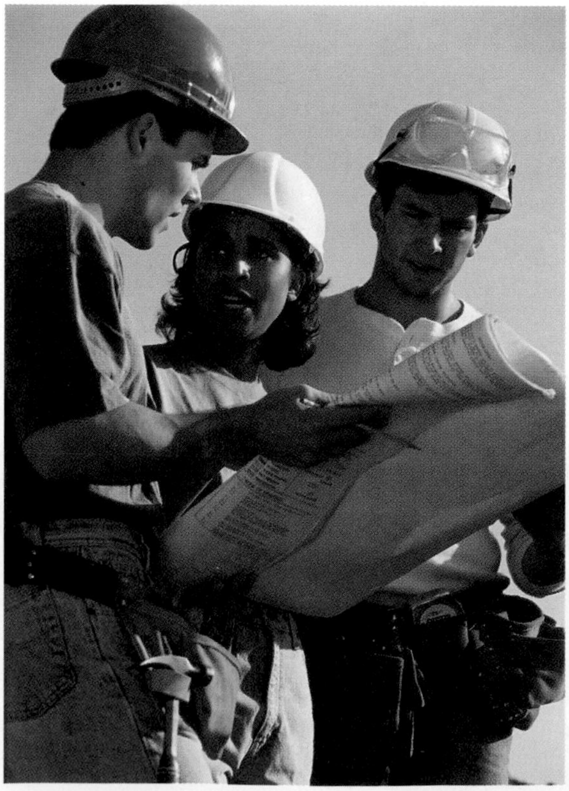

Your management role will focus on coordinating your resources. ***What type of resources might your business have?***

Directing. Employees require guidance and supervision. Directing means conveying your plans, assignments, and instructions to your employees. You will have to communicate your goals and motivate your employees to perform at their best. Effective directing also requires handling equipment, materials, and other resources.

Controlling. The final step in managing is controlling. Controlling is the process of comparing your expected results with actual performance. What can you do if there are significant differences between what you plan and what actually happens? If things aren't working out as expected, you will need to take corrective action.

Corrective action can take several forms. You might use a quality control program, a check for quality that is built into the production process to make sure products meet certain standards. You can use your budget to compare budgeted costs with actual costs. These gauges can help you replace people and resources to prevent things

Figure 14–2

Three Leadership Styles

Your choice of a leadership style can be a major factor in the success of your business. In general, there are three choices:

1. Power-oriented style.

Managers who use a power-oriented style try to maintain total control over their whole operation. This style works in large organizations and in situations where employees are untrained, inexperienced, or involved in a crisis.

2. Routine-oriented style.

Routine-oriented managers are primarily concerned with keeping the operation running smoothly rather than accomplishing other goals. This style is most appropriate in middle management in a large corporation.

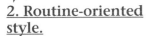

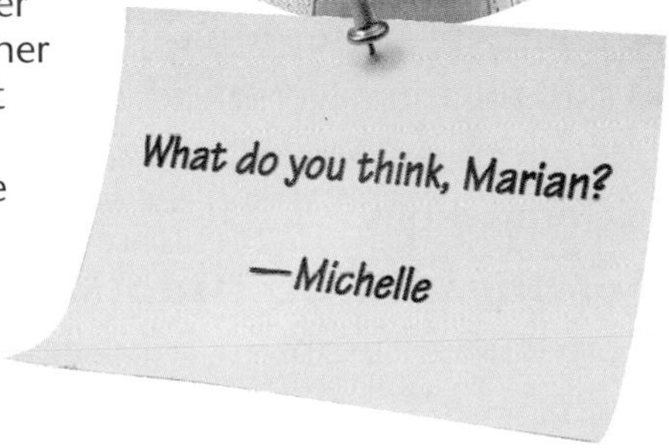
What do you think, Marian?
—Michelle

3. Achievement-oriented style.

Managers who are achievement oriented are open to new ideas and seek out employee suggestions. Achievement-oriented leadership is most effective where a manager is dealing directly with employees who are turning out work.

from going wrong in the future. Finally, you may decide to revise your goals.

Adopting a Leadership Style

Now that you know the functions of management, you need to choose a style. Leadership style is the manner in which you approach your management responsibilities. It is also a major factor in how you direct. **Figure 14–2** shows three styles of management.

Good managers are able to use whichever approach their circumstances dictate. This is called situational management. For example, you may have to take on a power-oriented approach if you are at risk of losing a major customer. Or you may have to become routine oriented in order to stabilize a part of your operation, like daily office procedures. Being flexible and able to change leadership styles is important for increasing profit.

Developing Management Skills

To manage activities successfully, you will draw on a specific set of skills. Some of these you already possess. Others can be gained through education and training. All of them can be improved with practice and experience.

Human Relations. Human relations skills help managers interact with employees, customers, and suppliers. These skills also help a manager lead and motivate employees. Human relations skills are generally considered the most important management skills. You will rely heavily on them no matter how large your operation becomes.

Communication. Communication is a foundational skill. It is essential to your effectiveness whether you are planning, organizing, directing, or controlling. You must be able to communicate to employees what you have in mind. If they don't know what you want them to do, it just won't happen.

Math. The ability to perform math computations is another foundational skill that managers need. Math is necessary for managing daily operations, evaluating business performance, and making long-range projections.

Problem Solving and Decision Making. Managers use the foundation skills of problem solving and decision making

Up & Coming Entrepreneur

Cleaning Entrepreneur

Kim Chuning began cleaning residential and commercial building interiors in her town of Orrville, Ohio. Through word-of-mouth referrals, her cleaning business tripled in one year. "It can be physically demanding, but I enjoy working my own hours. My clients are very appreciative and treat me with a lot of respect," says Chuning. She is currently considering expanding her business but worries about the reliability of possible employees.

Analyze **Kim Chuning's reputation is based on her work quality and reliability. How could she transfer her work ethic to future employees?**

frequently. Sometimes they use them to carry out planned actions. Other times they use them to handle situations that must be dealt with immediately.

Technical Skills. Technical skills involve the use of tools, equipment, procedures, and techniques that are critical to your business. In retail, technical skills would include mastery of the selling process. In food service, they would include the preparation of food. In manufacturing, they would include the operation of complex machinery. These skills ordinarily come from prior education and training. As your business grows, you may turn the management of technical aspects of your business over to supervisors that you hire.

Time Management. Managers are busy people. At any moment, they have many projects and activities in various stages of completion. In addition, they have to accomplish the objectives by a certain time. The process of allocating time effectively is called time management. **Figure 14–3** lists some useful time management techniques.

Conceptual Skills. Conceptual skills include the efficient use of thinking, reasoning, and logic. These skills help one to see the relationships among the parts of the enterprise and to visualize its future. As a small-business owner and manager, you will make day-to-day decisions against the backdrop of the bigger

Tips from the Real World

NETWORKING

Don't spend all your time in the office. Lillian Vernon, founder of the $258 million catalog company, says:

"*Time away from the business brings a fresh eye, broadens the horizon, and creates new contacts. Networking is an excellent way to find out what is going on.*"

Time Management Suggestions for Managers

1. Set and prioritize your goals.
2. Delegate work to others whenever possible.
3. Plan to spend blocks of time on specific activities that will help you achieve your goals.
4. Schedule your activities on a planning calendar.
5. Schedule your most important work for times (mornings, evenings, etc.) when you do your best work.
6. Group your activities for most efficient time use.
7. Handle or eliminate interruptions so they will take up as little time as possible.

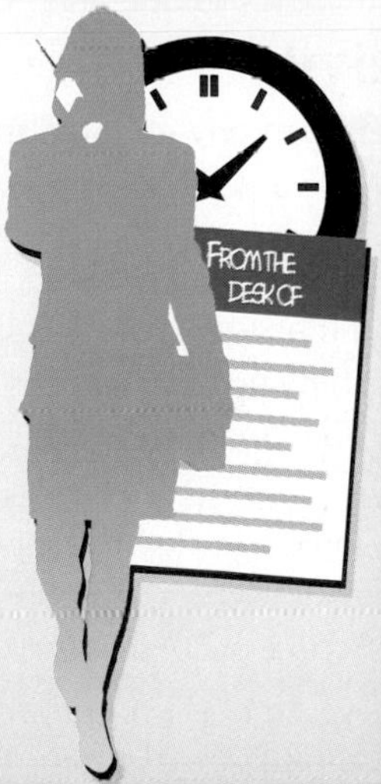

Figure 14–3
Study the time management techniques listed here. ***Why do you think they would be especially valuable to a new business owner?***

picture. Your conceptual skills will enable you to see how these decisions affect the future of your business. Conceptual skills will also help you make big decisions, such as when and how to expand your business.

No matter what business you start, management skills will help you succeed. Also, the skills you develop and experience you gain can be transferred from one business to another.

CHECK YOUR UNDERSTANDING

SECTION 14.1

Reviewing Key Terms and Concepts

1 What does a manager coordinate on a daily basis?

2 Your business needs to focus on improving sales. List possible strategic, tactical, and operational plans.

3 Are leadership styles fixed or interchangeable? Why?

Critical Thinking Activity

Choose a Risk Taker/Profit Maker from any chapter and describe which style of leadership the featured entrepreneur practices. Write a paragraph on why this style works for him or her.

Extension Lab—Leadership Skills

Out of Sync You are the owner and manager of a retail store. One of your sales clerks is always late to work, and sometimes doesn't even show up. Yet her monthly sales volume is two or three times higher than that of other salespeople. You don't want to fire this employee, but you need her to come to work every day and on time.

Role Play Demonstrate how you would handle this employee using the following leadership styles:

- Power-oriented
- Routine-oriented
- Achievement-oriented

SECTION 14.2

Management Planning

DEVELOPING A WORKING MANAGEMENT PLAN

Your original management plan included pre-opening staffing and day-to-day operating guidelines. Now you need to make the plan more organized, comprehensive, and flexible.

Designing Your Plan

A working management plan serves as a reference point for making short-term decisions. As you revise your long-range goals, you will also adjust your management plan. A working management plan includes tactical marketing objectives. These are marketing objectives that you plan to reach within one year. They provide the basis for immediate marketing decisions.

Day-to-day Operational Policies. Each day of business will be different. You will need a daily structure to stay focused on profits and survival. This daily structure will consist of routine operational policies. For example, you might allow

What you'll learn

- how a management plan can help to achieve your objectives
- what policies and activities make up a working management plan
- how to change from an average manager to an excellent one

Why it's important

You'll need an effective management plan to keep your daily business focused and your long-term goals attainable.

KEY TERMS

working management plan
tactical marketing objectives
organizational structure
total quality management

Figure 14–4
This chart shows the basic organizational structure of a new business. ***Do you think the communication channels in this business are open or closed?***

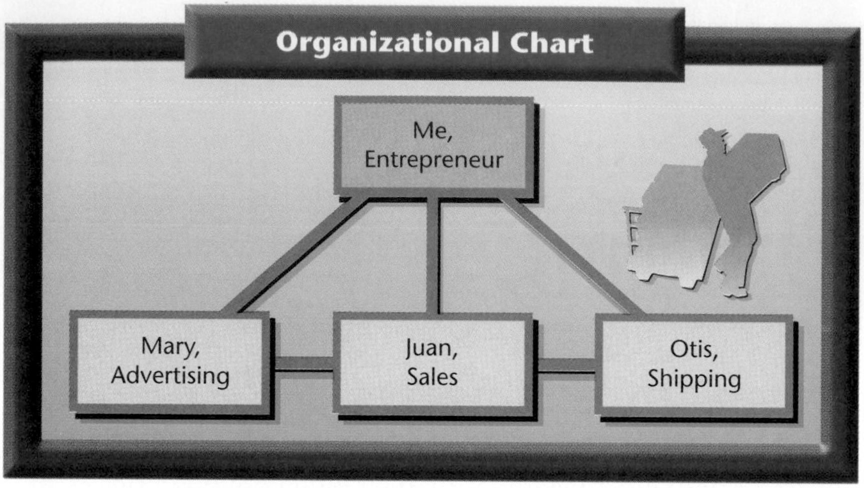

only a certain employee to handle your daily deposits. If you are a manufacturer, you may automatically shut down your plant after an accident to prevent further injuries.

Organizational Structure. Organizational structure shows how the departments in a business relate to each other. As an entrepreneur, you are the head of your organization. **Figure 14–4** shows a typical example.

The sales, shipping, and advertising departments work together closely. For example, if your advertising is effective, the sales and shipping departments will become busy handling orders. All departments will report their activity to you. At that time, you might discuss how increased sales will affect your management plan.

Hiring Policies. You will want sound policies in effect when it comes to human resources.

- *Employment resources*. To recruit the right people, you'll need to define the job, find skilled applicants, and then screen them accordingly. Will you use classified advertisements, employment agencies, or word of mouth to attract candidates?
- *Interviewing procedures*. Start with an application form, then follow up with a three-step process. First, ask the applicant general questions about his or her background. Then test his or her technical skills. Finally, continue the interview to confirm impressions and make a final decision.

Personnel Policies. Once they are hired, you'll need to keep your employees aware of the policies that affect them. These policies should be described in a booklet that includes the following information.

- *Working hours.* Here, a standard workday may be defined. Describe hours, including breaks and lunchtime. Observed holidays, vacation schedule, and sick leave policy may also be appropriate in this section.
- *Payment policies.* These can include the timing of paydays, the overtime pay rate, and how the pay for salaried employees differs from that of hourly employees.
- *Benefits.* Your health, dental, life, and disability insurance programs should be discussed in detail.
- *Termination policies.* These can include possible grounds for firing. Your policies on layoffs, resignations, and reemployment might also be mentioned.

Purchasing and Inventory Activities. Purchasing and inventory activities allow you to account for your inventory (the quantity of goods or materials on hand), supplies, and equipment. Perhaps an employee may notice an empty bin of bubble wrap. He or she might circulate a purchase order. This order would go to vendors for pricing and payment terms. A purchase order over a predetermined dollar amount may require your final approval before the order is placed. When the bubble wrap arrives, it will be received, inspected, and stocked.

Money Matters

OPENING BOOKS

Opening a company's books to employees allows them to see their impact on the business and encourages them to contribute. According to John Case, author of *Open-Book Management:*

"Open-book management transforms workers into active, involved, thinking employees."

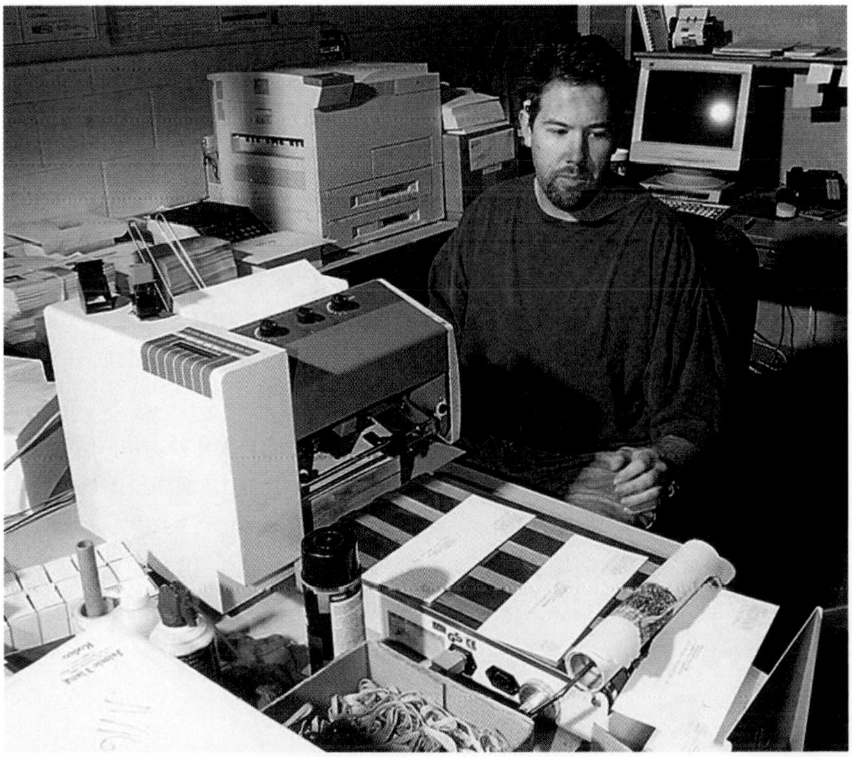

Being out of one part can disrupt the entire workflow. ***What types of controls can a business put in place to assure a complete inventory?***

RISK TAKERS PROFIT MAKERS

Name: Cris Coughlin
Company: Glacier Wilderness Guides
City, State: West Glacier, MT

Selling the Great Outdoors

When Cris Coughlin decided to begin an outdoor backpacking guide service in Montana's Glacier National Park, she didn't expect to find so much red tape. First she had to present her idea to park officials. Then she had to present her bid to the National Park Service. Eventually Coughlin's company, Glacier Wilderness Guides, won the exclusive role as the park's official guide service. By then the summer tourism season had arrived and she had no time left to advertise for her first year in business.

Today Glacier Wilderness Guides and Montana Raft Company is responsible for more than 8,000 rafting and hiking clients each summer. Although Coughlin still has to renew her stake for the exclusive concession every four years, she considers it a quality control measure, and declares "I don't blame the park service. They deserve the best: us."

Thinking Critically

Why is it important for private companies to bid for government contracts?

Production and Distribution Activities. Production includes production scheduling, controlling costs, and actual assembly. Distribution involves getting your products and services to the consumer. Where you locate your business is a distribution decision. Evaluating and choosing shipping companies, packaging supplies, and hiring temporary employees are also distribution activities.

Total Quality Management. Total quality management, is a style of management based on customer satisfaction. It consists of quality control taking place during production and continual market research efforts to verify your business's quality of work. TQM can be expensive, but it can pay off with loyal customers.

Using Principles of Management Excellence

In the book *In Search of Excellence*, managerial researchers Thomas Peters and Robert Waterman list eight keys to management excellence. These principles hold true in successful small businesses as well as large companies. Excellent managers do the following:

- They take action, rather than analyze plans to death.
- They listen to their customers and put themselves in their customers' shoes.
- They encourage their employees to act independently, be innovative, and treat the business as if it were their own.
- They stress respect for the individual.
- They instill commitment to values and objectives by keeping in touch with all employees.
- They keep the business focused on what it does best.
- They keep their organization simple, flexible, and efficient (and don't overstaff).
- They keep their operations under control and keep an eye on detail.

CHECK YOUR UNDERSTANDING

SECTION 14.2

Reviewing Key Terms and Concepts

1. What is a working management plan?
2. Ask an adult about the organizational structure at his or her workplace. Chart it.
3. How might using the principles of management excellence assist a business to reach its goals?

Critical Thinking Activity

Develop an "Employee Handbook" describing what your business's personnel policies might be.

Extension Lab — Problem-Solving Skills

Rumor Kathia manages a sales force of 200 people. Effective communication is a problem. The employees do not feel their problems are being heard and Kathia doesn't think her employees really understand the expectations she has for them. This leads to miscommunication and hurt feelings between management and staff.

Presentation Develop a system of communication that could improve the relations between Kathia and her employees. Be sure to address the following concerns:

- How can Kathia communicate with her employees more effectively?
- What can the employees do to communicate with Kathia more effectively?

CHAPTER 14 REVIEW

CHAPTER SUMMARY

- As an entrepreneur you will have a second role—that of a manager.
- Managers plan, organize, direct, and control, usually in that order.
- A plan determines the objectives or desired results of a business. There are three types of plans—strategic or long range, tactical or mid-range, and operational or short-term.
- Leadership styles include power-oriented, routine-oriented, and achievement-oriented. They are used by good managers according to the situation at hand.
- To manage a business successfully requires human relations, technical, time management, and conceptual skills as well as the foundational skills of communication, math, and problem solving.
- A working management plan serves as a guide for making short-term decisions and should include the marketing objectives you plan to reach within one year.
- Excellent managers adhere to some common management principles that include taking action, listening to customers, and encouraging independence and innovation among employees.

RECALL KEY TERMS

Imagine you have just completed a seminar for new managers. Write a summary of what you learned and use the following key terms in that summary.

manager
strategic plans
tactical plans
operational plans
quality control program
situational management
time management
conceptual skills
working management plan
tactical marketing objectives
organizational structure
total quality management

RECALL KEY CONCEPTS

1. What is different about an entrepreneur's role after the business opens?
2. List the four management functions managers use to achieve their goals.
3. What do managers do as part of the organizing function?
4. When is the power-oriented leadership style most effective?
5. Which one of the management skills is considered most important?
6. What policies, procedures, and activities are in the working management plan?
7. How do excellent managers deal with customers?

THINK CRITICALLY

1. Can an entrepreneur's hat and a manager's hat be worn at once? Explain.
2. How can the management function of controlling be used to prevent problems?
3. Compare the three leadership styles.
4. Which of the skills needed to be a good manager do you feel you possess? How can you improve or gain those skills? How could you attain the skills you don't yet have ?
5. Why should a manager encourage employees to treat the business as their own?

CHAPTER 14 REVIEW

CONNECT ACADEMICS TO THE WORKPLACE

Math

1. The amount you budgeted for long-distance telephone calls was $350. When you receive your phone bill, you find that long-distance expenses were actually $395. What is the difference between your budgeted and actual expenses in dollars and as a percentage?

Allocating Time

2. Ahmed, an entrepreneur and manager of a print shop, arrives at work and writes up the following "to do" list.

   - Order paper and ink for next week's projects
   - Evaluate last week's sale's figures
   - Attend luncheon at Chamber of Commerce
   - Check E-mail and voice mail
   - Review résumés for afternoon interviews

   Rank the tasks according to priority and explain your reasoning.

Speaking

3. Locate and read an article on one of the following topics: managing a small business, effective leadership styles, skills needed for management, or outstanding business managers. Prepare a summary and present it orally to the class.

WORK IN YOUR COMMUNITY

If you are employed, observe the activities of your manager for a one-week period.

- Record what he or she does at the end of each day.
- At the end of the week, make a chart categorizing each activity as planning, organizing, directing, or controlling.
- Make a separate category for those activities that were clearly non-management in nature.

(Note: If you are not employed, observe the activities of a particular teacher for one week.)

LINK SCHOOL TO CAREER

As a class, hold an "Entrepreneur of the Year" award ceremony.

- Identify entrepreneurs in your community who are successful and exhibit some or all of the eight principles of management excellence cited in the chapter.
- Invite them to a ceremony at your school and present them with a certificate or some other honorary token.
- Provide refreshments, take pictures, and seek publicity from school and local media.

*inter*NET CONNECTION

So Little Time

Denise is a full-time college student who owns and manages a children's bookstore. Since she is so busy, Denise has asked you for some time-management tips.

Connect

Using a variety of search engines, search the Web to find:

- Articles on time management
- Scheduling software programs that are available on-line for free
- Time-management software or books available for sale over the Internet

Summarize your findings.

CHAPTER 15

Managing Purchasing and Inventory

Learning Objectives

When you have completed this chapter, you will be able to:

- **Manage** your purchasing and inventory with profits in mind
- **Identify** the options faced by purchasing managers
- **Discuss** the methods of managing an inventory

You're the Boss!

Basket Case

As a retailer of camping supplies you've discovered a new market of upscale picnickers. You've decided to put together a new product—a straw picnic basket complete with linens, silverware, plastic cups, plastic dishes, serving containers, and a cutting board.

What Will You Do?

What factors will you take into account before you make purchases and how will you keep track of everything once it arrives?

SECTION 15.1

Purchase Planning and Management

PLANNING PURCHASES

Planning your purchases involves finding items that can be purchased at a low price and sold at a profit. First, you'll have to plan your **model inventory**, which is a target inventory of what you think you'll need to keep in stock. You will also need to identify your purchasing and sales objectives. What will you buy? How much inventory should you stock? Who will you buy it from? These questions are answered in your purchasing plan.

Purchasing Inventory

In this chapter, purchasing refers to buying inventory. Inventory includes products for resale or the materials to create such products. Inventory bought to sell is retail. Wholesale inventories can be for sale or used to make the end products.

Start-Up to Ongoing

The stage of your business will affect your perspective on purchasing. If you are planning a start-up inventory, you may

What you'll learn

- what to keep in mind when purchasing for the first time
- how to choose the right vendor
- when quality may be more important than price

Why it's important

Businesses owe it to their customers to get the best possible materials for the price. Dollars saved and spent in the right places can lead to better products and larger profits.

KEY TERMS

model inventory
vendors
trade discounts
cash discounts
secured funds

handle a small amount of goods. As you learn about what products work, you'll increase the quantities. You'll need to keep supply and demand, quality, and profitability in mind. Your ongoing inventory will benefit from the experience that you gain as you replace goods and test the success of new products. You'll become aware of inventory trends and cycles. You'll also become familiar with vendors, the businesses that will sell you inventory.

PURCHASING MANAGEMENT

Purchasing management is a primary concern to retail, wholesale, and manufacturing businesses. It may also be a concern to service businesses. For example, a copier repair business needs to purchase copier parts. Only extraction businesses, such as mining and farming, have a little concern with purchasing management.

Purchasing decisions can mean the difference between success and failure for an entrepreneur. If that seems extreme, consider how much money is invested in purchasing. Manufacturers spend up to 50 percent of every dollar they make on inventory. Wholesalers spend up to 85 percent, and retailers spend up to 70 percent. Even service businesses spend as much as 10 percent of their sales for materials that go into the services they create.

Managing purchases effectively should be a high priority for an entrepreneur. It involves making a number of basic choices.

Selecting the Right Quality

There is a rule for determining what quality of inventory to purchase. It is the same for any business: Buy the products or materials that match your needs. For example, if you manufacture

Up&Coming Entrepreneur

Folk Art Entrepreneurs

Griselda Arteaga and her sister, Omega Arteaga-Gamboa, opened San Antonio's ArteQuin as an outlet for their love of Mexican heritage and folk art. Arteaga regularly travels within Texas and over to Mexico to visit with local artists, from whom she selects pieces for sale back at her store. The name "ArteQuin" is a combination of the sisters' surname and the Spanish word for country house. "We want people to feel at home when they come into our store," says Arteaga, "and be able to take home a sense of our heritage."

Analyze **How does ArteQuin benefit cultural awareness?**

shelving, you should buy durable material. If you buy low-quality material, your products might not hold up. If you are a retailer dealing in moderately priced footwear, stick to that level of product. If you buy high-priced products or budget footwear, your customers will go elsewhere to find what they want.

Entrepreneurs are asked to handle numerous tasks at once. ***Why is it worthwhile to set aside time to read about business news and events?***

Buying the Right Quantity

How much inventory should you buy? Purchase enough to maintain your chosen inventory levels. Deciding on inventory levels is *inventory management.* This is discussed later in this chapter.

Timing Your Purchases

Time your purchases so that your money and storage space aren't tied up any longer than necessary. Also, take advantage of economic conditions. If prices are beginning to rise sharply, stock up before they go higher. If the economy is in a recession, keep purchases to a minimum. Making such timely buying decisions requires you to stay in touch with news and the economy.

Choosing the Right Vendors

Locating vendors is not a difficult process. However, choosing the right vendors will require a number of thoughtful decisions on your part.

- **Reliability.** Is the vendor able to deliver enough of the products or materials you need when they are needed? If deliveries are late or inadequate, you can lose sales and customers.
- **Distance.** How close is the vendor under consideration? The cost of transporting products or materials can be expensive. You are also more likely to get better service and coordination problems are easier to handle when the vendor is local.
- **Service.** What services will the vendor offer? You should inquire carefully. Will sales representatives call on a regular basis? Do they know the product line? Will they assist you with planning layouts, setting up displays, or solving production problems? If there is equipment involved, can they repair it? Will they make unscheduled deliveries in an emergency? What is their return policy? What other appropriate assistance can they provide?

Number of Vendors. Should you buy from one vendor or from several? **Figure 15–1** shows the advantages and disadvantages of both approaches. For a good combination, consider using one supplier for 70 to 80 percent of your purchases. Spread the other 20 to 30 percent of your business among other vendors.

Getting the Right Price

Contact several vendors to find the best price. In some instances, particularly when orders are large, prices may be negotiable. However, the lowest price is not always the right price. You have to factor quality and service into your decision. If the quality is below what your customers expect or if the materials aren't delivered when they are needed, you can lose more than you gain. The average dissatisfied customer tells 10 people about the poor products or services that he or she receives.

Purchase discounts can also affect prices. Depending on where you are in the channel of distribution, you may be able to take advantage of trade, quantity, or cash discounts:

- Many manufacturers grant trade discounts off the suggested retail price to wholesalers and retailers. For example, a manufacturer might give discounts of 50 percent to wholesalers and 40 percent to retailers. Manufacturers offer these discounts as a way to reward and recognize channel members for their role in getting their products to consumers.
- Quantity discounts are discounts that vendors give to buyers who place large orders.

Figure 15–1
Working with one vendor can be risky. ***What are some things that can go wrong?***

One or More Vendors?

One Vendor		Several Vendors	
Advantages	**Disadvantages**	**Advantages**	**Disadvantages**
Special treatment, possible quantity discounts.	Vulnerable if something goes wrong with working relationship.	Less risky, if one relationship goes amiss, the rest remain.	No special treatment, no discounts.

RISK TAKERS PROFIT MAKERS

Names: Tom First & Tom Scott
Company: Nantucket Nectars
City, State: Cambridge, MA

Bottling for Dollars

Tom First and Tom Scott met as freshmen at Brown University in the fall of 1985. In the summer of 1989, they created Allserve, a business that delivered newspapers, coffee, laundry, and other necessities to visiting yachts in the Nantucket Harbor.

Business was good until the onset of winter when tourism began to decline. During their first winter on Nantucket, they began a business centered on a fruit drink they made at parties from peaches, sugar, and water. They called it Nantucket Nectars.

The first summer, they sold 2,000 bottles of Nectars at $1 each. They knew they had a hit on their hands and enlisted the help of a bottler in Ohio. Unfortunately, they found that retailers turn away as many as 10 fruit juice makers per month. Refusing to give up, they set up tents at college campuses to promote their product. Today, Nantucket Nectars sells more than two dozen varieties of juice and has annual sales of $50 million.

Thinking Critically

Why was it important for Nantucket Nectars to distinguish themselves from other juice makers?

- Cash discounts allow buyers to deduct a percentage from the purchase amount if payment is received by a specified date.

Payment Methods

Until you establish a good working relationship, your new vendor may request *secured funds*. Secured funds are a form of guaranteed payment such as a credit card, cashier's check, wire transfer, or cash. As you establish credit, a vendor may be willing to accept a single company check. One may also arrange a series of post-dated checks to deposit into his or her account at specified times. It is important for you to pay your vendors on time so they will allow you to stretch your credit when you need it.

Receiving and Following Up on Purchases

Purchasing management doesn't stop with placing your order. You'll need to verify and record its arrival. If your customers are unsatisfied with your goods or services, you'll want to review quality issues with your vendors.

- *Accuracy and acceptability.* When you receive a shipment, check the purchase order against the invoice. Verify the identity, quality, and condition of your order. If there is anything wrong with the shipment or on the invoice, report it to the vendor. Keeping a close eye on incoming shipments will protect you from paying for somebody else's mistakes.
- *Controls.* If you are a retailer or wholesaler, you will have to mark your merchandise's size, cost, selling price, and other information on each unit. If you run a manufacturing or service business, you may need to mark the grade or source of materials.

Effective managers follow up on how their purchased inventory performs. Retailers and wholesalers follow up on complaints and returns. Manufacturers and service businesses follow up on the performance of materials used to make their products or perform the services they provide.

CHECK YOUR UNDERSTANDING

SECTION 15.1

Reviewing Key Terms and Concepts

1. What factors should you take into account when choosing a vendor?
2. List three types of discounts that can apply to purchasing.
3. What does a purchasing manager do when inventory stock arrives?

Critical Thinking Activity

Explain why manufacturers and service providers spend different percentages of their income on their inventories. Use an example for each type of business.

Extension Lab—Exercising Individual Responsibility

Balloon Controversy Your school is selling helium balloons to raise money for much needed computer equipment. Yesterday, the first shipment of balloons arrived and instead of 1,500 balloons, you received 15,000. The invoice shows that you will be billed for 1,500 balloons. Many students are excited that you now have 13,500 extra balloons to sell for 100 percent profit.

Role Play In groups of three or four, simulate a debate between students who are for and those who are against keeping the extra balloons. Center your discussion around the following questions:

- What kind of action should the school take?
- Is it ethical to keep and sell the extra balloons?

SECTION 15.2

Inventory Management

INVENTORY MANAGEMENT

The purpose of inventory management is to find and maintain inventory levels that are neither too small nor too large. Too little inventory can result in lost sales. It can lose customers and interrupt your operation. It also leads to frequent reordering. It takes time and energy to place these additional orders.

What you'll learn

- what costs are associated with managing your inventory
- how often you'll need to reorder your stock
- what systems work best to keep track of your inventory

Why it's important

Your main profit stems from the sales of your inventory. Precise controls should be kept over this valuable asset.

KEY TERMS

shrinkage costs
obsolescence costs
warehousing
lead time
usage rate
safety stock

However, too much inventory can add as much as 25 percent to the cost of your inventory. Added costs may include the following:

- *Financing costs*—the interest you pay to borrow money to purchase inventory
- *Opportunity cost*—loss of the use of money tied up in inventory
- *Storage costs*—the amount spent on renting or buying the space needed to store the inventory
- *Insurance costs*—the amount spent to insure the inventory on hand
- Shrinkage costs —money lost when inventory items are broken, damaged, spoiled, or stolen
- Obsolescence costs —money lost when products or materials become obsolete while in inventory

Unfortunately, there is no ideal way to determine and maintain an ideal inventory level. Inventories constantly change, and the "right" amount of inventory shifts with changes in demand and season. However, inventory planning can help you.

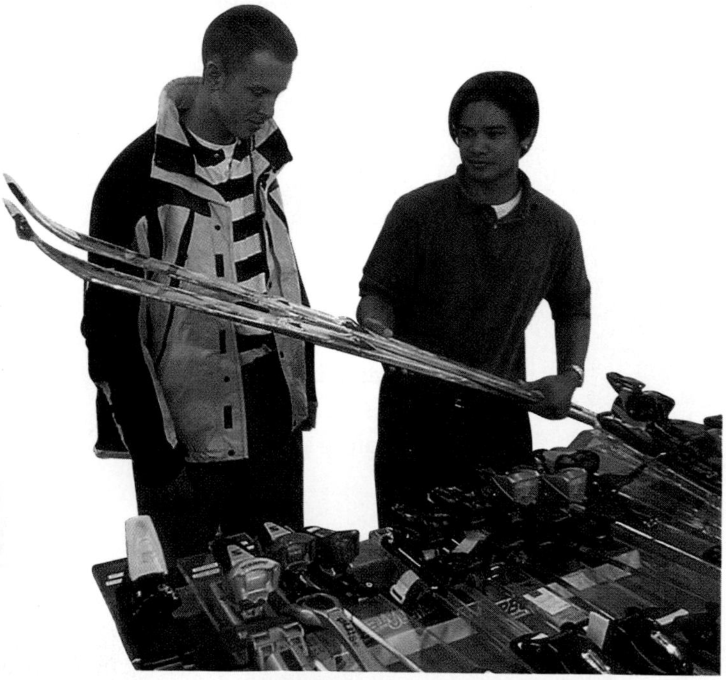

Certain businesses are seasonal. ***How can you adjust your purchasing strategy for the off-season?***

Planning Inventory

To determine a proper amount of inventory, you must consider time and money. Ask yourself two questions:

- How many months' supply should be on hand?
- How much of an investment would that represent?

Calculating Supply. For all industries, there is an average stock, or inventory, turnover rate. This is the average number of times the inventory is sold out during the year. For example, men's clothing stores have an average inventory turnover rate of 3; restaurants, 22; and some chemical manufacturers, as high as 100. Trade associations in your field can provide you with turnover rates for your type of business.

To find the number of months' supply you should keep on hand, divide your industry's average inventory turnover rate into

12 (the number of months in a year). If, for example, you sell men's clothing, the industry's average rate is 3, and this would be the calculation:

$$\frac{12}{\text{Average stock turnover rate}} = \text{How many months' supply to keep on hand}$$

$$\frac{12}{3} = \text{4 months' supply}$$

If you apply this calculation to the restaurant average of 22, you get .54. That's about a half-month's supply. Clearly, a restaurant depends on a constant supply of fresh inventory. It would also reorder more frequently than a clothing store.

Calculating Cost. Now that you have estimated how much inventory to keep on hand for a men's clothing store, you need to figure how much that will cost you. To find the inventory cost within a given turnover period, divide the cost of goods sold for your forecasted annual sales by the average stock turnover rate for your industry. Let's say you forecast sales for the coming year to be $100,000 and your cost of goods sold is 75 percent of sales. Using the average inventory turnover rate of 3, your calculation would be as follows:

$$\frac{\text{Cost of goods sold}}{\text{Average stock turnover rate}} = \text{Inventory cost}$$

$$\frac{\$100{,}000 \times .75}{3} = \frac{\$75{,}000}{3} = \$25{,}000$$

For your men's clothing store, you should keep 4 months of inventory on hand at a cost of $25,000.

This example suggests that one set of calculations applies to the entire inventory. Actually, you will have to make calculations

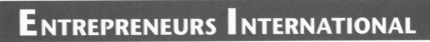

ENTREPRENEURS INTERNATIONAL

USA

Gretchen Porter's love for machine-made textiles and local handmade artisans' fabrics led her to open Portsmouth Fabrics. Over the years, Porter has doubled her New Hampshire business by hiring help and importing fabrics from around the world for her clients. Occasionally, working with other countries requires help. "I found this great hand-painted fabric from New Zealand once, but I had to get a customs broker to get it into our country," says Porter.

Apply **What are some problems that might arise when importing foreign goods?**

Money Matters

MARKET

In order for a business to grow and be successful, it's important to know the market. Richard Hirsh, of John Paul Richard Inc., says:

"We understand our market and . . . we have a keen understanding of what will sell at what price point."

for different product lines or types of materials. For example, socks have a higher turnover rate than raincoats. Each requires separate calculations.

Using Industry Averages. The average inventory turnover rate can help you gauge your inventory management. Compare the number of turnovers you have in a year to the industry average. If you are far ahead of the industry average, your prices may be too low. A lower-than-industry average may indicate that your inventory is tied up in slow-moving merchandise or material.

Keeping Track of Your Inventory

Keeping tabs on how much inventory you have in stock is the first step in controlling your inventory levels. When your business first gets under way, you may be able to keep track of your inventory by just looking at what you have. As your business grows, however, you will probably have to switch to more structured inventory control systems. To double-check any of those systems, you will also have to do a physical inventory count. **Figure 15–2** shows four systems used to keep track of inventories.

Physical Inventory Count

No matter which inventory control system you use, it's a good idea to conduct periodic physical inventory counts. Errors can occur in visual estimates or in recording changes in inventory. Items can be removed from stock and not recorded. Merchandise or materials can be lost, stolen, or go bad. Taking physical inventory will get your books in line with what you actually have in stock.

Taking physical count also helps you evaluate your inventory control system. Suppose your perpetual inventory system says you have 450 items of something in stock. If your physical count shows only 200, your perpetual system isn't very accurate.

Physical inventory counts usually involve two employees. One counts and calls out the item and number. The other records the count on a tally sheet.

Physical counts can be done often (the case when a JIT system is used) or as infrequently as once a year. If you plan to take a physical inventory count yearly, you can keep your counting costs down by getting your inventories as low as possible before the count. In retail this is often done through special year-end sales.

Figure 15–2

Inventory Systems

Here are four ways to keep track of your inventory:

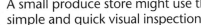

1. Visual inventory systems.

A small produce store might use this simple and quick visual inspection system: You look at how much inventory you have on hand and compare it to what you want to have on hand. This system usually works best where sales are steady, inventory is handled personally, and items can be obtained quickly.

2. Perpetual inventory systems.

As inventory is sold, it is subtracted from the inventory list. As new inventory arrives, it is added. Computerized cash registers allow retail businesses to use this accurate and instantaneous system, which is also popular with warehouses and storage facilities.

3. Partial inventory systems.

The partial inventory control system is a combination of systems. In this system, a perpetual inventory is maintained only for those items that account for a large share of the company's sales.

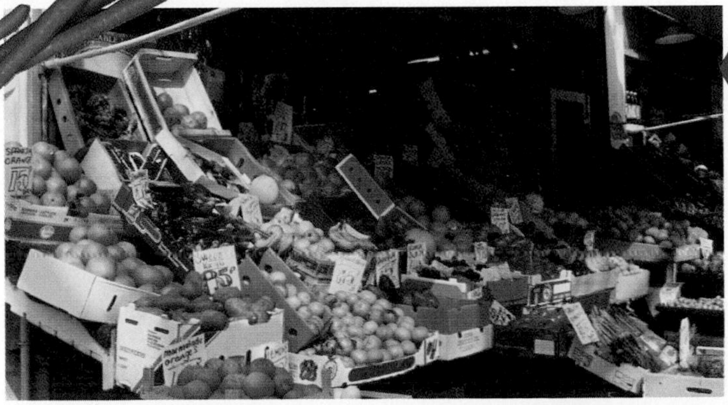

4. Just-in-time (JIT) inventory systems.

The JIT system shifts most of the inventory chores to the vendor. By having suppliers deliver inventory just before it is to be used, stocks are kept at a minimum. For many manufacturers, this can provide a very effective control.

Tips from the Real World

THE IMPRESSION

The success of a new product in a competitive market might depend on the impression you make. Pam Marker, an independent marketing and design consultant suggests:

"Give buyers something they can keep so they'll remember you. [A catalog] is your best salesperson."

Warehousing

Warehousing involves the operations that are associated with inventoried goods. The warehouse is where purchasing and inventory planning are put into effect. It can be an actual structure or just assigned space. When you plan your warehouse operations, keep the following points in mind:

- *Receiving and shipping docks.* Vendors and transportation companies will need easy access to and inside your facility. Keep their physical paths to you as clear as possible.
- *Bulk storage areas.* These are places where goods remain in their original crates, waiting to be broken down into more usable quantities.
- *Staging areas.* This is free space where your bulk inventory may be moved to free up space elsewhere. A staging area can help to organize your entire warehouse.
- *Picking rows.* These are rows of small and large inventoried goods that may be placed in bins or on pallets. Here they can be gathered as needed for assembly and packing.
- *Assembly areas.* In these spaces, goods are assembled individually or as kits.
- *Packing areas.* Boxing takes place in packing areas. Also, individual products that are ready for the consumer may need to be repacked in bulk units for shipping.
- *Management office and lockers.* Your employees will need space to work in and to keep their personal belongings.

Reordering

To maintain proper inventory levels, you will have to decide when and how much to reorder. The type of inventory you keep determines which reordering system is best for you.

Periodic Reordering. Products or raw materials that are inexpensive, used often, and easy to get should be reordered periodically. They should be automatically reordered to keep the inventory at the proper level. A manufacturer that uses nuts and bolts might restock such hardware every 60 days. A restauranteur might restock baked goods daily.

Nonperiodic Ordering. Inventory that is not suited to periodic reordering must be reordered in another way. Needs must be projected. To do this, consider three key questions:

1. What will be the gap in time between placing an order and receiving the delivery? This is called lead time.
2. How quickly will the inventory be used in a given period of time? This is known as the usage rate.
3. How much *safety stock* will be needed? Safety stock is the cushion of products or materials that keeps you from running out of inventory while you're waiting for an order.

Reordering Procedures

No matter what method of reordering is used, it is important for an entrepreneur to approach the matter systematically. He or she should do the following:

- Plan inventory
- Order and reorder in accordance with the plan
- Check to see how well the plan has worked
- Make any necessary adjustments

CHECK YOUR UNDERSTANDING

SECTION 15.2

Reviewing Key Terms and Concepts

1 Your industry's turnover rate is 11. Your sales are forecasted to be $90,000 and your annual cost of goods sold is 50% of sales. Find the number of months' supply to keep on hand and at what cost for inventory?

2 You run a small mailbox rental business and sell paper goods on the side. What inventory system will work best for you?

3 You've noticed that your inventory is suffering from excessive shrinkage. Develop and list some controls you can put in place to stop this.

Critical Thinking Activity

Draw your idea of the floor plan of a functioning warehouse for a business that sells kits of hair care products to individuals by mail order.

Extension Lab—Designing and Improving Organizational Systems

Account For It Your landscaping business is expanding, and managing your inventory has become a priority. Your inventory includes mowing and edging equipment; gardening tools; sod, plants, and trees; and fertilizers and pesticides. Right now, you keep most of the items in your garage and every so often you go out and count what you have left. It is time for a better system.

Presentation Explain how you will keep track of your inventory. Be sure to include:

- The system you will use to keep track of your inventory
- How often you will conduct a physical inventory count
- Where you will store the inventory

CHAPTER 15 REVIEW

CHAPTER SUMMARY

- Managing the purchasing and inventory process effectively should be a high priority for entrepreneurs and can mean the difference between success and failure.
- Purchasing management involves buying inventory of the right quality, in the right quantity, at the right time, from the right vendors, and at the right price.
- Purchasing management also includes verifying and recording the inventory when it arrives as well as marking the merchandise or materials.
- The purpose of inventory management is to find and maintain inventory levels that are neither too small nor too large.
- To determine the proper amount of inventory, you must calculate how many months' supply you should have in stock and how much that stock will cost you.
- There are several systems to keep track of your inventory, including visual, perpetual, partial, and just-in-time (JIT).
- Warehousing involves the operations that are associated with inventoried goods, including receiving and shipping docks, bulk storage areas, staging areas, picking rows, assembly areas, packing areas, and management offices and lockers.
- Reordering procedures are necessary to maintain inventory at a proper level.

RECALL KEY TERMS

As a new entrepreneur, prepare a one-page document stating your purchasing and inventory policies. Use the following key terms in your document.

model inventory
vendors
trade discounts
cash discounts
secured funds
shrinkage costs
obsolescence costs
warehousing
lead time
usage rate
safety stock

RECALL KEY CONCEPTS

1. How does the phase of your business (start-up or ongoing) affect the purchasing decisions you make?
2. What is the rule for determining the right quality of inventory to purchase for your business?
3. Why is timing so crucial to purchasing management?
4. When choosing a vendor, what factors should you consider?
5. Contrast trade and cash discounts.
6. What can happen if there is too little inventory?
7. What costs may result from too much inventory?
8. What are two questions that must be addressed in inventory planning?
9. Why isn't the just-in-time (JIT) inventory system practical for a retail business?
10. What do you need to consider when planning your warehouse operations?

THINK CRITICALLY

1. Compare the advantages and disadvantages of buying from one vendor or several.

2. How do you use stock turnover rate to determine the success you have had in managing your inventory?
3. How can you use industry averages to determine how successful you have been in managing your inventory?
4. As your business grows, what inventory control system will be most useful? Why?
5. Compare the periodic and nonperiodic ordering systems.

CONNECT ACADEMICS TO THE WORKPLACE

Math

1. You own a business in a field with an average yearly inventory turnover rate of 6. You have forecasted sales of $240,000 for next year. The cost of your inventory is 70 percent of your selling price.
   - How many months' supply of inventory should you keep on hand?
   - What would be the average dollar value of your inventory investment?

Work in Teams

2. You and a friend work as shipping and receiving clerks in a warehouse. You have noticed there are no procedures for receiving inventory when it arrives. With your friend, write a memo describing the procedures you think should be in place.

WORK IN YOUR COMMUNITY

Investigate the possibility of choosing a product line to sell in a business. Talk with at least three local vendors. Be sure to:

- Evaluate them based on reliability, distance, and service.
- Determine what discounts they offer.
- Ask about payment methods they require.

Based on the information you obtain, choose the vendor or vendors for your business. Explain your decision.

LINK SCHOOL TO CAREER

Interview a manager of a local business regarding the following:

- Purchasing and inventory procedures
- Purchasing and inventory problems
- How he or she handles or prevents common purchasing and inventory problems

Report your findings to the class. Compile the results and try to determine the similarities or differences between businesses.

*inter*NET CONNECTION

Job Hunt

Daunte plans to open his own business. To gain experience in purchasing and inventory management, he decides to search for a job in that field. He asks for your help.

Connect

Using a variety of search engines, conduct a job search on the Internet.

- Use keyword searches (inventory, purchasing).
- Access job-related sites such as CareerMosaic, Online Career Center, or Monster Board.
- Determine skills and experience necessary for a job in purchasing or inventory management.
- Determine starting salaries if possible.

Share your results with the class.

CHAPTER 16

Production Management and Distribution

Learning Objectives

When you have completed this chapter, you will be able to:

- **Describe** the nature of product development for entrepreneurs
- **Explain** the product development process
- **Discuss** how to manage production in your business
- **Identify** the various components of distribution management

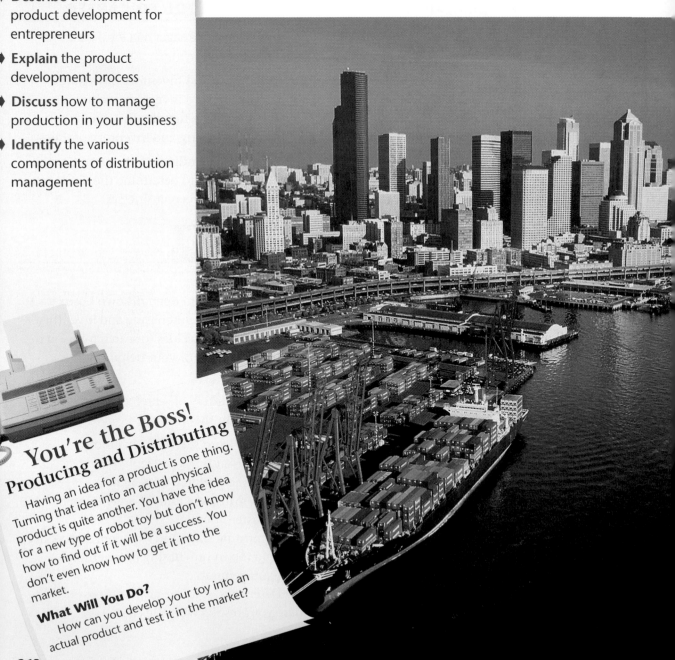

You're the Boss!

Producing and Distributing

Having an idea for a product is one thing. Turning that idea into an actual physical product is quite another. You have the idea for a new type of robot toy but don't know how to find out if it will be a success. You don't even know how to get it into the market.

What Will You Do?

How can you develop your toy into an actual product and test it in the market?

SECTION 16.1

From Idea to Product

PRODUCT DEVELOPMENT FOR ENTREPRENEURS

The transformation from idea to marketable product is a lengthy process. In this section you'll learn how entrepreneurs with limited resources develop products.

What Is Product Development?

Product development entails taking an idea, designing it on paper or with a computer, building a model, and testing it. Most large companies with big budgets have research and development departments to develop new products. They can make mistakes and still succeed. The same cannot be said for small business owners.

Some consider the product development stage of a new small business to be the highest-risk part of start-up. As a result it can be difficult for an entrepreneur to raise money to develop a new product. You will need to be creative in finding resources to turn your idea into a product.

Outsourcing Product Development

One of the ways that small business owners reduce the cost of product development is *outsourcing*. **Outsourcing** is the hiring of people and companies to handle tasks that you don't have the ability to do. Gregg Levin developed the PerfectCurve product that helped baseball caps retain their shapes when they were washed. However, he didn't have the knowledge, ability, or money to set up a manufacturing facility. So he outsourced it. He hired a plastic manufacturer to make the product. Then he had the finished product sent to a Boston rehabilitation program site. There, people with disabilities assembled and packaged it.

No matter what you're producing, you can use outsourcing. Someone else can create your design, decide what materials to use, manufacture it, assemble it, or package it. When your company gains profits, you can assume some of these tasks yourself.

What you'll learn

- how entrepreneurs develop new products with limited resources
- how the product development process works
- why it's important to make a prototype

Why it's important

Entrepreneurs often avoid production businesses because they don't think they have sufficient resources. However, there are ways to develop new products with limited resources.

KEY TERMS

product development
outsourcing
prototype

Tips from the Real World

QUALITY

Quality is a goal worth pursuing. A good product is sometimes its own best advertisement. Bert Suarez, founder and president of Diesel Radiator, Inc. remarks:

"Never underestimate the importance of a good product and word-of-mouth. About 25 percent of our new customers are referred to us by other customers."

THE PRODUCT DEVELOPMENT PROCESS

Product development for entrepreneurs isn't a linear process. There is no clear sequence. It has starts and stops. Sometimes it even goes backward, then forward again. The four steps of product development are described in **Figure 16-1**.

Designing It Right the First Time

It's best to design your product right the very first time. There are three very good reasons for designing it correctly at the outset.

1. *The cost of design.* The cost of product design is about 80 percent of your product's total budget. Starting over or redesigning is often more costly than the original work. You can save a lot of money by designing carefully.
2. *The quality and marketability of the product.* How well you design your product also determines how well it does in the market. The quality and time that are put into the product will affect the product's reliability.
3. *The time to launch.* If you design your product properly, you won't have to go back and make changes. Changes increase the production cost and lengthen the time it takes to release the final product.

Building a Prototype

The first prototype you build may not look like the final product. However, it should work like the final product. Gregg Levin built prototypes of the PerfectCurve out of clay, wood, and several other materials before he decided on the final one.
In the process, he fine-tuned the product. He can

ENTREPRENEURS INTERNATIONAL

Taiwan

In 1960, Sam Yu founded Tai Lung Chemicals Works to follow a childhood dream of manufacturing balloons. After finding success in his country, Yu began exporting his products around the world. Over the years, he has adapted his factory to accommodate a variety of styles for the global market. Today he produces party balloons, water balloons, rocket balloons, and promotional items for large corporations. Odds are you've been soaked with one of Yu's water balloons.

Apply **List some reasons why balloons make an easy product to export.**

Figure 16–1

An Overview of Product Development

There are four steps in product development:

1. Opportunity recognition.

Entrepreneurs are opportunity seekers. For example, the inventor of Nerf toys knew that parents wanted toys that children could throw indoors without destroying furniture.

2. Concept investigation.

Study the market to make certain there is sufficient demand.

4. Prototype building and testing.

A **prototype** is a working model of your product. Often you can't gauge a product until you can actually see, use, and handle it. Test the prototype or working model with actual customers.

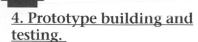

3. Product design.

Design the product on paper or on a computer. Make sure the needs and wants of potential customers are incorporated. Also include input from the people who are involved in marketing, producing, and financing the product.

Once a release date has been given for a product or service, it's very important to meet it. ***What are some reasons?***

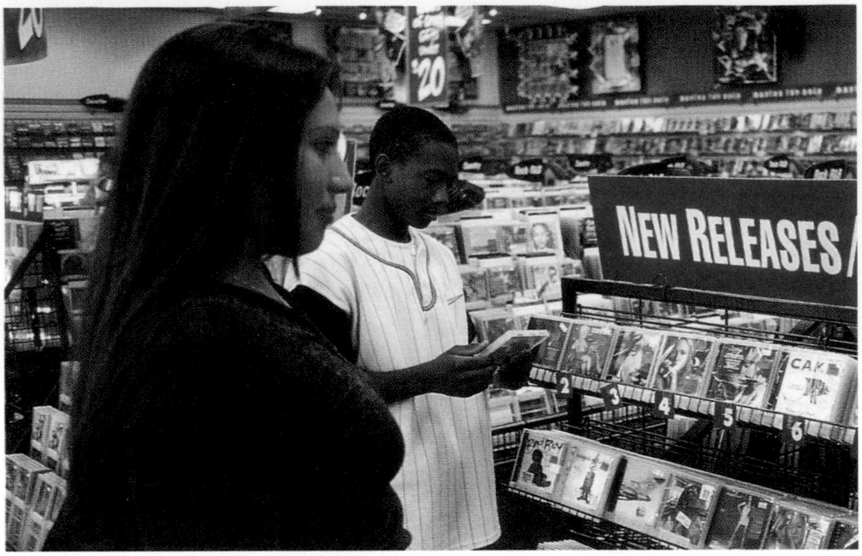

also get better customer input because they can actually see and use the product. It's amazing how close one can get to an actual working prototype of a new product by assembling items that already exist.

CHECK YOUR UNDERSTANDING

SECTION 16.1

Reviewing Key Terms and Concepts

1 What kinds of product development tasks can entrepreneurs outsource?
2 What are the basic steps in the product development process?
3 Why is product design so important?

Critical Thinking Activity

Interview an entrepreneur who has developed a new product. What steps did he or she take to move from idea to physical product?

Extension Lab—Decision-Making Skills

Paging All Entrepreneurs You work in research and development for a large company that manufactures pagers. Based on research you have completed at work, you came up with an idea for a new product. When you discuss your idea with friends, you find that everyone agrees you have a great product idea. Many people are even encouraging you to leave the company and develop it on you own, but a few have doubts as to whether it is legal or ethical.

Role Play In groups of three or four, take turns arguing for both views. Base your debate on the following:

- Does your company have any recourse against you for quitting and then developing this idea on your own?
- Is this ethical?

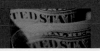

SECTION 16.2

Production and Distribution

What you'll learn

- how to manage the production aspects of a business
- how to use Gantt charts and PERT diagrams
- the elements of distribution management

Why it's important

Coming up with an idea for a product or service is only a small part of what it takes to make a successful business. You have to turn that idea into reality. Production and distribution are the ways that a business makes an idea come true and gets it to the customers.

KEY TERMS

Gantt charts
PERT diagrams
quality control
quality circles
productivity
automation
common carriers
contract carriers
private carriers
FOB
logistics

PRODUCTION MANAGEMENT

Once you have developed a prototype, you are ready to plan production. Outsourcing is one way for a new company to manufacture a product. However, you'll have more control if you produce your product in-house.

An Overview of Production

The principles of production management apply to all types of businesses, including service businesses. Production management has three functions:

1. Acquiring the resources needed to create a product.
2. Planning how to convert those resources into products.
3. Making sure that the products meet the standards set for them.

Chapter 15 described the acquisition of resources. This section focuses on scheduling and quality control.

Scheduling

Businesses plan their production by making schedules. These schedules describe each activity that must be completed to produce goods or services. They include estimates of how long each activity will take. There are two widely used graphic scheduling techniques, Gantt charts and PERT diagrams.

Gantt Charts. Gantt charts are an easy way to keep track of tasks to be performed. Tasks are listed on the vertical axis and the time required for each is

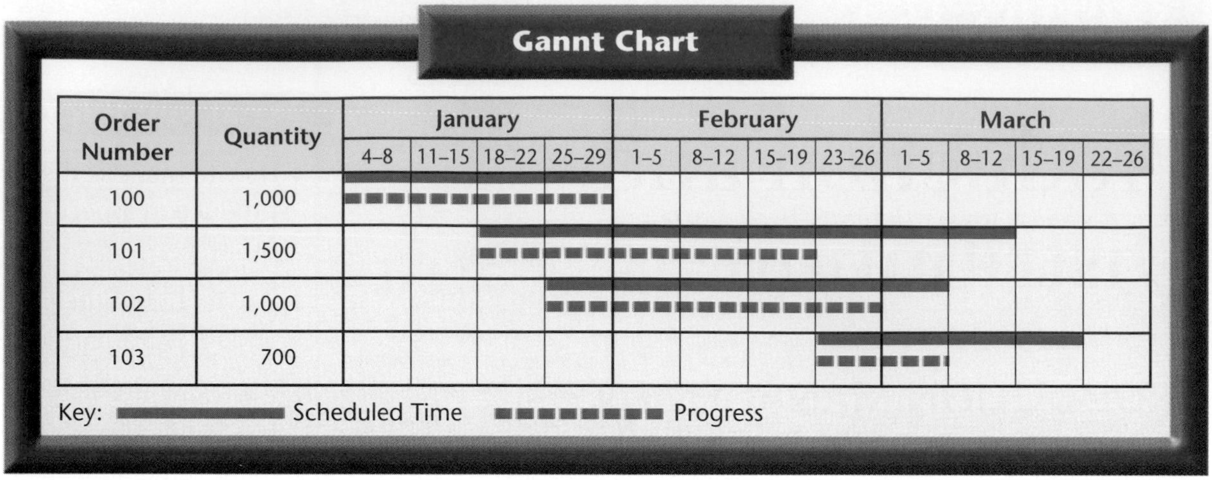

Figure 16–2
Gantt charts make it easy to compare planned work (solid lines) with actual progress (broken lines). For example, if you were looking at this chart on February 26, Order 100 would be completed and 102 would be on schedule. ***Where would Orders 101 and 103 be?***

shown on the horizontal axis. In **Figure 16–2**, individual orders are listed vertically. Solid bars span the period over which each order is scheduled to be produced. Broken bars indicate actual production activity.

Gantt charts are simple and helpful. They force you to think through the steps of a job and estimate the time needed for each part of it. They also provide a way to track actual progress against planned activities once the project is under way. Gantt charts are generally used for scheduling production activities or the beginning and ending dates of projects going on at the same time.

PERT Diagrams. PERT stands for *Program Evaluation and Review Technique*. PERT diagrams are useful for scheduling complex projects.

To use the PERT technique, identify the project's major activities. Then arrange the activities on the diagram in order. Connect with arrows activities that must occur in a fixed sequence. Finally, estimate and indicate the time necessary to complete each activity. An example of PERT scheduling is illustrated in **Figure 16–3**.

The longest path through the diagram is the *critical path*. Activities on this path dictate the time in which the project is completed. By completing critical path activities on schedule, you can control the project.

Controlling Quality

Quality control is the process of making sure that the goods or services you produce meet certain standards. Standards can be set for appearance, performance, and consistency. If you run a frozen yogurt shop, customers will expect the same quality and quantity every time they buy a cone. Quality control makes sure they get both.

The standards you set for your business will reflect the market segment you are targeting. Customers who want high quality will pay more for it. Customers who want low prices will expect reasonable—but not particularly high—quality.

Quality control takes time and costs money, but it is a way to ensure customer satisfaction. How do you achieve quality control? There are two major ways:

1. Quality Circles. Quality circles are groups of employees who handle problems regarding quality. This approach has been used successfully by large manufacturers such as Ford. However, the concept can also work for small operations. Quality circles improve quality because they require employees to be responsible for their work. It gives them the power to make decisions about quality.

2. Inspection. You can also inspect your products to control quality. If you do, you must decide whether to perform the inspection during the job or afterward. When you inspect your product depends on what you're selling.

If you manufacture complex equipment, you will probably inspect your product at several stages of the production process. That way, defects are caught and corrected immediately.

Figure 16–3
This PERT diagram lays out the process of remodeling a building for use as a food carry-out business. ***What is the minimal amount of time required for the completion of the project?***

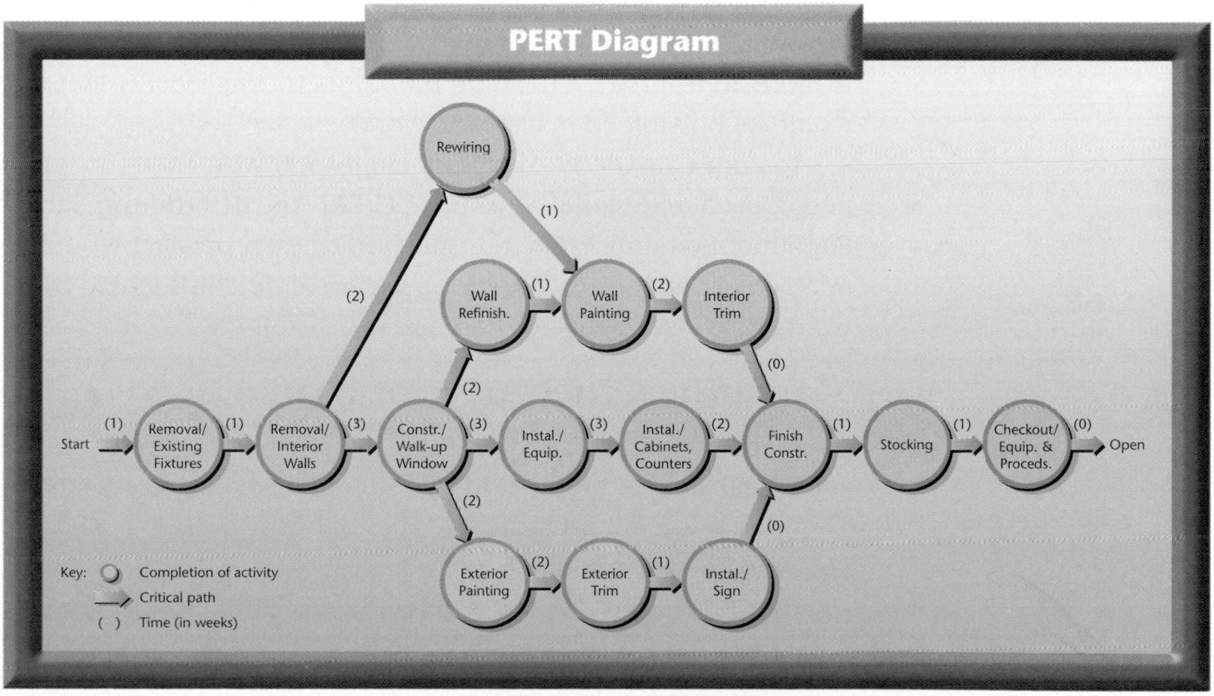

RISK TAKERS PROFIT MAKERS

Name: Windy Chien
Company: Aquarius Records
City, State: San Francisco, CA

The Age of Aquarius

"No one likes to sell something they don't believe in," explains Windy Chien. That's why her record store only carries music that she or one of her sales staff likes. This policy has created a unique inventory of music that includes independent rock, underground hip-hop, old reggae, and new dance music. The policy has also made Windy very successful.

After Windy bought the Aquarius Records shop in 1996, the number of sales quadrupled in two years. However, she doesn't measure her shop's success by its profits. She looks at her employees. "All of my employees have been with me for at least two years, which means they're happy," she says. "Keeping your employees happy—that's the most important thing."

In turn, the Aquarius staff keeps the customers happy and the customers keep coming back. "Once you turn someone on to a good record," suggests Windy, "you've got a friend for life."

Thinking Critically

What is the most important measure of success for a business?

If you provide a service such as dry cleaning, a final inspection is more appropriate. There are no points in the process where it would be possible to inspect the work.

You must also decide if you should inspect each and every product or just a representative sample. Cost is the determining factor. For a mobile-home builder, inspection of each product would be relatively inexpensive. However, a chocolate chip cookie baker would only check selected batches.

Managing Other Areas of Production

Productivity, automation, and preventive maintenance are additional areas of production that should be managed effectively. These areas are important to all types of businesses.

Productivity. Productivity is a measure of how much a business produces in a given time. It can also be expressed in terms of the output of each worker per unit of time. Machinists at a tool factory might have a productivity rate of 35 units per day.

Businesses can use productivity rates to measure and improve employee performance. For example, at a bakery one confectioner might bake two batches of pastries in an hour. Another might bake only one batch per hour, but produce pastries that are more elegant and tasty. With this information, an owner could find out what method increases sales, and adjust business practices.

Automation. Automation is the use of machines to do the work of people. Automation can cut production time, reduce errors, and simplify procedures. However, it can be expensive. Manufacturing and clerical tasks often lend themselves to automation.

Maintenance. The maintenance of machinery is a key factor in production management. There are three basic ways to manage maintenance.

1. *Organize your production process.* Arrange it so that when one machine is down, the work can be shifted to other machines.
2. *Build up inventories at each stage of the production process.* That way, other machines can continue to run.
3. *Conduct preventive maintenance.* This means fixing machines before they break down.

Money Matters

RESEARCH

A client can become a great source of profitable suggestions and ideas. According to Earl Bakken, co-founder of Medtronic:

"*We still do focus groups. . . . to make sure we're moving in the right direction.*"

Clothing is one product that is commonly checked by inspection. Often the checker leaves a tag in the articles of clothing he or she inspects. ***What might be some reasons for putting the tag in pants pockets, for example?***

DISTRIBUTION MANAGEMENT

Distribution management includes transportation, storage, materials handling, and specification of delivery terms. It controls the movement of a product from the manufacturer to customers.

Transportation

Shipping a product by plane, truck, railroad, pipeline, or waterway is regulated by federal and state agencies. Transporters are classified into three categories:

1. **Common carriers**, such as Federal Express and United Parcel Service, can be used by the general public.
2. **Contract carriers** have a contract with a particular shipper to handle their goods. A railroad is a contract carrier.
3. **Private carriers** are private companies that ship goods. A trucking company is an example.

Automated production can be faster and more precise than a human assembly line. ***What are some disadvantages?***

Storage

Entrepreneurs with limited resources might not be able to afford their own storage facilities. They may have a wholesaler store and distribute their products or store goods in a public warehouse.

Materials Handling

There's more to distribution than transportation and storage. You also need to handle the products without damaging them. This might include shipping containers, forklifts, and other aids.

Up&Coming Entrepreneur

Gourmet Cheesecake Entrepreneur

Before she discovered her talent for baking cheesecake, Lynn Carr moved from one friend's home to another while pursuing her high school equivalency diploma. Today, her Twainland Cheesecake Company and Café produces 116 varieties of cheesecakes with the help of ten employees, mostly high school dropouts and welfare moms, teaching them financial independence as a way of life. "Cheesecake is just a product. What we're really in is the people-growing business," Carr insists.

Analyze **How might Lynn Carr's hiring employees with misfortunes actually be a benefit to her business?**

Delivery Terms

On any shipment there will be delivery terms. Delivery terms identify who is responsible for the various components of distribution. As a small business owner, the most favorable delivery term is "free on board" or FOB. This means that the buyer pays all freight costs. In addition, the title to the goods passes to the buyer when the goods leave the manufacturer. Once the goods leave the warehouse, the responsibility for costs and loss go to the buyer.

Outsourcing Logistics

The details of a product's movement from the manufacturer to the customer are called logistics. You can handle the logistics yourself or outsource it. To decide, ask yourself three questions:

1. *Is your competition using transportation as a competitive advantage?*
2. *Are you seeking markets in other countries?*
3. *Are you having problems with shipments you're handling yourself?*

If you answer "yes" to any of these questions, you may need assistance from a logistics firm.

CHECK YOUR UNDERSTANDING

SECTION 16.2

Reviewing Key Terms and Concepts

1 What is the difference between Gantt charts and PERT diagrams?
2 What are two ways to approach quality control?
3 What is productivity, and what are two ways to increase productivity in your business?

Critical Thinking Activity

Investigate the various transportation modes a video game company might use to ship software from Atlanta to Singapore. Which mode seems to be the best for this type of product?

Extension Lab—Designing and Improving Systems

Campus Cafe Your entrepreneurship class has decided to run a food service on campus. You will be selling muffins and fruit to students. Every Friday, you will prepare and serve lunch to the faculty.
Presentation In groups of three or four, come up with a plan for quality control. Share your ideas with the class. Use the following steps for guidelines:

- Discuss the standards for the taste and appearance of your food.
- Determine how you will monitor the quality of the service you provide.
- Create a plan to achieve quality control of both the food and service.

CHAPTER 16 REVIEW

CHAPTER SUMMARY

- Product development is considered the highest risk part of start-up for a small business.
- Small business owners can reduce the cost and risks involved with product development by hiring other people to do the work.
- The four steps in product development are: (1) opportunity recognition, (2) concept investigation, (3) product design, and (4) prototype building and testing.
- Production management has three functions: (1) acquiring the resources needed for production, (2) planning the steps to convert the resources into products, and (3) making sure the products meet the standards set for them.
- Businesses plan their production through schedules. Two commonly used graphic scheduling techniques are Gantt charts and PERT diagrams.
- Quality circles and inspections are two ways to ensure that the goods and services you produce meet the standards you set for them.
- Productivity, automation, and preventive maintenance must be managed effectively as part of the production process.
- Distribution management concerns the physical movement of the product from the manufacturer to the customer.

RECALL KEY TERMS

Describe the production management and distribution processes you might use for the plastic key chains you plan to manufacture. Use the following terms in your description.

product development	**productivity**
outsourcing	**automation**
prototype	**common carriers**
Gantt charts	**contract carriers**
PERT diagrams	**private carrier**
quality control	**FOB**
quality circles	**logistics**

RECALL KEY CONCEPTS

1. Why would a small business owner outsource the product development process?
2. Why is it best to design a product right the first time?
3. Which scheduling technique would be most useful for complex projects?
4. What are the advantages of automating the production process?
5. What are the three basic ways to manage maintenance of machinery used in the production process?
6. Describe the three categories of transporters used to distribute products from the manufacturer to the customers.
7. What is the most favorable delivery term for a small business owner? Why?
8. When might you want to outsource a part of the distribution management process?

THINK CRITICALLY

1. Why is it essential to involve potential customers in the design and prototype process of a product?

CHAPTER 16 REVIEW

2. Briefly describe how production management can be applied to each of the five types of businesses: retail, wholesale, service, manufacturing, and extraction.
3. When and how could Gantt charts or PERT diagrams be useful in your selected business?
4. Why is quality control important?
5. Explain why distribution can make or break a business.

CONNECT ACADEMICS TO THE WORKPLACE

Math

1. Andrea works in a manufacturing plant and is paid a bonus based on her productivity. Using the following information, determine how much money Andrea earned last month.

Base salary	$320 per week
Bonus, Week 1	6.0%
Bonus, Week 2	2.6%
Bonus, Week 3	3.5 %
Bonus, Week 4	8.8%

Use Computers to Process Information

2. Select a class or school project. Prepare a Gantt chart using a word processing or spreadsheet program to schedule the tasks that make up your project. Estimate the time needed for each part of the project. Plan also to track the actual progress of your project against the planned activities.

WORK IN YOUR COMMUNITY

Interview someone in your community who has created a new product or service.

- Find out how the product prototype was developed.
- Ask if the production process was outsourced. If not, why not?
- Determine what quality control methods were used during the production process.
- Find out how the product is distributed to customers.

LINK SCHOOL TO CAREER

As a class, hold an "Invention Convention." Students can work individually or in groups to:

- Design a new product or invention.
- Build a prototype of the product and demonstrate its use to the class.
- Determine how much it might cost to develop the idea into a real product.

*inter*NET CONNECTION

Shipping Time

Dexter is ready to begin distributing a new line of watches to his customers. He wants to use a common carrier that is inexpensive yet reliable. He also would like to be able to track the progress of a shipment easily. You suggest he research the Internet to find out what is available.

Connect

Use a variety of search engines to create a report on using the Internet for research.

- Research the Web sites of common carriers like Federal Express and UPS.
- Determine shipping costs on comparable weights.
- Compare tracking procedures.
- Find out if international services are available.

CHAPTER 17

Managing Operations and Staffing

Learning Objectives

When you have completed this chapter, you will be able to:

- **Formulate** operating policies for your business
- **Write** personnel policies for your business
- **Prepare** an organizational chart for your business
- **Define** job descriptions and specifications
- **Determine** rules that apply to your business

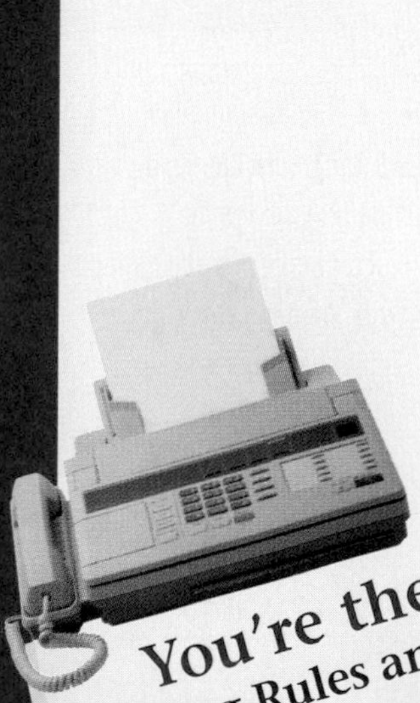

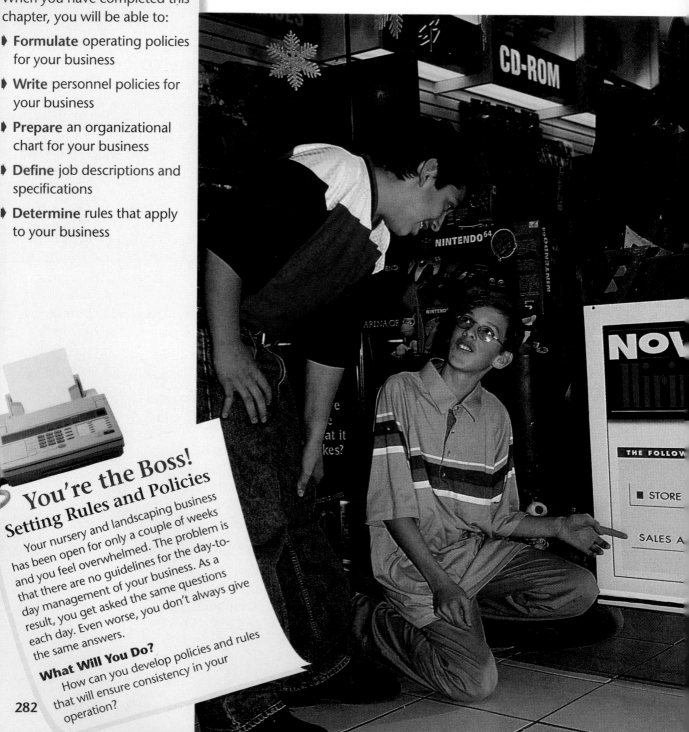

You're the Boss!

Setting Rules and Policies

Your nursery and landscaping business has been open for only a couple of weeks and you feel overwhelmed. The problem is that there are no guidelines for the day-to-day management of your business. As a result, you get asked the same questions each day. Even worse, you don't always give the same answers.

What Will You Do?

How can you develop policies and rules that will ensure consistency in your operation?

SECTION 17.1

Managing Operations

What you'll learn

- the role of policies and rules in managing operations
- the difference between policies and rules
- the process used to develop common operating policies
- operating policies and rules to consider for your business

Why it's important

For your operation to run smoothly, there has to be consistency in the way things are done and how people are treated. This is achieved by establishing and implementing policies and rules.

KEY TERMS

policies
rules
credit

IMPLEMENTING OPERATIONAL PLANS

The goal of managing a business is to put operational plans into action. These plans will govern your day-to-day business operations. They include productivity issues such as schedules and quotas. They also include the policies, rules, and staffing concerns that help keep a business going.

OPERATING POLICIES, RULES, AND REGULATIONS

When you start a business, you might manage the operation alone. However, as your business grows, it will become harder for you to make all the decisions. You may eventually need to delegate your responsibilities to employees.

Policies are general statements of intent about how to run your business. They simplify day-to-day management so you don't have to make the same decisions over and over again. A business may have a policy about working hours or overtime pay. Policies are meant to handle recurring situations, but they are flexible. They leave room for interpretation. Permitting an employee to come in late if he or she has a doctor's appointment is an example of policy.

In contrast, **rules** tell employees exactly what they should or should not do. They leave no room for interpretation. "Employees shall wear hard hats in all construction areas" is a rule. So is "All employees shall get two weeks' vacation after one year's service." They also can impose restrictions on customers: "Smoking is not permitted in the building."

Not all policies apply to all types of businesses. However, you can use the following examples as a starting point for policy statements that fit your business.

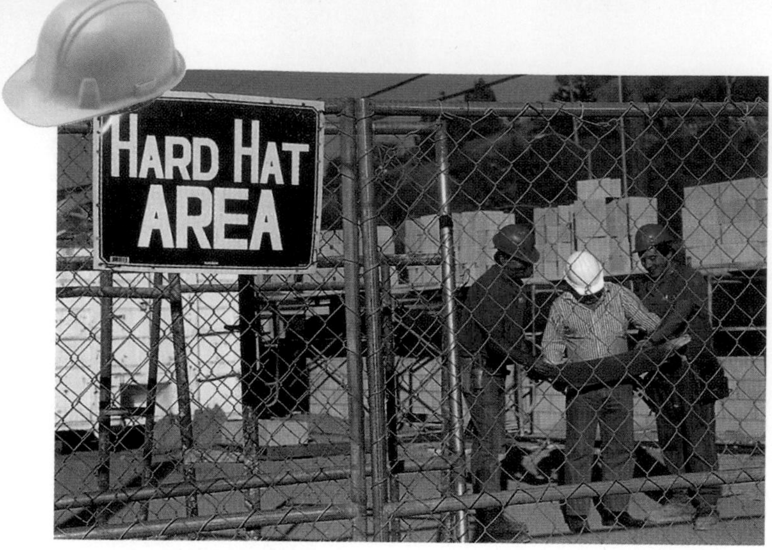

Certain work sites post clearly marked rules. ***Why is this important?***

Hours of Operation

Hours of operation are an important part of a business place strategy. When can your customers reach your location? When would it be most convenient for you to contact them? Will you be able to deliver your product to customers when they want it?

Hours should be set to suit the customers. For example, a movie theater might be open between noon and midnight on weekdays. It would be open later on Fridays and weekends when most people want to see movies. In contrast, a wholesaler might have much shorter hours. Office hours might be limited to 9:00–5:00 weekdays through Saturday. Those are the hours that their customers, typically businesses, phone in orders. On the other hand, delivery hours might be longer to accommodate the varying business hours of customers.

Credit Policies

Pricing does not only entail what you charge for your goods or services. It also addresses how much your customers can pay for them. One important part of your pricing strategy is *credit*. Credit is an arrangement in which a business or individual can obtain products in exchange for a promise to pay later.

Your first decision will be whether to accept or provide credit payments. A no-credit policy suits businesses that sell low-priced items and consumable goods. That is why some convenience stores and fast-food restaurants do not offer credit. However, if your business sells big-ticket items or if you encourage customers to buy in large quantities, you will want to make your products easy to buy.

If you allow credit, you will need to make a number of other decisions. You will have to select the form (or forms) of credit you will extend. You will also have to decide to whom you will offer credit and in what amounts.

There are several types of credit plans. Each has its own set of costs and advantages. Examples are shown in **Figure 17–1**.

The Three C's of Credit. Most businesses that offer credit have standards to determine who is eligible to receive it. One formula that is commonly used is known as the *three C's of credit*:

Figure 17–1

Credit Plans

Credit plans make it easier for a customer to make a purchase. However, each type has different costs and risks for the business.

1. Bank credit cards.

Many businesses accept bank credit cards. Since the bank that issues the card (not the customer) pays the bill, there is less risk for the merchant in this form of credit. However, bankcard issuers take a percentage of each charged purchase as a collection fee.

2. Charge accounts.

With this form of credit, the business gets the full purchase price plus a finance charge (a form of interest) if the balance is not paid within the established time limit. However, the business pays all the costs associated with collecting on these accounts. It also assumes the risk of nonpayment.

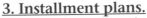

3. Installment plans.

Businesses that sell costly goods or services might offer an installment plan. For example, some furniture stores allow customers to make a down payment and then make regular payments. Some offer incentives such as no interest for a year. The costs and risks of installment plans are similar to those for charge accounts.

4. Financing.

Financing sales through a bank is usually reserved for very expensive goods, like new automobiles. With this form of credit, the business gets its money more quickly. However, the customer can be inconvenienced by delays at the time of purchase. His or her credit history and situation must be checked and approved.

- *Character*. Has the customer demonstrated responsibility in paying bills? You can find this out by contacting a credit bureau. Credit bureaus give good credit ratings to those who pay their bills on time. Poor credit ratings are assigned to those who don't.
- *Capacity*. Based on the customer's income and expenses, does he or she have the ability to pay? You can find this out by

asking credit applicants to report their income and monthly expenses on your credit application form.

- *Capital.* What are the customer's physical and financial assets? This information can be requested on your credit application form.

How much credit you extend to individual customers will depend on the three C's. You will probably set generous limits for those with higher incomes, good credit ratings, and substantial assets (such as a home or savings accounts). You will probably set lower limits for those with modest means. You will probably deny credit to those with bad credit ratings.

Return/Rework Policies

You may choose to have a return or rework policy. This means that your business will guarantee the quality of the goods you sell or the services you provide.

A fair policy regarding replacements, refunds, or repairs will help maintain customer goodwill. For example, you may consider something like "If we don't install it right, we'll fix it free." Many businesses offer a more limited guarantee, such as parts and labor free for six months, while others offer a "Money back guaranteed, no questions asked" return policy. The latter policy can be more costly than the others, but you may have to adopt it in order to be competitive.

Delivery Policies

Does your business need a delivery policy? For some service businesses, a delivery policy is the key to success. Domino's Pizza built a national reputation

ENTREPRENEURS INTERNATIONAL

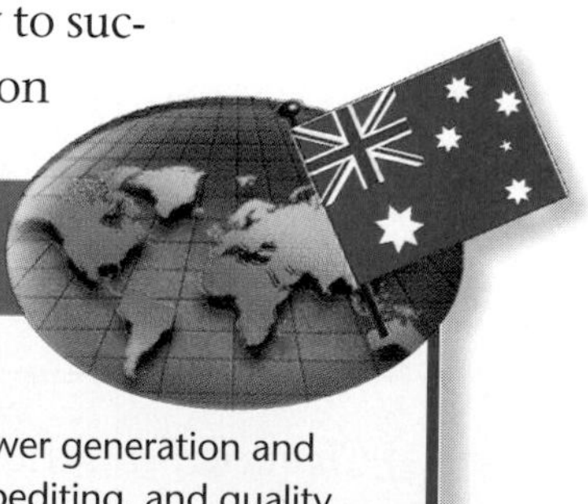

Australia

Phillip Wilton founded Q.A. Management Services in 1985 to gauge Australia's power generation and gas pipeline construction industries. Today, QAMS is one of the largest inspection, expediting, and quality assurance networks in the world. Major clients such as Hitachi and Shell can log into QAMS' network at any time for real-time project status information. "As a service provider rather than a manpower placement organization, we take full technical responsibility for the work undertaken," says Wilton.

Apply **Why might it be a good idea to look to an outside company to help implement quality assurance?**

with its original delivery policy. It promised "Delivery in 30 minutes, or it's free."

Delivery policies can be crucial for other types of businesses as well. Retailers who sell big-ticket items such as refrigerators risk losing sales if they don't deliver their products on time. Where will the customer store food if he or she doesn't receive the refrigerator on time? Wholesalers have to deliver goods on time to stay competitive as well.

If you decide to offer delivery, there are other aspects of the policy to consider. Will you charge for the service? Will you limit the delivery service to a certain area? Your resources and the competition will determine your answers.

Other Customer Service Policies

There are too many other service policies to list in detail. However, you should consider the following.

- *Handling complaints.* Most businesses use the policy, "The customer is always right."
- *Servicing what you sell.* If something you sell stops working within a certain time limit, will you fix it?
- *Courtesy to customers.* Some businesses require their clerks to ask departing customers, "Did you find everything you were looking for?"
- *Shopping climate.* Your business may have a policy of maintaining certain lighting or housekeeping standards.
- *Provision of restrooms.* Will these be open to the public or locked and usable by customers only on request?

Money Matters

LOANS

For entrepreneurs, nonbank lenders could be a good source of funding. Bill Sihler, finance professor at the University of Virginia, explains:

"In general, finance companies want to see strong assets to back up a loan and will monitor those assets much more carefully."

Delivering your goods or services adds convenience to your business. ***Where are some places that might be ideal for a restaurant that delivers food?***

- *Response time*. Some businesses advertise, "All orders filled within 48 hours of receipt."
- *Warranties*. Manufacturers usually guarantee the materials and workmanship that go into their products.

Employee and Customer Safety

The financial costs of an on-site accident can ruin a small business. However, you can take two basic precautionary measures.

First, train your employees in safety practices and procedures. Equipment may require protective gear or instructions for safe operation. There should also be emergency procedures in case of a mishap. Reinforce the training with signs posted throughout the workplace.

It's also important to protect your customers. A store can keep customers away from delicate or potentially damaging equipment with a warning: "Authorized personnel only." A restaurant can let guests know when a section of floor has been mopped. It's also important to make it clear to customers not to use certain facilities, such as elevators, during emergencies.

CHECK YOUR UNDERSTANDING

SECTION 17.1

Reviewing Key Terms and Concepts

1. What role do policies and rules play in managing operations?
2. Explain the difference between policies and rules.
3. Identify and list five common operating policies that could apply to any business.

Critical Thinking Activity

Make a list of the operational policies discussed in this section that may be applicable to a type of business you might be interested in starting.

Extension Lab—Speaking Skills

Credit Counts You are helping out at the family-owned furniture store. In addition to handling the billing and posting of customers' payments, one of your additional duties is to explain the various credit plans your store offers when prospective customers are thinking about purchasing an item.

Oral Presentation In groups of two or three, explain to the class the various credit plans listed as they relate to the furniture store.

- Bank credit cards
- Store charge accounts
- Installment plans
- Financing

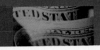

SECTION 17.2

Staffing and Company Policies

STAFFING YOUR OPERATION

If you intend to run a one-person operation, your staffing plan will be simple. However, for most businesses it is unlikely that you will be able to do all the work yourself. Even if you only plan on having one or two employees, you will have to familiarize yourself with the process of staffing.

To staff your business properly, you will use four types of forms. You will have to design an organization chart, write job descriptions, list job specifications, and compile professional summaries of yourself and your employees.

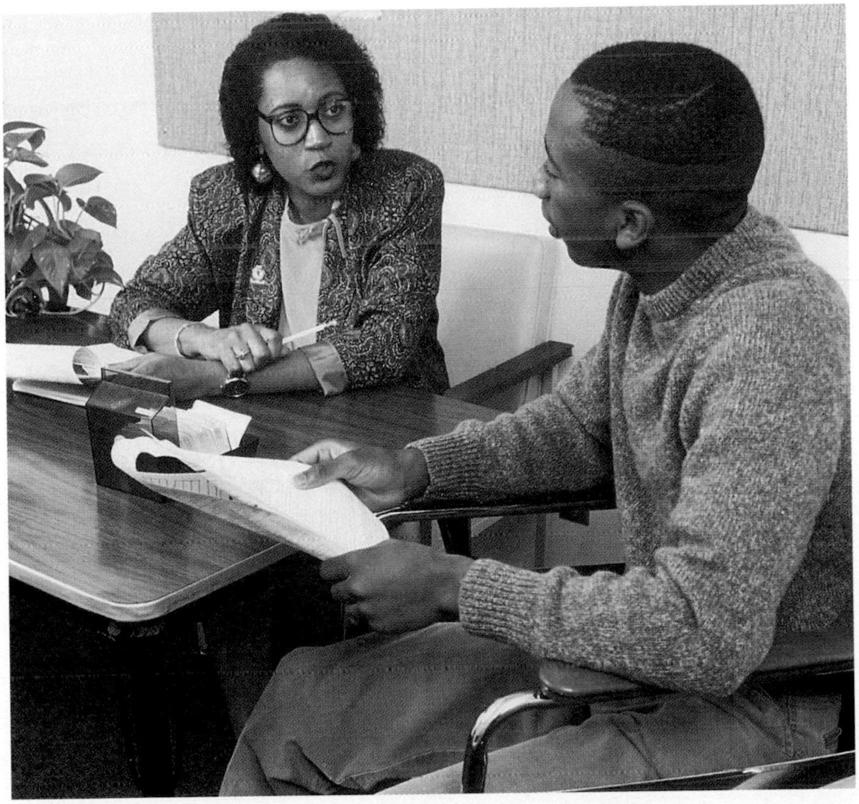

What you'll learn

- types of organizational structures
- the need for job descriptions, specifications, and summaries for your business
- the process for developing policies for your business

Why it's important

Staffing involves who does the work in your company and how your company is perceived. Consequently, your policies and decisions in this area have a direct bearing on its success.

KEY TERMS

line organization
staff
line-and-staff organization
job description
job specification
recruit
piece rate
commission

Figure 17–2
The line organization of this small owner-operated wholesale business shows who reports to whom. ***Who would the warehouse employee report to?***

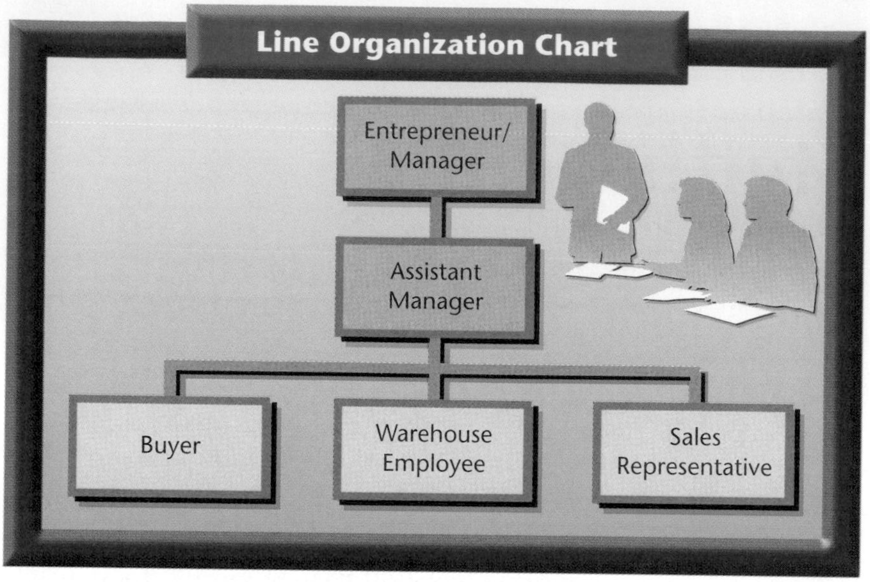

Types of Organization

What type of organizational structure will your business need? To decide on a structure, develop an organization chart. This diagram includes all the functional areas needed in your enterprise and shows how they are related to each other.

As you create your organization chart, keep in mind that its structure should help you delegate responsibility, authority, and work. Also, each job may not require a full-time employee. Stay open to other possibilities. For example, some jobs can be contracted out to consultants. Others may require only part-time employees.

There are several types of business organization. Here are some of the most common forms:

- *Line Organization.* Most small businesses use a line organization to structure their new business. An example is shown in **Figure 17–2**. This structure is effective if your employees will be involved in producing or distributing your product. It shows the various levels of positions, with you (as owner) at the top. Personnel who report to you are in the middle. Those who report to them are at the bottom.
- *Line-and-Staff Organization.* Your operation may become large enough to hire a staff. This term is often used for employees in general, but technically it refers only to those who provide

support for production and distribution people. Examples of staff might include those involved in bookkeeping or personnel activities. When diagramming a business that has a staff, you would use line-and-staff organization . The chart in **Figure 17–3** resembles the line organization chart. However, there are more positions and more levels of authority. The key difference is that a broken line ties in the bookkeeper and the personnel manager. That reflects the difference between staff and line personnel.

- *Project organizations.* Matrix and task-team organizations are temporary entities. They are used to supplement line or line-and-staff structures for special projects. Suppose that your company creates, manufactures, and sells greeting cards. If you are surprised by a huge order for Mother's Day cards, you may need to form a special task team to fill the demand. Employees assigned to such a task work on the project until the project is done. Then they return to their assignment in the formal organization. Large companies most often use these models, but small businesses can apply them as well.

Figure 17–3
A line organization chart shows the different roles of staff with different types of lines. ***What is the difference between the personnel, linked by solid lines, and staff positions, linked by dotted lines?***

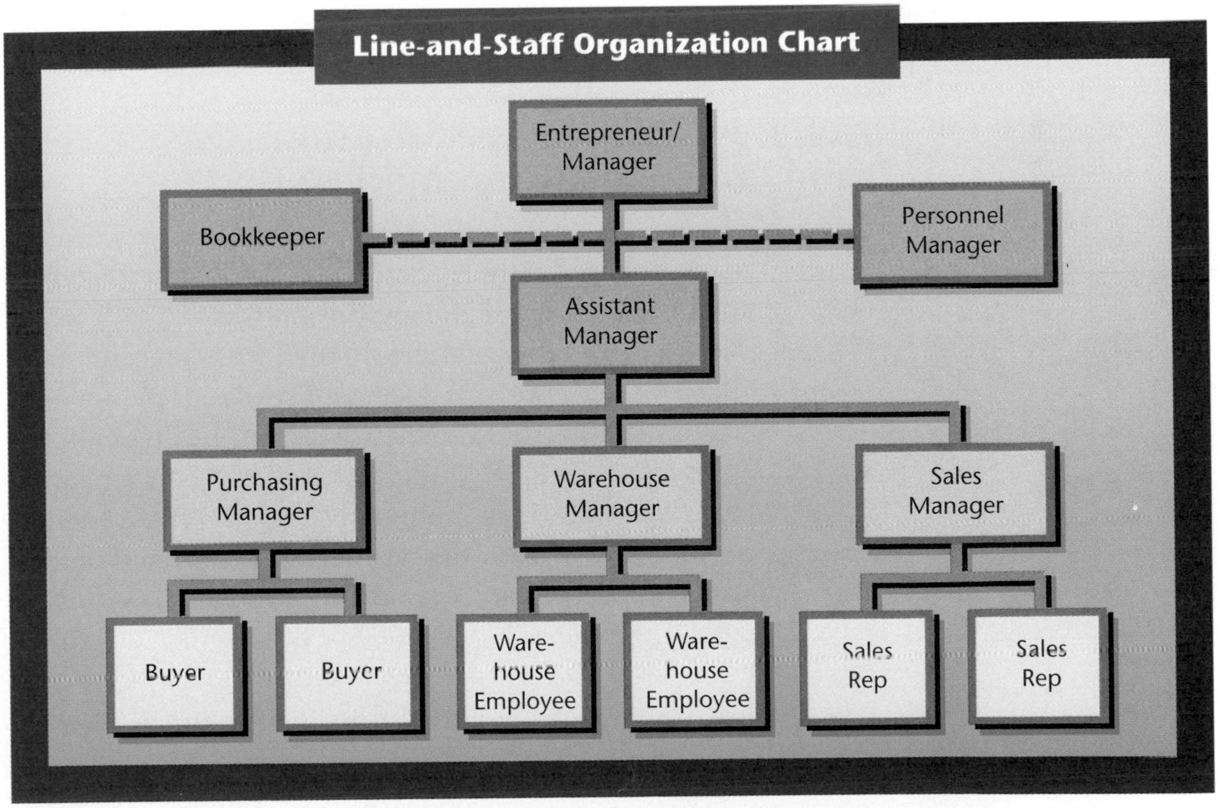

RISK TAKERS PROFIT MAKERS

Name: Lori Bowles
Business: Workforce 2000
City, State: Bedford, TX

Outsourcing Human Resources

Lori Bowles had an idea to develop an organization that managed employees for employers. She thought it would allow a business owner to concentrate on growing a core business while she took care of the red tape and paperwork associated with human resources. Workforce 2000 places employees in a client's business and retains the right to hire and fire them. It provides the payroll service as well as administers the benefits, job safety, and incentive programs. Since 1986, Bowles' Workforce 2000 has grown into a company with $38 million in annual sales and manages 2,100 employees in 14 states.

Workforce 2000 consults daily with clients and employees. "My clients may not think this is the fun part of the job, but I get a lot of satisfaction knowing that we're employing quality people and helping businesses succeed," says Bowles.

Thinking Critically

Could Workforce 2000 benefit a start-up business?

Job Descriptions, Specifications, and Professional Summaries

For each position in your organization chart, you will need to write a job description. This is a statement describing the objectives of the job and its duties and responsibilities.

For each job description, you should then write a second statement—a job specification. This document spells out the abilities, skills, educational level, and experience needed by an employee to perform the described job. Think of it as a kind of want ad.

Finally, create professional summaries of yourself and others you expect to be involved in the business. These should outline the skills and experience each person contributes. By comparing them with your job descriptions and specifications, you will be able to recognize gaps in your organization's staffing. These gaps highlight the areas where you will need to look for outside assistance.

Personnel Policies and Decisions

Before your begin to actively search for employees, think about the kind of people you want. Then decide how to find them.

Employee Standards. The people you hire affect what customers and clients think of your company. It is your employees who make up its face, voice, and reputation. That is why entrepreneurs establish hiring policies. All personnel decisions that you make will reflect this policy.

Define the traits you want on your policy statement. Your policy may be no more than the statement "Our organization will hire only the best people." Who are the best people? That will depend on the type of business you have. For a retail operation, you may want very social individuals; for a bookkeeping service, people who are detail oriented; for a custom carpentry business, people who share your high standards of quality. Under any circumstances, you will want people who project a positive professional image.

Recruiting Employees. There are many ways to recruit, or bring in, prospective employees. You can use classified ads, state-run and private employment agencies, school and college placement offices, union hiring halls, and word of mouth. Each recruitment method reaches a different type of applicant. Listing a job opening on an Internet job board would attract computer-literate applicants. Use the recruiting method that best suits the position you want to fill.

When you start to attract applicants, you will have to *screen* them. This can involve a number of steps. A common first screen

Up & Coming Entrepreneur

Floral Entrepreneur

Lorraine Willney gained experience in floral design and business management while she worked as an employee at various floral boutiques. In 1988, she purchased a small existing floral business, hired two employees, and was in business for herself. "We left the old shop name the same for a year so the customers would get to know us and get used to our new level of service," says Willney. Flowers By Lorraine has grown from $125,000 in sales since its beginning to over $500,000 annually.

Analyze **Why was it important for Lorraine Willney 's new customers to become familiar with her quality of service?**

Key Rules for Effective Interviewing

1. Define what you are looking for before the interview.
2. Conduct interviews in private. Don't use panel interviews.
3. Put the interviewees at ease. Treat them as equals.
4. Ask general background questions first, more specific questions later.
5. Encourage the interviewee to talk. Be a good listener.
6. Don't cut off the interviewee's answers, but interrupt when necessary to make a key point.
7. Confirm key observations several times during the interview.
8. Provide an opportunity for the interviewee to ask questions.
9. Look for how the interviewee conducts him or herself. Particularly note attitude and enthusiasm.
10. Look for what they will bring to the job.
11. Cover all your planned areas in enough detail to be able to make a sound decision.

Figure 17–4
These rules provide general guidelines for conducting an interview. ***What are some legal guidelines to consider?***

used by businesses is an application form or résumé. Either one will help you see how well an applicant matches up to your job specification. Those who don't fit your requirements can be eliminated from consideration immediately.

If you are impressed by an application or résumé, you can schedule an interview with the person. By meeting the applicant, you can find out more about his or her qualifications. You can also find out about the person's interpersonal and communication skills. **Figure 17–4** lists guidelines for conducting effective interviews.

During the interview, you may want to test the applicant. Tests can be used to evaluate an employee's intelligence, aptitude, achievement, interest, personality, and honesty. Be sure that your tests relate to the job.

Finally, you can request character references. Former employers can tell you about a person's previous job performance. Teachers, coaches, family members, and others can also help you find out about his or her reliability, work ethic, and other qualities.

Pay and Benefits. In order to attract and keep the kind of employees you want, you will have to do two things. First, you will have to pay a competitive wage or salary. This means paying a rate that is similar to the rates offered by other businesses with similar employee needs. Second, you will have to offer competitive employee benefits.

There are several ways to figure pay. One way is to pay wages based on the amount of time the employee works. You could, for example, pay an hourly rate or a flat salary per week, month, or year. Another way to pay is based on productivity. Productivity pay could be either a **piece rate** (so much per unit produced) or a **commission** (a percentage of sales). For example, a person who makes teddy bears may get paid by the unit. The person who sells them may get a percentage of the sales. It could also be a combination of productivity pay and salary. A person who sells cars may receive a salary and a commission. Base the way you pay on what is standard for your industry.

There are many kinds of employee benefits. Some are required by law. These include the employer's contribution to Social Security, unemployment compensation, and workers' compensation. Optional benefits include paid vacations, paid sick leave, health and life insurance, flextime, pensions, and child care. Companies offer benefits in conjunction with pay as a way to attract and keep good employees.

As you consider the benefits you will give your employees, you will want to keep their cost in mind. Compensating your employees is a major business expense. Typically, benefits for an employee run between 20 and 40 percent of salary. Therefore, if you pay an employee $1,700 a month, the cost of benefits for that employee will be between $340 and $680 a month.

Training and Development. You may hire very capable and intelligent people, but if they are not

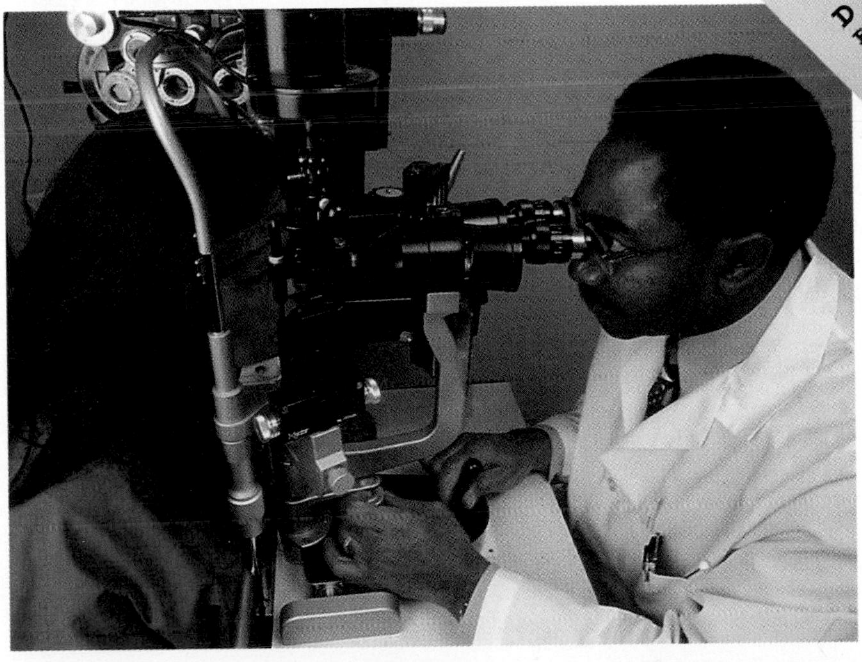

To compete with other employers, companies offer many forms of health care. ***How does this benefit the employer and the employee?***

Tips from the Real World

YOUR PEERS

Many entrepreneurs benefit from peer groups. Allen Fishman, head of a Denver-based peer group, points out:

> "*One of the major benefits is a cross-fertilization of ideas from people who are not in your field. . . . Some of the best ideas will come from people who aren't locked into your historical ways of thinking.*"

trained, they may not be beneficial to your company. New employees work better and are more efficient if they receive training immediately. Unless your business is highly technical, this early training will be given on the job—and you will be the trainer.

As your operation grows, you may need to hire a specialist to handle your training needs and the long-term development of your employees. You also have the option of contracting with outside consultants to provide these services.

Personnel Records. Staffing responsibilities don't end with the hiring and training decisions. You also have to make decisions about establishing and maintaining personnel files.

For your own use, you will need contact information and training and performance records. For government agencies, you will be required to keep certain documents for a specified period.

All of an employee's records can be kept in the same file. However, maintaining separate file categories facilitates auditing by government agencies. It also ensures privacy where necessary. Divisions for separate files may include primary personnel files, payroll records, medical records, and records of applicants not hired.

Other personnel file policies must be established with regard to security of the files, supervisor access, and employee access. Since every document has the potential for becoming a legal exhibit, a policy prohibiting personal notations on files should also be considered.

Keeping track of all the paper in personnel files can be a major job. You may want to use computer software to manage the personnel files.

DEVELOPING ADDITIONAL POLICIES FOR YOUR OPERATION

It is clear that there are many different policies and rules to consider for your operation. How can you be sure that you won't miss any that are vitally important to your business? Use the four-step procedure:

1. *Review operational processes.* Make a list of the operational rules and policies that apply to your business. Then, in your mind, go through a typical business day and note any situation that could require additional policies.

2. *Check competitor operations.* Observe and ask questions to determine your competitors' policies. Review their policy statements if obtainable. Find out which ones you're missing.
3. *Get feedback from potential customers.* Set up focus groups or survey potential customers. Record policies they want and the priority ratings they gave to those policies. Devise ways to monitor customer relations policies.
4. *Write policy statements.* Write a policy statement based on the data you've gathered.

As you work through these steps, remember that the intent of a policy is to simplify day-to-day management. Therefore, don't let your policies and rules get out of hand. Too many can limit your flexibility. Restrict your policy statements to situations in which they will eliminate the need to make routine decisions. Use rules only where they are necessary, in such areas as health and safety, fundamental fairness, and customer relations.

Once your business is under way, check to see that your policies are being implemented and that they are working. You can accomplish this through (1) periodic monitoring and (2) continued use of the customer feedback system you implemented for policy input.

CHECK YOUR UNDERSTANDING

SECTION 17.2

Reviewing Key Terms and Concepts

1 Draw examples of the two formal organizational structures described in this section.
2 Write a sample job description and a job specification for a position in your business.
3 List the steps in the process for developing a complete set of policy statements.

Critical Thinking Activity

Develop a complete set of policy statements for your proposed business.

Extension Lab—Decision-Making Skills

Work-out You co-own a retail exercise equipment store. When the business opened, you and your partner agreed on a "Money back guaranteed, no questions asked" return policy. However, you are now finding out that many customers would purchase equipment only to return it when they get tired of it. This return policy winds up costing you a lot of money.

Role Play In groups of two or three, enact a discussion between the partners. Bear in mind the following:

- Should you continue to offer this policy?
- Is there another policy that would be more cost-effective, yet would allow you still to be competitive?

CHAPTER 17 REVIEW

CHAPTER SUMMARY

- Managing your business requires you to put your operational plans into action.
- Operating policies include hours of operation, credit policies, procedures for returning/reworking a product, and delivery policies.
- The three C's of credit are character, capacity, and capital.
- As you begin to staff your organization, create an organizational chart to help you delegate responsibility, authority, and work.
- Three of the most common types of organizational structures are line, line-and-staff, and project organizations.
- Writing job descriptions and job specifications will help you determine the kind of employee you want.
- When trying to find prospective employees, use a recruiting method that best suits the position you want to fill.
- Try to avoid having so many policies, rules, and regulations that they limit your flexibility in managing your business.

RECALL KEY TERMS

Write a set of questions that you could use when interviewing prospective employees. Use the following key terms in your questions.

policies
rules
credit
line organization
staff
line-and-staff organization
job description
job specification
recruit
piece rate
commission

RECALL KEY CONCEPTS

1. How does establishing policies simplify the day-to-day management of a business?
2. Explain the differences between policies and rules and give two examples of each.
3. Describe the differences between bank credit cards, charge accounts, installment plans, and financing.
4. What is the difference between a line organization and a line-and-staff organization?
5. Compare a job description with a résumé.
6. What are some of the ways you can screen potential employees?
7. How can you be sure your business policies are being implemented and followed?

THINK CRITICALLY

1. What policies, if any, should every business have?
2. What factors will help you decide whether or not to offer credit to your customers?
3. Create a list of customer service policies from businesses in your community. Are they similar to those listed in the chapter?
4. What is the best way to get information to prospective employees about job openings that you have? Defend your choice.
5. Would your prospective business be better off trying to recruit and retain employees with an attractive pay and benefits package? Or would it be better off by hiring part-time people to carry out all or most of the job duties? How about by contracting

out all or most of the work you need done? Why?

CONNECT ACADEMICS TO THE WORKPLACE

Math

1. After screening all applicants, you hire the best candidate at a salary of $23,000 per year. Your benefits package normally amounts to about 25 percent of an employee's base salary. How much will your new employee's compensation add to your monthly operating expenses?

Individual Responsibility

2. Contact a bank or the consumer credit counseling service in your area. Find out how credit is established. Ask for an explanation of credit reports and how information is collected by credit reporting agencies. Develop a plan for your own use of credit and how you will maintain good credit records. Find out why good credit is important to a potential entrepreneur.

WORK IN YOUR COMMUNITY

Working in teams of three or four, collect at least three examples of organization charts from corporations and local businesses.

- Determine whether their structure is line or line-and-staff.
- Analyze any similarities and differences.
- Draw an organization chart of the administration of your school. Compare this chart with those you collected.

Share your findings with the class.

LINK SCHOOL TO CAREER

Choose a business you would like to own. Try to determine what the pay and benefits for your potential employees might cost your business.

- Gather information on current salaries and wage rates for the kind(s) of positions you will need to fill. As sources, use newspaper ads, occupational forecasting reports, state employment services, and personnel agencies.
- Contact the IRS, state tax office, and other appropriate agencies to obtain information regarding employer costs and withholding requirements.

interNET CONNECTION

Customer Service 101

As the proud owner of a record store, Blake believes that customer service is the key to a successful business. He wants all his employees to share this same belief so he's planning to provide specialized customer service training to his staff. Blake asks for your help in preparing this workshop.

Connect

Using a variety of Web browsers, research customer service techniques and tips.

- Prepare a five-minute presentation that emphasizes the importance of customer service.
- Incorporate specific examples that will be helpful in Blake's business.
- Use a presentation software package if possible.

CHAPTER 18

Managing Human Resources

Learning Objectives

When you have completed this chapter, you will be able to:

- **Plan** staffing procedures unique to ongoing businesses
- **Handle** human resource problems
- **Describe** how managers can influence and motivate employees

You're the Boss!

Managing and Motivating

You have a problem. Despite having a garage and staff whose size is comparable to other businesses, you have a long line of customers waiting for the oil in their cars to be changed. The mechanics have great references and their equipment is state-of-the-art, but they just don't do as much as they should. Now you wonder about your hiring tactics and motivational skill.

What Will You Do?
What can you do to increase your employees' productivity?

SECTION 18.1

Developing and Keeping Human Resources

STAFFING YOUR ONGOING BUSINESS

It's one thing to develop a staff for a new business. It's another matter to hire, keep, and develop employees while in operation. There are many staffing duties to handle when running a business.

Recruiting

As your business grows, you will have to add new employees. You will also have to replace employees. Fortunately, established businesses have forms of recruitment that new businesses do not. Additional sources include referrals from current and former employees and clients.

Recruiting from Within. Promoting or placing someone who already works for you reduces the cost of recruiting and training. It can also motivate employees to work hard for their own promotions. However, those who are not promoted can feel resentful. Using this procedure exclusively also can limit opportunities for bringing "new thinking" into the company.

Recruiting from Outside. There are many ways to recruit new workers. Advertising in newspapers and attending job fairs will help interested people find out about your company. School placement centers, employment agencies, and professional and labor organizations can refer you to candidates with specific backgrounds. Referrals can be the most helpful method of all. People are handpicked with skills, personality, and availability in mind.

Screening

An ongoing business owner uses the same screening methods as one who is starting up. Both review applications, conduct

What you'll learn

- techniques specific to recruiting employees for an ongoing business
- considerations for expanding employee pay and benefits packages
- steps in planning a complete training and development program
- procedures for resolving day-to-day employee problems
- considerations in dealing with unions
- your responsibility for ensuring a fair workplace
- considerations for handling termination

Why it's important

People are the most important resource of a small business. The employees that are found, hired, and kept have a great affect on its performance.

KEY TERMS

labor union
developmental activities
educational activities
cost-effective
employee complaint procedure
Pregnancy Discrimination Act

Many blue-collar workers belong to labor unions. ***What is the purpose of unions?***

interviews, and check references. However, more people are included in the hiring process of an established business. For example, in a business that is running, the prospective employee's immediate supervisor would be involved.

Unions and Your Business

Depending on your business, your employees may belong to *labor unions.* A labor union is an organization that is formed to represent workers. Most union members hold manufacturing, service, or blue-collar positions. By belonging to a union, they increase their ability to bargain for higher wages, increased benefits, better safety rules, job security, and other advantages.

As an employer, working with unions will cost you money. A union will require you to meet their standards of working conditions and wages. However, if their working conditions can be met without erasing your profits, everyone may benefit.

Training and Development

Training and developing employees will become more complex as your business grows. In addition to training new employees, you will have to upgrade the skills of current employees.

Training and development entails two types of activities. Developmental activities prepare managers to lead the company into the future. Conferences and classes can help them see where their industry is going and what new goals can be set. Educational activities prepare employees for promotion. These activities can help employees become more valuable and loyal.

A proper training and development program will take planning. There are four steps:

1. *Determine your needs.* Figure out your immediate, intermediate, and long-range training and development needs. Do you and your other managers lack strategic planning skills? You may need developmental activities. Do too many customers leave without buying? Your employees may need training.
2. *Design your program.* After you determine your needs, you will have to decide just how to meet them. Will you assemble a program yourself or will you designate someone else to do it?

If you decide to handle training and development yourself, start off by making a list of needs. **Figure 18–1** describes some of the techniques you can use.

3. *Implement your program.* Two things must occur. First you have to provide time and money for the program. Then you will have to follow up to make sure that what is learned through the program is actually implemented on the job.
4. *Evaluate your program.* Check to see if the program's objectives have been achieved. Was planning improved? Did sales improve? Then you will want to see if the program is cost-effective. Did the benefits outweigh the costs?

Money Matters

EMPLOYEES

Many employers are finding out that workers with disabilities make great employees. Phil Kosak of Carolina Fine Snacks says:

"*Initially ... I focused on what [my first employee with disabilities] couldn't do, not what he could. But that changed quickly because of his enthusiasm.*"

Training and Development Techniques

Technique	Description
On-the-job training	Employees learn the job on the job site under the direction of their manager or an experienced employee.
Vestibule training	Training takes place at a location away from the job that is equipped to simulate the actual work site.
Classroom teaching	Lecture, discussion, case studies, role playing, and other traditional classroom techniques are used to provide knowledge and problem-solving skills needed to perform the work.
Coaching	Employees receive ongoing instruction and feedback regarding job performance from their manager.
Mentoring	Employees receive one-on-one assistance from an established employee to help them get oriented within the organization and develop their potential.
Job rotation	Employees are moved from one job situation to another to provide them with a variety of job experiences and/or an understanding of the total operation.
Conferences and seminars	Several trainees or employees meet off the job with experts to learn how to deal with specific concerns or to exchange ideas.

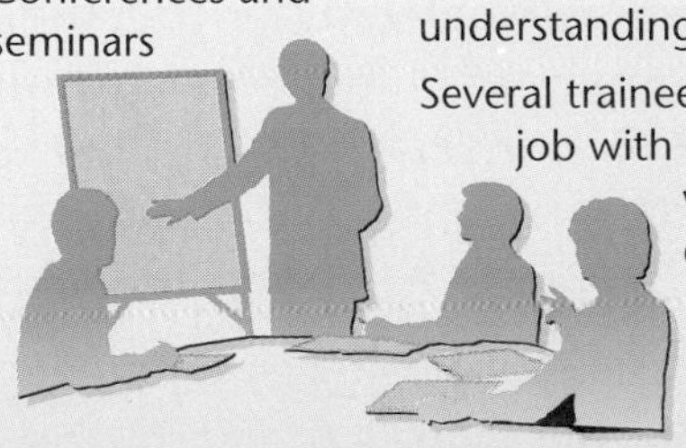

Figure 18-1
There are many types of training and development techniques for managers.
Which techniques count as learning by experience?

Tips from the Real World

STAND-IN

Train someone who can take over the business when you are away. Says Susan Stern, who took three years off from her public relations firm to recover from cancer:

"Anything could happen, and you need to be ready for it."

Pay and Benefits

Review your compensation package regularly. Be sure it includes the latest benefits required by law. Consider also adding benefits you couldn't afford initially. For instance, you can offer pensions, profit sharing, or bonuses to be competitive.

Expanding benefits will cost more than money. It can also add to your management responsibilities. For example, businesses that offer pensions are subject to the Employee Retirement Income Act. This act regulates pension plans and makes sure that eligible employees receive their pensions.

RESOLVING DAY-TO-DAY EMPLOYEE PROBLEMS

Encourage your employees to resolve disputes with their own problem-solving techniques and human-relations skills. However, some employee conflicts will require formal procedures.

Your formal procedure for handling employee complaints should be put in writing and distributed to all employees. This is called an employee complaint procedure. The first step may be the employee informing the immediate supervisor of the concerns. The second step could be an appeal to the next-level supervisor or an impartial committee. Many problems have no clear-cut solutions. Nevertheless, as a manager you must make a decision.

HANDLING DIFFICULT ISSUES

As a business manager, you will face many dilemmas. Two types are described below.

Discrimination

Employers must make sure that employees are not discriminated against on the basis of race, color, gender, religion, national origin, age, or handicap. Employers must also set standards for their employees' behavior. Employees must be told not to discriminate.

Laws and regulations designed to protect employees are enforced by the Equal Employment Opportunity Commission (EEOC). One law to know is the Pregnancy Discrimination Act. This act requires pregnant employees to be treated like all other employees when determining benefits. The EEOC's sexual harassment guidelines are also important. Sexual harassment is any unwelcome behavior of a sexual nature. The EEOC forbids sexual harassment of any kind.

A business cannot discriminate against people with disabilities. ***What are some aids that a business can provide?***

On-the-Job Problems and Employee Termination

Not all employees will work out. They may perform below expectations. They may disagree with your business goals. When this happens, try to help the individuals resolve the problem.

Ideally, you can develop a mutually acceptable way to change the person's thinking or actions. This can include upgrading skills or retraining. In some cases, the solution will lie in professional counseling or assistance.

The only realistic way to deal with the problem may be disciplinary action. This could include docking pay or termination (firing).

Terminating Employees. Not all of the problems you will deal with are brought on by employees. You may find it necessary to terminate an employee because of a drop in business. Give the employee the exact reasons for termination, and explain severance pay and unemployment compensation. Let him or her know that it is best for both parties to part ways.

CHECK YOUR UNDERSTANDING — SECTION 18.1

Reviewing Key Terms and Concepts

1. Explain the purposes of forming labor unions.
2. List the steps in setting up a procedure for handling employee complaints.
3. Summarize your responsibility for making sure that your employees are not discriminated against.

Critical Thinking Activity

Design a plan for handling employee complaints in your proposed business.

Extension Lab—Monitoring and Correcting Performance

Mystery Shopper For your mystery shopper service, you send out employees as "shoppers" to evaluate the quality of customer service at a variety of retail stores in the community. Recently, you found out that one of your employees was not taking the time needed to shop each store. He would file the reports, but some of the information would be inaccurate.

Role Play Working in pairs, take turns role-playing a conversation between owner and employee. Consider the following:

- What steps would you take to resolve this problem?
- What procedures could you put in place so this won't happen again?

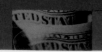

What you'll learn

- what really motivates employees
- techniques for motivating employees
- the advantages and disadvantages of delegating responsibility

Why it's important

One of an entrepreneur's tasks is to motivate employees. Employees who are motivated produce more and better work.

KEY TERMS

Theory X
Theory Y
motivating factors
hygiene factors
job enlargement
job enrichment
flextime
telecommuting
family leave
management-by-objectives
work team
performance evaluation

Motivating Your Employees

HOW DO MANAGERS INFLUENCE MOTIVATION?

Communication is a key factor that affects your employees' motivation. You must communicate your goals and objectives clearly if your employees are to meet them. You also have to provide feedback.

How employees are regarded and treated also affects their motivation. There are many theories about how this works. Douglas McGregor and Frederick Herzberg provide two theories that apply to small businesses.

What Managers Assume

In *The Human Side of Enterprise*, Douglas McGregor identifies two sets of assumptions managers make about employees: Theory X and Theory Y. The theories are defined in **Figure 18-2**.

Assumptions Managers Make

There are cases where it's necessary for a manager to make Theory X assumptions. Not all employees are right for a job. However, most small businesses benefit from using Theory Y.

Hygiene Factors vs. Motivating Factors

Most people assume money is a worker's principal motivator. According to the research of Frederick Herzberg and others, this is not so.

Herzberg concluded that compensation, working conditions, and fair company policies only motivate employees in the short-run. The really effective motivating factors in the workplace include

Assumptions Managers Make

Managers who make *Theory X* assumptions believe the following:

- People do not like work and try to avoid it.
- Managers have to push people, closely supervise them, or threaten them with punishment to get them to produce.
- People have little or no ambition and will try to avoid responsibility.

Managers who make *Theory Y* assumptions hold these views:

- Work is natural to people and is actually an important part of their lives.
- People will work toward goals if they are committed to them.
    - People become committed to goals when it is clear that achieving them will bring personal rewards.
    - Under the right conditions, people not only accept responsibility but also seek it out.
    - People have a high degree of imagination, ingenuity, and creativity, all of which can be used in solving an organization's problems.
    - Employees have much more potential than organizations actually use.

Figure 18-2 Douglas McGregor contrasts two sets of assumptions managers make about employees. ***Why would most small business situations benefit from using Theory Y?***

achievement, recognition, responsibility, advancement, growth, and the work itself. Sound familiar? Many of these are part of Theory Y's assumptions. Both McGregor and Herzberg emphasize the value of work, the importance of achievement, and need for responsibility.

Herzberg suggests that the real value of motivating factors lies in keeping employees from becoming dissatisfied. They function much like good health habits, such as brushing your teeth. Motivating factors don't make conditions better, but they do keep them from going bad. For this reason, Herzberg calls them hygiene factors .

Getting the Most from Your Employees

As a small business manager, you will probably want to apply Theory Y assumptions. You will want to benefit from what your employees have to offer. How will you do this? Here are a few techniques:

Provide Meaningful Work. Employees who are motivated by their work relate to it in a special way. They derive satisfaction from it. They take pride in it. To prompt such feelings, a job must be meaningful. It must offer a range of duties and responsibilities.

If your employees' jobs do not fit this description, consider redesigning them. You could add more tasks of the same skill level to them. This is called job enlargement. An example would be having a production worker perform an increased number of operations. You could also give employees more responsibility and control. (Here you would add elements at a different or higher skill level.) This is called job enrichment. For example, give the accounts receivable clerk responsibility for following up on past-due accounts.

Give Scheduling Flexibility. Allowing employees to plan and manage their own work schedules sends a clear message of Theory Y-type trust. Flexible scheduling can take a variety of forms. Examples are shown in **Figure 18-3**. These techniques can lead to increased productivity but do not lend themselves to every work situation. An auto mechanic cannot work at home. Neither can an electrician.

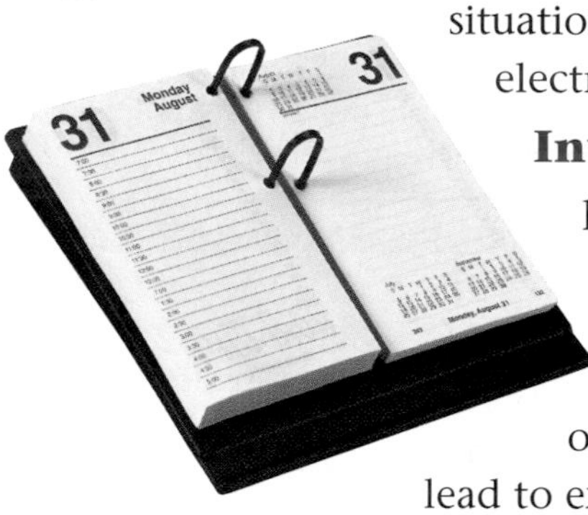

Involve Employees in Decision Making. Give employees opportunities to make suggestions about where the organization is going and what their role in it will be. This management approach has two positive outcomes. First, it gives employees a strong sense of purpose. Second, it allows them to see their own ideas put to work. Both lead to extra motivation and a sense of ownership.

There are many ways to involve employees in decision making. One is quality circles, which were described in Chapter 16. Another is *management-by-objectives*. In management-by-objectives, employees set their own objectives and gauge their own progress. A third is *work teams*. In a work team, a group

ENTREPRENEURS INTERNATIONAL

Mexico

Rodolfo Nelson Barbara is known as the father of the Mexican maquiladora, a Mexican assembly plant that uses foreign materials to manufacture a product that is exported to a final customer. In the mid-1960s, Nelson Barbara introduced this concept to foreign countries based on Mexico's inexpensive labor rates and built his first maquiladora in Mexicali. Today, the Nelson Group employs 50 people to engineer industrial and commercial buildings throughout Baja California for foreign clients.

Apply **How might a company oversee the quality of its products if they are assembled elsewhere?**

Figure 18–3

Workplace Flexibility

Many businesses are offering a more flexible workplace as a convenience to employees and to improve their productivity.

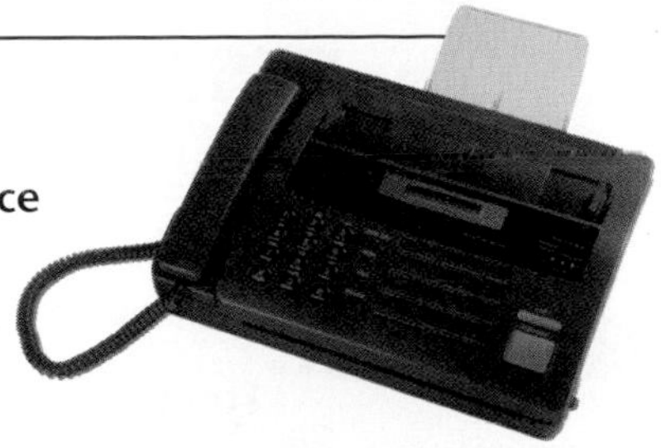

1. **Telecommuting** involves performing some or all of the job away from the business. The key is technology. Computers, cellular phones, FAX machines, and overnight delivery services allow employees to work at home or while traveling.

3. **Flextime** allows employees to choose the work hours and days they think will be most effective. It might result in four ten-hour days or working afternoons and evenings, or some other combination.

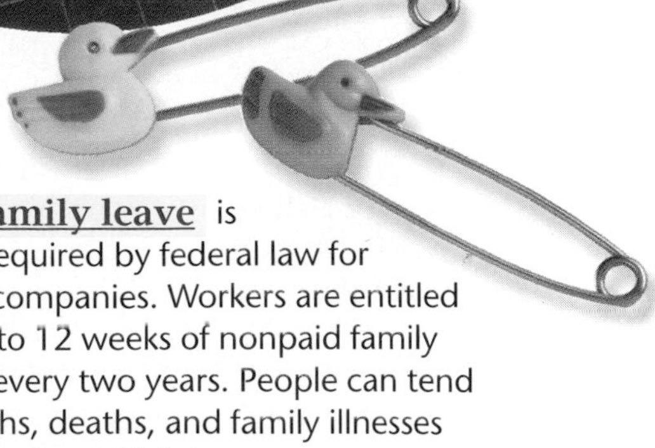

2. **Family leave** is now required by federal law for large companies. Workers are entitled to up to 12 weeks of nonpaid family leave every two years. People can tend to births, deaths, and family illnesses without fear of job loss.

RISK TAKERS PROFIT MAKERS

Name: Jake Burton
Company: Burton Snowboards
City, State: Burlington, VT

Boards by Jake

In 1977, Jake Burton left his Wall Street job for a town in Vermont. With a $20,000 inheritance from his grandmother, he vowed to turn his snow surfing idea into a sport that would rival skiing. Jake spent his days making snowboards and was soon able to make 50 boards in one day. However, he only sold 300 boards his first year in business. "My whole circle thought my concept was whacked," Burton recalls. "I ended up a hundred grand in the hole before I turned things around." Then Burton faced another obstacle—getting riders on the mountains. He visited resorts throughout the country, working with the management to allow snowboarders on the slopes.

Today, Burton Snowboards is the world's number-one manufacturer of snowboarding equipment. Burton hasn't lost his love for the sport and passes it on to his employees and fellow riders around the world.

Thinking Critically

What are some of the benefits that Burton Snowboards would reap from encouraging its employees to snowboard often?

of employees is assigned a task without direct supervision and with responsibility for the results.

You can increase the effectiveness of group decision making with training. **Figure 18–4** shows some group decision-making guidelines.

Give Recognition. It's important to acknowledge an employee's contributions in the workplace. You can give recognition informally every day. You can praise an employee for doing a good job or give credit for a useful idea. Employees can also be formally recognized. They might receive a plaque or award at a meeting or banquet. When you recognize an employee's contributions,

Group Decision-Making Guidelines

Leading a Small Group Meeting

1. Open the conference with a brief statement of the problem.
2. Ask for contribution.
3. Make frequent summaries.
4. Minimize your personal contributions.
5. Keep the meeting moving and on track.
6. See that each person participates, but don't go around the table asking each person for views.

Participating in Small Group Meeting

1. Keep your contributions brief and to the point.
2. Take up only one topic at a time.
3. Support your contributions with statistics, examples, analogies, expert opinions, and other evidence.
4. Listen attentively.
5. Don't interrupt other participants.
6. If you disagree with an individual, ask him or her why in nonaggressive way.

Figure 18–4
The leader of a small group meeting should not make personal contributions.
Why?

he or she will probably continue to perform well. In addition, you might increase the morale and motivation of your other employees.

Provide Performance Evaluations. A performance evaluation is a review of how well an employee does his or her job. Formal evaluations are usually done once a year. In a private meeting with the employee, you can evaluate the person's strengths and weaknesses. You can also give tips to help the employee become more productive. Informal evaluations may be given more often.

Up&Coming Entrepreneur

Investigating Entrepreneur

In 1994, John Mowell started Mowell Investigations. Today Mowell, his wife Shelly, and five employees work on corporate investigations ranging from background checks to surveillance of people who have made workers' compensation claims. "I've taken photos of people claiming to be bedridden who are out changing the motors in their cars," says Mowell. Through his service, Mowell has narrowed down employee theft investigations from 7,000 suspects to 1. He's also spent three consecutive 12-hour days sitting in his car.

Analyze **If you were an employee, would you consider corporate investigations an intrusion of privacy? What if you were an employer or business owner?**

Figure 18–5
Each type of performance has strengths and weaknesses. ***What are the strengths and weaknesses of the Performance Factor Form?***

Types of Performance Evaluations

Evaluation Form	Performance Evaluated
Performance Factor Form	Focuses on personality traits (cooperativeness, flexibility, etc.) important to job effectiveness.
Job Specific Form	Measures effectiveness in carrying out job duties and responsibilities.
Management-by-Objective Form	Evaluates progress toward individual objectives designed to support company objectives.
Combination Form	Combines measures from two or more of the above forms.

Evaluations can be very motivational. They can provide the basis for pay increases and promotions in the future. Some types of performance evaluations are shown in **Figure 18–5**.

Reward Performance. It is important to acknowledge and reward employee achievement. Usually the reward is financial. Does that contradict the idea that money is a hygiene factor, and not a motivating one? Not really. Money can represent both recognition and achievement.

Other rewards may include special assignments, job titles, or promotions. These, too, can represent acknowledgment and achievement. Many employees measure their value and success with their salaries and bonuses. Salespeople may look at their commissions as a way to "keep score."

WHERE DOES DELEGATING RESPONSIBILITY FIT?

When you delegate a task to an employee, it allows you to work on other things. It also motivates the employee. It demonstrates confidence in him or her and prepares the person for more responsibilities.

Of course, certain conditions have to exist before you should delegate responsibility. The employee must be capable and willing. You have to trust that he or she can handle the job. You also should be aware that the final responsibility rests with you.

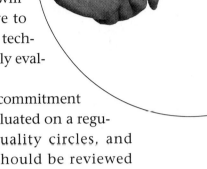

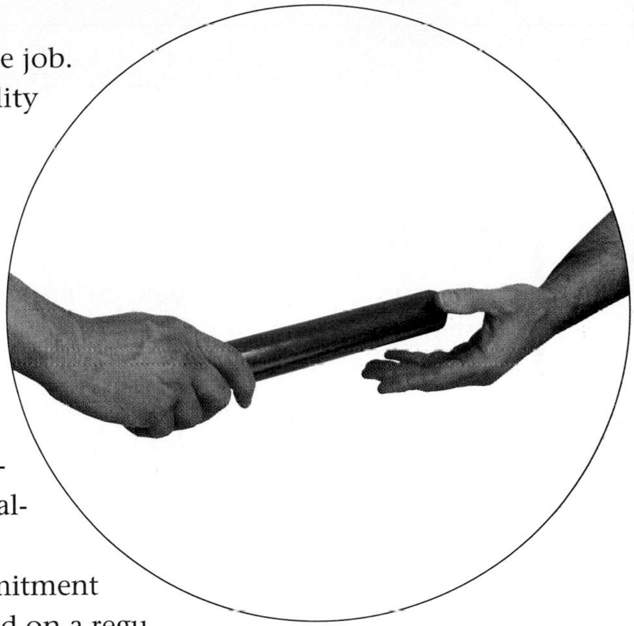

HOW DO YOU DETERMINE IF YOU ARE MOTIVATING YOUR EMPLOYEES?

Motivational techniques used every day will usually yield quick feedback. You might have to make some adjustments in how you apply the techniques, but you probably won't have to formally evaluate their effectiveness.

In contrast, techniques that require a large commitment of company time and resources should be evaluated on a regular basis. A program such as flextime, quality circles, and employee award banquets, for example, should be reviewed in terms of the following questions. Is it working as a motivator? Does it need revision? Is it worth the cost? Can we do it better another way?

CHECK YOUR UNDERSTANDING

SECTION 18.2

Reviewing Key Terms and Concepts

1 What is the difference between hygiene factors and motivating factors?
2 List three ways to motivate employees.
3 What are four questions to ask about an employee motivation program?

Critical Thinking Activity

Make a chart that lists hygiene and motivating factors. With overlapping sections or colored labels, visually indicate how some factors belong to both groups.

Extension Lab—Interpreting Information

Going Global The shortage of skilled employees has forced some entrepreneurs to recruit globally. Mark Grank, co-owner of a machine shop, recruited a South African worker and sponsored him for a green card, which allows immigrants to work for the United States.

Research Applying the group decision-making guidelines on page 311, answer the following questions.

- What are pros and cons in recruiting internationally for small business owners?
- How can small business owners compete with corporations when vying for potential employees?

CHAPTER 18 REVIEW

CHAPTER SUMMARY

- Staffing a business, whether ongoing or start-up, requires the same steps—recruiting, screening, setting pay and benefits, and providing training and development. The ongoing business, however, has more options and personnel to work with, making it much more complex.
- As a business manager, you will have to develop procedures to resolve disputes among employees, to ensure that employees are not discriminated against, and to deal with employees who are performing below expectations.
- Managers influence employees by making Theory X or Theory Y assumptions and using motivating factors.
- In order to get the most from their employees, managers can (1) provide meaningful work, (2) allow for schedule flexibility, (3) involve employees in decision making, (4) give recognition, (5) provide performance evaluations, and (6) reward performance.
- Delegating responsibility expands an owner's ability to manage in the workplace. In addition, it can be very motivating to employees.

RECALL KEY TERMS

Your boss has asked you to attend the local job fair and recruit new employees for your company. To prepare, write a summary of human resource issues that potential employees might want to know. Use the key terms:

labor union
developmental activities
educational activities
cost-effective
employee complaint procedure
Pregnancy Discrimination Act
Theory X
Theory Y
motivating factors
hygiene factors
job enlargement
job enrichment
flextime
telecommuting
family leave
management-by-objectives
work team
performance evaluation

RECALL KEY CONCEPTS

1. What are the advantages of recruiting from within?
2. Why is it important to review your compensation package regularly?
3. What is the purpose of developmental activities?
4. What are Theory X assumptions? Theory Y assumptions?
5. Name two motivating factors. Name two hygiene factors.
6. How does involving employees in the decision-making process motivate them?
7. What is the value of formal performance evaluations?
8. When you delegate responsibility to an employee, who has the final responsibility?

THINK CRITICALLY

1. How can business owners benefit by hiring employees who belong to labor unions?
2. Would you provide training to your employees that was effective but not cost-effective? Why or why not?

CHAPTER 18 REVIEW

3. Are most employees like those described by Theory X or Theory Y? Why? If you work, what type of employee are you?
4. Identify three businesses in your community where you think:
   - Flextime would be an acceptable option
   - Telecommuting would not be feasible.
5. What do you think motivates employees most? Defend your answer.

CONNECT ACADEMICS TO THE WORKPLACE

Math

1. Errors by your telephone sales staff are costing you $12,000 per year. You'd like to send four telephone salespeople to a three-day training seminar to correct the situation. The expenses will be as follows:
   - Registration costs: $500 per employee
   - Travel and lodging: $625 per employee
   - Salary and benefits: $125 per day per employee
   - Temporary replacement staff for three days: $1,500

   Will the training be cost-effective? How many years will it take for the training to pay for itself?

Negotiate

2. Forrest pays his employees a salary that is slightly under the industry standard. Consequently, employees often work for him to get experience but then leave to earn more money. What can he do to retain employees besides raising salaries?

WORK IN YOUR COMMUNITY

Choose a business you would like to open. As you consider the training and development of your employees, prepare a plan that will include the following:

- Immediate, intermediate, and long-range training and development needs
- Type of programs you will offer
- Who will design the programs
- Implementation procedures
- Evaluation procedures

LINK SCHOOL TO CAREER

Interview an entrepreneur or small business manager in your community regarding the following:

- Techniques used to motivate employees
- Most and least effective techniques

As a class, compile your results. Are there similarities between companies? Which techniques would motivate you?

interNET CONNECTION

Cyber-Employer

One of your employees has requested permission to telecommute from home. You know that telecommuting is becoming popular, but need more information.

Connect

Using a variety of Web search engines, research telecommuting. Find out the following:

- What types of jobs are appropriate for telecommuters
- The benefits of allowing employees to telecommute
- Appropriate ways to supervise an employee who telecommutes
- Methods you could use to evaluate an employee who telecommutes

MANAGING OPERATIONS

OVERVIEW

How entrepreneurs plan and manage their businesses will have a large impact on their success or failure. Considerations include purchasing, production, distribution, and operations. In the long run, well-managed and efficient business operations will be more profitable. In this unit lab, you will examine, plan, and develop steps that entrepreneurs can use to manage processes.

TOOLS

- Copies of *Product Sheet*
- Rolls of tape without dispensers
- Scissors
- Word processor (optional)
- Graph paper or spreadsheet program

PROCEDURES

STEP A

Identify jobs in your community that require employees to perform repetitive tasks, such as assembly line workers or office workers.

1. Get permission to observe one of these workers. Note the tasks performed.
2. In detail, describe the steps necessary to complete a specific task:
   - List two tasks the employee performed.
   - Identify the steps of each task.
3. Identify ways to improve the efficiency of each task.

STEP B

Individually or in a group, complete the activity that follows.

1. Obtain copies of the *product sheet* you or your group will be producing. You will also need scissors and one roll of tape (without a dispenser). Your task is to cut out the design, tape the sides, and produce a box that has five sides and is open on top.
2. Before beginning production, identify steps needed to accomplish this task.
3. Produce boxes for *three minutes*. Record the number of boxes produced.
4. Now identify steps that might increase box production. Using these new steps,

produce boxes again for *three minutes*. Record the number of boxes produced.

5. Next, identify different steps or procedures for producing these boxes. Using these steps, produce boxes for *three minutes*. Record the number of boxes produced.
6. If time permits, experiment with other steps. Each time, identify the steps, produce boxes for three minutes, and record the number of boxes produced. Record the results on the Unit 4 worksheet or a clean sheet of paper.

STEP C

Once you have identified the steps that you or your group believes are most efficient, set up a competition. Designate students to be quality control experts.

1. Give students or groups copies of the *product sheet*, scissors, and one roll of tape without a dispenser.
2. Produce boxes for *three minutes*.
3. The "quality control" experts will then determine the number of acceptable boxes produced by each student/group and announce the winner—the individual or team that developed the most efficient production process.

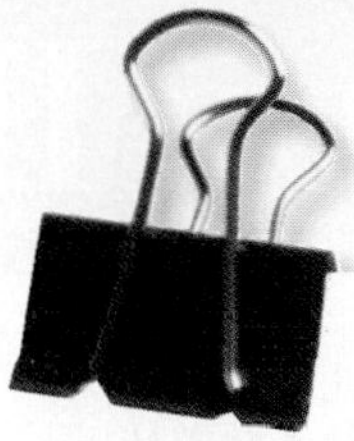

LAB REPORT

STEP D

Using a word processor, create a two-page report that describes what you learned about planning and managing business operations. Your report should contain the following:

- A description of the different steps with which you experimented to produce the boxes
- The benefits of the steps you selected for competition
- An explanation of what allowed the winning team to produce the most boxes
- An illustration of your findings in line graph form, created on graph paper or with a spreadsheet program
- Suggested tools or steps that your group could have used to improve its production efficiency

UNIT 5
MANAGING THE FINANCES OF YOUR BUSINESS

UNIT OVERVIEW

Money fuels your business from start-up to growth to maturity. How well you manage your finances will determine whether or not your venture opens its doors, stays in business, and grows.

As an entrepreneur, you will need to analyze finances, prepare statements, keep accurate records, and create budgets. Keeping control of your finances will take time and effort. However, it is necessary to make the best use of your resources and maximize your profits.

Entrepreneurship: What It Takes

What do you know about starting your own business?

1. Where can you go for start-up money?
2. What does a bank look for in a loan applicant?
3. Where can you find resources for expansion?
4. How do you determine the amount of start-up capital that you need?
5. Where can you go for help in making financial decisions?
6. How do you maximize your profits?
7. What are the pros and cons of offering credit to customers?
8. What is the best way to keep business records?
9. How can you organize data in your financial records?
10. How do you read financial statements?

CHAPTER 19

Financing Your Business

Learning Objectives

When you have completed this chapter, you will be able to:

- **Discuss** the resources available to entrepreneurs to start their businesses
- **Distinguish** among the various types of financing for start-up
- **Explain** how to obtain financing
- **List** the types of growth financing available to entrepreneurs
- **Describe** how to calculate your start-up capital needs

You're the Boss!

Financing Resources

After months of hard work, you're coming close to starting your tutoring and orientation service for international students. You've even come up with leads for possible lenders. The only problem is you don't know how much money you're going to need and which source is the best one for your business.

What Will You Do?

How much capital do you need to start your business and where will that money come from?

SECTION 19.1

Financing the Small Business Start-up

ENTREPRENEURIAL RESOURCES

Finding the resources to launch your business is a creative process. In this section, you'll learn how to find start-up capital.

Bootstrapping

Most entrepreneurs get their businesses off the ground by *bootstrapping*. Bootstrapping involves operating as frugally as possible and cutting all unnecessary expenses. This means getting by using as few resources of your own as you can.

- *Hire as few employees as possible*. Employees are generally the greatest single business expense. Instead, use workers from temporary services. That way you do not have employee tax and insurance payments. The temporary service handles them.
- *Lease anything you can*. Don't buy it. That way your money is not tied up in equipment or in a building. With leasing, you have no down payment and costs are spread over time.
- *Be creative*. When Marianne Szymanski started her toy research company in Milwaukee, she knew she couldn't afford a test center. Instead, she asked a friend at Marquette University to let her use the basement of the child-care center. The children at the center tested her toys and student interns provided help for free.

There are other bootstrapping techniques. You can ask suppliers to give you longer terms, so you don't have to pay them as quickly. You can require customers to pay in advance. You can also sell your accounts receivable to a *factor*. A factor is an agent who handles your transactions for a fee. He or she pays you cash and charges a fee of 1 or 2 percent on each account, plus interest on the cash advance. The factor then assumes the responsibility of collecting the accounts receivable from your customer.

What you'll learn

- how to bootstrap the start-up of your business
- the difference between debt and equity financing
- the types of debt and equity financing available

Why it's important

Most businesses are started with limited resources. You need to understand what resources are available to you and which ones make the most sense for your type of business.

KEY TERMS

bootstrapping
factor
equity
risk capital
angels
venture capitalists
line of credit
trade credit

Money Matters

FUNDING

Networking is an important business factor for men and women alike. Patty Abramson, of the Women's Growth Capital Fund, observes:

"Women don't get [start-up] money [because] they don't have relationships within venture funds . . . I wouldn't say this is about discrimination; it's about not having the relationships."

Start-Up Money

Because a new business has no track record to prove that it will survive, it can be hard to attract investors. As a result, the main source of start-up money for entrepreneurs is personal resources. These can include savings, credit cards, family, and friends. If you plan to start a business, it's smart to begin saving beforehand. Then start to identify outside sources.

FINANCING THE START-UP

To finance a new business, entrepreneurs must know where to look. Some sources, such as banks and finance companies, are obvious. Others, like investment companies, may be less familiar. Your business plan should state your preference for sources of new capital. There are two types of financing for new capital: equity and debt sources.

Equity Sources

Equity sources trade cash for some portion of ownership, or equity, of a business. For example, an investor might give you a certain amount of money if you give him or her a 10 percent interest in your company. Equity funding is sometimes called **risk capital**. This is because an individual who invests in a business puts his or her money at risk. If the business is successful, the investor makes a profit. However, if the business fails, he or she can lose it all.

The entrepreneur's own savings is the number-one source of business start-up income. ***Why would an entrepreneur's own investment be important to an outside investor?***

There are many forms of equity financing:

- *Personal savings.* The number-one source of start-up capital for new businesses is the entrepreneur's own personal savings. The U.S. Department of Commerce reports that 67 percent of all new businesses were started without borrowing any money. When a business does borrow money, the entrepreneur should chip in more than half the start-up capital. By doing so, he or she keeps control of the business.
- *Friends and family.* Entrepreneurs often borrow money from friends and relatives. However, you have to consider whether the relationships can survive if the business fails and the investment is lost.
- *Private investors.* Private investors are nonprofessional financing sources. Sometimes they are called angels because of the help they give new businesses. They often become involved in start-up financing of one or two new local businesses a year. Angels usually prefer to keep a low profile and are not easy to locate. The most common way to find them is through networking in your community. Also, some nonprofit organizations have established networks of angels. Be very careful about choosing private investors. Put the terms in writing and have an attorney check it.
- *Partners.* By finding a partner with compatible goals, you can share the costs of a business. If you have complementary skills, you can divide the responsibilities as well. Your business can also form a strategic alliance with another business. That occurs when two companies each have special skills that the other needs. (Reread the section in Chapter 7 on the advantages and disadvantages of partnerships.) When entering a partnership with another company, be sure to put the agreement in writing and have it reviewed by an attorney.
- *Venture capitalists.* Venture capitalists are individuals or firms that invest capital professionally. They make investments to make money. As a result, they expect a large portion of the business and look for high growth potential. Because venture capitalists are so expensive and demanding, they are not good sources of start-up capital for most small businesses. However, venture capitalists are a good source of money for established businesses that seek funding for growth.
- *State-sponsored venture capital funds.* Some states use funds to start businesses and create jobs. Because they are not as

Tips from the Real World

AUTONOMY

While many entrepreneurs hire subcontractors to handle aspects of their businesses, Gail Mosley Conner of G&C Environmental Services is getting her own environmental law degree. Conner believes:

"*Business owners should never offer a service that they have to hire someone else to do.*"

The SBA has established the MESBICs to support female, minority, and disabled entrepreneurs. ***How do MESBICs function?***

focused on making a profit, they are likely to support a small business. Check with your local economic development corporation for help in locating such funds.

Debt Sources

Sources of debt capital are far more numerous than sources of equity capital. With debt financing, an entrepreneur borrows money and has to repay it with interest. When an entrepreneur raises capital by borrowing, he or she retains full ownership of the business. However, the loan must be carried as a liability on the business balance sheet.

- *Banks.* Banks were once the primary source of operating capital, or the money that businesses use to support their operations in the short term. With a line of credit, a bank agrees to lend a business a certain amount of money at a certain interest rate. The company can then borrow against that credit line as its needs dictate and pay back the money on a regular basis. Today, banks are very conservative in their lending practices. They are not inclined to lend to businesses unless they are well established.

  After your business is up and running, however, banks may make some types of financing available. For example, you may be able to borrow money using your business assets as security for the loan. If you don't pay back the loan, the bank can take these pledged assets. What kinds of assets can you use as security? One possibility is your inventory. Another is your accounts receivable.
- *Trade credit.* Trade credit is a source of short-term financing in which you get credit from within your industry or trade. Suppose you purchase goods from a supplier on 30–90 days of credit, interest free. This means that you would have the use of your money for at least an extra 30 days. If your customers pay promptly, they could provide you with the money you need to pay your bill.
- *Minority Enterprise Small Business Investment Companies (MESBICs).* The SBA has also established MESBICs to provide funding to businesses whose ownership is at least 51 percent minority, female, or disabled.

- *Commercial finance companies.* Commercial finance companies provide a more expensive alternative to commercial banks. Finance companies are less conservative than banks and they typically take more risks. They also charge more. Some form of security is usually required for a loan. Typically, the security is the entrepreneur's home. However, finance companies may also accept receivables and inventory.
- *Small Business Administration (SBA).* If the SBA approves your request for a loan, it will use a commercial bank to process and release the money. It will also guarantee repayment of up to 90 percent of the loan should your business fail. If your business fails, the SBA assures the bank that it can only lose the portion of the loan that is not guaranteed. The SBA also lends public funds to qualified veterans and persons with handicaps.
- *Small Business Investment Companies (SBICs).* These companies are licensed by the SBA to provide equity and debt financing to young businesses. They invest about twice as often in start-up ventures as do venture capitalists. Each SBIC is privately owned, and their requirements vary.

CHECK YOUR UNDERSTANDING

SECTION 19.1

Reviewing Key Terms and Concepts

1 What is bootstrapping and how can it help entrepreneurs?
2 What is the difference between debt and equity financing?
3 What is the most common source of start-up capital for entrepreneurs?

Critical Thinking Activity

Visit either a bank or a commercial finance company and inquire about the requirements for a loan for a new business. How difficult will it be to meet their requirements?

Extension Lab—Speaking Skills

Machine Chow You are very excited about a business idea: food service vending machines at school cafeterias. You have already filed for permission from the school system and all you need now is funding. You believe your Aunt Elizabeth might consider investing in the business. You are also hoping for backing from several friends or from the local bank.

Role Play With a classmate, take turns role playing the following scenarios.

- Convince Aunt Elizabeth to give you $5,000 for your business.
- Convince someone who is not a relative to invest in your business.
- Make a presentation to a bank requesting the money.

SECTION 19.2

Obtaining Financing and Growth Capital

What you'll learn

- what financiers look for
- the types of growth financing available
- how to calculate your start-up capital needs

Why it's important

Before looking for financing, you should know how much money you need and why. You should also know what kind of financing is available for growing your business.

KEY TERMS

capacity
collateral
due diligence
private placement
initial public offering (IPO)
stock
working capital
contingency funds

HOW TO OBTAIN FINANCING

Once you have identified potential sources of financing, you need to be sure that your business plan addresses the very specific needs of your financial sources. Your business plan must include projected-income statements, cash-flow statements, balance sheets, and a break-even analysis. Your plan is the financial road map for the business. These financial forms will be discussed in more detail in Chapter 21. In this section, you'll learn what financiers look for in a new business.

What Venture Capitalists Look For

As an entrepreneur, your goal is to have your business survive and grow. However, the goal of the venture capitalist is to achieve capital gain through investment and then cash out. You and the venture capitalist do not have the same goals.

When venture capitalists do invest in start-up companies (and that isn't often), they are looking for high-growth firms. What is "high growth"? They want a 30–50 percent return on their investment. Using a simple example, suppose venture capitalists give your business $50,000 for five years. At the end of that period, they will want to receive their investment back plus an additional $15,000–$25,000.

Above all, venture capitalists look for a business with a good management team. They firmly believe that a good team can take a mediocre product and make it successful. However, a mediocre team cannot take even a good product and build a successful business. They also look at the market potential for the product or service of the company.

The process of obtaining funding from venture capitalists is a slow one. They will examine every facet of your business. Therefore, don't go to a venture capitalist when you are desperate for money.

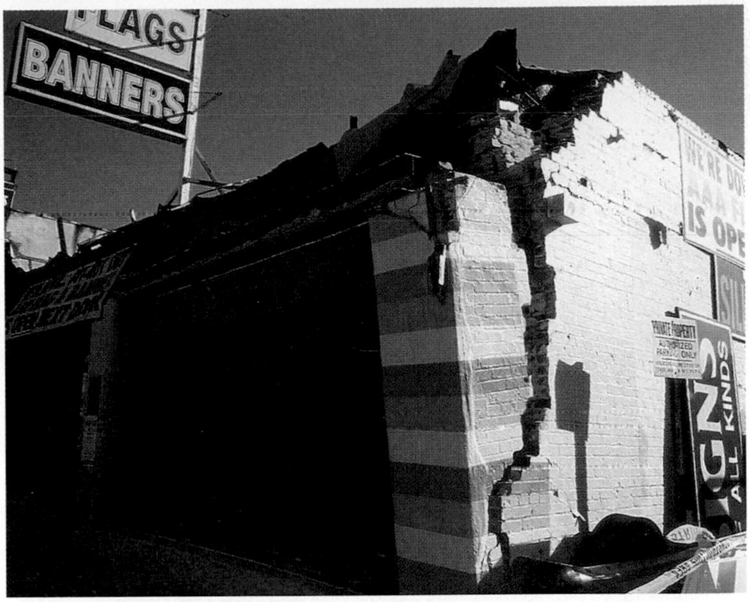

In addition to the five C's of credit, many bankers look at insurance coverage when screening business loan applications. ***Why is this?***

As with bankers, the paradox is that you should go to them when you don't need money, or at least long before you do need it.

What Bankers Look For

In contrast with businesses that use the three C's of credit, bankers rely on five C's to determine the acceptability of a loan applicant. Their requirements are greater because they lend larger amounts of money. The bankers' five C's are:

- *Character.* The bank needs to believe in the character of the entrepreneur and the people with whom he or she is associated. Like venture capitalists, bankers recognize the value of a good management team.
- *Capacity.* Capacity refers to the ability of a business to pay in view of its income and obligations. Banks look for businesses with a sufficient cash flow to pay back a loan.
- *Capital.* Banks place a strong emphasis on whether a business has a stable capital structure. They look for businesses that don't have too much debt.
- *Collateral.* Banks are more likely to lend to businesses with collateral, things of value they can claim if a business does not repay its loan.
- *Conditions.* Banks will consider all the conditions of the environment in which the business will operate. Business conditions include potential for growth, the amount of

ENTREPRENEURS INTERNATIONAL

United Arab Emirates

Ajmal Ali Haji Abdul Majid founded House of Ajmals in Dubai. His experience in the art and technique of extracting pure oils from natural substances has made House of Ajmals a world leader in the manufacturing of exotic perfumes. "My quest for natural and exclusive fragrances has taken us from the forests of North East India, to Burma, Cambodia, the continent of Africa, the Middle East, and Europe." The scent of the Middle East is conveyed in perfumes named Red Carpet, Flame, and Raheeb.

Apply **How does Ajmal's quest for exotic fragrances affect his financial plans?**

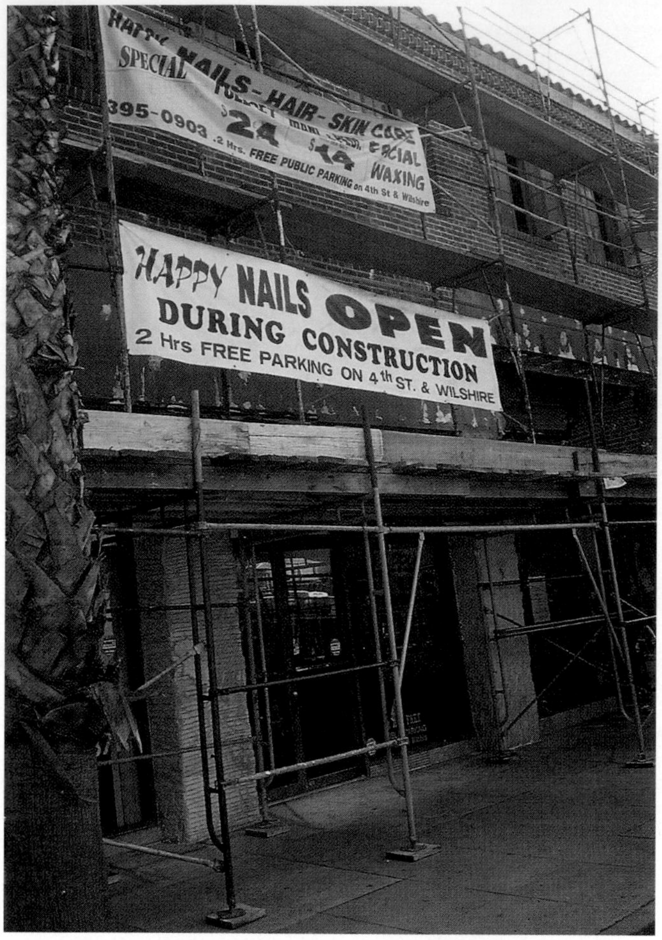

After a business has established a track record, financing growth can be easier to secure. *Why are some reasons for growth?*

competition, the location of the business, and the form of ownership. They may even check coverage by insurance.

To be considered for a commercial bank loan, you and your business will need to score very high on all five C's. It's also important to establish a relationship with your banker before you ask for money.

What Private Investors Look For

Private investors tend to be conservative in their investments. They prefer manufacturing, energy and natural resources, and some service businesses. They usually avoid retail businesses because such enterprises have a higher failure rate.

Most private investors put between $10,000 and $500,000 into a new business. Usually located near the investor, such businesses are often found through friends and business associates. On average, these investors aim to get 10 times their investment at the end of five years. Like bankers and venture capitalists, private investors look for a strong management team.

TYPES OF GROWTH FINANCING

When your business is ready to grow, you may seek a second round of financing, or growth financing. In this section, you'll learn about some of the types of financing available to grow your business.

Venture Capital Companies

Most venture capital *companies* expect returns that range between 60 and 70 percent. They may also require a significant ownership interest of the company and a seat on the board of directors. The older and more established your business, the less risky it will be for the venture capital company and the less it will want in return for its investment.

RISK TAKERS PROFIT MAKERS

Name: Kristen Lauer
Company: Blue Potato Installations
City, State: W. Roxbury, MA

Scene–Stealing Window Displays

"It's all about attention and image. I do what I can do to make sure my client will get a consumer's dollar and not go elsewhere for a similar product," says Kristen Lauer. Her company Blue Potato Installations, designs windows and in-store environments. To attract business, she has chopped the toes off of shoes for a "2/3–Off Sale." For other retail stores, she has created underwater scenes complete with periscopes. Lauer hires specialized artisans from cabinet builders to mural painters to assist with installations.

Big-name clients such as House of Blues and Reebok now call on Blue Potato regularly. Where did the company's unusual name come from? Lauer explains, "For my first job I placed piles of spray-painted electric-blue potatoes against an acid-green background, complete with shiny chrome potato peelers. People kept asking me, 'Are you the one who did the blue potatoes?'"

Thinking Critically

There are many ways to promote a business besides the common printed advertisement. What are some other advertising methods?

The best way to locate a venture capital company is to be introduced by someone close to it. You will be asked to supply a business plan. If the plan looks good, you will be asked to present it formally. If the venture capital company decides that your team can deliver its claims, it will begin due diligence. This means that its team of experts will run background checks on you, your team, and your business. If the experts like what they see, the terms of the agreement will be negotiated and an agreement made. Don't expect the money to show up very quickly because the venture capitalists don't contact their investors until the deal with you is completed.

Private Placements

Private placement is a way to raise capital by selling ownership interests of your private corporation or partnership. These ownership interests that you sell to private investors are also called *securities*. If you decide to raise capital through private placement, it's best to follow Regulation D of the Securities and Exchange Commission (SEC).

Regulation D states that your investors must be "sophisticated." That means they invest on a regular basis and have a net worth of at least a million dollars. That may sound like a lot of money, but the investors' home, cars, bank accounts, insurance policies, and other properties do add up.

Initial Public Offerings (IPOs)

The initial public offering (IPO) is the sale of stock (ownership interests) in your company on a public stock exchange. An IPO is a popular way to raise a lot of money for growth because all the proceeds of the initial public offering go to the company. However, once you've made an IPO, your company is no longer private. It is public. Public companies are regulated heavily by the Securities and Exchange Commission and the federal government. All of the company's information must be made available to the public. The CEO is now responsible primarily to the stockholders.

The expensive and lengthy IPO process is illustrated in **Figure 19–1**. Entrepreneurs devote up to a year in preparation for the date of a public offering. Such thorough preparation will make your company's stock easy to buy and sell. In addition, you can then use company stock to attract and reward employees.

Up&Coming Entrepreneur

Fitness Entrepreneur

Rodney Taylor once had to scramble to be on time for all the personal training sessions he taught. When Rodney was late to an appointment a second time, his client suggested that he start a business where the clients come to him. Taylor agreed. To help cut start-up costs he traded his training services for various things ranging from construction work to towels and carpeting. "Of course, I'll be training some people for life, basically," says Taylor about his bartering. Taylor, 51% owner of Taylor Made Bodies, is thinking about expanding into other southwestern cities.

Analyze **What type of costs might be involved with starting your own personal training business?**

Figure 19–1

The Initial Public Offering Process

There are five steps to becoming a public company with stock for sale on a public stock exchange:

1. Choose an underwriter or investment banker.

These professionals sell securities and help you through the initial public offering process, much like a tour guide.

2. Draw up a letter of intent.

This letter outlines the terms and conditions between you and the underwriter and gives the price range for the stock.

3. File a registration statement with the SEC.

This document is called a "red herring" or prospectus. It spells out the potential risks of investing in the initial public offering. You will also need to choose the stock exchange where your stock will sell.

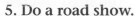

4. Announce the offering in the financial press.

The advertisement you place in the financial paper is called a "tombstone."

5. Do a road show.

This is a whirlwind tour of all the major institutional investors (insurance companies, pension plans, etc.) to market the offering. This is done so that the offering can be sold in one day, the "coming out" day.

Figure 19–2
This financial statement identifies start-up costs. ***Which of the items listed will also become operating expenses?***

Summary of Start-up Costs

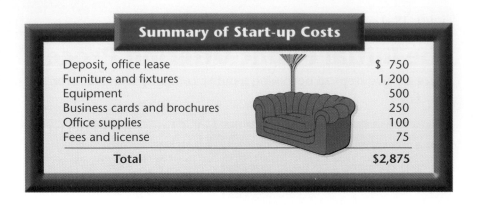

Deposit, office lease	$ 750
Furniture and fixtures	1,200
Equipment	500
Business cards and brochures	250
Office supplies	100
Fees and license	75
Total	**$2,875**

CALCULATING YOUR START-UP CAPITAL NEEDS

Once you know you can acquire money to start or grow your business, you'll need to calculate exactly how much money you need. This will require estimating start-up costs, working capital, and contingency funds.

Start-up Costs

Start-up costs are those costs that you incur before you actually start the business. You may need to rent space, lease equipment, purchase phones, and train employees. All these expenses occur before you ever make a sale to the customer.

To figure your start-up costs accurately, you will need to talk to suppliers, vendors, manufacturers, distributors, and others in your industry. They will help you determine what you need and how much it will cost.

Suppose you are starting a shop that customizes bicycles. Once product development is completed, your list of start-up costs might look like that found in **Figure 19–2**.

Working Capital

Working capital is the amount of cash you need in order to carry on your daily operations. It ensures that the business has a positive cash flow. Working capital covers the time between selling your product or service and receiving the money from the customer.

In the next chapter you will learn how to do a cash-flow statement that will help you decide just how much working capital you need to maintain a positive cash position.

Contingency Funds

No one can predict the future. That's why it's important that you include some extra funds, called contingency funds , when calculating start-up needs. These funds are used if you're not paid on time. They'll also cover unforeseen business expenses.

How much to figure for contingencies will depend on your type of business, the dependability of your customers, and other factors. Some business owners keep enough money in reserve to cover two or more months of fixed costs. (That would include salaries, rent, and so on.) Those who operate in seasonal industries, such as umbrella factories or ski resorts, might put as much as 6 to 12 months' worth of capital in reserve.

CHECK YOUR UNDERSTANDING

SECTION 19.2

Reviewing Key Terms and Concepts

1 What do private investors look for when they invest in a new business?
2 Why is venture capital not a good source of start-up capital?
3 What are the three types of money you need to calculate in order to determine your start-up needs?

Critical Thinking Activity

Go to your library's periodical section and look for an article about a company that recently made an initial public offering. How did their experience compare with what you read in the chapter?

Extension Lab—Decision-Making Skills

Creative Financing Tomorrow, the board of directors at the bank will be voting whether to loan you $30,000 for your new business, "Creative Touch." One of the board members is also a friend and tells you that if the loan is approved, he will invest an additional $10,000 of his own money. In return, you will give him a 10 percent interest in the business.

Presentation Discuss the following questions in groups of three or four. Present your thoughts to the class.

- Should you keep your friendship a secret until after the loan is approved?
- Should the board member abstain from voting so as not to show favoritism?
- Is it ethical to apply for a loan at a bank where a friend sits on the decision-making board?

CHAPTER 19 REVIEW

CHAPTER SUMMARY

- Many entrepreneurs start up their businesses very frugally by hiring as few employees as possible, leasing rather than buying, and being creative.
- Equity sources of financing involve giving up some ownership in the company. Debt sources of financing involve borrowing money and paying it back with interest.
- Once you have identified potential financial sources, you need to make sure that your business plan meets their criteria. Banks look for evidence of the five C's: character, capacity, capital, collateral, and conditions. Venture capitalists and private investors look for a strong management team and a good return on investment.
- Once the business is up and running, you might seek a second round of financing for expansion. Venture capital companies, private investors, and IPO's are ways to finance a growing business.
- To determine how much money you will need for start-up or for growth, estimate your start-up costs, working capital, and contingency funds.

RECALL KEY TERMS

For each of the following terms, write a sentence that describes what role the term might play in financing your start-up and/or growing business.

bootstrapping
factor
equity
risk capital
angels
venture capitalists
line of credit
trade credit
capacity
collateral
due diligence
private placement
initial public offering (IPO)
stock
working capital
contingency funds

RECALL KEY CONCEPTS

1. Name five sources of equity financing.
2. How do banks and finance companies differ in the way they lend money?
3. How do the goals of the entrepreneur differ from those of the venture capitalist investing in the business?
4. Describe the five C's of credit that bankers use to judge a loan applicant.
5. Define the five steps in the Initial Public Offering (IPO) process.

THINK CRITICALLY

1. How might you use bootstrapping to help your new business get off the ground?
2. If you wanted to retain as much control of your business as possible, what sources of financing would you consider? Why?
3. What advantages does equity financing have over debt financing?
4. A hi-tech company pays over a million dollars to develop a television satellite that may or may not ever be launched into orbit. Why would a venture capitalist be willing to finance such a risky project?
5. Describe the differences between private placements and initial public offerings.

CHAPTER 19 REVIEW

CONNECT ACADEMICS TO THE WORKPLACE

Math

1. Roberto has estimated start-up costs for his new business to be $6,500. He projects that for the first six months his ongoing operating costs will be $4,300 and personal expenses will total $8,200. Roberto has saved $12,780 to put toward the new business. How much money will he need to borrow? What percentage of his total costs will he borrow?

Use Computers to Process Information

2. Choose a company that has made an IPO within the last year. Using a spreadsheet program, track the stock price from its initial offering to today. (You could track it daily, weekly, or monthly depending on the amount of time it has been publicly traded). Create a line graph and present your findings to the class.

WORK IN YOUR COMMUNITY

Research sources of financing for your new business. As part of your decision-making process, evaluate each type of financing based on these questions:

- What type of financing is most advantageous?
- What is the risk to the business?
- If you borrow money, how will the loans be repaid?
- If you finance through an equity source, how will the investors be paid?

Based on your research, which funding source is the best for your business? Add your findings to the class resource log.

LINK SCHOOL TO CAREER

Obtain a loan application from a local bank.

- Fill it out to the best of your ability.
- Make a list of questions about the things you do not understand.
- Go back to the bank and get the answers.
- Ask how the bank deals with applicants under the age of 18.

If possible, invite a banker to your class to answer questions regarding loans to small business owners.

*inter*NET CONNECTION

Public Showing

Your business has been open for about two years and has shown sound financial performance. You are ready to expand and know that a good way to raise money is by "going public."

Connect

Using a variety of Web browsers, research three companies that have recently sold stock on a public stock exchange for the first time. Find out about:

- The advantages and disadvantages of selling shares of ownership in their companies
- The Securities and Exchange Commission (SEC) regulations for IPOs
- How the companies marketed their offerings

Present the results of your research in chart form and determine whether "going public" is right for your business.

CHAPTER 20

Financial Management

Learning Objectives

When you have completed this chapter, you will be able to:

- **Explain** how to analyze your business's finances
- **Describe** procedures for planning and managing your company's finances
- **List** considerations involved in the decision to extend credit
- **Identify** steps involved in the process of extending credit

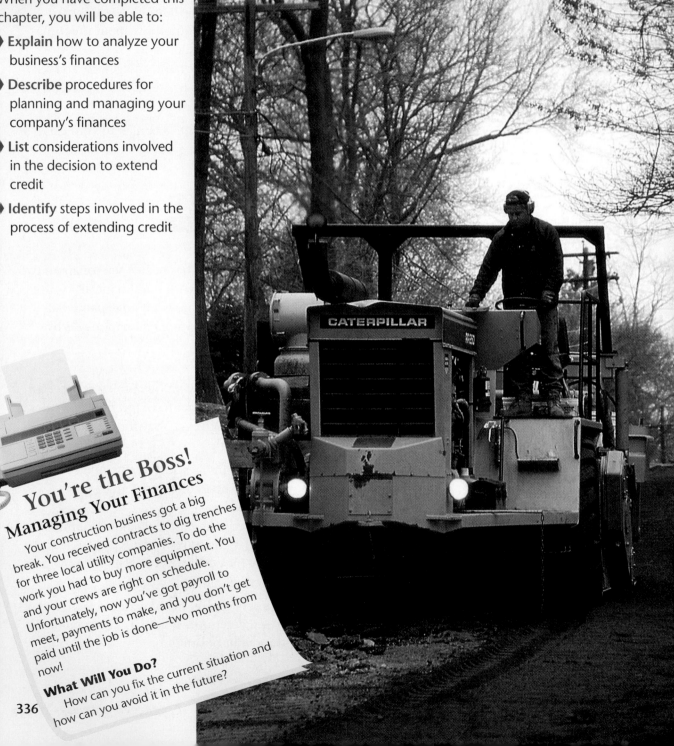

You're the Boss!

Managing Your Finances

Your construction business got a big break. You received contracts to dig trenches for three local utility companies. To do the work you had to buy more equipment. You and your crews are right on schedule. Unfortunately, now you've got payroll to meet, payments to make, and you don't get paid until the job is done—two months from now!

What Will You Do?

How can you fix the current situation and how can you avoid it in the future?

SECTION 20.1

Analyzing Your Finances

USING FINANCIAL STATEMENTS

How can you keep track of your business finances? Study your financial statements. The same forms you used to start your business do more than help you borrow money. They are also the financial plans for operating your business.

Start with two forms. An **income statement** is a financial report that shows how much a business has earned or lost during a year. It is also called a *profit-and-loss statement.* A **balance sheet** is a financial statement that tells you what your business is worth at any given time.

Comparing Financial Statements

By comparing current and past income statements and balance sheets, you can spot trends in your sales, cost of goods sold, or

What you'll learn

- how to obtain information from your balance sheets and income statements to determine your company's financial position
- how to do ratio analysis
- how to interpret key ratios
- the advantages of using computers and financial advisors to assist with financial analysis

Why it's important

Understanding your financial documents will help you keep control of your company's financial situation.

KEY TERMS

income statement
balance sheet
ratio analysis
current assets
current liabilities
return on equity

Income Statement (Year 1)

Martin's Moccasins
Income Statement
Year Ended December 31, ____

Revenue from Sales		
Gross sales	$1,750,000	
Less sales returns and allowances	15,000	
Net Sales		$1,735,000
Cost of Goods Sold		
Beginning inventory	$ 695,500	
Purchases	846,000	
Total goods available for sale	$1,541,500	
Less ending inventory	388,000	
Total Cost of Goods Sold		1,153,500
Gross Profit on Sales		$ 581,500
Operating Expenses		
Salaries	$ 190,000	
Advertising	133,000	
Sales promotion	2,000	
Travel and entertainment	5,200	
Depreciation—store equipment	8,000	
Miscellaneous selling expenses	1,500	
Rent	15,000	
Depreciation—delivery equipment	5,000	
Depreciation—office furniture	1,200	
Utilities	4,500	
Insurance	40,000	
Telephone	2,200	
Miscellaneous general expenses	2,000	
Total Operating Expenses		409,600
Net Income from Operations		$ 171,900
Less interest expense		24,000
Net Income Before Taxes		$ 147,900
Less federal income taxes		40,950
Net Income After Taxes		$ 106,950

Figures 20–1 and 20–2
The firm whose statements are shown here increased sales but still suffered a loss of income. *Why?*

operating expenses. Look at **Figure 20–1** and **Figure 20–2**. Even though net sales have increased, net income after taxes is down. You can see which expenses have increased and caused the lower income.

Another financial gauge is the *ratio analysis*. A ratio analysis compares numbers from a balance sheet or income statement.

Income Statement (Year 2)

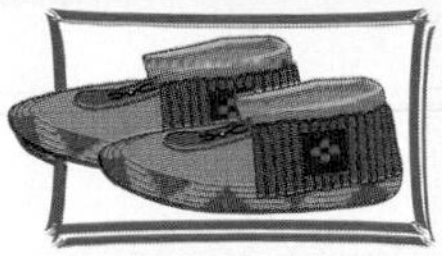

Martin's Moccasins
Income Statement
Year Ended December 31, ____

Revenue from Sales		
Gross sales	$1,845,750	
Less sales returns and allowances	16,500	
Net Sales		$1,829,250
Cost of Goods Sold		
Beginning inventory	$ 388,000	
Purchases	1,218,000	
Total goods available for sale	$1,606,000	
Less ending inventory	376,000	
Total Cost of Goods Sold		$1,230,000
Gross Profit on Sales		$ 599,250
Operating Expenses		
Salaries	$ 203,200	
Advertising	152,950	
Sales promotion	2,150	
Travel and entertainment	10,500	
Depreciation—store equipment	8,000	
Miscellaneous selling expenses	1,600	
Rent	15,000	
Depreciation—delivery equipment	5,000	
Depreciation—office furniture	1,200	
Utilities	4,800	
Insurance	42,000	
Telephone	2,250	
Miscellaneous general expenses	2,200	
Total Operating Expenses		450,850
Net Income from Operations		$ 148,400
Less interest expense		28,000
Net Income Before Taxes		$ 120,400
Less federal income taxes		40,150
Net Income After Taxes		$ 80,250

You can compare your ratios to the industry standards found in Dun & Bradstreet's *Cost of Doing Business*.

Current Ratio

The *current ratio* compares current assets (cash or things that can be converted to cash and that are used up by a business within a year), with current liabilities (debts due within a year). These

Balance Sheet Used to Compute Current Ratio

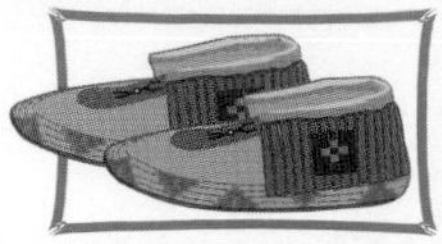

Martin's Moccasins
Balance Sheet
December 31, ____

ASSETS			
Current Assets			
Cash		$ 45,500	
Accounts receivable	$162,000		
Less allowance for bad debt	5,500	156,500	
Notes receivable		6,000	
Inventory		388,000	
Total Current Assets			$596,000
Fixed Assets			
Delivery equipment	$120,000		
Less accumulated depreciation	30,000	$ 90,000	
Furniture and store equipment	$ 79,000		
Less accumulated depreciation	23,200	55,800	
Total Fixed Assets			145,800
Total Assets			$741,800
LIABILITIES			
Current Liabilities			
Accounts payable		$147,000	
Notes payable		78,000	
Salaries payable		15,900	
Income taxes payable		48,000	
Total Current Liabilities			$288,900
Long-term Liabilities			
Mortgage payable on equipment		$ 70,000	
Note payable		92,000	
Total Long-term Liabilities			162,000
Total Liabilities			$450,900
OWNER'S EQUITY			
Martin's Moccasins, Capital			290,900
Total Liabilities and Owner's Equity			$741,800

Figure 20–3
Suppose total current assets for this firm are $335,000. *What would be its current ratio?*

numbers can be found on the balance sheet. The current ratio indicates the ability of a business to pay its bills. It is determined as follows:

$$\frac{\text{Current assets}}{\text{Current liabilities}} = \text{Current ratio}$$

RISK TAKERS PROFIT MAKERS

Name: Enrique Galvez
Company: Banzai Anime
City, State: Los Angeles, CA

Imported Animation

"I didn't intend to open a business," explains Enrique Galvez. "It was just for fun." At the time, he was a college student who enjoyed watching Japanese animation. The imported cartoons feature martial artists, alien encounters, robot armies, and other fantastic subjects that American cartoons don't touch.

Unfortunately, when he set up his booth with 75 dollars' worth of merchandise at an animation convention in 1991, there wasn't enough interest to turn a profit. "I wanted to see if it would work," he remembers, "Basically, it didn't."

Enrique didn't give up. He fine-tuned his business, experimenting with his product line and promotions at later conventions. Eventually, his booth evolved into a mail-order operation called Banzai Anime, which became a full-fledged store and Internet site. He now sells videos, DVDs, toys, and soundtracks to a customer base that grows as more people discover the imported cartoons. "We get all kinds of people," he says. "Japanese animation has a little bit for everyone."

Thinking Critically

What can you do if your original business idea doesn't work as well as you had hoped?

Figure 20–3 shows a sample balance sheet. Martin's Moccasin Company's total current assets are \$596,000. The total current liabilities are \$288,900.

$$\frac{\$596{,}000}{\$288{,}900} = 2.06 \text{ to } 1$$

Martin has about \$2 of current assets for every \$1 of current liabilities. A current ratio of 2:1 usually suggests sufficient capital.

Working Capital

Businesses also use a *working capital* calculation. It shows the capital a firm has to carry out its daily operations. To determine the working capital use the same numbers from the current ratio calculation, but subtract current liabilities from current assets.

Use the figures from Martin's Moccasin Company.

Current assets	$596,000
– Current liabilities	$288,900
Working capital	$307,100

Martin's Moccasin Company has $307,100 of working capital.

Some companies and organizations hire big-name accounting firms for prestige and reputation. *What needs does an entrepreneur have?*

Debt Ratio

The *debt ratio* measures the percentage of total dollars in the business provided by creditors. The debt ratio is calculated below:

$$\frac{\text{Total liabilities}}{\text{Total assets}} = \text{Debt ratio}$$

$$\frac{\$450{,}900}{\$741{,}800} = 61\%$$

Martin is in debt for 61 percent of his assets. Business owners prefer to have a high debt ratio, with creditors and others financing the business.

Net Profit on Sales

Net profit on sales shows the number of cents that are left from each dollar of sales after expenses and income taxes. The net profit on sales for Martin's Moccasins is figured below:

$$\frac{\text{Net income after taxes}}{\text{Net sales}} = \text{Net profit on sales ratio}$$

$$\frac{\$106{,}950}{\$1{,}735{,}000} = 6.16\%$$

Compare your ratio to other companies in the field. If it is lower than average, your prices may be too low or your costs too high.

Operating Ratio

Operating *ratio* shows the relationship between each expense on the income statement and sales. Use the following formula:

$$\frac{\text{Expense}}{\text{Sales}} = \text{Operating ratio}$$

If sales for the month were $10,000 and the monthly rent was $1,000, the lease expense would represent 10 percent of sales. If that percentage is higher than what is average in its field, it could mean that Martin is spending too much on his lease.

There are two more useful ratios. The *quick ratio* shows whether a company is liquid without having to depend on inventory:

$$\frac{\text{Current assets} - \text{inventory}}{\text{Current liability}} = \text{Quick ratio}$$

Return on equity represents the amount of money earned for each dollar invested by the owner:

$$\frac{\text{Net income}}{\text{Total owner's equity}} = \text{Return on equity}$$

USING TECHNOLOGY AND PROFESSIONAL ASSISTANCE

As your business grows you should consider using computer software and a financial advisor. Software can organize payroll, manage invoicing, and prepare income tax returns. Working with an accountant or other financial advisor also has advantages. These experts will make sure your records are in order. They can also help you set realistic goals and evaluate your progress.

CHECK YOUR UNDERSTANDING SECTION 20.1

Reviewing Key Terms and Concepts

1 What information can be obtained by comparing current and previous income statements?
2 Explain the steps in arriving at an operating ratio.
3 List advantages of obtaining professional assistance to do financial analysis.

Critical Thinking Activity

Obtain information on at least two computer programs that perform financial analyses for your proposed business. Write a report explaining which is best for you.

Extension Lab – Speaking and Listening Skills

Delivery Deal For your delivery service, two employees drive company cars and the other ten drive their own cars. You feel that your business is ready for more growth.

Interview Talk with a local entrepreneur for insights into the following:

- What changes to your marketing mix could you make to increase sales?
- What cost-control adjustments might you make?
- How could you include your employees in the decision-making process?

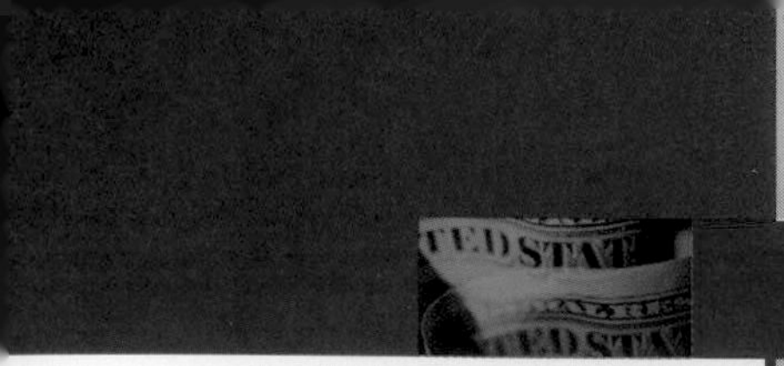

SECTION 20.2

What you'll learn

- how to plan for profits
- procedures for managing your cash flow
- general steps in planning for capital expenditures
- tax considerations in managing your finances
- managing credit

Why it's important

Effective management of your company's finances enables you to anticipate and solve financial problems. It also helps you to maximize profits and plan for future expenditures.

KEY TERMS

variable costs
fixed costs
pro forma income statement
cash budget
capital expenditures
credit bureaus
trade credit agencies

SPRINGBOARD: Ask students: What should a business take into consideration when planning for profits?

Managing Your Finances

PLANNING FOR PROFITS

Profits don't just happen. The owners of businesses have to plan for them. This includes forecasting sales, evaluating profit potential, controlling costs, and budgeting.

Forecasting Sales

To begin profit planning, you have to forecast sales. As an ongoing business, you can base your projections on sales records. You can also use the current rate of sales growth in your field or the rate of growth of the Gross National Product. Then adjust your forecast based on economic factors such as inflation or recession.

Suppose that in the car accessory industry, sales have been up 5 percent per year for the last three years and inflation rates have been stable at 2 percent. If you sold $300,000 of cup holders and air fresheners last year, this is how you could forecast sales:

$$5\% + 2\% = 7\%$$
$$.07 \times \$300{,}000 = \$21{,}000$$
$$\$300{,}000 + 21{,}000 = \$321{,}000$$

Evaluating Profit Potential

If you are satisfied with your forecast, you don't need to adjust your profit planning. However, you probably want to improve your profit picture. One way to increase sales revenue is by going after additional market share. You might add new products (such as tissue holders), raise prices, or increase advertising.

Before you decide to invest in a change, you have to evaluate its profit potential. One way to evaluate profit potential is with a variation of the break-even analysis. This shows how many units of product must be sold to make a profit based on the change:

$$\frac{\text{Fixed cost}}{\text{Selling price} - \text{variable cost}} = \text{Break-even point}$$

Variable costs are business expenses that change with each unit of product produced such as utilities, wages, and production materials. Fixed costs are expenses that don't change with number of units produced. Examples include insurance and rent.

Suppose you read about a potential market in making portable backboards for basketball tournaments. The article predicts sales of 100 units in your region. You can sell each backboard for $250. The materials, labor, and other variable costs will be about $150. Because you have to buy equipment, your fixed costs will be $5,000. How many units would you have to sell to break even?

$$\frac{\$5,000}{\$250 - \$150} = \frac{\$5,000}{\$100} = 50 \text{ units}$$

The break-even point is 50 units. For every unit over 50, you will have $100 ($250 – $150) going toward profit. However, if sales are fewer than 50, there would be no profit. If you had to spend more than $10,000 for fixed costs, there would be no profit. You would have to sell more than 100 of the backboards, which would exceed the predicted sales.

You can use this analysis to evaluate any change in your marketing mix. The costs of launching a new advertising campaign, hiring salespeople, or changing location can be factored.

Controlling Costs

Remember operating ratios? If there's a big difference between your costs and the industry average, you should investigate further.

Assume your percentage of lease expense compared to sales was 10 percent. If others in your industry are only paying 5 percent, you may have a larger facility than you need. Suppose that others are paying 15 percent. This might mean that you could increase profits by paying more for a better location.

In other instances, referring to your previous experience might give you a better comparison. Let's say your shipping costs have doubled over the previous year. You may be able to increase your profit by finding a different

Variable costs are business expenses that change with each unit of product produced. ***What are some variable costs of a basketball shoe manufacturer?***

Figure 20-4

Ways to Control Costs

There are many ways to control costs.

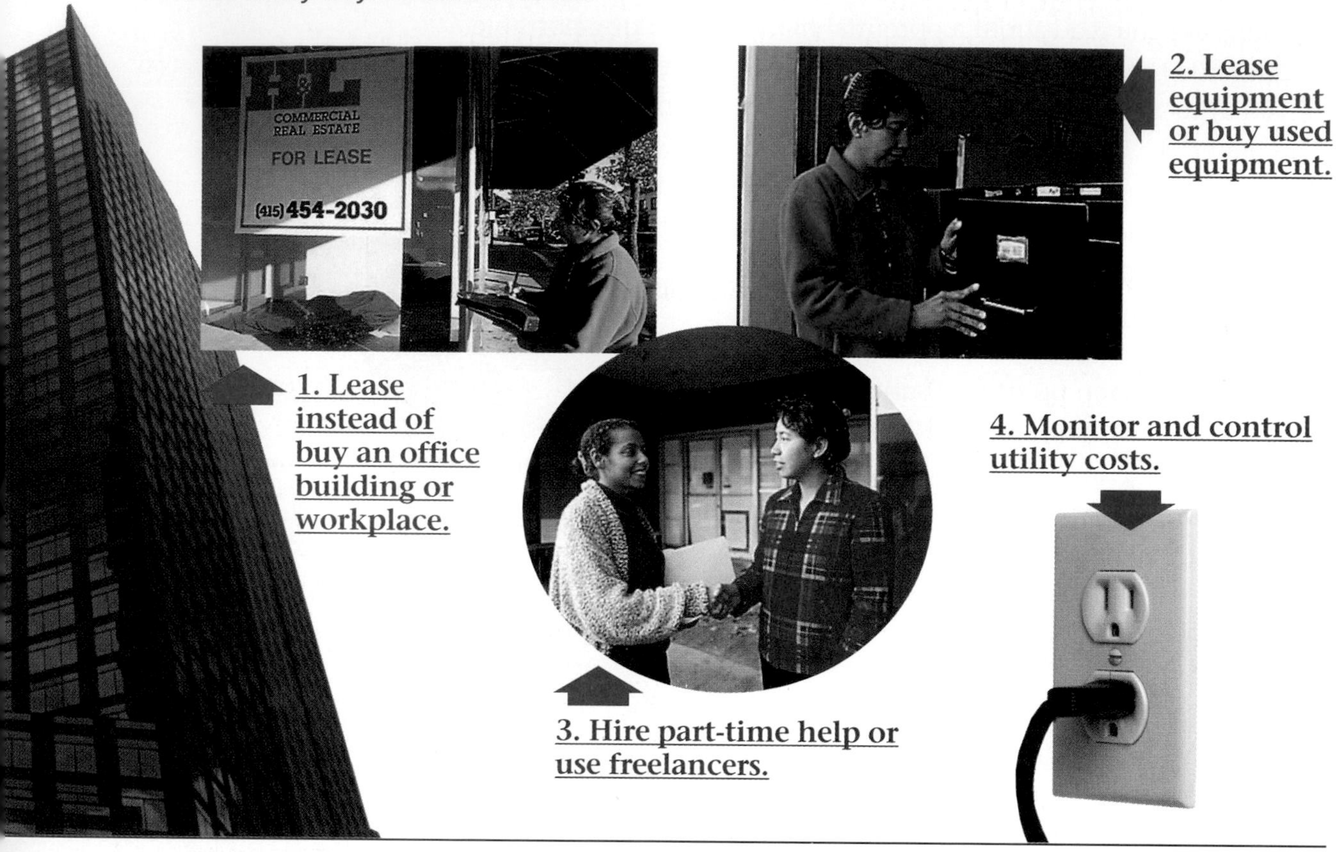
COMMERCIAL
REAL ESTATE
FOR LEASE
(415) 454-2030
1. Lease instead of buy an office building or workplace.
2. Lease equipment or buy used equipment.
3. Hire part-time help or use freelancers.
4. Monitor and control utility costs.

trucking contractor or leasing your own trucks. **Figure 20–4** lists additional ways to control costs.

Budgeting

At the beginning of each planning period, prepare a pro forma income statement, which estimates income, and a balance sheet. Use the financial statements from your previous operating period to make adjustments and create a master budget.

MANAGING CASH FLOW

A business can be growing and profitable and still fail if it runs out of cash. Profits are often "plowed back" into new inventory and equipment and into expanding facilities. The problem is that you can't pay employees, lenders, or suppliers with profits that have been reinvested. You need cash.

Using a Cash Budget

A *cash budget* (sometimes called cash forecast) like the one shown in **Figure 20–5** is an important cash management tool. For the cash budget your projections of cash receipts and disbursements will be based on past operating records. It shows estimated cash flow, actual cash flow, and the difference between the two.

Figure 20–5
The cash budget form has three columns for each month. ***What is the purpose of such a layout?***

Cash Budget

For Quarter Ending ____________

	MONTH 1			MONTH 2			MONTH 3		
	EST.	ACT.	DIF.	EST.	ACT.	DIF.	EST.	ACT.	DIF.
Projected Cash Receipts									
Cash sales									
Collections on accounts receivable									
Other income									
Total Receipts									
Projected Cash Disbursements									
Purchases (raw materials, merchandise)									
Advertising									
Dues, subscriptions, licenses									
Insurance									
Interest									
Legal and professional expenses									
Office supplies									
Payroll taxes									
Rent									
Salaries									
Sales taxes									
Telephone									
Travel and entertainment									
Utilities									
Notes payable									
Other ____________									
____________									
____________									
____________									
____________									
____________									
Total Disbursements									
Net Cash Increase (Decrease)									

Most businesses prepare cash budgets in three-month periods. With a cash budget, you can make sure you meet cash needs and anticipate shortfalls. If your budget indicates that you are going to be short $6,000 cash at the end of the month, you can secure short-term financing. If you foresee a sizable cash surplus, you can put the money to work. Options are highlighted in **Figure 20–6**.

Improving Your Cash Flow

Certain areas in a business operation have more room for improving cash flow than others. Some are described below:

- *Tighten up your credit and collections.* If a customer goes past due, follow up immediately.
- *Set up a cash reserve for bad debts.* Create a cash fund to counterbalance the effect of unpaid receivables.
- *Take advantage of credit terms.* Pay your bills on time, but take all the time that is available to you.
- *Offer cash discounts.* Give cash discounts to customers for prompt payment.
- *Manage inventory carefully.* Excess inventory can tie up cash. If inventory doesn't sell, cut prices and turn it back into cash.
- *Put cash surpluses to work.* When you temporarily have more cash than you need, invest it.

Figure 20–6
The Cash Budget Summary shows the outcomes of your financial planning. ***If you used such a form during a quarter, why wouldn't you have an entry for every space on every line?***

Cash Budget Summary

For Quarter Ending ___________

	MONTH 1			MONTH 2			MONTH 3		
	EST.	ACT.	DIF.	EST.	ACT.	DIF.	EST.	ACT.	DIF.
Estimated beginning cash balance									
Plus net cash increase (or minus net cash decrease)									
Estimated ending cash balance									
Necessary cash balance									
Short-term loan needed (if cash is less than amount required)									
Cash available for short-term investment (if cash is greater than amount required)									

- *Keep your payroll under control.* Contracting work out or hiring part-time people may cost less than full-time employees.
- *Cut expenses.* You may be tempted to spend freely when money is rolling in, but remember that bills may not be far behind.

PLANNING FOR CAPITAL EXPENDITURES

Capital expenditures are long-term commitments of large sums of money to buy new equipment or replace old equipment. How do you plan for capital expenditures? First determine if you can pay for the equipment. Then consider the revenue it will generate and how long it will take to pay for itself.

When you make a capital expenditure, you will probably have to pay for some of it yourself and borrow the rest. To borrow, you will have to make your debt ratio low and attractive for lenders. This means paying off some debts before incurring new ones.

MANAGING TAXES

We discussed your legal obligations to pay taxes in Chapter 8. However, there are some additional tax considerations:

- *Time income so that you can control when it is taxed.* Scheduling sales for the beginning of the upcoming year will defer taxes.
- *Time your deductions.* During high income years, identify costs that can be deducted during that year.
- *Choose the depreciation method that is most beneficial.* Because new businesses often have more to write off than they have income, it is better for them to spread write-offs over time.

Tips from the Real World

FOCUS

Hard work, personal service, and focus have led many entrepreneurs to success. Kathleen Bobe of Chrispanic Enterprises Inc. says:

"We answer the phone, we don't have voice mail, and we're in tune with what customers need."

ENTREPRENEURS INTERNATIONAL

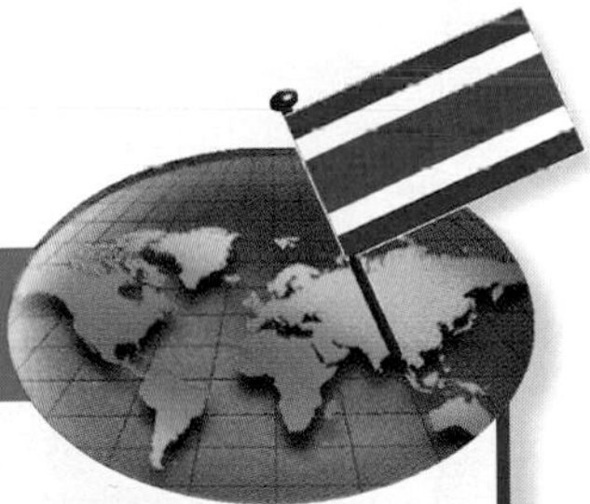

Thailand

In 1992, Guy Hopkins and his wife, Toi, opened The Spa Resort on Lamai Beach in the Gulf of Siam. Worldwide guests travel to the Hopkins spa. They indulge in stress-free vacations including mountain biking, hiking, yoga, health food, and massages. Due to the exchange rate, an all-inclusive week costs about US$210. "We are a small, family-run oasis for self-improvement. My wife Toi and her family offer splendid home cooking with superb Thai vegetarian and seafood cuisine," adds Hopkins.

Apply **How can an exchange rate affect your purchasing power of non-U.S. goods and services? Give examples.**

Advantages and Disadvantages of Extending Credit

Advantages

- You can build closer relationships with customers by making purchasing easier.
- Selling by telephone or mail is made easier.
- Credit account records provide a useful marketing tool.
- Credit can increase and broaden sales.

Disadvantages

- Slow-paying customers can affect cash flow.
- Capital can be tied up in goods sold on credit.
  - If you borrow money to extend credit, interest is added to the cost.
  - You have the additional costs of credit checking, additional bookkeeping, billing, and collections.

Figure 20–7
There are benefits and drawbacks to extending credit. ***What are some other advantages?***

- *Write off bad debts.* If you are extending credit, you can write off accounts deemed uncollectible.
- *Claim research and development expenses.* You may not have many of these, but be aware that they are deductible.
- *Keep records of all expenses.* Any honest expense is deductible, but it is up to you to keep the records.
- *Keep up-to-date on tax laws.* You may need to consult with a financial advisor, an attorney, or the IRS for advice.

MANAGING CREDIT

The advantage of offering credit is increased sales volume. Advantages and disadvantages are presented in **Figure 20–7**.

Granting Credit

Credit management begins before credit is given to a customer. The granting process involves five steps.

Up&Coming Entrepreneur

Publishing Entrepreneur

Colin Kane claims he isn't as interested in the product as he is in the opportunity. "As long as there is a potential niche, low development costs, and a low overhead, I'm in!" Thirty-one-year-old Kane runs Simply Media, an upstart business focusing on straightforward, colorful, and humorous guides to help people get through tedious tasks from taxes to wedding planning. Eventually, Kane hopes to build a brand name for his $8 books by distributing them in bookstores and national retail chains.

Analyze **What costs might be considered "business development" costs? What costs might be considered "business overhead" ?**

1. Obtaining Information. Have the customer submit information on employment, income, assets, and credit references.

2. Checking Credit and Background. Credit bureaus can provide a person's credit information to their member businesses. Trade credit agencies also provide credit information for a fee.

3. Evaluating Credit Applications. Ask for the three C's of credit: character, capacity, and capital.

4. Making Your Decision. You can require a cosigner, collateral, a down payment, or shorter terms.

5. Closing. The amount due, interest, payments, and due date must be clear. You must indicate how the interest is computed. Thoroughness in closing is required by the Truth-in-Lending Act.

Collecting Accounts

A business can collect accounts internally or externally. The most effective internal collection procedures involve progressively forceful steps. Start with timely notification *before* the bill is due. Once an account is past due, send a reminder notice to the customer. If there is no response to numerous mailings, contact the customer by telephone. If you cannot collect an account yourself, you have to get help externally. One option is to hire a collection agency. The agency will pursue collection for a fee—usually 33 to 50 percent.

Money Matters

QUALITY

Seen in a positive light, even government regulations can benefit a small business. Valerie Skonie, founder of Skonie Corp., recalls:

"*The IRS was so demanding on our contractor arrangement . . . [it] actually made some of our breakthroughs [in management] possible.*"

CHECK YOUR UNDERSTANDING

SECTION 20.2

Reviewing Key Terms and Concepts

1. List the four steps involved in planning for profits.
2. What are the broad steps in planning for capital expenditures?
3. What would be the three most important tax considerations for your proposed company?

Critical Thinking Activity

Evaluate the profit potential of adding one product to your proposed business mix, using your best estimate for costs

Extension Lab—Serve Customers

Rock and Roll Last year, you began offering credit to customers of your custom rocking-chair business. One of your best customers has become delinquent in her payments. Whenever you call, this customer has become angry and threatened to purchase the rocking chairs from a competitor.

Role Play With a classmate, take turns role-playing one of such calls. Keep these considerations in mind:

- How can you defuse the customer's anger and collect your money?
- What can you do to help retain customers who are delinquent in their payments?

CHAPTER 20 REVIEW

CHAPTER SUMMARY

- The same financial statements you used to start up your business—the income statement and balance sheet—can help you with planning the operation of your business.
- You can analyze your business finances by comparing completed financial statements and calculating certain ratios.
- As your business grows, you may need to use computer technology and professional consultants to help you make sound financial decisions.
- Business owners must plan for profits by forecasting sales, evaluating profit potential, controlling costs, and budgeting.
- In addition to planning for profit, the cash flow of the business must be managed effectively to ensure that enough money is on hand to meet expenses.
- Capital expenditures must be planned for long before they are needed.
- Taxes can be managed to enhance the financial position of the business.
- The advantage of offering credit to increase sales volume must be weighed against the cost of extending credit.

RECALL KEY TERMS

Working with a team, create a bulletin board explaining financial management. Be sure to include the following key terms. As a class, vote on the best one and display it.

income statement
balance sheet
ratio analysis
current assets
current liabilities
return on equity
variable costs
fixed costs
pro forma income statement
cash budget
capital expenditures
credit bureaus
trade credit agencies

RECALL KEY CONCEPTS

1. What does a current ratio indicate?
2. What does debt ratio measure?
3. How would you determine whether the net profit on sales ratio was a good ratio?
4. Name the growth rates you could use to forecast sales.
5. How can you analyze the profitability of a change in your marketing mix?
6. List four ways to control costs to improve profitability.
7. How is a cash budget designed?
8. Describe four ways to improve cash flow.
9. Explain the five-step process for granting credit.

THINK CRITICALLY

1. Why would creditors prefer you have a moderate debt ratio?
2. The chapter cites two ways to improve profits (increasing market share and controlling costs). Are there other ways? What are they?
3. What is the difference between controlling costs to improve profits and the steps that can be taken to improve cash flow? Explain your answer.
4. What is the best way to improve cash flow?

Defend your answer.

5. Is it ethical to try to minimize your business taxes? Why or why not?
6. How is cash flow related to credit management?

CONNECT ACADEMICS TO THE WORKPLACE

Math

1. You own a small teen dance club. For the past year you have had a live band on Saturday nights and have drawn an average of 150 teenagers. Many of the regulars have told you that you could increase business by enlarging the dance floor. That remodeling would cost $12,000. You calculate that each teen spends $15 and your variable cost is $10 per teen. By enlarging the floor, you figure you can increase the business to 200 teenagers. How long would it take to break even? (Assume 200 teens would come every Saturday night.) Would enlarging the floor be profitable?

Writing

2. Think about a business that you might like to open. Write to trade associations requesting information about industry averages for net profit on sales, operating ratios, and other important statistics in your field of interest.

WORK IN YOUR COMMUNITY

Interview an accountant or CPA who specializes in small business management. Ask about the following:

- The services provided to small businesses
- The costs of those services
- Recommended software packages to be used for financial management
- What small businesses should do to position themselves for the best possible tax situation
- The most common financial mistakes a small business owner makes

LINK SCHOOL TO CAREER

Working in teams of three or four, offer a "financial check-up" to small businesses in the community or clubs in the school. Provide the following service:

- Complete ratio analyses (current, debt, net profit on sales, operating costs, and so on)
- Sales forecast for the coming year
- Suggestions for improving profitability
- Suggestions for improving cash flow

Present your "check-up" in a professional format.

*inter*NET CONNECTION

Finance Facts

Rosa owns a toy store. You offer to show her some Internet sites that will provide her with financial information.

Connect

Using a variety of search engines, locate sites offering the following:

- Free accounting software for financial statement preparation
- Financial advice for small businesses
- Tax advice for small businesses

Add these sites to your resource log.

CHAPTER 21

Accounting and Record Keeping

Learning Objectives

When you have completed this chapter, you will be able to:

- **Discuss** the importance of record keeping
- **List** records that should be kept on a daily basis
- **Explain** which records are kept on a weekly and monthly basis
- **Determine** who should do the record keeping for your business
- **Discuss** the financial statements your business will need to prepare

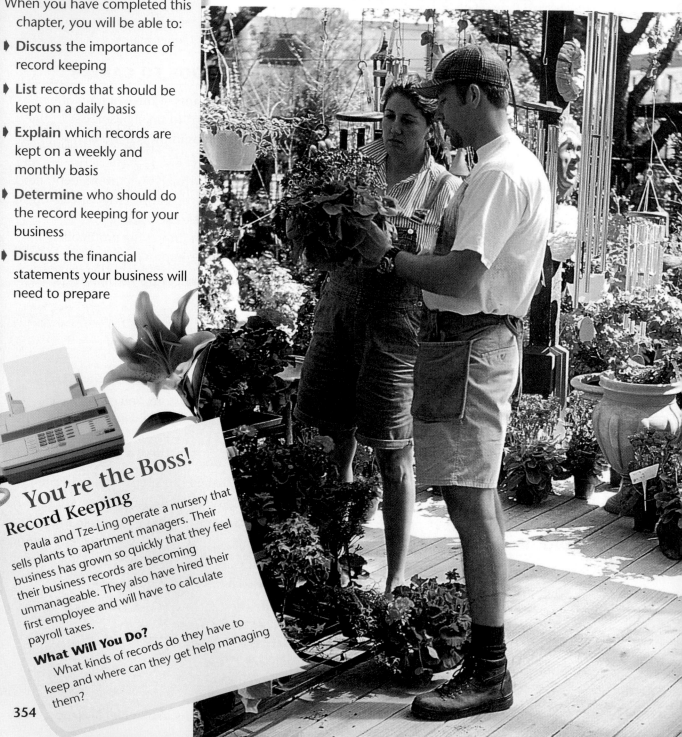

You're the Boss!

Record Keeping

Paula and Tze-Ling operate a nursery that sells plants to apartment managers. Their business has grown so quickly that they feel their business records are becoming unmanageable. They also have hired their first employee and will have to calculate payroll taxes.

What Will You Do?

What kinds of records do they have to keep and where can they get help managing them?

SECTION 21.1

Keeping Records and Accounting

THE IMPORTANCE OF RECORD KEEPING

In business, change is swift and constant. Change can come from many sources. Your customers and your competitors can be located down the street, across the country, or halfway around the world. The challenge of the entrepreneur is to respond to the shifting demands of such a marketplace.

Good record keeping keeps the owner and others informed about cash flow, sales, inventory, production, taxes, and payroll. In this section, you will learn how to set up an accounting system. You will also learn how to keep track of important business information on a daily, weekly, and monthly basis.

After poor management, most of the major causes of business failure are directly related to faulty record keeping. If you do keep sound records, your business will have an advantage.

How to Set Up a Record-Keeping System

Before you can set up a record-keeping system, you must make some basic decisions determined by the specific needs of your business. Here are some of the decisions you must make.

Choose a Fiscal Year. The first thing you need to do is decide on a *fiscal year*. A fiscal year is a tax year selected by a business for accounting purposes. Your business will pay its income taxes based on the fiscal year you select. A fiscal year may be different from the calendar year, which runs from January 1 to December 31. However, it must be the same 12-month period year after year. Once you have chosen your fiscal year, you cannot change it without approval from the IRS.

How do business owners choose a fiscal year? Often they look for their slowest quarter, the one in which they are likely to have the lowest sales. A Travel agency may avoid ending a fiscal year in a summer month, during peak sales. Tax preparers are busiest in

What you'll learn

- the difference between single- and double-entry systems of accounting
- how to keep daily, weekly, and monthly business records
- the different types of records
- who should keep the records for your business

Why it's important

Many entrepreneurs fail because they don't monitor the financial health of their businesses.

KEY TERMS

fiscal year
cash basis
accrual basis
accounts payable
accounts receivable
single-entry system
double-entry system
debit
credit
journals
cash receipts journal
cash disbursements journal
sales journal
purchases journal
ledger

Many companies use the calendar year as their fiscal year because it ends with the holiday season. ***Why would they want to end it with the slowest season?***

April. Bookstores, clothing stores, and shoe stores conduct brisk business in September, before school starts.

Choose a Cash or an Accrual Basis. Next, you need to choose how to record income and payments. If you use a cash basis, you record your income when it is received and your expenses when they are paid. (You use this same system with a personal checking account.) This is the easiest method.

If inventories are a big source of income for your business, you are required by the IRS to use an accrual basis. This means you record income when it is earned and expenses when they are incurred. In other words, you record the right to receive income and the obligation to pay expenses at some future date.

Businesses that use the accrual basis describe costs that have been incurred but not paid as *liabilities*. Accounts payable, for example, are amounts you owe for items bought but not yet paid for. Sales that have been made but not collected are called accounts receivable, an *asset* account.

Choose a Single- or Double-Entry System

The third and final decision concerns how you will enter items in your records. Many start-up businesses use the single-entry system because it is a simple accounting system noting only amounts due to and owed by a business. You simply record the daily income and expenses. At the end of the month, you prepare a summary of the receipts and dis-

ENTREPRENEURS INTERNATIONAL

Austria

Artweger & Co. is an Austrian family business founded in 1923. They began by manufacturing wooden clothespins until the factory was shut down during World War II. After the war Artweger reopened, introducing aluminum kitchen products to its line and expanding into plastic manufacturing. Artweger soon became world famous for its accordion-style clothes dryers. Today Artweger employs 250 people and manufactures all types of cabinetry and high-quality products for the bath.

Apply What last-minute steps would Artweger have needed to take during World War II to prepare its business for closing and reopening after the war?

bursements (or payments). The problem with this method is that it does not balance itself.

Most businesses use a double-entry system. This system is a bookkeeping method in which each transaction is entered twice in the ledger—as a *debit* to one account and a *credit* to another account. A debit is an item that increases the balance of an asset account. A credit is an item that decreases the balance of an asset account.

Money Matters

SCORECARDS

Short, one-page reports called Scorecards provide a good way to keep track of progress, especially toward specific goals. At Certifiedemail.com, says owner Court Coursey:

"*[Scorecards had shown] me a way to save money by cutting waste. It was something I may not have seen without this feedback.*"

DAILY RECORD KEEPING

The best way to monitor the financial health of your business is to keep records on a daily basis. It makes it more likely that you will catch errors when they occur.

Using Journals

The daily record keeping of a double-entry system uses books called journals to record business transactions. The types and number of journals you use will depend on the size and scope of your business.

A very small business may use just one journal to record all its daily transactions. This would be a *general journal*. **Figure 21–1** shows two transactions recorded in such a journal. On March 7, cash was spent to pay the rent. On March 8 inventory was purchased on account (or with credit).

Eventually a business may find that using one journal is not sufficient to keep track of all of its transactions. At that point, the business will set up separate, special journals. The special journals

Journal Entry

PAGE NO. 2

DATE	ACCOUNT	ACCT. #	DEBIT	CREDIT
MAR. 7	RENT EXPENSE	51	1425 00	
	CASH	12		1425 00
MAR. 8	PURCHASES	58	10500 00	
	ACCOUNTS PAYABLE	23		10500 00

Figure 21–1
A journal is a daily record of business transactions.
Is this journal single- or double-entry accounting?

Figure 21–2

Special Journals

Commonly used special journals include the following:

1. Cash receipts journal—
Cash (and checks) received are posted in a cash receipts journal.

2. Cash disbursements journal—
Payments made in cash or check form are posted in a cash disbursements journal.

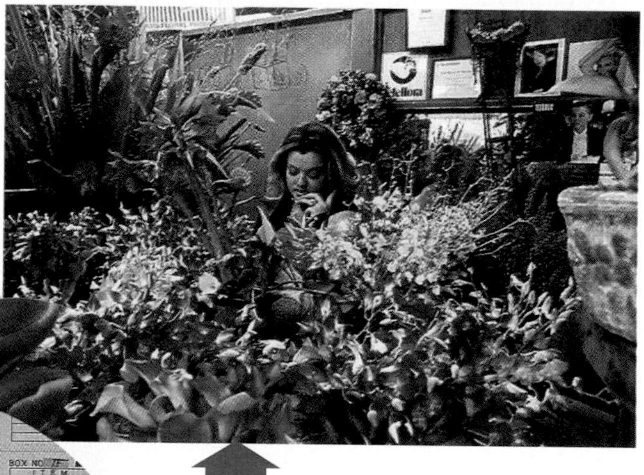

3. Sales journal—Sales on account are posted in a sales journal.

4. Purchases journal—
Purchases on account are posted in a purchases journal.

most often used are shown in **Figure 21–2**.

Using Summary of Sales and Cash Receipts

Businesses that have regular daily sales should keep a daily summary of sales and cash receipts. The summary allows you to see your total daily sales at a glance. It also verifies the total of your cash receipts. **Figure 21–3** shows a sample summary. There are three main headings: *Cash Receipts, Cash on Hand,* and *Sales*.

Figuring Cash Receipts. The Cash Receipts section lists *cash sales, collections on account,* and *miscellaneous receipts*. Miscellaneous receipts are items that you don't normally receive during a day's business.

Counting Cash on Hand. The Cash on Hand section of the summary shows the amount in the register broken down into coins, bills, and checks. It also includes the opening cash fund, which may double as a petty cash fund.

At the end of the Cash on Hand section, calculate how much

Tips from the Real World

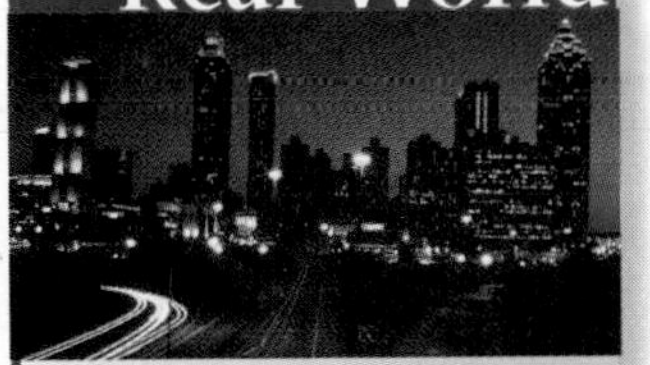

START SMALL

One of the advantages of starting small is the ability to test the market. Mary Anne Johnson, co-owner of The Chandlery, advises:

"Develop some accounts that give you enough capital to figure out what really sells . . . then you can approach buyers on a grander scale."

Summary of Sales and Cash Receipts

January 20, ____

Cash Receipts		
Cash sales		$2,160.85
Collections on account		160.35
Miscellaneous receipts		69.77
Total Cash Receipts		$2,390.97
Cash on Hand		
Cash in the register		
Coins	$ 75.31	
Bills	780.00	
Checks	1,635.66	
Total Cash on Hand		$2,490.97
Less opening cash/petty cash fund		
Petty cash slips	$ 20.55	
Coins and bills	79.45	
Opening Cash Fund		100.00
Total Cash Deposit		$2,390.97
Sales		
Cash sales		$2,160.85
Credit sales		465.39
Total Sales		$2,626.24

Figure 21–3
A summary tells you your total daily sales. ***How and where?***

Ledger Entry

ACCOUNT *CASH* ACCOUNT NO. *11*

DATE	ITEM	J.R.	DEBIT	DATE	ITEM	J.R.	CREDIT
MAR 1	BALANCE	✓	14390 00	MAR 7		G2	1425 00

Figure 21–4
Journal entries are posted to various accounts in a ledger. ***What is this account's name?***

cash to deposit in the bank at the day's end. To do this, subtract the opening cash fund total from the amount in the register.

Use your amount of deposit to verify your cash receipts total. The amounts should be equal. If they are not, look for a mistake:

- Did you record all transactions?
- Did you record a transaction for less than the correct amount?
- Did you give a customer too little change?

If you are depositing less than your total receipts, ask yourself:

- Was money taken from the register without recording it?
- Did you record an amount higher than the correct amount?
- Did you give a customer too much change?

Recording Sales. The final section of the summary tells you your total daily sales. It adds up your cash and credit sales.

WEEKLY RECORD KEEPING

Conduct additional record keeping every week. This practice will help you simplify end-of-the-month calculations.

Posting to a Ledger

A ledger is a collection of all the accounts of a business. Examples of accounts include *cash, sales, accounts receivable,* and *accounts payable.* These allow you to see what is happening in each of those accounts.

Look at the ledger account of cash in **Figure 21–4**. You can see that the cash account had a debit balance of $14,390. Then the account was credited $1,425. (In other words, the rent payment was subtracted, although the calculation was not shown.) At that point, the account had a debit balance of $12,965.

Post your journal entries to a ledger as often as necessary to keep your accounts up-to-date. However, posting weekly is probably enough to give you a good idea of how your business is doing.

Keeping Track of Payments

It's important to keep track of your business bills. Some of these are monthly bills such as rent, telephone, and utilities. By reviewing which of these bills are due on a weekly basis, you can be sure they are paid on time.

Other bills might include suppliers of either inventory or raw materials. Remember how suppliers often offer discounts for early payment? Keeping track of supplier bills on a weekly basis will help you take advantage of these discounts.

Aging Amounts Owed to You

One way to keep track of what people owe you is by setting up an aging table. In this case, *aging* means categorizing a customer's account by the length of time since the bill was incurred.

Figure 21–5 shows how to age an account. First, list all customers in a column. Then across the top of the page, write column headings such as *Current, 31–60 Days, 61–90 Days,* and so on. This chart will show you who has owed you money for how long.

Figure 21–5
Aging your accounts receivable can tell you how promptly your customers are paying. ***What percent of your customers have accounts aged 60 days or less?***

Aging Table

Customer	Amount	Current	31–60 days	61–90 days	Over 90
C. Appelgren	40.55	40.55			
M. Neumann	120.54		120.54		
C. Canedo	395.00		395.00		
R. Vasquez	59.45				59.45
Percent of Total	**100%**	**6.6%**	**83.7%**		**9.7%**

RISK TAKERS PROFIT MAKERS

Name: Joel Rayden
Company: Datascan, Inc.
City, State: Ventura, CA

Filing Files Forever

Through research, Joel Rayden found that senior employees waste nearly four full work weeks per year searching through file cabinets for files. Administrative employees spend even more time retrieving documents than their senior supervisors do!

Rayden's Datascan electronically automates paper files through digitally scanning their images onto CDs, then indexes each page for easy computer referencing. Rayden calls the process Electronic Document Warehousing.

"In an instant, an entire warehouse of archived files could be on your desktop," Rayden explains, "but more important, in the event of a disaster, all documentation is saved on and off site in a medium that can get a business up and running immediately." Rayden hopes that his system of filing will be the standard one day, and he is looking into franchising his company across the nation.

Thinking Critically

What type of records would a business need to recover quickly from a natural or man-made disaster?

Keeping Payroll Records

If you have employees, you need to figure how much to pay and how much to withhold for taxes. The *payroll register* provides the information you need to report the taxes you need to pay. Make a general journal entry when you pay your employees.

Keeping Up with Taxes

Business owners are responsible for sales tax, payroll taxes, and federal business income tax. Keeping track of collections or withholding for these taxes on a weekly basis makes sure you have money to meet your tax obligations.

Maintaining Other Records

There are nonfinancial records that you will want to maintain. **Figure 21–6** lists some of the records most businesses keep.

Other Business Records

Record Types	What to Include
Insurance	Record the types and amounts of insurance you carry. Include policy numbers, premiums, and payment dates.
Maintenance	Record all maintenance work performed on plant and equipment. Include dates, costs, and type of service or repair.
Quality control	Monitor complaints about product quality. Keep track of returns and repairs.
Inventory	Track changes in inventory. Note items and quantities sold, purchased, and currently in stock.
General office records	Keep documentation for all business transactions.

Figure 21–6
Updating records is important for keeping track of your business and your bills. ***Where would you file insurance receipts concerning a company vehicle that had gotten in an accident?***

Retain invoices, purchase orders, contracts, and business correspondence. You might want to make a similar list for yourself.

MONTHLY RECORD KEEPING

Certain records will have to be updated on a monthly basis. In many instances, these updates will result in prepared statements.

Financial Statements

Financial statements are documents that reflect the financial health of the business. They include the cash flow statement, income or profit-and-loss statement, and balance sheet.

Up&Coming Entrepreneur

Administrative Entrepreneur

Carolyn Sims Akens was employed for 15 years in administrative support and human resource management positions. "I wasn't happy with the quality of personnel that our office would hire on a temporary basis, so I decided to use my skills to help others become more effective." For a flat fee of $20 per hour, Akens works from her office in Florida as a one-person Virtual Partner, accomplishing administrative tasks her clients don't have time to handle themselves.

Analyze **Why might Akens have gone from being in personnel management to becoming a temp herself?**

Figure 21–7
Many stores allow customers to use bankcards to draw money directly from their accounts as payment. ***How would these be treated when balancing a checkbook?***

Steps for Balancing a Checkbook

Step 1 ***Write the bank statement balance on the first line of the reconciliation form.*** This is called the *bank balance.*

Step 2 ***List outstanding deposits on the appropriate line and add them to the bank balance.*** Outstanding deposits are those that have not yet been added to your bank statement.

Step 3 ***Compare the canceled checks or those checks listed on your statement with your check register or check stubs.*** Check off all items that have been returned to you or listed as paid. These are amounts that the bank has subtracted from your account.

Step 4 ***List outstanding checks on the appropriate line and subtract them from the bank balance.*** Outstanding checks are checks you have written that do not yet show on your statement. They represent money you have paid that has not yet been removed from your account. The result of these calculations is the *adjusted bank balance.*

Step 5 ***Compare the balance from your checkbook to the adjusted bank balance.*** The two figures should be the same.

Step 6 ***If there is a difference, go back and check your work.*** Be sure that all your calculations are correct. Verify that all checks and deposits have been accounted for in the reconciliation. Finally, be sure you have recorded all service charges in your register and subtracted them from your balance.

Reconciling a Bank Statement

Once a month you will receive a statement from the bank that describes the status of your business checking account. When you receive this statement you should reconcile, or balance, your checking account right away. This allows you to verify that neither you nor your bank has made any errors in record keeping.

Balancing a Checkbook

Balancing a checkbook is not difficult if you enter transactions throughout the month. The reconciliation form is on the back of the bank statement. The process is listed in **Figure 21–7**.

Balancing a Petty Cash Fund

If your business has a petty cash fund, you will need to balance it monthly. Each time money is withdrawn from the petty cash fund, a receipt should be prepared. At the end of the month, the amount of money left in petty cash plus the total of the receipts should equal the fund's fixed amount.

Paying the Payroll Tax Deposits

You will need to create records to show that all tax deposits for payroll withholding have been made monthly. You will also need to record that federal and state employer taxes have been paid.

WHO SHOULD KEEP THE RECORDS?

How can you keep records and still find time to run a business? Fortunately, there are many options. You can hire a bookkeeper to handle forms, journal entries, and payroll. You can also hire a CPA (certified public accountant) to audit your books. With computerized software, it's easier than ever to keep your own books.

CHECK YOUR UNDERSTANDING

SECTION 21.1

Reviewing Key Terms and Concepts

1. Which records should be kept on a daily basis and why?
2. Which records should be kept on a monthly basis and why?
3. Who should do the record keeping in your business?

Critical Thinking Activity

Meet with an accountant to get his or her opinion on how to set up your business records.

Extension Lab—Monitoring and Correcting Performance

Correct Change Paul manages the College Corner, a store that sells books and supplies for the local community college. At the end of each working day, he prepares a summary of sales using figures supplied by his sales clerks. Over the last two months, his summaries have not balanced with the sales reports generated by the computerized cash registers.

Investigate In groups of two or three, research different ways of accounting and preparing a summary, then discuss the following:

- What is a better way for Paul to balance his reports?
- What procedures could he put in place to ensure customers were charged the right amount and were given the correct change?

Financial Statements

What you'll learn

- how to prepare a cash flow statement, income statement, and balance sheet
- how to prepare a personal financial statement

Why it's important

Financial statements are the way we look at the financial health of a business. They indicate how a business is doing at any time.

KEY TERMS

cash-flow statement
profit-and-loss statement
balance sheet
assets
owner's equity

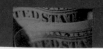

PREPARING YOUR BUSINESS FINANCIAL STATEMENTS

You need to prepare certain financial statements so that outside users, such as investors and bankers, can study your business. You also need financial reports for yourself and others inside the business. These include a cash flow statement, which describes the flow of cash into and out of a business. Financial statements for outside users include an income statement and a balance sheet. In this section, you will learn how to create all these statements.

Preparing a Cash Flow Statement

The cash flow statement is one of the most important statements you create at the end of each month. Cash flow is important because you cannot pay your expenses with sales. You can only pay them with cash. The cash flow statement helps you do the following:

- *Estimate sales.* This figure is based on how quickly your customers pay their bills. It is also affected by seasonal changes in your industry. If you study your industry carefully, you will have a good sense of such patterns.
- *Estimate operating expenses.* A cash flow statement helps you estimate ongoing operating costs. These are the costs of running the business, such as rent, salaries, supplies, and so forth. A new business may often show negative

cash flow (a minus amount) during the first few months.

- *Construct the statement.* If you look closely at the cash flow statement in **Figure 21-8**, you can see how one is constructed. It follows this pattern:

$$\frac{\textbf{Cash receipts}}{\textbf{(inflow)}} - \frac{\textbf{Disbursements}}{\textbf{(outflow)}} = \textbf{Net cash flow}$$

The business took in $23,000. It spent $16,620. This leaves a positive cash flow of $6,380.

Preparing a Profit-and-Loss Statement

A profit-and-loss statement compares revenues and expenses over a specific period. It is also called an *income statement*. Usually prepared monthly, it shows the following:

Revenues – Expenses = Net income (or loss)

The profit-and-loss statements for different types of businesses may vary in format. For a service business, you would subtract expenses from revenues. For retail and wholesale businesses, however, you must first compute the cost of goods sold. The income statement includes sales and expenses you may have incurred but haven't paid. **Figure 21–9** is an example of an income statement.

Cash Flow Statement

March 31, ____

Cash Receipts		$23,000
Disbursements		
Equipment	$12,000	
Cost of goods	2,500	
Selling expense	200	
Salaries	700	
Advertising	130	
Office supplies	20	
Rent	500	
Utilities	90	
Insurance	170	
Taxes	70	
Loan principal and interest	240	
Total Disbursements		16,620
Net Cash Flow		$ 6,380

Figure 21–8
If a business has more money coming in than going out, it has a positive cash flow. If more money goes out than comes in, it has a negative cash flow. ***Which situation does this statement illustrate?***

Figure 21–9
An income statement for a business shows how much it earned after paying all of its expenses. ***Is this income statement for a service business or for a retail business?***

Swim World Income Statement

Year Ended December 31, ____

Revenue		
Sales		$450,000
Cost of goods sold		250,000
Gross Profit		$200,000
Operating Expenses:		
Salaries	$70,000	
Advertising	12,000	
Rent	14,000	
Utilities	3,600	
Maintenance	1,200	
Insurance	1,500	
Miscellaneous	1,000	
Total Expenses		103,300
Net Profit (before taxes)		$ 96,700

Preparing a Balance Sheet

A balance sheet tells an entrepreneur what his or her business is worth. It is based on an equation that states that business assets (the things of value that belong to a business) are equal to the financial rights people have in those assets:

Balance Sheet

March 31, ____

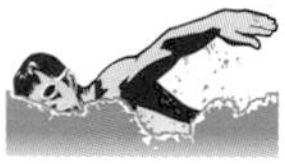

Assets		
Cash	$10,745	
Accounts receivable	868	
Inventory	5,799	
Supplies	433	
Total Assets		$17,845
Liabilities		
Accounts payable	$ 3,444	
Notes payable	5,705	
Total Liabilities		$ 9,149
Owner's Equity		
Joseph Conrad		8,696
Total Liabilities and Owner's Equity		$17,845

Figure 21–10
A balance sheet shows how much a business is worth and how much of that amount actually belongs to the owner. ***How much equity does the owner have in the business?***

Assets = Liabilities + Owner's equity

Liabilities are what are owed to others. The owner's equity is the amount left over after liabilities are subtracted from assets.

Look at **Figure 21-10**. The first section shows the assets of the company. The second section shows the business's liabilities. The last section is the owner's equity. At swim world, assets are $17,845, liabilities are $9,149, and owner's equity is $8,696

$17,845 = $9,149 + $8,696

PREPARING YOUR PERSONAL FINANCIAL STATEMENT

Potential investors or bankers will be interested in studying your *personal financial statement*. Create this statement like a balance sheet. First, list your personal assets (such as a savings account or house), then your personal liabilities (or debts). You arrive at your personal net worth by subtracting your liabilities from your assets.

Net worth = Assets – Liabilities

This figure will help people gauge your financial health.

CHECK YOUR UNDERSTANDING

SECTION 21.2

Reviewing Key Terms and Concepts

1 What is the difference between a cash flow statement and an income statement?
2 Why is it important to do a personal financial statement?
3 What does a balance sheet tell you about the business?

Critical Thinking Activity

Construct a personal financial statement for yourself. Include all your assets and your liabilities.

Extension Lab—Organizing and Maintaining Files

Tax Time Last year, Cyrena started selling custom T-shirts. Her business has been good, but never kept records or paid taxes. Yesterday, the IRS informed her that they will close down her business if she doesn't pay back taxes.

Research Visit the library to find out more information about income tax regulations, and present your results to the class. Keep the following questions in mind as you research:

- What should Cyrena do so she can pay her taxes and remain in business?
- How can she avoid these problems in the future?

CHAPTER 21 REVIEW

CHAPTER SUMMARY

- Keeping good business records ensures that the entrepreneur will be informed about the financial status of the enterprise.
- Before a record-keeping system can be set up, the entrepreneur needs to select a fiscal year, choose a cash or accrual basis, and decide whether to use single- or double-entry accounting.
- Records that should be kept daily include sales, cash receipts, cash disbursements, and purchases journals, as well as a summary of sales and cash receipts.
- Records that should be kept weekly include postings to a ledger, bills to be paid, amounts owed to you, payroll, taxes, insurance, maintenance, quality-control information, inventory, and general office records.
- Each month, an entrepreneur should prepare financial statements, reconcile the bank statement, balance the checkbook and petty cash accounts, and pay federal tax deposits and FICA.
- An entrepreneur can do his or her own record keeping or hire someone else to do it—a CPA or bookkeeper.
- Financial statements reflect the health of a business. They include cash-flow statements, a profit-and-loss statement, and a balance sheet.

RECALL KEY TERMS

You have just hired your first employee to keep your books. With a partner, role-play how you will teach the record-keeping system of your business. Use the following key terms:

fiscal year	**sales journal**
cash basis	**cash receipts journal**
accrual basis	**cash disbursements journal**
accounts payable	**purchases journal**
accounts receivable	**ledger**
single-entry system	**cash-flow statement**
double-entry system	**profit-and-loss statement**
debit	**balance sheet**
credit	**assets**
journals	**owner's equity**

RECALL KEY CONCEPTS

1. What factors usually determine how a business chooses a fiscal year?
2. Which basis for recording information does the IRS require you to use if inventory is a big source of income for your business?
3. Why would you use more than one journal to record transactions?
4. What is a petty cash account?
5. What does the information from an aging table help the entrepreneur do?
6. List the six steps of balancing a checkbook.
7. Why is a cash-flow statement important to the business?
8. What is the accounting equation?

THINK CRITICALLY

1. If you owned a small business, would you use the cash or accrual system for recording the income of your business? Explain why.
2. You are using an aging table like the one shown in **Figure 21–5** to track your

accounts receivable. How would you react to the following results?

- The *Over 90* column accounts for half the money owed to you.
- The *61-90 Day* column accounts for 85 percent of the money owed to you.

3. Why would a cash flow statement be more useful to a new business than a profit-and-loss statement?
4. Could a business operate without financial statements? Defend your answer.
5. Can you keep too many records? Why?

CONNECT ACADEMICS TO THE WORKPLACE

Math

1. You are the bookkeeper at a travel agency. Last month, the following transactions occurred:

• Sales:	Credit	$15,000
	Cash	6,000
• Expenses:	Credit	$ 6,000
	Cash	7,000

For that month, compute the firm's net cash flow and net income.

Decision Making Skills

2. Your aunt has opened an insurance agency and is ready to hire her first employee—a bookkeeper. She has asked you to help her choose just the right employee. Make a list of the skills and characteristics the new employee should have.

WORK IN YOUR COMMUNITY

Your new business is ready to open and you need to set up your record-keeping system. Develop the components of your system. Include the following:

- Fiscal year
- Cash or accrual basis
- Single- or double-entry system
- Daily, weekly, and monthly record keeping
- Journals used
- Accounts receivable and accounts payable tracking methods
- Who will be doing the record keeping

LINK SCHOOL TO CAREER

Contact two local business owners about how they keep their records. Choose two different types of businesses and find out:

- How they chose their fiscal year.
- Which basis they use—cash or accrual.
- Whether they do their own record keeping.

As a class, compile your information and compare the results.

*inter*NET CONNECTION

Cyber Theft

You have also been researching electronic commerce and think that within a year or two your business will be buying and selling over the Internet.

Connect

Using a variety of search engines, research Internet security and find out about the following:

- On-line security sources
- How to protect your business from "hackers"
- Future trends in Internet security related to electronic commerce

UNIT 5 LAB

Business Plan Basics

ESTIMATING AND OBTAINING FINANCING

OVERVIEW

Deciding how much money they will need to open a new business is a critical decision that all entrepreneurs must answer. Too often, many entrepreneurs attempt to open a new business without enough capital. They inevitably start facing financial problems from the first day of operation. Entrepreneurs need to estimate all expenses associated with opening a business. They must identify and compare various types of financing available to them. In this unit lab you will calculate how much you would need to open a new business and explore where you can obtain the financing.

TOOLS

- TV and radio advertisements
- Financial newspapers and magazines
- Telephone directories
- Internet
- Graph paper or spreadsheet program
- Word processor (optional)

PROCEDURES

STEP A Work individually or in a small group of not more than three.

1. List items or equipment that would be needed to open the following businesses:
   - Telephone directories
   - A business that makes buttons for school and community groups
   - A home-based cake decorating business
   - A water-ski instructor
   - A neighborhood lemonade stand
2. Record the equipment on the Unit 5 worksheet or a clean sheet of paper.
3. As a class, compile a complete list of expenses for each business enterprise.

STEP B Select one of the businesses identified in Step A.

1. Through shopping trips, telephone contacts, or the Internet, identify costs of the items needed to start your business.
2. Record the items and costs on the Unit 5 worksheet, a sheet of graph paper, or a spreadsheet program.
3. On graph paper or with the spreadsheet program, create a pie chart.

STEP C

Once entrepreneurs know what they need and how much it will cost, their next step is to obtain funds. Assume that you are starting a business, like the ones previously listed, and your new enterprise requires $10,000 to start up.

1. Identify three sources of funding. Through a personal interview or telephone contact with these sources, ask the following questions:
   - What type of loan would be granted for this amount of money?
   - What is the interest rate on the $10,000 loan?
   - How many months would you have to repay the loan?
   - What amount needs to be repaid each month?
   - Are there special requirements to obtain the loan, such as length of time living in the community or collateral?
   - What happens if payments are missed or the loan is not repaid?
2. Record the items and costs on the Unit 5 worksheet, graph paper, or using the table function of a word processor.
3. Develop a chart that compares the three sources against these criteria.

LAB REPORT

STEP D

Select a small business that you may be interested in starting in the future. Complete a two-page report that includes the following:

- Identify all the items/equipment that you would need to start this business.
- Find the cost of each item. Record this information and create a pie chart.
- Determine how much money you would need to cover these expenses.
- Identify a commercial, private, or government source for obtaining funding.
- Describe the advantages and disadvantages of using this source.
- Identify all the terms associated with the loan, such as interest rate, repayment schedule, special requirements to obtain the loan, etc.

UNIT 6
GROWING YOUR BUSINESS

UNIT OVERVIEW

It is never too early to prepare for potential risks and plan for growth. The research, planning, and management skills it takes to start and protect your business will also allow it to survive, grow, and profit.

Ethics must also be considered. Treating employees, customers, and the community responsibly is proper. It can also enhance your venture's reputation. Protecting your business, planning for growth, and practicing ethics are steps that will help your business prosper in the future.

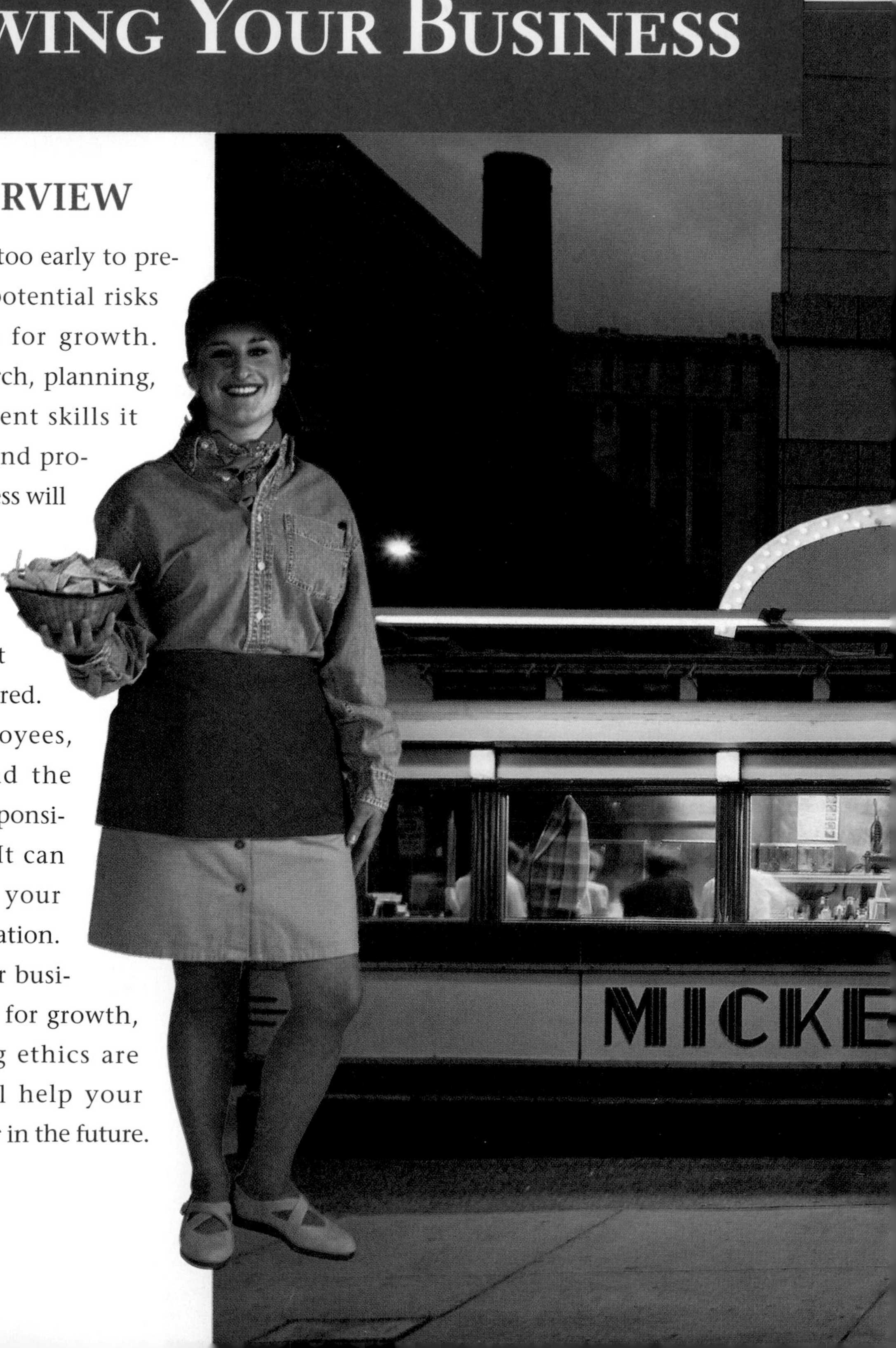

Entrepreneurship: What It Takes

What do you know about starting your own business?

1. What kinds of risk does a new business face?
2. How can a business prevent shoplifting and theft?
3. What are the ways to reduce unavoidable risks?
4. Where can you find growth opportunities?
5. How can you determine the growth potential within your market?
6. How can you find opportunities outside of your industry?
7. Where are the potential sources of growth funding?
8 What social responsibilities does a company have?
9. Why does a business need a written code of ethics?
10. What are some common ethical problems that a business will face?

CHAPTER 22

Risk Management

Learning Objectives

When you have completed this chapter, you will be able to:

- **Describe** the risks facing a new business
- **Define** the four approaches to managing risk
- **Identify** steps new business owners should take to prepare for handling risks

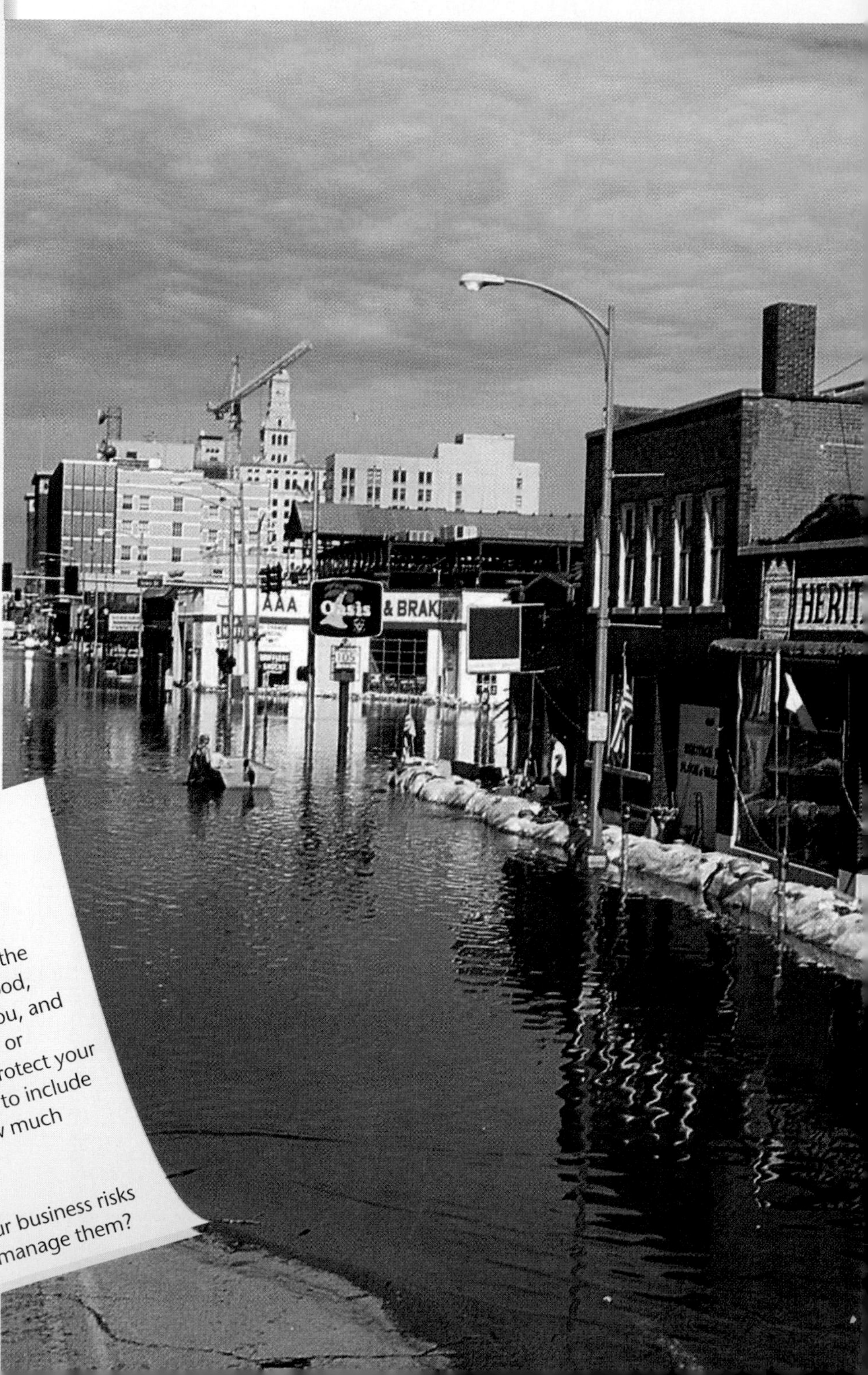

You're the Boss!

Being Prepared

As you've planned your business's growth, you've been thinking about the things that might go wrong. Fire, flood, burglary, and shoplifting can cost you, and what about employees, customers, or delivery people getting hurt? To protect your business, you have to know what to include in your insurance policy and how much coverage is enough.

What Will You Do?

How can you identify your business risks and what are the ways to manage them?

SECTION 22.1

Identifying Business Risks

SPECULATIVE RISK

Speculative risk involves taking a chance for profit or loss. When you buy machinery, obtain new inventory, or construct a building, you are taking a speculative risk. You are risking loss to make a profit. We will explore speculative risks when we discuss managing growth in the next chapter.

PURE RISK

Pure risk is the threat of a loss to your business without any possibility of gain. The threat of burglary, robbery, and employee theft are pure risks to your business. So are natural disasters (such as floods, earthquakes, and tornadoes) and accidents involving customers or employees.

In this section, we will identify the major risks that new businesses face. We will also suggest some ways of addressing those risks.

Crime

The U.S. Department of Commerce has stated that small businesses are 35 times more likely than large businesses (those with annual sales in excess of $5 million) to be victims of crime. Of all businesses, retail enterprises are the most susceptible to crime. This is because so many people pass through retail stores in the course of a business day. As a result, the cost of crime is also highest for retail operations.

Consider an example. Suppose a music store loses a CD worth $15 every day for a year. In that case, it would lose $5,475 a year.

$$\$15 \times 365 = \$5,475$$

If the store operates at a 10 percent profit margin, it must sell

What you'll learn

- the types of risk business owners are concerned with
- the kinds of crime faced by business owners
- the risks of natural disaster faced by business owners
- the risks of accident and injury faced by business owners

Why it's important

Risk is a fact of life for entrepreneurs. To build a successful business and maximize profits, one must understand risk and make effective decisions to deal with it.

KEY TERMS

speculative risk
pure risk
burglary
robbery
electronic credit authorizers
negligence

an additional $54,750 worth of merchandise to make up the loss!

$$\frac{\$5,475}{.10} = \$54,750$$

How does one "lose" merchandise? There is a number of ways.

Shoplifting. Shoplifting is one of the most common crimes in the retail business. It accounts for about 3 percent of the price of any item. A shoplifter is anyone who takes an item from a store without paying for it.

Shoplifting often takes place when stores are understaffed. You can reduce your risk by considering these techniques:

- Recognize potential shoplifters. Individual shoplifters may act nervous and spend a great deal of time looking around the store. They may carry large bags or wear bulky clothing.
- Keep your store well lit and your display cases low so you can see your entire operation at a glance.
- Employ two-way mirrors, peepholes, or closed-circuit TV.
- Use tamper-proof price tickets or electronic tags.
- Hire a uniformed security guard.

If you spot a shoplifter, the safest approach is to alert a police officer and let him or her confront the person. Usually this is done outside the store.

Although the laws regarding shoplifting vary from state to state, in general, the store owner must do the following:

- See the person take the merchandise
- Be able to identify the merchandise as belonging to the store
- Confirm that it was taken with the intent to steal
- Prove that it was not paid for

Up & Coming Entrepreneur

Seafood Buying Entrepreneur

When his boss defaulted on a bank loan, Hugh Reynolds purchased his employer's pier in a Maine Real Estate Foreclosure Auction. Today, Reynolds' Green Head Lobster Company is a seafood "buying station" for large food resellers. "It's all about service. If we can provide the best bait and coffee, sell gas at a reasonable price, and offload lobsters the most efficiently, then the boats will keep returning here," says Reynolds.

Analyze **What are some of the risks of dealing with seafood as a commodity?**

Figure 22–1

Reducing Employee Theft

Businesses that do not establish policies, controls, security procedures, and penalties send a message. They tell their employees that those who steal will probably not get caught. To discourage employee theft, observe the following procedures:

1. Let employees know that employee theft is not tolerated.

2. Lock all doors that do not need to be used for entry or exit.

4. Control the distribution of keys and other security devices.

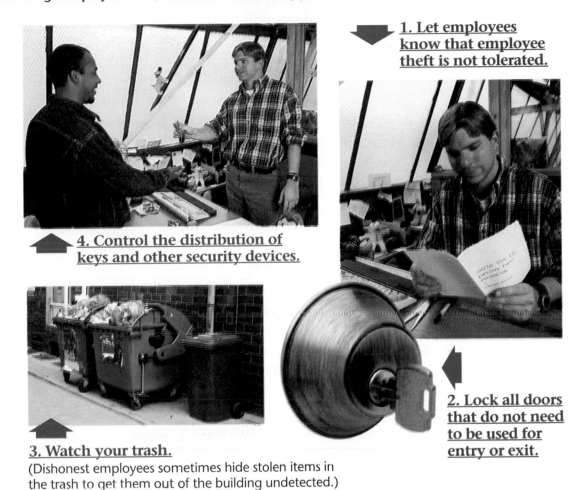

3. Watch your trash.
(Dishonest employees sometimes hide stolen items in the trash to get them out of the building undetected.)

Once a shoplifter has been caught, you will need to decide whether to prosecute. If you drop charges, you give a person a second chance. If you proceed with charges, you tell would-be shoplifters that crime will not be tolerated in your store.

Employee Theft. The Department of Commerce reports that about 50 percent of all retail crime is employee theft. Businesses may lose as much as one third of their profits to it. The cost to the consumer is about 15 percent of retail prices. **Figure 22–1** shows ways to discourage employee theft.

Some business owners are careless how they handle cash. Money frequently coming in and going out can tempt workers to be dishonest. A large number of voided or no-sale transactions could be a signal that an employee is covering up theft. A good rule is not to let a single person control a transaction from beginning to end. Instead, have one person handle the funds and another record or account for them.

Hiring honest people is one of the keys to preventing employee theft. At the very least, use application forms when interviewing prospective employees. Ask applicants for an employment history and character references. Then check the information.

Aptitude and psychological tests can also be helpful. You may also be able to require applicants to take a polygraph, or lie-detector, test. (Check a government representative to see if it is permitted in your state.) These can screen out applicants who are likely to steal.

Burglary. The act of breaking into and entering a home or business with the intent to commit a felony is called a burglary. (A felony is a serious crime, such as stealing.) The problem of burglary is growing, but there are ways to minimize your risk.

- *Site selection.* An entrepreneur's best defense is to select his or her business site carefully. This means considering the overall level of crime in the area. Specifically, check the level of burglaries. Then select a secure building for the enterprise.
- *High-quality locks.* The next-best defense is to install high-quality locks and control who has the keys. Solid locks are useless if someone untrustworthy has the keys.

ENTREPRENEURS INTERNATIONAL

Chile

In 1982, Ignacio Iensen began his security business, Seguridad y Servicios, when foreign corporations began moving to Chile. Iensen's company provides security services from alarm monitoring, to guard services for businesses and individuals in need of protection while in his country. Seguridad y Servicios also provides analyses and reports of political and terrorist risks. His clients include large multinational corporations as well as local firms.

Apply **Why might a company thinking of expanding into Chile hire Ignacio Iensen to provide a report on political risk?**

- *Alarm systems.* There are two systems—supervised and nonsupervised alarms. With a supervised alarm system, all points of entry to the business are monitored all the time from a central location. An alarm alerts police to trouble. A nonsupervised alarm is active only when the owner arms it. These alarms may also be set to alert the police.
- *Security guards.* Some businesses choose to employ a security guard. He or she patrols the premises during the night and at other times when the business is closed. Hiring a security guard may help prevent additional crimes such as vandalism.
- *Proper lighting.* The use of sufficient lighting also deters burglars. Many owners leave lights on in their businesses all night. Floodlights in parking lots and on rear entrances can also make it difficult for someone to break in unnoticed.

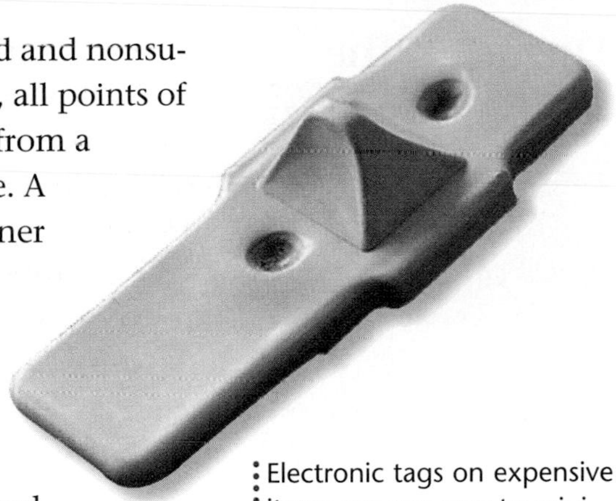

Electronic tags on expensive items are one way to minimize losses to shoplifting. ***What are two ways they help?***

Robbery. Robbery involves the taking of property by force or threat. Most robberies involve a weapon and a person who is not afraid to use it. It is the business owner's responsibility to protect employees and customers. This means allowing the person to take what he or she came for and leave without harming anyone.

If you are robbed, try to give a good description of the person (or persons) committing the robbery. Noting a robber's height, hair color, and any distinguishing features or mannerisms can help the police identify the thief.

One security measure you can take is to use a safe. That way you can minimize the amount of cash you keep in your register. Surveillance cameras are another valuable measure. When placed where potential robbers can see them, they, too, can deter criminals.

Stolen Credit Cards and Bad Checks. Using credit cards or checks to pay for purchases is a major convenience for consumers. To businesses they can also be a source of financial loss. Credit cards can be stolen and used to run up huge bills. Customers may write bad checks.

There are ways to identify an invalid or stolen credit card. Many businesses use electronic credit authorizers, machines that verify if a credit card is good. They are linked to a central credit bureau that identifies stolen or invalid cards. Other companies call a central authorization phone number to check credit cards.

Tips from the Real World

CHANGE

Change can be frightening, but the ability and willingness to grow is the key to success for entrepreneurs. Harry Quadracci, CEO of Quad/Graphics remarks:

"Our employees look at change and learning as job security."

Bad checks represent another problem for businesses. As a deterrent, companies usually charge a service fee if a customer's check is returned. In addition, many states have passed laws making the writing of bad checks a crime and imposing stiff fees. In California the penalty is three times the face value of the check. Many businesses place signs by their cash registers announcing these penalties to discourage bad check writers.

Business owners can also reduce the number of bad checks with a check reader. This is similar to an electronic credit authorizer. It tells the business owner if the account on which the check was written is open and whether it has a history of bad checks.

In any case, it is wise to write the driver's license number on his or her check. That way, if anything is wrong with the check and the address is not current, you will have a way to track down the individual. Always ask check writers for photo identification.

Computer Crime. The increasing number of computers and people with computers has been accompanied by the emergence of computer crime. Computer criminals have developed a variety of ways to access computers and steal or alter information. Computer hackers penetrate the security of computer systems for mischievous purposes. Disgruntled employees erase thousands of hours' worth of work or install viruses. Some companies even engage in industrial espionage.

The simplest and least inexpensive way is to secure your computer with a key. This locks the machine and prevents an unauthorized user from starting it. You can also secure important data by using passwords, encoding programs, and virus detectors.

Fireproof safes can be used to protect cash and important documents.
What are some other ways to protect valuables from natural disasters?

Natural Disasters

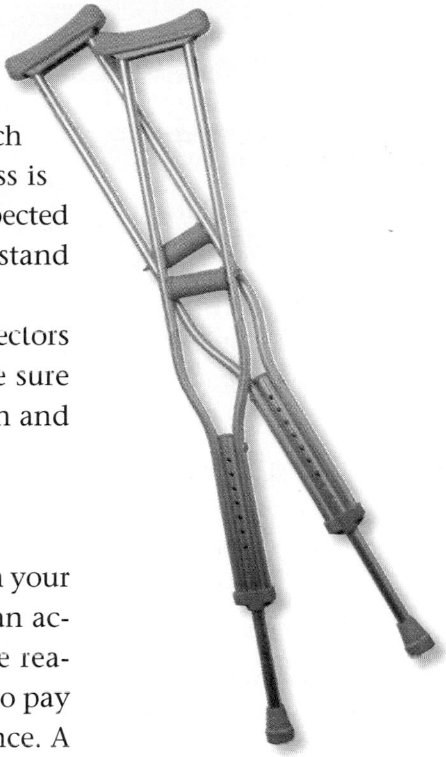

Crime isn't the only risk a new business faces. Many owners have lost everything as a result of natural disasters such as fires, earthquakes, tornadoes, and floods. If your business is in an active earthquake zone, you can have your building inspected by a structural engineer and, if necessary, reinforced to withstand tremors.

Protecting your business against fire is simpler. Smoke detectors and sprinkler systems will help protect your staff and make sure fires are extinguished before they become too big. Store cash and important documents in a fireproof safe.

Accidents and Injury

What if an employee or customer slips and gets injured on your business premises? A company can be held responsible for an accident that results from **negligence**, the failure to exercise reasonable care. At the very least, a business would be required to pay the medical expenses of someone injured due to its negligence. A jury might award additional amounts in a lawsuit.

CHECK YOUR UNDERSTANDING

SECTION 22.1

Reviewing Key Terms and Concepts

1 What is the difference between speculative risk and pure risk?
2 Why do employees steal?
3 Describe how a natural disaster that occurs in your community affects its businesses.

Critical Thinking Activity

Create a three-column chart, labeled *Crime, Natural Disaster,* and *Accidents and Injury*. Identify risks your proposed business would face in each category.

Extension Lab—Creative Thinking Skills

Risky Business Your company has been hired by Jacque to do a complete risk analysis of the retail computer store he owns. As background information, Jacque tells you that he has five employees and a computer inventory worth $1.5 million and that he repairs an average of 30 computers per week.

Presentation Prepare a presentation for Jacque by completing the following.

- Recommend methods to prevent loss of merchandise (by both shoplifters and employees).
- Recommend security measures for Jacque's business.
- Develop an emergency response plan for Jacque and his employees in the event of a natural disaster (like a hurricane, earthquake, or tornado).

SECTION 22.2

Dealing with Risk

What you'll learn

- steps to risk reduction
- the risk transfer strategy
- the risk retention strategy procedures for purchasing insurance
- considerations for determining security needs
- steps to take before contracting with a security company
- the importance of planning for emergencies

Why it's important

It is impossible to completely protect your business from pure risks, but you can lessen their impact through risk-management and planning.

KEY TERMS

premium
business interruption insurance
casualty insurance
errors-and-omissions insurance
product liability insurance
fidelity bonds
performance bonds
workers' compensation
independent insurance agent
direct insurance writer

RISK REDUCTION

If a business cannot avoid risks, its chances for success, or even survival, will be greatly reduced. Many of the procedures and practices recommended in the first part of this chapter are examples of risk-reduction strategies.

Suppose you own a retail store. Installing a sprinkler system will not eliminate the chance of fires, but it does reduce damage. Similarly, placing electronic tags on expensive merchandise does not eliminate theft, but it does discourage it.

To reduce the likelihood and amount of loss, take the following steps:

- *Design work areas so that the chances of accident or fire are lowered.* This includes offices, retail spaces, and manufacturing floors.
- *Hold meetings with employees to educate them about the safe use of equipment.* Make sure they know how to handle emergencies.
- *Check and service safety equipment.* Test fire extinguishers and smoke detectors regularly. Do the same for security equipment such as burglar alarms.
- *Stress the limits of your company's products.* Inform consumers about how to use the products safely. Provide instructions for correct use of products, as well as warnings about possible hazards.

RISK TRANSFER

Let's say you have located your business in a relatively crime-free part of town. You have also installed locks, burglar alarms, and sufficient lighting. You may still experience a robbery, theft, accident, or disaster. How will you cope financially? Most likely, you'll transfer the risk. You will buy insurance to cover your losses. A fee called a premium is required to transfer risk to an insurance company.

It's easy to be overwhelmed by the many different types of insurance available. There are four basic types of business losses that require coverage.

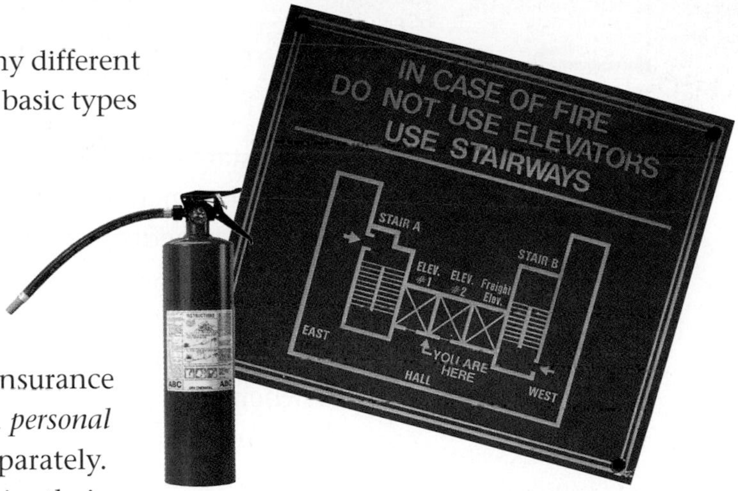

Planning how to handle emergencies is an important way to reduce risk. ***How can you make sure the plans are carried out?***

1. Property Insurance

Property insurance covers the loss of physical property such as cash, inventory, vehicles, and buildings. Business owners usually purchase several property insurance policies. *Real property* (like buildings) and *personal property* (like vehicles) must be insured separately. Risks such as floods and earthquakes require their own policies, too.

One kind of insurance deals with the consequences of property damage. Business interruption insurance pays net profits and expenses if a business is shut down for repairs or rebuilding. The insurance makes up for lost income and allows a business owner to continue making rent, salary, and other key payments.

2. Casualty Insurance

Casualty insurance protects a business from lawsuits. If a person gets injured on your business premises or one of your workers causes damage, you may be sued. Casualty insurance will pay the claim. It also covers the costs of defending your business in court.

There are many types of casualty insurance. Companies that advertise can purchase errors-and-omissions insurance, which protects them against lawsuits for mistakes in advertising. Manufacturing firms can purchase product liability insurance, which protects them against claims for injuries that result from using their products.

Bonding is another type of casualty insurance. Fidelity bonds protect a company in case of employee theft. Performance bonds protect a business if work is not finished on time or as agreed.

3. Life Insurance

Imagine the loss a new business would incur if its creator and owner died unexpectedly. Life insurance pays a business in the event of the insured person's death. Among other benefits, the payments give a business time to make a decision about replacing the key person. It offsets some of the losses that may occur because of work delays during the transition.

4. Workers' Compensation

Business owners are required by law to make contributions to the state workers' compensation plan. Workers' compensation is a government-regulated program that provides medical and income benefits to employees who are injured on the job. Job-related illnesses are also covered.

The amount of compensation a worker receives is based on the wages or salary of the employee, the seriousness of the injury, and whether the injury is permanent or not. To file for compensation, an injured or ill employee must submit a claim with the compensation board. The board decides how much money to pay out.

The program is designed to free businesses from the threat of employee lawsuits. Workers who accept benefits under the program are barred from suing their employers over their injuries. However, workers' compensation premiums are a major financial burden for businesses in some states. As a result, many people consider workers' compensation costs to be a key indicator of a state's attitude toward business.

Money Matters

EXPERT ADVICE

Listening to expert advice can save you from losing money. According to Michael E. Gerber, the author of The E-Myth Revisited:

"The problem with most failing businesses is. . . . that [their owners] spend their time and energy defending what they think they know."

SELECTING AN INSURANCE AGENT

Before you talk to an insurance agent, become knowledgeable about the needs of your business. Identify the risks and require-

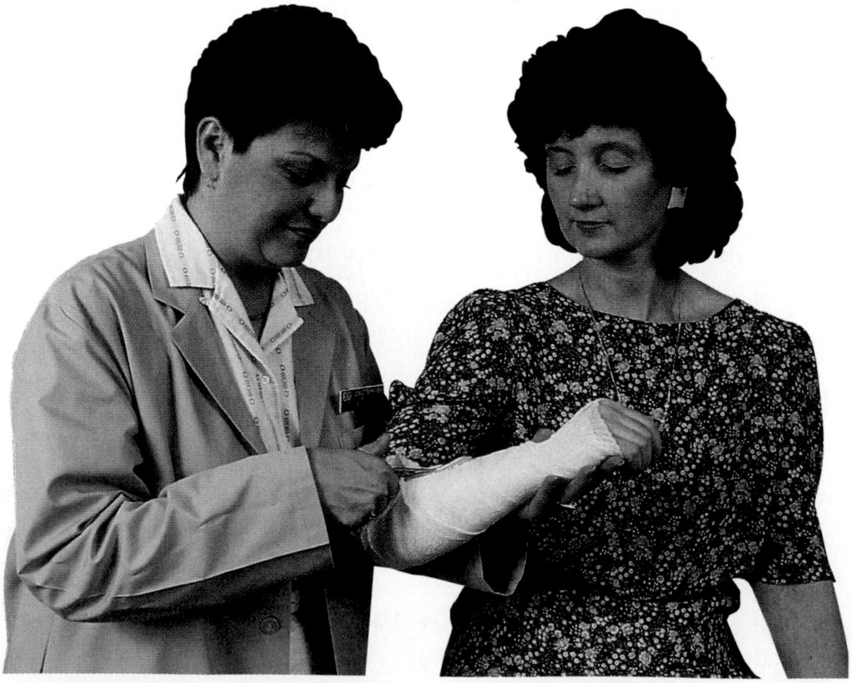

Workers' compensation helps people who are hurt on the job. ***What is the cost to employers?***

RISK TAKERS PROFIT MAKERS

Name: The Shepherd Family
Company: Camp Winding Gap
City, State: Lake Toxaway, NC

The Family That Camps Together . . .

In 1978, Marilyn and G. O. Shepherd decided to build their own children's summer camp on some lakefront property they had recently purchased. With the help of their children, who ranged from 13 to 27 years of age, Camp Winding Gap became a reality. Camp Director Ann Shepherd Hertzberg recalls, "We put everything we had into the start-up. We built two cabins, a lodge and two bathrooms from scratch and by hand—all for 12 campers!"

Camp Winding Gap has indeed come a long way. Its cabins now have electricity and are winterized. There are also many more buildings, including an infirmary, an Arts and Crafts studio, and a photo lab.

Although Camp Winding Gap is only open in the summer, Hertzberg claims to be marketing the rest of the year through advertising, the Internet, and slide shows in people's homes. The campaign is apparently a success. This year they had 11 countries represented among their 85 campers.

Thinking Critically

Camp Winding Gap is considered a "seasonal business." What major concerns are associated with a seasonal business?

ments that your business will face. Find out what types of insurance you are required to carry in your state. You can do this by talking to your local business development agency or the SBA.

There are two types of insurance agents. An independent insurance agent works in a specific geographic area and represents several insurance companies. Such agents offer fast service and competitive rates. In addition, some specialize in a field, such as bonding, or a certain type of business. For example, one might handle construction businesses, which are risky to insure. The other type of agent is the *direct insurance writer*. A direct insurance writer works for one insurance company. Most business owners buy life and automobile insurance from direct agents.

CHOOSING SECURITY MEASURES

You can install secure doors and windows, alarm systems, panic buttons, card-access systems, and closed-circuit TV monitors. For protection from fires, there are alarms, smoke detectors, and sprinkler systems. Some monitoring systems can send out calls for fire, medical, and police assistance. There are guards, guard dogs, and patrol services. You can even get security for your computers.

How do you decide which security systems are right for your company? First assess the security needs related to your situation. Consider your type of business, location, number of employees, and so on. Then list specific problem areas. Is there exposed outdoor equipment? Is vandalism common in your neighborhood?

When you have completed your assessment, find a security company and check its background. Then hire them to conduct a review. They should spot weaknesses, show areas of concern, and help you prioritize your security needs.

PLANNING FOR EMERGENCIES

No matter how many preventive measures you take or how much insurance you buy, fires, floods, earthquakes, explosions, hazardous spills, and other disasters do happen. When they occur, they can overwhelm a small business.

It's important to have procedures in place *before* a crisis occurs. Emergency response planning will minimize your losses and get you back in business quickly. Although there will be similarities in the actions taken during different kinds of emergencies, plans

Figure 22–2
Creating response plans can help you handle emergency situations more smoothly. ***Why do you need more than one plan?***

Emergency Response Plan

1. Assess the damage or emergency.
2. Call 911 to report the disaster/emergency.
3. Call for evacuation.
4. Designated persons collect priority items for removal.
5. Designated person secures premises to people (such as looters) from entering.
6. Designated person moves to gate or entry to provide direction to rescue people.
7. Evacuated employees report to a central location.
8. Check presence of all employees. If someone's missing, direct rescue workers to the person's work station.
9. Those trained in first aid administer treatment to injured people or help rescue workers.
10. Depending on extent of damages, dismiss employees. Management team waits for cleanup or repair people.

should be drawn up for each eventuality. Each plan should include a list of priorities and actions to take. **Figure 22–2** provides a sample plan.

To prepare for emergencies, emergency phone numbers and floor plans for rescue teams should be compiled. Key records should also be tagged for quick removal. Once your plans are completed, let employees know about them. Copies should be provided and posted. Run emergency drills on a regular basis.

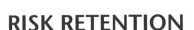

RISK RETENTION

In some instances it is impossible for a company to transfer a business risk. The firm may be unable to get insurance or afford the policies. In these circumstances, the business must self-insure. This strategy is called *risk retention.* The owner puts aside money every month to help cover the costs should a loss occur.

CHECK YOUR UNDERSTANDING

SECTION 22.2

Reviewing Key Terms and Concepts

1 List specific steps you can take to reduce risk.
2 Explain the value of casualty insurance.
3 How can you determine the proper amount of insurance coverage for your business?

Critical Thinking Activity

Develop an emergency response plan for flood conditions for your proposed business.

Extension Lab—Reasoning Skills

Fake Figures You own an automobile detailing business where you clean cars until they look like new. Last night your shop was burglarized and all your cleaning supplies were stolen. Your insurance company requested an itemized list of the stolen goods. When you told your in-house accountant, he offered to help you pad the numbers.

Role Play With a partner, enact a discussion between you and your accountant. Keep in mind the following.

- Is this ethical? Why or why not?
- Suppose there would be no way for the insurance company to find out you padded the figures. Would you be tempted to accept payment for inventory you really never had?

CHAPTER 22 REVIEW

CHAPTER SUMMARY

- The major risks facing a business are crimes, natural disasters, and accidents and injuries.
- Crimes that especially affect businesses are shoplifting, employee theft, burglary, robbery, the use of stolen credit cards, bad checks, and computer crime.
- Shoplifting accounts for about 3 percent of the price of any item purchased. It is one of the most common crimes in the retail business.
- Businesses should establish policies, controls, procedures, and penalties to prevent both shoplifting and employee theft.
- If a business cannot avoid risks, three strategies can be employed: risk reduction, risk transfer, and risk retention.
- As an entrepreneur, you will probably need property, casualty, life, and workers' compensation insurance.
- There are two types of insurance agents—the independent agent (who works for many insurance companies) and the direct insurance writer (who works for only one company).

RECALL KEY TERMS

Working in teams of three or four, create a crossword puzzle using the following key terms. Make sure your definitions are short and clear. Exchange with other teams in your class to solve the puzzles.

speculative risk
pure risk
burglary
robbery
electronic credit authorizers
negligence
premium
business interruption insurance
casualty insurance
errors-and-omissions insurance
product liability insurance
fidelity bonds
performance bonds
workers compensation
independent insurance agent
direct insurance writer

RECALL KEY CONCEPTS

1. Which type of business is most susceptible to crime? Why?
2. List five ways retailers can reduce shoplifting.
3. List three ways to prevent employee theft.
4. Contrast burglary and robbery.
5. What can businesses do to prevent customers from writing a bad check?
6. What other risks do business owners face besides crime?
7. What type of insurance would you purchase to cover:
   - Theft (of inventory)
   - Business closed down for two weeks (due to flood damage)
   - A customer fell in your store
   - One of the partners dies
   - An employee fell in your store
8. What does workers compensation insurance protect your business against?
9. Describe how risk retention works.

CHAPTER 22 REVIEW

THINK CRITICALLY

1. Compare and contrast shoplifting and employee theft in terms of who commits these crimes and how they affect a business.
2. What is the difference between credit card theft and writing bad checks? How can a store owner deal with them?
3. Does insurance eliminate risk? Why or why not?
4. How would you address the business owner who complains, "If I put the proper procedures in place to avoid risks, I don't need to purchase insurance."
5. Describe how you will select an insurance agent.

CONNECT ACADEMICS TO THE WORKPLACE

Math

1. Preliminary calculations show that this year your business earned profits of $50,000. In past years, however, the company has lost up to one third of its profits to employee theft and 3 percent to shoplifting. Given these figures, how much do you think your profits actually were?

Acquire and Evaluate Data

2. You have decided to install an alarm system in your retail business. Call several companies in your community and ask them to send you information about their systems. Evaluate the products and choose the one that best serves your needs.

WORK IN YOUR COMMUNITY

Select a business you are interested in owning. Working in teams of three or four, consider the risks that your business might face. Create a chart (use a spreadsheet program if possible) with the following headings:

- *Potential Risks*
- *Ways to Avoid Risk*
- *Ways to Reduce Risk*
- *Type of Insurance Necessary*

Compare your findings with the class.

LINK SCHOOL TO CAREER

Interview two insurance agents (one independent and one direct writer) that specialize in business insurance. Ask them about:

- The insurance needs of your own business
- Type of insurance they recommend
- Approximate cost of the policies

How do their recommendations differ?

interNET CONNECTION

Crime Stoppers

You own a chain of gift boutiques that cater to teenagers. You have a policy in place to deal with shoplifting, but it is time to develop one for employee theft.

Connect

Using a variety of Web browsers, research ways to deter employees from stealing. Include information about:

- Surveillance methods and equipment
- Screening of potential employees
- Employees and computer crime

Use your research to create a report outlining what you will do to prevent employee theft.

CHAPTER 23

Making Your Business Grow

Learning Objectives

When you have completed this chapter, you will be able to:

- **Explain** how to time the expansion of your business
- **Discuss** the various growth strategies
- **Recognize** the challenges that come with growth
- **Explain** what it takes to find growth capital
- **List** the growth funding options

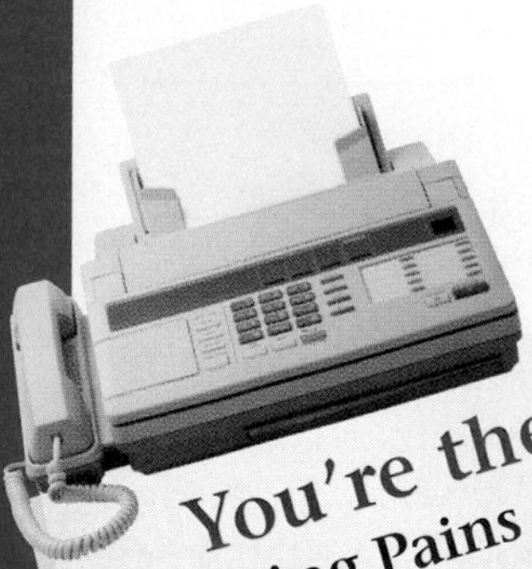

You're the Boss!

Growing Pains

Your gardening supply business has been growing for three years and has reached a crossroad. You have no doubt that you want to make the business grow more. The question is how. Should you open a second store? Take on new products? It's a difficult decision.

What Will You Do?
What strategies can you take when growing a business?

SECTION 23.1

Managing Growth

TIMING YOUR EXPANSION

If an entrepreneur puts together a good team and develops a viable concept, his or her new business will not remain small for long. A successful business will grow. How should you expand your business? This section will look at the various methods you can use to grow the business.

Using Intensive Growth Strategies

Intensive growth strategies exploit opportunities within a current market. A business that wants to increase sales to its target customers might use this approach. Sales can be drummed up in one of the following ways:

Market Penetration. **Market penetration** is an attempt to *increase sales* in your current market. You can do this in a variety of ways:

- *Get your customers to use your product more often.* The makers of Arm & Hammer Baking Soda increased sales by suggesting new ways to use it. Customers once purchased baking soda only for cooking. Now they brush their teeth and keep their refrigerators smelling fresh with it.
- *Attract your competitors' customers.* A retail store owner might locate near a competitor to encourage comparison shopping.
- *Go after people in your present market who are not using products like yours.* Marcel Ford found new customers for his silk plant cleaner by demonstrating the product in Price/Costco outlets.

What you'll learn

- what kinds of growth strategies to use and when to use them
- the difference between horizontal and vertical integration
- how to recognize factors that affect your ability to grow

Why it's important

The growth period of a business is risky. Growing a business requires research and planning.

KEY TERMS

intensive growth strategies
market penetration
market development
integrative growth strategies
vertical integration
horizontal integration
diversification
synergistic diversification
horizontal diversification
conglomerate diversification

Market Development. With market development, a business expands its product to *reach new locations*. A business can open a branch in another community, nationwide, or go international.

Franchising is one of the most popular ways to expand a business. California Pizza Kitchen, Chief Auto Parts, and most automobile dealerships are examples of franchises. Franchisers sell the right to do business under a company's name. For a fee, the franchiser also provides training and other assistance. One of the biggest advantages of franchising your business is that you can expand it with someone else's money.

Franchising also makes it easier for you to manage your growing organization. With franchising you personally train your franchisees. They in turn hire and are responsible for the employees who work for them. You do not have to oversee them.

However, franchising is not perfect. It is like starting your business over again. You must prepare training manuals, write instructions on how to run the business, and make an analysis of the market and your competitors. In addition, the costs of setting up the franchise structure add up. There may be legal, accounting, consulting, and training costs. Also, it may be a long time before a franchise turns a profit. One company in Memphis sold more than 70 franchises but did not show a profit for a year. Waiting three to five years for a profit is not uncommon.

One way to increase sales is to introduce new uses for existing products. ***How are disposable cameras used differently than traditional ones?***

How do you know if your business is ideal for franchising? Ask yourself the questions illustrated in **Figure 23–1**. Franchising is a very complicated process that will require help from experienced attorneys and accountants.

Don't limit your growth to the United

Figure 23–1

So You Want To Start a Franchise

If you decide to franchise your business, these are some of the questions you should ask yourself:

1. How long have you run the business?

Experience will help you. You will have a clearer understanding of how a successful business should be run.

2. Is your business one that will grow?

Be careful that it's not a fad. To be a good franchise prospect, your business should have a large potential market.

3. Will it be easy to take your product to other geographic areas and other markets?

Generally, seasonal items are not good choices for franchises.

4. Can your business generate a high percentage of gross profit?

The production costs for your product must be low enough to ensure a gross profit.

5. Can your business be systematized and duplicated?

You must be able to teach your business operations to others. If it is too complicated, the cost and time to train franchisees may be too much.

States. Increasingly, franchises are exploring the Pacific Rim and Europe. Franchises are becoming common in those areas. You can find a Hard Rock Café in Beijing and a Timberland shoe store in London. Other businesses form partnerships and enjoy tremendous success. Calcorn Inc.'s Popcorn Palace has flourished in Japan. Businesspeople from other countries actually come to the United States looking for franchisers and partners who can profit in their cultures.

Expanding into the former Soviet Union has become very popular, but it still has many problems. You need to form a partnership with a company native to the region and go through reams of bureaucratic paperwork. Also, your profits cannot be taken out of the former Soviet Union in the form of dollars. Because rubles have little value outside Russia, many companies like Pepsi are taking their profit in trade goods.

Product Development. Another way to increase sales to existing customers is product development, the introduction or improvement of products. You probably notice companies advertising "new and improved" versions of existing products. Shampoo, paper towels, toothpaste, and cereal are frequent examples.

You can also develop new packaging and sizing for your product. Detergent manufacturers have begun to offer their products in concentrated form. These small containers are easier to handle.

Using Integrative Growth Strategies

Integrative growth strategies involve your company's expansion within the industry you are operating in. Your business can grow by integrating either vertically or horizontally.

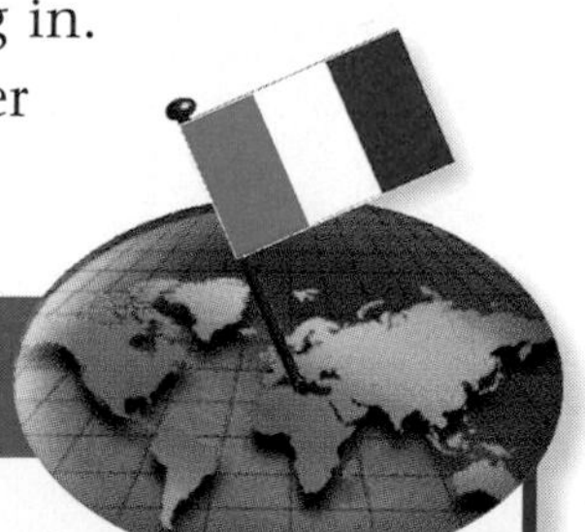

ENTREPRENEURS INTERNATIONAL

Italy

The Argentina Valley is part of the San Remo countryside where the cultivation of olive trees has been a tradition since ancient Roman times. There, the Boeri family has been involved in agriculture since 1900, when they formed ROI Company. Today, Franco Boeri spends his time working at the family olive press just as his ancestors have done for four generations. ROI has updated its pesticide-free farm and production facility to manufacture products such as olive-oil–based cosmetics and olive-wood utensils.

Apply **How has Franco Boeri extended his family agriculture business? List some other possible ideas for expansion.**

Vertical Integration. With vertical integration, a company expands by moving earlier or farther along in its channel of distribution. In most instances, this means taking over either suppliers or distributors or both.

If you employ *backward integration*, you attempt to gain control of the supplies you use to make your products. Suppose you are a manufacturer of plastic items. You could buy the company that supplies your plastics if the firm is profitable. This would help you cut costs and expand your business.

If you choose *forward integration*, you attempt to gain control of the distribution systems for your product. You can do this in two ways. First, you can eliminate intermediaries by selling directly to your customers. Second, you can gain ownership of the distributors or dealers of your products. More manufacturers, such as Nike and Levi-Strauss are opening their own retail stores.

Horizontal Integration. Horizontal integration entails increasing your market share and expanding your business by buying up your competitors. For example, you may decide to purchase a company that has a product and market compatible with yours. You may also purchase a troubled company with buildings

Money Matters

LARGE LOANS

Getting a large start-up loan can be daunting, but it's not impossible. According to Arthur Lipper III of British Far East Holdings Ltd.,

"*Angel investors . . . [can] provide loan guarantees. It's not cheap, and sometimes it's not easy. But for companies with explosive growth opportunities, it can be the best way to go.*"

One way to expand a business is to diversify. ***What kind of diversification is shown here?***

Tips from the Real World

GROWTH

One of the greatest challenges of growing big is in staying intimate. Says Howard Schultz, CEO of Starbucks Corp.,

"You can't let relationships get buried while you focus on sales, profits, competition, your investors, and so forth."

and distribution channels already established in a different geographic area. That way your product can move into a new geographic market without the expense of locating or constructing buildings or setting up distribution channels.

Using Diversification Growth Strategies

Diversification means investing in products or businesses that are different from the products you sell or the business you own. Businesses that have exhausted the opportunities within their present industry or market often diversify. In contrast with intensive or integrative strategies, diversification exploits opportunities outside a business market or industry.

Synergistic Diversification. Trying to find new products or businesses that are in some way *technologically compatible* with yours is called synergistic diversification . You may purchase the rights to make a product that is made in a manner similar to your own. You may buy another business that is technologically similar to yours.

Consider a specific example. Say you own a bakery. You may decide to establish or buy a small gourmet restaurant, figuring that it can be a showcase for your baked goods.

Horizontal Diversification. To seek products that are *technologically unrelated* to yours is horizontal diversification . However, you want them to be salable to your present customers. For example, Bell Sports, which manufactures bicycle helmets, began selling cycling clothing with the Bell logo as well as other cycling accessories.

Conglomerate Diversification. If you decide to choose conglomerate diversification to expand, you look for products or businesses that are *totally unrelated* to yours in terms of technology or markets. Why would you want to do that? You may be looking for an enterprise that fills a gap in your own business. For example, suppose your primary business involves a great deal of traveling. You may purchase a travel agency to cut costs and provide convenience. Or you may decide to buy the building in which your company is located for much the same reasons. You could then lease the extra space to another business, thereby becoming a landlord.

Be Realistic

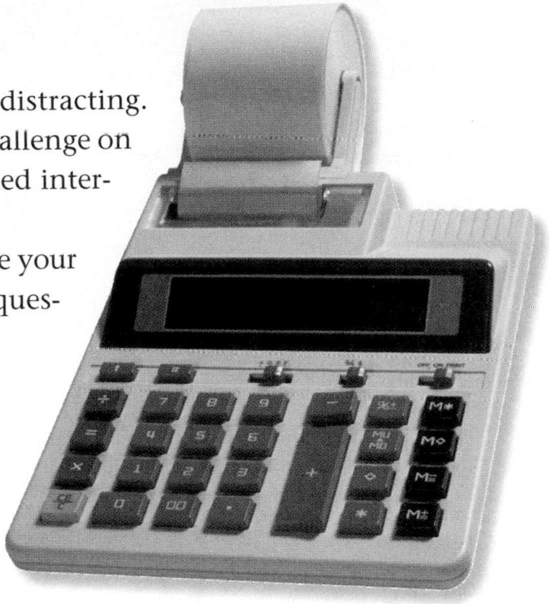

Diversification can be profitable. It can also be distracting. Starting and running a single-focused business is a challenge on its own. To juggle the original venture with diversified interests is an added challenge.

Before you choose to diversify, make sure you have your primary business under control. Then ask yourself questions such as the following:

- Am I knowledgeable about the new product or service?
- Can I manage the extra paperwork, finances, and decisions?
- Will the new venture require additional staff?
- Is the workspace able to handle the new operations?
- How much will new material, staff, or equipment cost?

Answering such questions will help you determine if the potential for growth outweighs the costs and risks.

CHECK YOUR UNDERSTANDING

SECTION 23.1

Reviewing Key Terms and Concepts

1 Describe the difference between market development and product development.
2 List drawbacks to franchising your business.
3 What are some strategies for expanding your business to another country?

Critical Thinking Activity

Interview a franchisee—the owner of a franchise—to find out what was involved in purchasing the franchise and how the owner can grow the business.

Extension Lab—Communicating Information

Clip & Dip Garth owns a successful pet grooming service called "Clip & Dip" and thinks he would like to open a second location in a nearby city. He decides to hire a manager for the current store so he will have time to work in the new one. Garth knows there are challenges that come with opening a new store but believes his new manager will be a great asset.

Role Play With a partner, take turns discussing the following topics with the new manager:

- Your overall growth vision for Clip & Dip
- Your marketing plans for the new store
- Management and communications procedures to follow

Challenges of Expansion

What you'll learn

- challenges of growth
- what it takes to acquire growth capital
- the types of growth funding available

Why it's important

It costs money to make money. You need to understand the type of money you're looking for as well as how much it will cost in time and money to get it.

KEY TERMS

second-round financing
prospectus
public stock offering
employee stock option plan (ESOP)

CHALLENGES THAT COME WITH GROWTH

Expansion is a natural outgrowth of a successful business. In an age when consumer tastes and preferences are constantly changing, a business that has expanded and diversified will have the advantage. However, when considering growth, you must consider whether your business is suited for it. Factors that affect the ability of a business to grow include the following:

1. *The characteristics of your target market.* If the niche you created is too small, your ability to grow will be limited.
2. *How innovative your industry is.* If your industry thrives on innovation, you must learn to do it better and faster to grow.
3. *Your ability to delegate responsibility to someone else.* Many entrepreneurs are successful at recognizing opportunity and starting a business, but they don't have the skills to manage. You will need to hire someone who does.
4. *Your ability to get everyone to think like an entrepreneur.* Everyone in your company must have the growth vision and work to achieve it.

When expansion begins, it brings concerns that shouldn't be overlooked. These involve areas as diverse as management, marketing, finances, and record keeping.

The Challenge of Multiple Sites

When you move from an owner-operated business to two or more additional sites, you can become distanced from your customers and employees. Consequently, it is not as easy to keep apprised of their needs. Also, you have to decide whether to transfer your present business image to the new location or establish a different image. Many times, particularly in retail, an image that

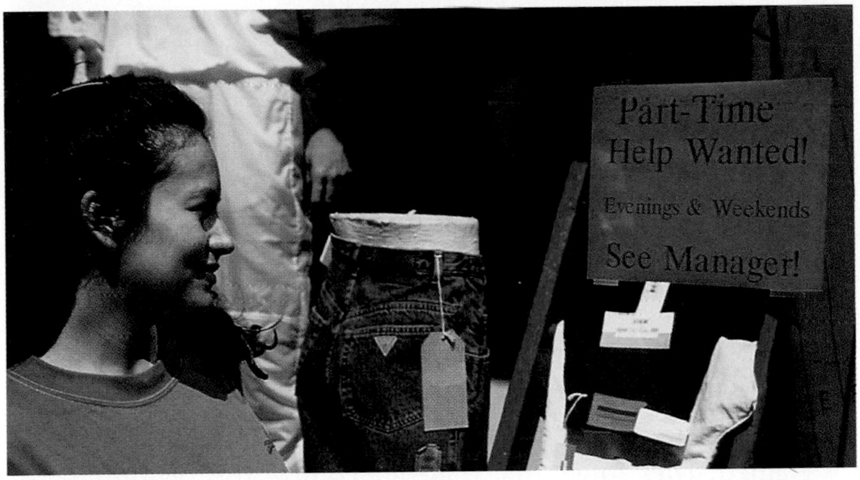

Expansion of a business requires additional staff. ***What will this cost the entrepreneur?***

works in one community will not meet the needs of another. You will have to expand and change your marketing.

In the management area, you will need to decide if your new store or stores will operate independently or be controlled by the main store. Sometimes the main store will control the marketing, accounting, finance, and purchasing functions. This arrangement leaves the branch store to concentrate on its day-to-day operations. (The branch will keep detailed records on its transactions and send this information to the main store on a regular basis.)

Expansion also requires additional managerial staff. This can be expensive and difficult. It's hard to find people who have the necessary skills and who can be trusted. You will be entrusting a portion of your business to any manager you hire, so it's important to hire carefully. One of the best ways to accomplish this is to hire someone who is referred to you by a business associate.

Up & Coming Entrepreneur

Beauty Entrepreneur

At the age of 18, Marcy Cona opened a small two-chair hair salon. Now, nearly 18 years later, she is running M.C. Hair Consultants, which employs 40 people in a 5,000-square-foot refurbished old house and offers much more than just a hairdo. Her employees currently include massage therapists, aestheticians, hair stylists, and manicurists. "We continually strive to better ourselves," says Cona. It must be working. M.C. Hair Consultants was voted one of the top 200 salons in the country.

Analyze **Managing 40 employees might distract one from growing a business. List some ways to simplify employee management.**

The Effect on Record Keeping

Finally, with expansion your record-keeping requirements will become more complicated. You will need to develop an accounting system that can track sales, net income, expenses, and other key data at all your locations. Usually the system that worked when you had only one location will not be adequate to keep track of the accounting at additional locations.

The Problem with Success

Successful growth can be a trap if you let it happen. This is because people who have become successful often take that success for granted. They forget that there are competitors waiting for an opportunity to take your customers.

With success comes a healthy cash flow and this is the biggest trap for the entrepreneur. Many business owners start pulling money out of the business or investing in expensive overhead such as furniture, facilities, and cars. It's a way of celebrating their victory. What they forget is that if the market changes and business slows, they could be saddled with payments they can't make.

When your business is growing, it's important to put your extra cash back into the business to produce more revenues. Then you will be assured of reaching a point where the business has created wealth that you can take out.

Businesses that deal in technology may grow faster than others. ***What are some reasons?***

WHAT IT TAKES TO FIND GROWTH CAPITAL

When financing the expansion of your business, try the same sources you used to start the business. These include personal savings, friends and family, private investors, and banks. Some of these options were described in Chapter 19. However, the amount you need to grow the business is often greater, so this section will look at what it takes to raise more money to grow the business.

RISK TAKERS PROFIT MAKERS

Name: David Filo, Jerry Yang
Business: Yahoo!
City, State: Santa Clara, CA

From Thousands to Millions. Yahoo!

In 1994, David Filo and Jerry Yang were two PhD. candidates in Electrical Engineering at Stanford University who kept track of their personal interests on the Internet. When they found that their own lists were becoming too cumbersome, they decided to start an on-line navigational guide serving the needs of Internet users.

"What we did took 20 hours a day, but we were one of the first to [try and organize the Web], and we did it better than anyone," says Yang. Yahoo! stands for *Yet Another Hierarchical Officious Oracle.*

Today, income is generated mainly from advertisers, and revenues reported for the first quarter of 1998 totaled $30 million. Yahoo! generates 95 million daily page views and now serves more than 30 million users per month.

Thinking Critically

What are some of the challenges in having a business like Yahoo! that grows from thousands to millions of users in just a few years?

The Process of Raising Money

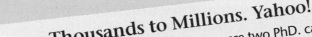

Growth is a very costly proposition. It can put a great strain on the limited resources of your business. That's the bad news. The good news is that if you can demonstrate that your business has excelled in sales and earnings, you will have an easier time raising capital. Second-round financing, or growth capital, involves acquiring funds to move a venture out of the start-up phase and toward becoming a stable business.

Because growth is expensive, most entrepreneurs decide to take it slowly. However, growing too slowly can actually hurt the business. You can miss opportunities and your competitors can pass you by. When you decide to raise money to grow your business, be aware of three things:

1. Raising money takes time. Plan on it taking several months to a year to find the money you need. Then it may take several more months for the potential investor or lender to check out you and your business. Finally, it may take up to six months to actually receive the money. So don't wait until you need the money to begin looking for it.

2. Your money deal may not work out. After months of working with your investors or lenders, they may change their mind and not go through with the deal. To avoid being left with no alternatives, always have a backup waiting in the wings in case your perfect investor doesn't come through.

3. You may have to buy out your relatives. Second-round investors often want to buy out the first-round funders. These first-round funders are often friends and family. The professional investors do not want to deal with your relatives and they really have nothing to lose by demanding a buyout. There are plenty of other deals out there.

It takes money to raise money. As the entrepreneur, you pay all the costs of raising the money before the money is received. Costs to maintain the capital once you have it can often be paid from the proceeds of the loan or investment capital.

TYPES OF GROWTH FUNDING

As more cash comes into the business and less cash leaves, the excess can be used to fund expansion. If you have enough, this is an excellent source of expansion. You won't have to give up any equity in your business and you won't have to take on any debt.

Unfortunately, most fast-growing businesses require more cash than they can generate. Other sources of financing must be considered. A few alternatives are listed below. Some of these sources were discussed in Chapter 19. Because expansion is so costly and borrowing money can be tricky, it will pay to research the sources' expectations.

One way companies can raise money for expansion is by offering stock to the public. ***What are some drawbacks to this method?***

- *Private placement.* To sell investment interests in your businesses to private investors, or to raise money through private placement, you need to develop a type of business plan called a *prospectus.* A prospectus spells out the risks involved in the private placement. Get help from an attorney to help you do this correctly.

- *Public stock offering.* Only corporations can raise money by selling shares of stock, or making a **public stock offering**. To make a public offering, your company should have a track record of increasing revenues for several years. This process is regulated by the Securities and Exchange Commission to protect the public from illegal or poorly prepared offerings.
- *Employee Stock Option Plan.* **Employee stock option plan (ESOP)** is a source of financing in which a company gives its employees the opportunity to buy a portion of the business. To raise money with an ESOP, a company must have at least 25 employees and revenues of $5 million. An attorney can let you know if you meet the additional requirements. In an ESOP, a company either takes existing stock or borrows money to buy stock. The stock is bought by the company's employees and placed in a trust fund. The company makes tax-deductible contributions to the trust fund to repay the bank debt, while the stock serves as collateral for the bank note.

Growing a business requires planning, but it is exciting. You get to see your hard work translated into tangible rewards.

CHECK YOUR UNDERSTANDING

SECTION 23.2

Reviewing Key Terms and Concepts

1 What are some challenges of operating multiple sites?
2 What are two types of growth funding available to the small business?
3 What is an employee stock option plan?

Critical Thinking Activity

Visit a banker or someone you know who invests in businesses to find out how much money it costs to raise capital through a bank loan or a private investment.

Extension Lab—Improving Systems

Shop 'Til You Drop Two years ago, Juan started a personal shopping service. His clients are busy professionals who work downtown and don't have time to take care of errands during the day. Juan picks up dry cleaning, purchases gifts for family members, and even plans and purchases his clients' wardrobes. His business is growing so fast, however, that recently the personal care his clients have come to expect is slipping. Currently, Juan has no competition, but he is afraid this may change.

Research

- What challenges is Juan facing because of the success of his business?
- What should Juan do to improve the quality of service his clients expect?

CHAPTER 23 REVIEW

CHAPTER SUMMARY

- Intensive growth strategies provide opportunities for growth within a current market. These strategies include market penetration, market development, and product development.
- Integrative growth strategies give you the opportunity to grow within your industry either vertically or horizontally.
- Diversification growth strategies provide opportunities outside the market or industry in which your business normally operates. There are three diversification growth strategies: synergistic, horizontal, and conglomerate.
- When considering expansion, entrepreneurs should consider the characteristics of their target markets, how innovative the industry is, their ability to delegate responsibility, and whether they can get everyone else in the company to think like an entrepreneur.
- Expansion often complicates business management, marketing, finances, and record keeping.
- Three sources of funding for expansion are private placement, a public stock offering, and an ESOP.

RECALL KEY TERMS

Create a series of questions and answers using the following key terms. When you are finished, trade with a partner and see if you can answer each other's questions.

intensive growth strategies
market penetration
market development
integrative growth strategies
vertical integration
horizontal integration
diversification
synergistic diversification
horizontal diversification
conglomerate diversification
second-round financing
prospectus
public stock offering
employee stock option plan (ESOP)

RECALL KEY CONCEPTS

1. What is the difference between market development and market penetration?
2. List five questions you should ask yourself before you consider franchising your business.
3. Describe the difference between backward and forward vertical integration.
4. What are the differences between synergistic, horizontal, and conglomerate diversification growth strategies?
5. Why would you need a new accounting system if you were expanding to several locations?
6. How can success be a problem?
7. How can growing too slowly hurt a business?
8. What is the advantage of an ESOP over other types of expansion financing?

THINK CRITICALLY

1. Your product, a new kind of cereal, seems to have reached a plateau in the growth of

CHAPTER 23 REVIEW

its market share. Which growth strategies could you use to increase its sales? Explain.

2. Choose a business with which you are familiar and identify ways to expand it using integrative growth strategies.
3. What are some problems associated with conglomerate diversification?
4. To expand an innovative bicycle business internationally, what steps would you take?
5. What are the advantages of a private placement over a public offering for a growing business in need of expansion financing?

CONNECT ACADEMICS TO THE WORKPLACE

Math

1. Your business revenues in its first six months of operations were as follows: \$2,500; \$2,800; \$3,050; \$3,500; \$4,200; and \$4,900. By what percentage did your monthly revenues grow from each month to the next?

Sociability

2. You are ready to expand your business and will need to hire a general manager. Your two best employees have applied for the position. Daphne is the most qualified on paper, but Geri is more experienced in the field. You need to make the best decision for your business without alienating the other employee. Write a memo to the employee you did not select explaining why she did not get the job.

WORK IN YOUR COMMUNITY

Imagine that your business has been very successful over the last five years. You have been thinking about expanding internationally. Prepare a written document justifying your expansion plans. Include the following:

- The international market(s) where you think expansion is appropriate
- Growth strategy options
- Management, marketing, and record-keeping policies
- Method(s) for raising expansion capital

LINK SCHOOL TO CAREER

Research examples of businesses that have used the following growth strategies:

- Franchising
- Vertical integration
- Horizontal integration
- Synergistic diversification
- Conglomerate diversification

Use your findings to determine which strategy was the most successful.

*inter*NET CONNECTION

Export Expansion

Ian wants to expand his import/export business. He thinks that an ESOP might be an excellent way to finance the expansion.

Connect

Using a variety of search engines, research sites that provide information about ESOPs. Find out the:

- Advantages and disadvantages
- Requirements for raising money with an ESOP
- Process a company uses to start an ESOP

CHAPTER 24

Social and Ethical Responsibility

Learning Objectives

When you have completed this chapter, you will be able to:

- **Explain** how entrepreneurs can become socially responsible
- **Discuss** ways that small businesses can perform community services
- **Define** what it means to be ethical
- **Explain** how to develop a code of ethics
- **List** some special ethical problems that entrepreneurs face
- **Discuss** the effect of culture on ethics

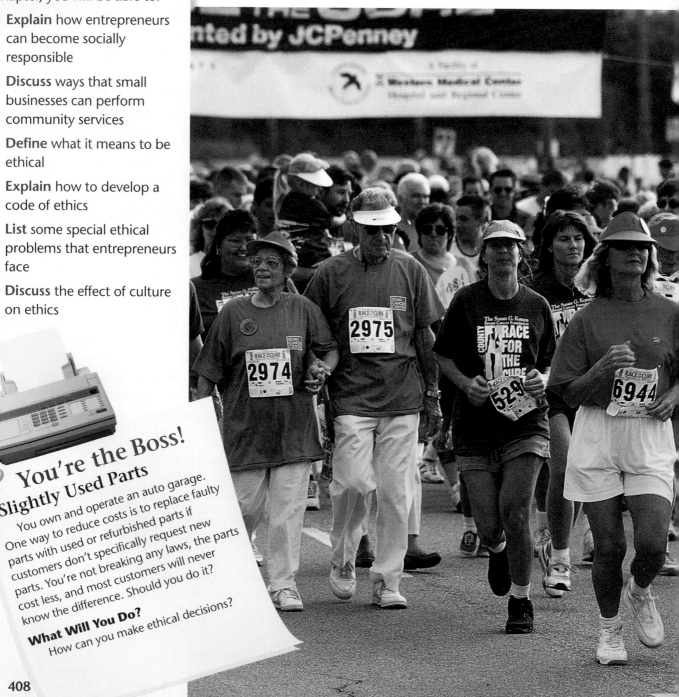

You're the Boss!

Slightly Used Parts

You own and operate an auto garage. One way to reduce costs is to replace faulty parts with used or refurbished parts if customers don't specifically request new parts. You're not breaking any laws, the parts cost less, and most customers will never know the difference. Should you do it?

What Will You Do?
How can you make ethical decisions?

SECTION 24.1

Social Responsibility

ENTREPRENEURS AND SOCIAL RESPONSIBILITY

History is rich in stories of entrepreneurs such as J. P. Morgan, John D. Rockefeller, and Andrew Carnegie. Some of these men were considered ruthless in business. However, they all chose to make generous and enduring contributions to society.

Morgan gave books and art to libraries and museums. His library was turned over to research. Rockefeller gave away more than a half billion dollars to charity. His money fights hunger and disease even today. Carnegie set up more than 2,800 libraries. He also founded the Carnegie Institute for science.

Being a responsible entrepreneur, however, takes more than philanthropy, or making donations. It involves how you run your enterprise every day.

Social responsibility requires a business to acknowledge it has a contract with society. This contract includes many duties. A business must make safe products. It should treat customers well and employees fairly. It should be run honestly. Being socially responsible can inspire loyalty in employees and customers.

What you'll learn

- how entrepreneurs can become socially responsible
- how entrepreneurs can contribute to their communities

Why it's important

It's not enough for a business to provide jobs and make a profit. Companies are expected to run their businesses responsibly.

KEY TERMS

philanthropy
social responsibility
Environmental Protection Agency (EPA)

RISK TAKERS PROFIT MAKERS

Name: Ann Schewe
Company: AMS Imports
City, State: Amherst, MA

Weaving Success

Ann Schewe (pronounced shoo-ee) modestly describes her million-dollar business as if she were telling a good friend about her life's adventures. Shewe's AMS Imports scours the planet for unique flat-weave rugs, pillows, and throws. She began the business out of her home in 1980 by importing rugs designed in Sweden and manufactured in Egypt. Today, AMS Imports wholesales its products to small and large businesses through their showrooms in Georgia and North Carolina. AMS Imports also sells samples and seconds (just below first-quality merchandise) at its main office and showroom in Amherst, Massachusetts.

"It's all about relationships," Schewe insists, "through a non-profit group called Aid to Artisans, I've been contracted as the sole importer of a Bedouin tribe's weavings." AMS Imports helps bring a unique product into the world market.

Thinking Critically

How does AMS Imports and Aid to Artisans help improve the world's economy?

Your Responsibility to Customers

All businesses must act responsibly toward their customers. Companies must not mislead customers about a product's quality, performance, or safety. Information must be given about proper use, and unsafe products must be labeled as such.

The free market is the consumer's best protector. When businesses are free to compete with one another in satisfying consumer wants, they are highly motivated to offer the best quality products at the lowest prices.

Two other forces that protect customers are the *consumer movement* and *government regulation*. In 1965, Ralph Nader started the consumer movement with his book, *Unsafe at Any Speed*. In the book, he argued that American autos were unsafe. Then he branched out to other areas where he felt consumers were being treated unfairly. Since then, institutions such as Consumers Union have formed. These groups' tests and findings have provided consumers with information about the relative quality, safety, and costs of competing products.

Laws also affect how business is run. The Truth-in-Lending Act requires businesses to fully inform their customers about purchases. The Fair Credit Billing Act requires businesses to respond quickly to consumer complaints. Breaking such laws results in fines and punishment.

Rating and regulation have both led businesses to improve their service to customers. However, most successful businesses see that customer service is a competitive advantage on its own.

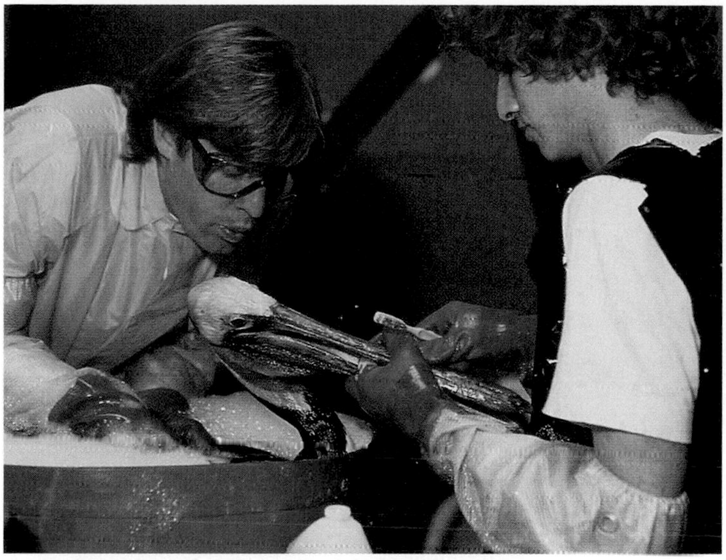

Businesses must be more environmentally aware than they were in the past. ***What is the likely result if they are not?***

Your Responsibility to the Environment

Have you noticed how many ads are environment oriented? Oil companies show how they protect rare birds. Chemical companies describe how they can protect crops without poisoning the soil. Soap companies advertise recyclable boxes.

To create and enforce environmental standards, the U.S. government formed the Environmental Protection Agency (EPA) in 1970. Among other duties, it researches pollution and creates laws to regulate it. For example, the EPA banned the use of harmful fluorocarbons in aerosol products such as hairspray in 1978. It also makes sure that businesses properly dispose of hazardous wastes. Those who don't follow the standards can be fined or the responsible parties can even be imprisoned.

The media and the public also promote environmentalism. They criticize any business that pollutes the environment. When the Exxon Valdez oil tanker spilled in Prince William Sound in 1989, a public furor resulted. The company's reluctance to take full responsibility seriously damaged its image. More than a decade later, Exxon's reputation remains stained.

You can learn from the mistakes of Exxon and others. You can adopt a proactive policy on the environment. In other words, establish a record of sound environmental decision making before problems occur. What will do you if an accident occurs? Better yet, what can you do to prevent one from happening? Then promote

Figure 24–1

Making a Contribution

These are some ways you can give to your community:

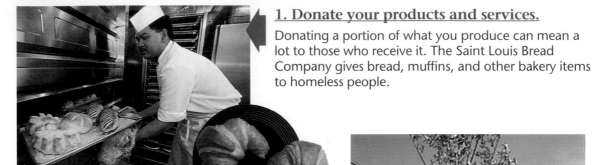

1. Donate your products and services.

Donating a portion of what you produce can mean a lot to those who receive it. The Saint Louis Bread Company gives bread, muffins, and other bakery items to homeless people.

2. Get your employees involved in philanthropy.

Encourage your employees to give something to the community as well. Offer them some time off each month or a certain number of hours a year to do community service.

3. Join with other companies to promote social responsibility.

Organize a group of small businesses to work on a community project. Just Desserts, a San Francisco bakery, put together a group of 35 businesses. Each of them adopted an elementary school. Then they did such things as paint classrooms and plant trees on the campus.

your efforts. Recycle products. Reduce waste. Then let your customers know how they can help the environment, too.

Ways to Contribute to the Community

You do not have to have a big corporation to be able to make a contribution to your community and to society at large. Many smaller businesses have found creative ways to be generous. Some examples are shown in **Figure 24–1**.

Being a Responsible Employer

As a small business owner, you have a responsibility to treat your employees fairly. Additional benefits are up to you. The government encourages businesses to offer flextime schedules, health care, and assistance to the physically challenged. Some businesses offer other perks, such as telecommuting options and on-site childcare. These benefits may cost you money. However, having happy workers can make up for the loss with effort and loyalty.

CHECK YOUR UNDERSTANDING

SECTION 24.1

Reviewing Key Terms and Concepts

1 What does it mean to be socially responsible?
2 What are two areas in which your business can become socially responsible?
3 What are two ways you can contribute to your community?

Critical Thinking Activity

Find a business in your community that you believe is socially responsible. What kind of contribution is it making to the community?

Extension Lab—Decision-Making Skills

Ticket Taker You work for a company that makes gift baskets for all occasions, especially birthdays, anniversaries, and holidays. You job is to purchase the baskets and the products that go into them. One of your suppliers brings you small gifts—calendars, pencils, and flowers—every time he comes to call on you throughout the year. Yesterday, the supplier called and offered you two tickets to the sold-out basketball game Friday night. You have been trying for weeks to get tickets to that game.

Role Play With a partner, take turns enacting a discussion between yourself and the supplier. Keep in mind the following.

- Should you accept the tickets to the game?
- How will you feel about purchasing products from this supplier if you take the tickets?

Ethical Responsibility

What you'll learn

- what it means to be ethical
- how culture affects ethics
- the special ethical problems entrepreneurs face
- how to develop a code of ethics

Why it's important

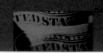

Once lost, a good reputation can be hard or impossible to regain. It's important to learn how to conduct business in a way that demonstrates integrity and builds your reputation.

KEY TERMS

ethics
code of ethics
conflict of interest
bribes
dumping

WHAT DOES IT MEAN TO BE ETHICAL?

Ethics are guidelines for human behavior. They help people decide how to act in situations where moral issues are involved. Ethics set the standards for moral behavior. In this section you'll learn about ethics and how they affect your business conduct.

What Are Your Values?

In Chapter 5 we discussed the importance of creating a vision for your company that is based on your value system. For example, if the values of honesty, integrity, and responsibility are the basis of your ethics, your business will be shaped by those values. They will govern your actions in dealing with others and they will be reflected in your reputation in the community. Here are some of the benefits of understanding your value system.

- It's easier to make decisions if you don't consider actions that go against your values.

- When you are confident about your values, it is easier to persuade others to agree with you.
- You will probably not regret decisions made based on your value system.

What Are Business Ethics?

Businesspeople are often portrayed as ruthless individuals who will do anything for money. However, most businesses do not earn their profits by unethical means. In fact, many entrepreneurs start their businesses for reasons other than money. They are motivated by independence, adventure, achievement, and the like.

Are Everyone's Ethics the Same?

All people do not share the same ethical values. For example, many employees realize that equipment is provided at the workplace to complete particular jobs. Others feel that it is acceptable to steal from their employers. They may take pens and computer disks or use company E-mail or mail services for personal use.

Employers can be dishonest, too. They may try to avoid paying taxes by not reporting employee earnings or by hiding money abroad where the IRS can't find it. They may fail to report or remedy unsafe working conditions.

Because not everyone has high ethical standards, it's important for the entrepreneur to create a clear policy. He or she should make clear what is acceptable in the business. He or she should also state what is not acceptable.

At Special Risk—Small Businesses

Because large businesses are in the public eye, they have to be careful about how they do business. Small businesses aren't watched as carefully. They may be more vulnerable to unethical practices than large businesses for other reasons as well. Small companies are generally less structured and formal. They don't take the time to identify potential ethical problems. The environment in which small businesses operate can often propel them toward unethical conduct.

DEVELOPING A CODE OF ETHICS

A **code of ethics** is a set of guidelines for living morally. Many entrepreneurs find it helpful to develop an explicit code of ethics

Tips from the Real World

COMMUNITY

Starting a business in your community is a chance to give back to it. Former L. A. Laker, Earvin "Magic" Johnson, opened a chain of theaters in his old neighborhood:

"African-Americans make up more than 30 percent of all the movie-going business . . . [but] there were no theaters in our neighborhoods. Now we have [them] in our own communities."

In some small businesses salespeople are not allowed to accept gifts from clients. ***Why might a free meal be unethical?***

that spells out appropriate conduct for their business.

Written Versus Unwritten Codes

Codes of ethics can be written or unwritten. Unwritten codes are simply norms, or ways of doing things that have come about over time. For example, in your business it may be understood that salespeople do not accept any gifts. This may include meals. This rule would not be written down. It is just passed on verbally from one salesperson to another.

Formal, or written codes, usually grow out of unwritten ones. As a company's business and its number of employees grows, so does the potential for misunderstandings. A larger company will also have more to lose if it engages in unethical practices. Valuable relationships and goodwill can be lost quickly as a result of unethical behavior. Once a reputation has been tarnished, it can be impossible to regain.

A written set of guidelines will reduce the chance of unethical behavior. Follow these steps to create a code of ethics:

1. *Brainstorm some ethical dilemmas.* Do this with your employees. Hypothesize about potential ethical problems the business might face.
2. *Discuss potential solutions.* Have your employees offer suggestions on how they might handle these situations.

Up&Coming Entrepreneur

Entertainment Entrepreneur

Bob Zettlemoyer truly enjoys being Zeppy the Clown. Although it is just a sideline to his more usual job inspecting copper beryllium strips, he performs between 80 and 90 shows a year at children's events. "It takes me 45 minutes just to apply my makeup but it's worth it. At the end of the show when the kids come up to me and give me a hug, I see that sparkle in their eyes and know I've made a difference," says Zettlemoyer.

Analyze **"Making a difference" can be as important as a making a profit. List some not-for-profit organizations in your community.**

Discussing them will give you a sense of your employees' values and help everyone reach a positive outcome.

3. *Write a set of general guidelines.* Base these on your discussions. The guidelines should offer a range of acceptable ways to deal with different situations.
4. *Improve your code.* When a new situation or solution occurs, discuss it. Then add it to your guidelines.

As part of its code of ethics, Cray Research, Inc., asks its employees to use the following question as a standard of conduct: *How would I feel if my actions appeared on the front page of the newspaper for my family and friends to see?* You may want to incorporate this computer company's standard into your own personal ethical values—and into your business from the moment you start up.

Money Matters

RULES & ETHICS

With so much competition, entrepreneurs are sometimes tempted to cut corners. That's not necessarily a step they should take, says Tom Scott, of Nantucket Nectars:

"*[We] operated from the shared belief that there are no rules in life; there are laws, there are ethics.*"

SPECIAL PROBLEMS FOR ENTREPRENEURS

Entrepreneurs, by definition, operate in dynamic environments under a great deal of pressure. In such situations, some people may be tempted to put aside ethics to meet a short-term obligation or make a short-term gain. Some typical ethical problems include the following.

Conflict of Interest

A conflict of interest is a conflict between an individual's private interests and his or her responsibilities as a person in a position of trust. Consider an example. Let's say a newly opened resort in Florida offered free stays to journalists and securities analysts nationwide. The amount of publicity and goodwill such a gesture could create would be immeasurable. However, the gesture would also create a conflict for the journalists and securities analysts. Why? They are supposed to have an objective point of view. How could they report anything negative about the resort after they had been treated so well by that firm? Their gratitude toward the resort and their responsibility to their readers were in conflict.

What should the journalists and analysts have done? Many would say that they should have turned down the trips. That would be a sacrifice to most of them, but it's the right thing to do.

During earthquakes, hurricanes, or blackouts, the demand may rise for provisions such as canned food, clean water, and batteries. ***Should a business be able to raise prices on such items during such adversities?***

Desperate Measures

There is a saying that "you do what you have to, to survive." For example, a storeowner in debt may be tempted to help circulate negative advertisements against a competitor in hopes of gaining more business. It is important, however, to live by your code of ethics in all situations, no matter how tough that may be.

Cultural Differences

Dealing in international business presents some challenging ethical dilemmas for Americans. In fact, some businesspeople choose to avoid international markets entirely because of such difficulties. Here are some areas in which different ethical standards may come in conflict.

Bribes. Bribes are payments made to secure special services for a business or special consideration for its products. In the United States, bribes are illegal. In many other parts of the world, they are an accepted part of doing business. They are seen as courtesies or gifts. Therefore, it is important that you determine your company's policy on giving or accepting bribes before you begin doing business abroad.

Patent or Copyright Infringement. Some governments are not respectful of patents and copyrights held by people in other countries. They

ENTREPRENEURS INTERNATIONAL

Canada

In 1986, Charlie Goodman left the insurance industry and turned his hobby of racing cars into a full-time business. Goodman Motorsports teaches short- and long-term driving courses to a worldwide clientele under the sponsorship of Bridgestone Tires and Pontiac Automobiles. Its schools offer selected car-racing techniques while promoting safety to the everyday driver. It also trains advanced race-car driving on his track to up-and-coming professionals.

Apply **How is Goodman Motorsports serving the community as well as the professional driver?**

infringe on the rights of a foreigner and force the person to go to court to enforce them. Other countries have a long patenting or copyrighting process that foreigners must go through. The delay sometimes allows local businesses to familiarize themselves with the item and submit similar patents or copyrights first.

Unfair Pricing. Dumping occurs when a nation sells its products abroad at below cost. It is probably the most commonly protested form of unfair pricing. For example, if a company in another country has a surplus of calculators, they may ship them to the United States and sell them for below cost. That way they don't flood their own country with products and they gain sales in another market. Being aware of such practices will help you evaluate your business prospects realistically, both in the United States and abroad.

It may seem that businesses that put ethics aside gain the profits. In the short term, they may. However, you are in business for the long run. Your integrity and your reputation will be what keep your customers coming back. Following a moral code of behavior consistently is the way your business will grow and thrive.

CHECK YOUR UNDERSTANDING

SECTION 24.2

Reviewing Key Terms and Concepts

1. Why is it important to understand your value system?
2. Why are small businesses at special risk for ethics violations?
3. What are two types of ethical problems entrepreneurs face?

Critical Thinking Activity

Interview an entrepreneur to find out how he or she deals with ethical issues in the business. Does the business have a formal code of ethics?

Extension Lab—Acquiring and Evaluating Data

Double Dip Ben & Jerry's, Vermont's Finest Ice Cream and Frozen Yogurt, was founded in 1978 by friends Ben Cohen and Jerry Greenfield. They are committed to a "values-led" corporate concept of linked prosperity—where both the company and the world can profit. Ben and Jerry believe that business has a powerful influence on society and is responsible for the welfare of that society and the people in it.

Research Through research, answer the following questions:

- How does Ben & Jerry's philosophy permeate all aspects of their business?
- Could a values-led philosophy actually hurt a business?
- Are there other companies that have a similar philosophy?

CHAPTER 24 REVIEW

CHAPTER SUMMARY

- A socially responsible company is one that makes safe products, treats its customers and employees fairly, and operates honestly.
- A company has a duty to protect its customers from unsafe products and misinformation.
- The Environmental Protection Agency (EPA), the media, and the public all promote environmentalism among businesses.
- Entrepreneurs can contribute to the community by donating products or services, encouraging employees to participate in community service, and by joining with other companies to work on projects in the community.
- An entrepreneur should develop a written code of ethics to reduce the chance of unethical behavior occurring in the business. Involve your employees in the development of your code of ethics.
- Businesses often face ethical problems when there are conflicts of interest, when their economic survival is threatened, and when doing business abroad (where ethical practices may differ).

RECALL KEY TERMS

Select a business in your community and create a poster that promotes social and ethical responsibility in that company. Use the following key terms and be creative.

philanthropy
social responsibility
Environmental Protection Agency (EPA)
ethics
code of ethics
conflict of interest
bribes
dumping

RECALL KEY CONCEPTS

1. How did the legendary entrepreneurs of American history demonstrate social responsibility in their time?
2. What are two forces that protect consumers with regard to product safety and quality?
3. Name two groups that monitor businesses and make sure they are not damaging the environment.
4. Why are small businesses more vulnerable than large businesses to unethical practices?
5. What are the steps to follow when creating a code of ethics?
6. What ethical standard does Cray Research Inc. suggest that its employees use to evaluate their conduct?
7. Describe three business practices that are unethical in the United States but may be acceptable abroad.

THINK CRITICALLY

1. What is the difference between social responsibility and ethical responsibility?
2. Do you believe most businesses act responsibly toward consumers? Can you think of a company that has not? Describe the company's behavior and the consequences.

CHAPTER 24 REVIEW

3. How do socially responsible firms improve the quality of life for everyone?
4. What is the value of developing a written code of ethics?
5. Should American businesses pay or accept bribes when operating in countries where bribes are the norm? Explain your answer.

CONNECT ACADEMICS TO THE WORKPLACE

Math

1. A school-wide project has a goal to help 200 families with holiday baskets. Each basket will contain at least 10 cans of food. Sixteen groups of students are competing to see who can collect the most cans of food.
   - How many cans are needed to meet the school's goal?
   - How many cans would each group need to collect to meet the school's goal?
   - If each group collects 150 cans, what percentage of their goal did they collect?

Speaking

2. Working with a partner, research a famous entrepreneur (past or present). Find out how he or she demonstrated social and ethical responsibility. Report your findings to the class in an oral presentation.

WORK IN YOUR COMMUNITY

Create a formal code of ethics for your business. Be sure to include the following sections:

- Purpose of the code
- Social principles (general guidelines)
- Ethical principles (general guidelines)
- Potential ethical dilemmas and solutions

Compare your code of ethics with others in the class. Analyze the similarities and differences.

LINK SCHOOL TO CAREER

As a class, develop and implement a service project to promote the idea of social responsibility in your community. Divide into teams to complete the following assignments:

- Project selection
- Coordination of students
- Marketing and promotion of event
- Implementation of event

If possible, make this activity an ongoing project.

interNET CONNECTION

Dirty Dungarees

You own a company that manufactures blue jeans for several distributors worldwide. You have decided to become a more environmentally friendly company but need help to achieve this goal.

Connect

Using a variety of search engines, research the Internet to develop a proactive policy on the environment as it relates to your business. Be sure to include:

- Measures for conserving resources
- Methods to reduce waste and pollution
- Recycling plans
- Promotion activities

UNIT 6 LAB

Business Plan Basics

Analyzing Risk and Identifying Trends

OVERVIEW

Protecting and growing a new business requires entrepreneurs to carefully analyze their operations. Entrepreneurs need to determine the risks they face, such as crime, natural disasters, employee accidents, and customer injuries. In addition, they must be aware of market trends that could cause their business to stop growing. In this unit lab, you will analyze market trends and identify business risks, which all entrepreneurs must prepare for.

TOOLS

- Current news magazines/newspapers
- The Internet (optional)
- Word processor (optional)
- Graph paper or database program

PROCEDURES

STEP A Work individually or in a small group.

1. Identify risks that each of the following types of businesses would probably face:
   - warehouse
   - fast-food restaurant
   - barber shop
   - toy store
   - insurance agency
2. Then, identify any risks faced by *all* the businesses listed. You may want to visit local businesses of these types, and/or interview their owners or managers to collect information. You can also base your responses on previous visits to similar businesses.
3. Organize the business types and risks on the Unit 6 worksheet or a clean sheet of paper.

STEP B

Identify specific activities or strategies that entrepreneurs could use in dealing with the risks that you listed.

1. Categorize the strategies and activities as risk avoidance, risk reduction, risk transfer, or risk retention.
2. Organize your work on the Unit 6 worksheet, graph paper, or using the table function of a word processor.

STEP C

Using the library, community resources, or the Internet, complete the following steps for each of the types of business listed in Step A:

1. Identify market trends that could have a *negative* impact on each of the types of businesses listed. A news article about e-coli bacteria being found in food at a local fast food restaurant could greatly decrease business.
2. Identify market trends that could have a *positive* impact on each of the types of businesses listed. For example, consumers wanting more convenience would probably cause the need for fast food restaurants to grow.
3. Organize your findings on the Unit 6 worksheet, graph paper, or using the table function of a word processor.

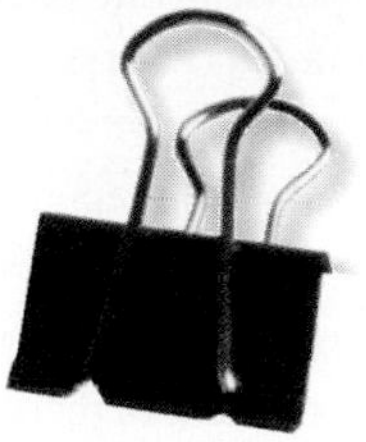

LAB REPORT

STEP D

Select a business that you might be interested in starting in the future.

1. Tour a similar business in your local community and interview the owner. Take descriptive notes on business risks that you detect. Ask the owner about types of insurance that are carried for the business. Make a list of the risks faced by that business.
2. On a clean sheet of paper or using a database program, list the possible activities or strategies that entrepreneurs could use to deal with those risks. Include an estimation of how much it costs to handle these risks on a monthly basis. With the database or on paper, list the risks in order of their expense.
3. Next, using the library, community resources, or the Internet, identify market trends that could have either a positive or negative impact on the type of business that you are researching. Write a two-page report using your research and analysis. In your report, describe how entrepreneurs could protect and grow this type of business.

Glossary

A

accounts payable Expenses that have been incurred but not yet paid for; money owed by a business. (356)

accounts receivable Sales that have been made but not yet collected; money owed to a business. (356)

accrual basis A method of recording income and expenses in which income is recorded when it is earned and expenses when they are incurred. (356)

advertising Paid presentation of ideas, goods, or services directed toward a mass audience by an identified sponsor. (202)

advertising agencies Companies that can handle all phases of advertising. (212)

angels Coined term for nonprofessional investors who tend to put their money into local businesses. (323)

appointments Interior design equipment and furnishings such as fish tanks and planters, used to define corridors or aisles. (155)

assets Items of value that belong to a business or an individual. (368)

automation The use of machines to do the work of people. (277)

B

bait-and-switch Advertising using a bargain-priced item to lure potential customers into a store, then a salesperson tries to sell them higher-priced merchandise. (135)

balance sheet Financial statement that tells an entrepreneur what his or her business is worth at any given time. (337)

balance sheet Financial statement that tells an entrepreneur what his or her business is worth at a given time. (368)

barriers to entry Conditions that keep new busi-
esses either from entering an industry or succeed-
in that industry. (101)

it Feature that promotes or enhances the
a product or service to the customer. (76)

pect" list A list of products that other countries are looking to purchase. (64)

bootstrapping Operating a business as frugally as possible and cutting all unnecessary expenses. (321)

brand Name, symbol, or design used to identify a product. (164)

brand loyalty The practice of customers to purchase products and services from companies they know. (100)

break-even point The point at which the money from product sales equals the costs of making and distributing the product. (189)

bribes Payments made to secure special services for a business or special consideration for its products. (418)

burglary The act of breaking into and entering a home or business with the intent to commit a felony. (380)

business broker Someone whose job is to bring buyers and sellers together. (47)

business concept An idea for a new business that can be tested. (75)

business failure A business that files Chapter 7 bankruptcy and loses money for creditors, the people who lent them money, and their investors. (14)

business interruption insurance A type of insurance which pays net profits and expenses if a business is shut down for repairs or rebuilding. (385)

business plan A document that describes a new business, explaining to lenders and investors why the new business deserves financial support. (80)

buying process The series of mental steps that a customer goes through when making a purchase. (221)

C

campaign A series of related promotional activities with a similar theme. (201)

capacity Element of a legal contract stating that you are legally able to enter into a binding agreement. (126)

C-corporation A form of corporation which protects the entrepreneur from being sued personally for actions and debts of the corporation. (114)

capacity The ability of a business to pay in view of its income and obligations.

capital The buildings, equipment, tools, and other goods needed to produce a product, or the money used to purchase these items. (22)

capital expenditures Long-term commitments of large sums of money to buy new equipment or replace old equipment. (349)

cash basis A method of recording income and expenses in which income is recorded when it is received and expenses when they are paid. (356)

cash budget A financial report showing a business's projected and actual receipts/disbursements and the difference between the two. (347)

cash disbursements journal Special journals for all payments made in cash or check form. (358)

cash discounts Discounts that allow buyers to deduct a percentage from the purchase amount if payment is received by a specified date. (257)

cash flow statement A financial statement that describes the flow of cash into and out of a business. (366)

cash receipts journal Special journals for all cash (and checks) received. (358)

casualty insurance A type of insurance which protects a business from lawsuits. (385)

census tracts Subdivisions of SMSAs containing 4,000-5,000 people. (142)

channel of distribution The path a product takes from producer (or manufacturer) to final user (or consumer). (166)

code of ethics A set of guidelines for living morally. (415)

collateral Items of value that a lender can claim if a business does not repay its loan. (327)

commission A percentage of sales given in place or as part of a salary. (295)

common carriers Transporters used by the general public. (278)

competition Striving for the same customer or market. (21)

competitive grid A way to organize important information about the competition. (78)

conceptual skills Skills that help one to see the relationships among the parts of the enterprise and to visualize its future. (243)

conflict of interest A conflict between an individual's private interests and his or her responsibilities as a person in a position of trust. (417)

conglomerate diversification Growth strategy in which a business looks for products or businesses that are totally unrelated to it in terms of technology or markets. (398)

consideration Element of a legal contract speaking of that which is exchanged for the promise and causing the contract to be binding. (125)

consumer pretests Procedure in which a panel of consumers evaluates an ad before it runs. (212)

contingency funds Extra funds that are calculated into the start-up needs, and can be used to cover unforeseen business expenses. (332)

contract A binding legal agreement between two or more persons or parties. (125)

contract carriers Transporter under contract with a particular business to handle their goods. (278)

cooperative advertising, An arrangement whereby the suppliers or manufacturers of goods that a business sells agree to share that business's advertising costs. (212)

copyright A grant to an author that protects his or her original works. (123)

corporation A business that is chartered, or registered, by a state, and legally operates apart from its owner or owners. (113)

cost-effective The benefits outweigh the costs. (303)

credit An arrangement in which a business or individual can obtain products in exchange for a promise to pay later. (284) Also, an item that decreases the balance of an asset account. (357)

credit bureaus Collection agencies which provide a person's credit information to their member businesses. (351)

current assets Cash (or things that can be converted to cash); also, items that are used up by a business within a year. (339)

current liabilities Debts due within a year. (339)

customer benefits The advantages or personal satisfaction that customers will get from the product. (218)

Glossary

customer needs analysis A way to pinpoint exactly which features and benefits of your goods or services your customers value. (103)

customer profile A complete picture of a venture's prospective customers. It includes geographic, demographic, and psychographic data. (102)

D

debit An item that increases the balance of an asset account. (357)

demand The amount or quantity of goods or services that consumers are willing and able to buy. (7)

demographics Characteristics of human populations and population segments, especially when used to identify consumer markets. (40)

descriptive research Market research design used to determine the status of something. (95)

developmental activities Activities that prepare managers to lead the company into the future. (302)

diminishing marginal utility The principle establishing that price alone does not determine demand. (8)

direct channel The procedure of delivering a product or service directly to the customer. (84)

direct insurance writer An agent who works for one specific insurance company. (387)

discontinuance A business that is operating under a new name or a business that has been purposely discontinued to start a new one.(14)

disposable income Money to spend after necessary expenses are paid. (65)

distribution channel The means for supplying a product to the customer. (84)

diversification A method of expansion in which a company invests in products or other businesses that are different from the products it sell or the type of business itself. (398)

double-entry system A bookkeeping method in which each transaction is entered twice in the ledger—as a debit to one account and a credit to another account. (357)

due diligence Background checks on a business, its owner, and its team. (329)

dumping Selling one's products abroad at below cost prices. (419)

E

economic base A community's main source of income. (141)

economics The study of the decisions or choices that go into making, distributing, and consuming products. (4)

economies of scale The phenomenon by which businesses can churn out products more cheaply and quickly as they grow bigger. (100)

educational activities Activities that prepare employees for moving up in the organization. (302)

elastic Term to describe a product for which a small change in price causes a significant change in the quantity demanded. (7)

electronic credit authorizers Machines that verify if a credit card is good. (381)

emotional buying motives Feelings the buyer associates with the product. (220)

employee complaint procedure Formal written procedure for handling employee complaints. (304)

employee stock option plan (ESOP) A source of financing in which a company gives its employees the opportunity to buy a portion of the business. (405)

entrepreneur An individual who undertakes the creation, organization, and ownership of a business. (3)

entrepreneurial Of or having to do with an entrepreneur or entrepreneurs. (4)

entrepreneurship The process of getting into and operating one's own business. (4)

enterprise A company that is organized for commercial purposes. (22)

enterprise zones Specially designated areas of a community that provide tax benefits to new businesses locating there and grants for new product development. (12)

environment Elements affecting a business that are not controlled by the entrepreneur. (12)

Environmental Protection Agency (EPA) Federal agency formed to create and enforce environmental standards. (411)

Environmental Protection Agency (EPA) Federal agency formed to create and enforce environmental standards. (411)

Equal Employment Opportunity Commission (EEOC) Federal agency charged with protecting the rights of employees. (128)

equilibrium The point at which consumers buy all of a product that is supplied, leaving neither a surplus nor a shortage. (8)

equity Ownership. (322)

errors-and-omissions insurance A type of insurance which protects a business against lawsuits for mistakes in advertising. (385)

ethics Guidelines for human behavior, especially in situations involving honesty, integrity, and fairness. (414)

exclusive distribution Placement of a product in a limited number of outlets to one per area. (168)

executive summary A brief recounting of the key points contained in a business plan. (83)

exploratory research Market research design used to expand knowledge when little is known about a problem. (94)

export management company A company handling all the tasks related to exporting for a manufacturer for a commission (or a percentage of sales). (67)

exporting The selling and shipping of products to another country. (53)

F

FICA Federal Insurance Contribution Act, or social security. (135)

façade The face of a building. (155)

factor An agent who handles another person's business transactions for a fee. (321)

factors of production The resources that businesses use to produce the goods and services that people want. (6)

family leave A leave from work when people can tend to births, deaths, and family illnesses without fear of job loss. (309)

feasibility analysis Process used to test a business concept. (76)

feature A distinctive aspect, quality, or characteristic of the product or service. (76)

fidelity bonds A type of casualty insurance which protects a company in case of employee theft. (385)

fiscal year A tax year selected by a business for accounting purposes. (355)

fixed costs Expenses that don't change with number of units produced. (345)

flextime Allowing employees to choose the work hours and days they think will be most effective. (309)

FOB Delivery term for "free on board," meaning that the buyer pays all freight costs. (279)

foundational skills Math, communication, and decision-making skills that entrepreneurs use regularly in setting up and running a business. (26)

franchise A legal agreement to begin a new business in the name of a recognized company. (45)

franchisee The buyer of a franchise. (45)

franchiser The seller of a franchisee. (45)

free enterprise system Economic system in which people have the right to make economic choices of what products to buy, whether or not to own private property, or to start a business and compete with other businesses. Also called *capitalism* or a *market economy*. (4)

freight forwarder Someone who will handle overseas shipments for a fee. (67)

G

Gantt charts Scheduling charts that show tasks to be performed on the vertical axis and time required on the horizontal axis. (273)

general partners Partners who share unlimited personal liability and take full responsibility for the management of the business. (109)

global economy The economies of countries are linked in the marketplace. (53)

goodwill Customers' approval and support of a business. (45)

gross domestic product (GDP) The total value of all goods produced during the year. (55)

guarantees An assurance of the quality of a product. (173)

H

historical research Market research design used to explore past occurrences, including their causes and effects. (95)

horizontal diversification Growth strategy in which a business seeks new products that are technologically unrelated to it. (398)

horizontal integration Growth strategy in which a business increases its market share and expand by buying its competitors. (398)

hygiene factors Aspects of a job such as compensation, working conditions, and fair company policies, that keep employees from becoming dissatisfied. (307)

I

image Beliefs, ideas, and impressions that people have about a business. (199)

importing The buying and shipping of goods from other countries to sell in their own country. (54)

incentives Advantages that help businesses, such as lower taxes, cheaper land, and employee training programs. (141)

income statement A financial statement that shows how much a business has earned or lost during a year. (337)

independent insurance agent A person who works in a specific geographic area and represents several insurance companies. (387)

indirect channel Selling a product to a wholesaler who will find retail stores to carry the product. (84)

industrial markets Customers who buy goods or
services for business use. (93)

industrial parks Areas communities have set aside for industrial uses. (146)

industry A collection of businesses with a common line of products or services. (91)

industry average The standard used to compare costs. (211)

inelastic If a change in price has little or no effect on the quantity demanded, we say that demand for the item is. (7)

initial public offering (IPO) The selling of a company's stock on a public stock exchange. (330)

innovation Finding new ways of doing things. (39)

integrative growth strategies A method of expansion in which a company grows within the industry it is operating in. (397)

intensive distribution Placement of a product in all suitable sales outlets. (167)

intensive growth strategies A method of expansion in which a company grows through exploiting opportunities within its current market. (393)

intermediaries People or businesses that move products between producers and final users. (166)

International Business Exchange (IBEX) The U.S. Chamber of Commerce's electronic commerce system. (64)

Internet A large computer network linking smaller computer networks worldwide. (27)

interpreter A person who translates from one language to another. (63)

interrelationships Access, arrangement, and flow among all the activities in a layout plan. (151)

investment The amount of money one puts into a business as capital. (22)

J

job description Statement that describes the objectives of the job and its duties and responsibilities. (292)

job enlargement Adding more tasks of the same skill level to an employee's job. (308)

job enrichment Adding tasks of a higher skill level to an employee's job, thus giving the employee more responsibility and control. (308)

job specification Document that spells out the abilities, skills, educational level, and experience needed by an employee to perform a given job. (292)

joint venture A partnership created by two or more companies for a specific purpose over a set period of time. (67)

journals Books used to record business transactions for the daily record keeping of a double-entry system. (357)

L

label The part of the package used to present information. (164)

labor union An organization that is formed to represent workers. (302)

layout A floor plan or map that shows how a business intends to use the space its site provides to conduct business. (150)

lead time The gap in time between placing an order and receiving the delivery. (265)

ledger A collection of all the accounts of a business. (360)

liability Money owed to others. (108)

limited liability A form of business ownership in which the owners are liable only up to the amount of their individual investments. (115)

Limited Liability Company (LLC) Form of business organization with limited liability and has pass-through tax advantages. (117)

limited partners Partners whose liability is limited to their investment. (110)

line-and-staff organization Form of business organization used when a company is large enough to hire staff. (291)

line of credit An amount of money that a bank agrees to lend a business at a certain interest rate. (324)

line organization Form of business organization used when all employees are involved in producing or distributing a company's product. (290)

logistics The details of a product's movement from the manufacturer to the customer. (279)

M

management-by-objectives Motivational technique that involves employees in decision making by having them set their own objectives and gauge their own progress. (308)

manager Person who coordinates the people, pro-cesses, and other resources of your operation on a daily basis. (238)

markdown The amount of money taken from the original price. (191)

market A group of people or companies who have a demand for a product or service and are willing and able to buy it. (92)

market development Growth strategy in which a business expands its product to reach new locations. (394)

marketing mix The particular combination of product, price, place, and promotion strategies that you use to reach your target market. (163)

marketing objectives What a business wants to accomplish with its marketing efforts. (163)

marketing plan A plan for a business to reach its marketing objectives through the four main strategies of product, place, price, and promotion. (163)

market penetration Growth strategy in which a business attempts to increase sales in its current market. (393)

market research The process of investigating the areas of the market. (94)

market segments Small groups of buyers within a larger market with similar needs and interests (92)

market share A portion of the total sales generated by all the competing companies in a given market. (101)

markup The amount added to the cost of item to cover expenses and ensure a profit.

model inventory A target inventory of business needs to keep in stock. (2

motivating factors Things such as recognition, responsibility, advancement, and the work itself, that encourage better job performance. (306)

N

negligence The failure care. (383)

new venture organiz rounds all the produ that are part of the

news releases B sent to the medi

niche A sma based on cus ket research

nonprofit corporations Legal entities that make money for reasons other than the owners' profit. (117)

O

obsolescence costs Money lost when products or materials become obsolete while in inventory. (260)

odd/even pricing Pricing an item at an odd price to suggest a bargain, or an even price to suggest higher quality. (186)

operational plans Plans that address short-range objectives for the implementation of tactical plans. (239)

opportunity An idea that has commercial value. (13)

order getting Seeking out buyers and giving them a well-organized presentation. (217)

order taking The completion of a sale to a customer who has sought out a product. (218)

organizational structure Explanation of how the departments in a business relate to each other. (246)

outsourc Contract with other companies for services. (3)

outsourcing Hiring people and companies to handle tasks at a business doesn't have the ability to do. (269)

owner's equity The amount left over after liabilities are subtracte from assets. (369)

P

kage The physic container or wrapper that ds it. (164)

nership Form of b iness where more than erson shares the bu ess's decisions and mes. (109)

A grant to an inve r that gives him or exclusive right to pro e and sell an n. (121)

pplied-for Status of a ent while the rches the patent applica n. (122)

nding Status of a paten nce the PTO t the claims are accepted t before s actually issued. (123)

penetration pricing Method of introducing a product by charging a low initial price to keep unit costs to customers as low as possible. (187)

performance bonds A type of casualty insurance which protects a business if work or a contract is not finished on time or as agreed. (385)

performance evaluation A review of how well an employee does his or her job. (311)

personal selling The oral presentation made by a salesperson to help a customer make a buying decision. (217)

PERT Diagrams. Scheduling diagrams that show a project's major activities in sequence, with the most time-consuming arranged along the critical path. (274)

philanthropy The promotion of human welfare through giving. (409)

piece rate Set amount of money paid per unit produced. (295)

policies General statements of intent about how to run your business. (283)

Pregnancy Discrimination Act Law that requires pregnant employees to be treated like all other employees when determining benefits. (304)

premium Something of value that a customer receives in addition to the good or service purchased. (208) Also, a fee required to transfer risk to an insurance company. (384)

preselling Influencing potential customers to buy before contact is actually made. (200)

prestige pricing Pricing an item at a higher than average price. (186)

price discrimination The act of selling the same product to different people at different prices. (131)

price lining Pricing an item according to its category. (186)

price skimming Method of introducing a product by charging a high price to recover costs as quickly as possible. (187)

primary data Information obtained for the first time and is specificto the problem studied. (96)

private brand Products packaged with the retailer's rather than the manufacturer's name on them. (173)

private carriers Private companies that ship goods. (278)

private placement A way to raise capital by selling ownership interests of a private corporation or partnership. (329)

product development Process that entails taking an idea, for a new or improved product, designing it on paper or with a computer, building a model, and testing it. (269)

productivity A measure of how much a business produces in a given time. (276)

product liability insurance A type of insurance which protects a business against claims for injuries that result from using its products. (385)

product mix All the products a company makes or sells. (165)

product positioning How consumers see a product in terms of quality, availability, pricing, and uses. (164)

profile A set of characteristics or qualities that iden-tify a type or a category of person. (27)

profit Money that is left after all the expenses of running a business have been deducted from the income. (4)

profit-and-loss statement A statement that compares revenues and expenses over a specific period to see if the business has made a profit. (367)

pro forma income statement Financial statement which estimates the income of a business. (346)

promotional mix The combination of promotional media used to reach a target market within the promotional budget. (202)

promotional pricing Pricing an item at a low price for a limited period to generate sales. (186)

proprietary technology Know-how that is owned and often protected by patents. (100)

prospecting Looking for new customers. (222)

prospectus A type of business plan that spells out the risks involved in the private placement. (404)

prototype A working model of a product. (271)

psychographics A segmentation of the consumer market, including personality, opinions, and lifestyle elements, including activities and interests. (93)

psychological pricing Pricing strategy based on the belief that customers base perceptions of a product on price. (186)

public domain Condition a product or original work enters when it is unprotected by copyright or patent, and could be used by anyone free of charge. (123)

publicity The placement of newsworthy items about a company or product in the media. (206)

public relations Activities designed to create goodwill toward a business. (207)

public stock offering The sale of shares of stock on a stock exchange to raise money for a business. (405)

purchases journal Special journals for all purchases on account. (358)

pure risk The threat of a loss to a business without any possibility of gain. (377)

Q

quality circles Groups of employees who handle problems regarding quality. (275)

quality control The process of making sure that the goods or services produced meet the standards set for them. (274)

quality control programs A check for quality that is built into the production process to make sure products meet certain standards. (240)

R

ratio analysis Way of analyzing the financial condition of a business by comparing certain numbers from a balance sheet or income statement. (338)

rational buying motives Conscious decisions for making a purchase. (220)

rebates Return part of the purchase price as an incentive for customers to purchase a product. (208)

recruit To bring in prospective employees. (293)

return on equity The amount of money earned for each dollar invested by the owner of a business. (343)

risk capital Equity funding. (322)

robbery The taking of property by force or threat. ([illegible]1)

role model A person whose attitudes and achievements they tried to emulate. (24)

rules Guidelines telling employees exactly what they should or should not do. (283)

S

safety stock The cushion of products or materials that keeps a business from running out of inventory while it's waiting for an order. (265)

sales call reports Salespeople's record reporting information such as the number of calls made, orders taken, miles traveled, days worked, new prospects contacted, and new accounts sold. (226)

sales forecast An estimate of sales for a specified period. (227)

sales journal Special journals for all sales on account. (358)

sales potential The projected or estimated figure of the amount a product can realistically be expected to sell. (99)

sales quota A goal assigned to a salesperson for a specific period. (228)

scarcity When wants are greater than resources. (6)

secondary data Information that has already been collected for a purpose other than the one under study. (96)

second-round financing Growth capital that involves acquiring funds to move a venture out of the start-up phase and toward becoming a stable business. (403)

secured funds A form of guaranteed payment such as a credit card, cashier's check, wire transfer, or cash. (257)

selective distribution Placement of a product in a limited number of sales outlets in an area. (167)

service mark A design or symbol that describes a service business. (124)

services Intangible (or conceptual) products that our economic system produces to satisfy our wants. (5)

shrinkage costs Money lost when inventory items are broken, damaged, spoiled, or stolen. (260)

single-entry system A simple accounting system noting only amounts due to and owed by a business. (356)

situational management The use by managers of whichever leadership style their circumstances dictate. (241)

Small Business Administration (SBA) A federal agency that provides services to small businesses and new entrepreneurs. (86)

social responsibility Responsibility of a business to acknowledge it has a contract with society. (409)

sole proprietorship Form of business where the owner is the only one responsible for the business activities. (107)

special market circumstances Circumstances calling for a temporary price increase. (194)

specialty items Giveaways such as pens and T-shirts that have a business name or logo. (205)

specialty magazines Periodicals targeting people with special interests in sports, camping, fashion, and a variety of other areas. (41)

speculative risk Risk that involves taking a chance for profit or loss. (377)

staff Employees who provide support for production and distribution people. (290)

Standard Industrial Trade Classification (SITC) codes The United Nation's numeric system for classifying goods sold in the international market. (63)

Standard Metropolitan Statistical Areas (SMSA) Geographic areas that usually include a metropolitan area such as Chicago or Atlanta. (142)

start-up resources Resources an entrepreneur needs to have when starting a business, including capital, skilled labor, management expertise, legal and financial advice, a facility, equipment, and most importantly, customers. (13)

stock Certificates indicating the amount of equity each investor has in a business. (330)

strategic alliance Forming a partnership with another company. (38)

strategic plans Plans that map out a business course for the next 3-5 years. (239)

Subchapter S corporation Form of corporation which is taxed like a sole proprietorship or partnership. (115)

sweepstakes Games used by businesses to get customers thinking and talking about what the company has to offer. (208)

synergistic diversification Growth strategy in which a company finds new products or businesses that are in some way technologically compatible with itself. (398)

T

tactical marketing objectives Marketing objectives that a business plans to reach within one year. (245)

tactical plans Plans that focus on a period of one year or less. (239)

target customers Consumers most likely to buy a product and service. (77)

target market The particular group a business is interested in making the focus of all the company's efforts. (92)

tariffs Taxes imposed by a government on imported or exported goods. (54)

telecommuting Performing some or all of the job away from the business location, using modern technology like computers, cellular phones, FAX machines, and overnight delivery services. (309)

Theory X A set of negative assumptions about employees based on the premise that people do not like work and will try to avoid it. (307)

Theory Y A set of positive assumptions about employees based on the premise that work is natural to people and an important part of their lives. (307)

time management The process of allocating time effectively. (243)

total quality management A style of management based on customer satisfaction. (248)

trade area The region or section of the community from which a business can expect to draw customers. (143)

trade associations Organizations offering technical and general assistance to entrepreneurs in a specific profession or industry. (86)

trade barriers Taxes, quotas, and other restrictions on goods entering or leaving a country. (54)

trade credit Credit obtained from within one's industry or trade, usually from one's suppliers. (324)

trade credit agencies Agencies that collect credit information on other businesses. (351)

trade discounts Discounts off of the suggested retail price to wholesalers and retailers. (256)

trade magazines Periodicals published for specific types of businesses or industries. (41)

trademark A word, symbol, design, or combination of these that a business uses to identify itself or something it sells. (123)

trade missions Opportunities that the U.S. government and private agencies offer small business owners to meet and talk with foreign agents, distributors, or potential business partners. (64)

trade shows Shows and exhibitions allowing vendors and manufacturers to introduce new items and promote established products and services. (42)

U

Uniform Commercial Code (UCC) A group of laws that covers everything from sales to bank deposits and investment securities. (133)

unlimited liability The debts incurred by a firm may have to be paid from the owner's personal assets. (108)

usage rate The speed at which inventory is used in a given period of time. (265)

V

variable costs Business expenses that change with each unit of product produced. (345)

vendors Businesses that will provide inventory as opposed to supplies. (254)

venture A business undertaking involving risk. (3)

venture capitalists Individuals or firms that invest capital professionally. (323)

vertical integration Growth strategy in which a company expands by moving earlier or farther along in its channel of distribution. (397)

vision The main concept you have for your business. (81)

W

warehousing The operations associated with inventoried goods. (264)

warranty of merchantability A guarantee assuring the buyer that the product he or she is purchasing is of at least average quality and fit for the purpose for which it was intended. (134)

workers' compensation A government-regulated program that provides medical and income benefits to employees who are injured on the job. (386)

working capital The amount of cash a business needs in order to carry on with its daily operations. (332)

working management plan A plan that serves as a reference point for making short-term decisions. (245)

workstations Specific areas with equipment for a single worker. (152)

work team Motivational technique that involves employees in decision making by assigning a group of employees to a task without direct supervision and with responsibility for the results. (308)

wrongful termination When an employee is fired for wrongful reasons. (129)d

Index

A

B

C

D

E

F

G

H

I

J

K

L

M

N

O

P

Q

R

S

T

U

V

W

Y

Z

Cover Photo

Michael Simpson/FPG, Inc.

Photos

Mike Powell/Allsport 191
A. Ramey/PhotoEdit 184, 342
Mark Richards/PhotoEdit 43, 253, 300
Jon Riley/Tony Stone Images 240, 263, 285, 285, 356
Elena Rooraid/PhotoEdit 20
George Rose/The Gamma Liason Network 198
Michael Rosenfeld/Tony Stone Images 241
Andrew Sacks/Tony Stone Images 109, 278
Jeff Sciortino/Sciortino Photography 3
Brian Seed/TSW 234
Mark Segal/Tony Stone Images 63, 83
Siu/Visuals Unlimited 386
Don Smetzer/Tony Stone Images 23
Don Spi[illegible]o/Tony Stone Images 309
Mary Stei[illegible]acher/PhotoEdit 171, 282
David R. Sto[illegible]klin 174
Vince Streano/[illegible]ony Stone Images 268
Superstock Inte[illegible]tional 6, 201, 331, 358
David Sutherland/[illegible]ny Stone Images 60
Taylor Photographi[illegible] [illegible]6
Ed Taylor/FPG Intern[illegible]nal 110
Telegraph Colour Libra[illegible]PG International 379
Charles Thatcher/Tony St[illegible] Images 252, 337
Bob Thomason/Tony Stone [illegible]ges 180
Pierre Tremblay/Masterfile 2[illegible]
Susan Van Etten/PhotoEdit 33[illegible]
Jeff Vinnick/Reuters 418
Rudi Von Briel/PhotoEdit 66
Sandra C. Wallace 362
Dave Wehr/Wehr, Inc. 204
Larry Williams/Masterfile 94
Keith Wood/Tony Stone Images 100
David Young-Wolff/PhotoEdit 2, 75, 91, 98, 106, 107, 162, 176, 210, 255, 277, 322 , 41[illegible]
David Young-Wolff/Tony Stone Images 120, 309, 345

Illustrations

Randy Miyake 7, 8, 9, 29, 55, 77, 92, 114, 129, 132, 142, 151, 154, 166, 167, 183, 203, 207, 239, 246, 256, 274, 275, 290, 291, 294, 303, 307, 311, 312, 332, 338, 339, 340, 347, 348, 350, 357, 359, 363, 364, 367, 368, 388
Corel Clip Art 13, 25, 44, 64, 84, 96, 109, 131, 147, 175, 184, 206, 220, 238, 243, 261, 270, 286, 308, 327, 349, 356, 380, 396, 418